Unpublished Correspondence
of Henri de Toulouse-Lautrec

Unpublished Correspondence of Henri de Toulouse-Lautrec

273 letters by and about Lautrec
written to his Family and Friends
in the Collection of Herbert Schimmel

Edited by Lucien Goldschmidt and Herbert Schimmel
With an Introduction and Notes by
Jean Adhémar and Theodore Reff

PHAIDON

The translation of the letters from the French is by Edward B. Garside

All rights reserved by Phaidon Press Ltd.
5 Cromwell Place, London S.W.7
First published 1969
Phaidon Publishers Inc., New York
Distributors in the United States: Frederick A. Praeger, Inc.
111 Fourth Avenue, New York, N.Y. 10003
Library of Congress Catalog Card Number: 69–19811
SBN 7148 1389 3
Made in Great Britain
Printed by Robert MacLehose & Co Ltd, The University Press, Glasgow

Contents

Acknowledgments

The letters of Toulouse-Lautrec and those about him have never been assembled before now. Even the family holdings were spread among numerous owners. Beginning around 1955 Herbert Schimmel and Lucien Goldschmidt undertook a strenuous search for the surviving autographs, following leads too numerous to mention. In almost all cases individual items only were located, except for the 24 autographs already assembled by the late Ludwig Charell and for the discovery of a group tied up in a canvas bag formerly at the Château de Malromé. This bag contained the moving sequence of Berthe Sarrazin letters and some other items.

The Museums in Europe and in America contain only a few pieces which are discussed in the introduction or the notes. The editors wish to thank the following whose help has done much to make this volume as inclusive as it is:

Dr. A. Aisenberg, Edmond Alphandéry, Mary Comtesse Attems, Mme Huguette Berès, Pierre Berès, Bibliothèque Nationale, Jacques Bourges, Louis Carré, Mme G. Dortu, Mrs. Marguerite Goldschmidt, Robert Goldschmidt, Ferdinand de Goldschmidt-Rothschild, Mme de Gouttes, Mme Simone Groger, Jacques Guignard, Harvard University, H. Imart-Rachou, Miss Anahid Iskian, Francis A. Kettaneh, B. Kist, E. Kornfeld, F. Lachenal, Jean Lapeyre, Herman W. Liebert, Mme Alice Dethomas Macé, S. Marcy, Paul Marionnet, Henri Matarasso, Miss Grace Mayer, Mrs. Nadine Mendelson, Musée Clemenceau, Musée du Louvre, Musée Toulouse-Lautrec, Musées Royaux des Beaux-Arts de Belgique (Mme Ph. Mertens), Lionel Prejger, Mme G. Privat, Claude Roger-Marx, Mr. and Mrs. P. Roland, Lessing J. Rosenwald, Mme G. Séré de Rivières, M. Sérullaz, Marc Tapié de Céleyran, Antoine Terrasse, Marcel Thomas, Mario Uzielli and a private collector.

Introduction

THE COLLECTION of over 230 letters by Toulouse-Lautrec that is published here is by far the largest in existence, and constitutes an invaluable source of information on him both as an artist and as an individual. Dating from every year of his life between 1871, when he was only six, to 1900, when he had only months to live, these letters permit us to follow the history of his art and life in an incomparably detailed manner. A number of Lautrec's letters have already been published in biographies of him and in a few miscellaneous sources, but from none of them do we gain as vivid a picture of his daily existence, both private and professional, as from those which are published here. Indeed, the majority of them were written to members of his family, above all to his mother, but also to his grandmothers, uncles, aunts, and cousins, and are fascinating as documents of the life of a great family of that period. Superficially, they appear to repeat the same themes: I am well despite various indispositions . . . I am working and it is hard . . . no details, because it wouldn't interest you . . . I have seen various members of the family. . . . But when they are read more closely, the living Lautrec can be seen in them in a gripping manner. A new Lautrec can in fact be recognized, one whose preoccupations are in process of emerging, whose talent is swiftly developing, and who is driven by an ambition that has not been recognized previously.

Outside of family letters, we find in this collection a number addressed to dealers in paintings and the graphic arts such as Kleinmann, Manzi, and Pellet; to critics and editors such as Alexandre, Geffroy, Roger Marx, Deschamps, and Dujardin; and to a few friends and anonymous collectors. Distinctly different in style from the first group, they reveal the professional aspects of Lautrec's life, and also provide new information on works he completed, exhibited, or sold, information which in many instances corrects that which was previously available. In addition to the letters by Lautrec himself, there are the fascinating one written by his father immediately after his death, and the series of 35 letters sent to his mother by her maid Berthe Sarrazin, who was charged with reporting to her during the crisis in 1899 which ended with Lautrec's confinement in a mental hospital. These poignant documents, which reveal the artist abandoned at a time when he desperately needed affection, are not only deeply moving in themselves, but shed new light on his attitudes and behaviour during the crisis. Both his father's letter to Manzi and those of Berthe Sarrazin are published here in an appendix.

All the letters in this collection are the property of Mr. Herbert D. Schimmel of New York, and have been acquired during the past fifteen years. Many of them come from the Tapié de Céleyran and Séré de Rivières collections, that is, directly from relatives of the artist or their descendants. A small number of the letters have been quoted by the Countess Attems (née Mary Tapié de Céleyran) in *Notre Oncle Lautrec*, but in a very fragmentary form, and with either no dates or incorrect ones. An equally small number have been published by Mme Dortu and Philippe Huisman in *Lautrec par Lautrec*, but sometimes without dates and in an occasionally incomplete form. As for the letters, both published and unpublished, which are not included in the present edition, the interesting information in them has been incorporated into the footnotes wherever it is relevant.

What do we learn from his correspondence about Toulouse-Lautrec, an artist to whom art historians, students of manners, chroniclers in search of scandal, and above all doctors and psychiatrists have devoted their attention since 1930? Intellectually, he was surely not an original thinker. He frequented a rather limited circle of men-about-town and 'petits journalistes' such as Jules Roques, Jean Lorrain, Lucien Muhlfeld, Maurice Donnay, Jean de Tinan, and Arsène Alexandre (one of them, Hugues Rebell, made him the hero of a novel of artistic life, *La Câlineuse*, published in 1899). To some extent, however, Lautrec was also in contact with the more sophisticated circle of the *Revue Blanche* and Tristan Bernard, as is evident from letters of around 1895. Among the painters of his period, he admired the works of Degas and Bonnard, but actually associated primarily with such minor Nabis as Sérusier, Ranson, and Valtat, and with such popular figures as Dethomas, Somm, and Maurin. During his student years he was closest to Anquetin, Rachou, and Gauzi, of whom Anquetin alone achieved some fame, while his relations with Van Gogh and Bonnard a little later were very brief. This is less true, however, of Vuillard, who painted a brilliant portrait of him and later wrote a fine memoir of his former colleague.

In general, Lautrec's intellectual style was that of the periodical *Fin de Siècle*, the only one which consistently supported him and responded to him and his particular milieu. It was a kind of man-about-town publication, full of advertisements for preservative injections and remedies for impotence, for books like *Introduction to Sin*, Maupassant's *Maison Tellier*, and Dujardin's *About Love*, as well as for 'rarities gallant and literary' and art photography. It also flourished on its articles on the world of fashionable courtesans, its images of contemporary fashion, its reviews of plays and novels such as *The Consecration of Venus* and *The Bazaar of Adultery*.

In contrast to all this, however, the correspondence published here shows that Lautrec had in addition a highly developed family feeling, a great respect for his grandmothers, a tender affection for his mother (which was not always reciprocated when she was preoccupied with the affairs of her large family), and an interest in his uncles, cousins, and nephews, from Uncle Odon to Cousin Gabriel. Indeed, thanks to his mother and his frequent sojourns in the family residences, Lautrec was for a long time deeply involved in family affairs; and many times, by sheer grumbling and grousing, he succeeded in straightening them out.

What was Lautrec's physical appearance? Surprisingly, it is still a matter of dispute, although we know that he was not quite five feet, one inch tall. Because of his long torso and short legs, he gave the impression of being a dwarf, a sort of gnome, and he tended to exaggerate this effect by going about with extremely tall men like Anquetin, Dethomas, and Gabriel Tapié de Céleyran. As for his attitude towards his physical appearance, he was by no means satisfied with it and cheerful, as is often maintained today. In his correspondence, he often returns to his physical misfortunes, which seem to have befallen him without interruption after a rather short childhood period of happiness and health. He describes himself ironically as 'the darling of the Graces', states bluntly that 'gracefulness is not my gift', and admits that 'my figure is devoid of elegance'. He feels that he has 'a loud, ugly voice', a 'bearded face which recalls that of a water carrier', a chin 'like an old shoe-brush', and 'an Auvergnat beard', as a result of which he must give 'Auvergnat-style kisses'. Yet he was also proud of his beard, which he allowed to grow more or less untrimmed, since it was, as he told his friend Gauzi, 'a sign of virility'.

Lautrec was often very ill, not only after the accidents which crippled his legs, forcing him to 'trot' on little legs in the streets, as he wrote in 1885, but before the accidents as well. Moreover, his letters are filled with reports on scores of minor annoyances; warts on his nose, frequent constipation, pimples, piles, toothaches, at least three bouts of influenza or the grippe. He was declared 'unfit for military service' in 1884 and three years later was having himself 'electricized' (a popular treatment at the time) by his friend Dr. Bourges. These deformities and illnesses, and above all of course his misshapen legs, desolated Lautrec. He told Coquiot that he would like 'to find a woman who had an uglier lover' than himself, and described himself in a letter to his mother as 'the abject being who makes for your despair'. On another occasion he reproached himself for the 'impure kisses' that he sent her. His sadness, at least at certain moments in his life, emerges strongly from his letters and the accounts of those who knew him. Several times he wrote that he was 'a disillusioned old man', even in 1884, at the age of twenty. What added to this feeling was the presence within his family, and rather close to him, of a relative who was his absolute opposite. This was his cousin Louis Pascal, whom he described as an elegant, gracious man, a likeable pleasure-seeker, although he also recognized that Louis would probably never amount to much more than the husband of a rich heiress, and was relieved when instead he found a position in an insurance company.

Yet Lautrec, despite his physical condition, and unlike so many of his colleagues, was very much interested in sports. He could hardly ride a horse after his accidents as his father and uncles loved to do; but he enjoyed the sea and all kinds of activities associated with it—swimming, sailing, fishing with cormorants—and for that reason spent several weeks every year at Arcachon, Taussat, and other seaside resorts. Shortly after his leg injuries, he was already beginning to swim again, at Nice; a few years later he was looking forward to 'soaking himself' at Arcachon; and in 1890 he enjoyed salt-water bathing at

Biarritz. At the end of his life, when he was no longer strong physically, he installed a rowing-machine in his studio. In addition to swimming, he liked to sail, dressing up as 'a merchant marine captain', and above all to fish with his pet cormorants. He mentioned them in several letters, and according to Coquiot, he used to walk on the beach at Taussat, waddling like them. Joyant, too, reports an incident concerning cormorants—that the biggest blow of Lautrec's life was the accidental shooting of one of them by a hunter. Appropriately enough, when Lautrec got a commission to do a binding design in 1893, he drew a cormorant.

Lautrec's interest in sport was not confined to the sea. He also enjoyed hunting crows with Anquetin in Normandy, and spoke with admiration of his father's prowess with the gun. In addition, he liked to watch bullfights, bicycle races (he even accompanied a French team to England to observe a meet and to make sketches of it), and toward the end of his life he watched horse races, returning in this to a much earlier interest that had been fostered by his acquaintance with Princeteau, a specialist in hunting and racing pictures. Among Lautrec's lithographs, there is also one that depicts an early automobile.

Like the other members of his aristocratic family, Lautrec was fond of fine food and drink. 'He likes to eat', remarked his friend Natanson, 'like those in the know'. Eating and drinking were, after all, important events for the hosts, all older than he, of Le Bosc, Céleyran, and Malromé. His father was famous for his culinary fantasies, all of which Lautrec imitated. Again and again in his letters food and drink are the subject, so much so that on one occasion he admitted, 'I am re-reading my letter and find it to have a gastronomic character.' He was indeed forever asking his mother to send him, as he did in that letter, the products of his native region—pâté de foie gras, truffles, capons, and of course wine from the vineyards of Malromé. Even in Paris he could visualize others eating them in the South, and concluded one letter to his mother, 'I kiss you on your cheeks, stuffed with asparagus, at least as I suppose.' He was curious about recipes, liked to entertain, and to be congratulated on the results. It was hardly by chance that he designed many menu cards, especially in 1896 and 1897. On the one he drew in honour of his friend Sescau in March 1895, he offered his guests 'opossum, *en liberty*', playing on the words 'liberty', a new kind of fabric, and 'opossum', an allusion to the kangaroo which Zola had recently served.

Given his appreciation of food, it is hardly surprising that Lautrec frequented the finest restaurants in Paris. Like his father, he seems to have dined regularly at Lucas', one of the best of the boulevard restaurants; he also ate at Weber's, at the Royale, at Claudon's Café Américain, and in bars. As for the connoisseurship of alcoholic beverages, he was acknowledged by many acquaintances to be an expert, a fine judge of wines, and an enthusiastic experimenter with liquors. Indeed, it was he who taught the French how to make and drink cocktails, and many stories circulated about the potency of the ones he served.

From his childhood, Lautrec never ceased to love the countryside and animals.

He enjoyed spending part of his summer vacations at Le Bosc, and regretted deeply that a property division within his family deprived him of it. Consequently, he was elated when his mother bought the estate of Malromé, a fine old house on a large piece of land, near Bordeaux. Occasionally he went to Rivaude, his Uncle Amédée's hunting property, and to Respide, which belonged to the Pascals, also relatives. His love of animals was indeed in an old family tradition. At Le Bosc his grandmother had monkeys, including a tame pouch-monkey; she also kept many dogs, cats, and horses, with which Lautrec was familiar at a very early age. Moreover, his father was something of a professional sportsman,· who fished with cormorants, hunted with hawks (he is shown as such in one of Lautrec's first paintings), and even kept a tame ferret. Characteristically, after he had left his wife alone in the Midi he sent her a telegram with the one message he felt was important: 'Send ferrets.' During the years he spent in Paris as a child, Lautrec never had enough of the Zoological Gardens, and he continued to return there until the end of his life. He raised birds, grew fond of a toad, admired the apes and llamas, the parakeets and pelicans of the Botanical Gardens. The title of a book on the latter, illustrated with drawings by Crafty (Victor Géruzez), appears in one of his earliest letters; and in one of the last ones, he is concerned with his own illustrations for Jules Renard's celebrated *Histoires Naturelles*. It can even be maintained that he would never have produced them without the earlier experiences described above.

From the letters published here, it can be seen that Lautrec was very much attached to his family's homeland, the region of Languedoc, in which his forebears had lived since the Middle Ages. Proud of this attachment, Lautrec acquired a perfect knowledge of the Gascon dialect and used it often in his speech and writing. His relative, the Countess Attems, reports that he liked to sing the Christmas Carol, 'Daré la porto dé la glèiso' (Open the door of the church). In his correspondence, Gascon words such as 'cagonit' (a small child or bird) and 'poutous' (kisses) often occur; and to them he added his own invention, 'poutounégeades' (a flood of kisses). Once, too, he quoted the Provençal proverb, 'Canta abaud d'avé fa l'iovu' (Don't count your chickens before they are hatched), and at other times he employed such phrases as 'Chés, semblo sa mairé' (Oh God, they're just like their mother!), 'esperpil' (gay), and 'bouillaque de l'Aveyron' (mud of the River Aveyron).

Although he used Gascon phrases to identify himself with a region and a tradition, and at times simply to amuse himself, Lautrec preferred English as an alternative to French. This Anglomania was also a part of family tradition, coming to him from both his mother and his father. The former liked to speak in English; the latter had 'lads' and English coachmen. Moreover, many Frenchmen of their class shared this attitude: certain sections of Paris, precisely the ones where the Lautrecs lived, had a decidedly English appearance, both in the architecture of the houses with their English basements and in the behaviour of the inhabitants. And this was especially true of the late nineteenth century, when Anglomania was the height of fashion, and characters in the novels of

Paul Bourget and Anatole France frequently shifted into English to convey their most intimate or enthusiastic ideas.

Among these Anglomanes, Lautrec was one of the noted figures. His mother normally spoke to him in English at the dinner table; his father hoped that his English groom and the latter's children would correct his pronunciation, though it is likely that they contributed nothing but a Cockney accent. Lautrec had an Irish governess, Miss Braine, with whom he was still in contact many years later. One of his letters to his mother is written in English, as is one of those to his friend Adolphe Albert, written twenty years later. He always preferred English expressions to any other, using the word 'fuss', for example, in speaking of the excitement of a departure, and frequently signing himself, in letters to his mother, 'Yours'. Once he spoke of 'l'horizon de five o'clock teas', and on another occasion he used the phrase, 'that is the question'. Many of his friends and models were English—May Belfort, May Milton, and Lona Barrison, all well-known entertainers, and the anonymous girl of the Le Havre cafe, 'The Star'. He was on intimate terms with the English artists Conder and Rothenstein, and admired Whistler. Indeed, it was partly thanks to Lautrec that some of his friends developed British manners; he nicknamed Leclercq 'Petit Gentleman' and Bouglé 'L'Anglais d'Orléans'. In 1892 he spent ten days in London; in 1894 and again in 1895, at least a week. His father even advised him to settle there, because it was the only country where a man could drink as he pleased. During one of his visits to London, Lautrec attended the trial of Oscar Wilde, of whom he made a penetrating portrait.

Lautrec's knowledge of English obviously enabled him to speak and write it with ease, yet he seems to have read little of the literature in that language. At least, there are no references to it in his letters; and this is also true, to a large extent, of French literature. The only quotations from it are a few familiar phrases: 'autre guitare' (another matter) from Victor Hugo; 'Je suis seul avec mon désespoir' (I'm alone with my despair) from an opera; 'fallait pas qu'il aille' (he didn't have to go), a popular idiom; and several lines from the *Fables* of La Fontaine, which of course are learned by every schoolchild. Quick-witted and intelligent but never a great reader, Lautrec read mostly at night, in order to fight insomnia, as his cousin Gabriel reported. This does not invalidate what we have already learned of his intellectual style in discussing his affinities with the magazine *Fin de Siècle* and his friendship with the 'petits journalistes'.

If Lautrec was, at least up to a point, a Paris 'Englishman', he was also an authentic Parisian, and this, too, is reflected in the language he employed in his correspondence, which undoubtedly reflects that of his everyday speech. He knew how to write to his mother in an easy, lively style, using rather abbreviated, often incoherent punctuation. Among his colleagues, he boasted of knowing argot, of having 'a profound knowledge of slang'. Indeed, the one extant letter to a painter written prior to 1893, namely, the one to Eugène Boch, contrasts absolutely with those he sent to his family. He signed it 'jeune pourriture' (literally, young putrefaction, or Old Stinker); evidently because this was a nickname given to him by studio comrades, and one which speaks volumes. He described his works as 'vachages' (literally, cowages, or direction-less, like a cow wandering in a field), and elsewhere, too, he took great liberties with the language. In all this he undoubtedly showed the influence of the coarse Montmartre milieu in which he was then living, above all that of the singer Aristide Bruant, whose specialty was an insolent slang. But he was also influenced by his friend Goudezki, whose 'slow, monotonous, bored way of talking [showed] a brutal disdain for the public'. Hence it was appropriate for the Socialist periodical *Le Père Peinard* (April 30, 1893) to congratulate Lautrec for not being among the 'flossies who wouldn't want to peck at anything but pap'.

Unfortunately, rather few of his letters to friends have survived—only some short notes to Bruant, to journalists and editors, to publishers for arranging appointments. Nothing is known of what he might have written to Grenier, Anquetin, Sescau, Guibert, or Rachou. But one letter to the sculptor Carabin, which has been reproduced by Coquiot, gives an idea of what these letters were probably like. He calls Carabin 'viande crue' (literally, raw meat) and concludes 'Tout va bien, Canrobert' (Everything's okay, Canrobert), an allusion to a famous order of the day by that general. From the accounts of Lautrec's conversation, we get a similar impression of his language. With artists and friends he liked to speak without pulling his punches, and in a voice 'so strong and resonant that his friends used to call [it] the "golden voice", carrying every word he said far and wide.' Moreover, he had a twangy way of speaking, some-thing of a lisp, as other contemporaries recalled, and with that a gift for turning a neat phrase. His sallies were 'caustic and sharp, summed up in a few words, sometimes in just one, always precise and unexpected'. Like the witticisms of Degas, with which his own had an affinity, they circulated in the studios of Paris. His speech was punctuated with phrases like 'pas beau, ça', 'hein?' and 'quoi?' In addition, he invented phrases which were familiar only to his friends, yet seemed more expressive than conventional ones; a number have been quoted: 'os clavicule' (literally, collarbone, for a place best not to go for fear of breaking one's neck); 'ouax rababaou' (an imitation of a fox-terrier's barking, to describe a disagreeable person); also 'moustache', 'Croxi (for Croques-y) Mar-gouin', and others. In his *Journal*, Jules Renard speaks of Lautrec's desire to say things 'so foolish that they are good', a Flaubertian attitude which resulted in such celebrated descriptions as 'il est beau, il a l'air d'une sole' (he's handsome, looks like a sole [fish]).

The Lautrec who loved to talk in an original and vivid style was also a prolific letter writer. In the correspondence published here, the greatest concentration is in the years from 1871 to 1892, after which there is a progressive decrease, especially in letters to his family. Before about 1890, he wrote regularly to his grandmothers, to keep up the conversation, as it were, when he was absent; and in the same spirit he wrote to his mother, his uncles and cousins. Often, he had spent the summer with them at Malromé and Le Bosc, and was now informing them of events in Paris during the winter. In 1890, however, there are signs of a break with his family, a break between the radically Bohemian artist and the conservative, aristocratic family which did not understand him or wish to. Aware of this, he would write: 'I'd like to talk to you about my painting, but *it is so special*', and in fact it was so special, so remote from his closest relatives' interests, that he stopped writing to them. It was only with his mother that he maintained a correspondence; his letters to her were affectionate and spontaneous, but were also concerned frequently with financial and other practical matters. The far fewer letters to his friends were largely written to arrange a meeting in a café or studio; and it was there that he could communicate directly, while looking at his companion and even sketching him, imposing a vision on him, a conception of life. Of course, these letters help us to bring the memory of his friendships, and their chronology, into focus, but only rarely do they contain important new facts. For Lautrec evidently did not want to expose himself in them: the self revelation which we do find is unintentional, just as that in Van Gogh's letters is purposeful and indeed the very reason for their existence.

On the other hand, Lautrec's early letters, almost entirely unknown until now, are invaluable documents of the formative years between the ages of six and twenty-six, years which were decisive in establishing the friendships and shaping the tradition in which he lived. Let us examine these early years in greater detail.

About twenty of the letters date from the period 1871–78, in other words, up to the time of the first accident to his legs, which occurred when Lautrec was fourteen. Largely the traditional New Year's letters, they show that he had a very affectionate nature, and felt a special fondness for his cousin Madeleine Tapié de Céleyran, whose premature death in 1882 was to sadden him greatly. In these letters also appear the relatives and friends of whom he would almost never lose sight later, notably his cousin and schoolmate Louis Pascal, his cousin and future companion Gabriel Tapié de Céleyran, and his teacher, the Abbé Peyre. In these letters, too, Lautrec already reveals some characteristic traits: his affection for animals and birds, his taste for good food. Apropos the latter, we may note that the phrase 'élève crottinophage' (literally, horse-manure-eating pupil), which he uses in signing a letter of around 1875, is not, as his biographers have assumed, an allusion to his passion for horses, but rather an expression of his fondness for 'crottins,' the famous chocolate drops of the Midi. During these early years, he lived not only in the South, but in Paris, where he attended a *lycée* while living with his mother at 'Aunt Pérey's,' the Hôtel Pérey in the fashionable Cité du Rétiro, which was directed by a distant relative of theirs.

In 1878 and 1879, spaced only fifteen months apart, occurred the accidents to his legs, and from his correspondence it is evident that they had a profound effect on the young Lautrec. After the first one, in which he fractured one of his thigh bones, he described himself as a 'béquillard' (a cripple on crutches) and signed himself 'Henry patte cassée' (Henry Broken-Paw). After the second accident, which he likewise attributed to his own clumsiness, not understanding the inevitable physiological causes, he rarely mentioned the resulting infirmity;

14

for thereafter his legs had ceased to grow, and the long sojourns in spas at Barèges and Nice, the treatments with electric brushes, and so on, did not alter this tragic condition. These years are in any event inadequately represented in his letters, since his mother was with him constantly while he was taking cures, and the only letters he wrote were to his grandmothers and his friend Etienne Devismes.

In 1880, when he failed to pass the baccalaureate examinations, Lautrec expressed his feeling of wounded pride in a characteristically ironic manner: he had name-cards printed with the legend 'Henry de Toulouse-Lautrec, retoqué ès-lettres' (flunker of the arts). At this time, his letters were still rather immature and centred on family affairs. But their tone changed abruptly in August 1881, when he decided to paint and almost immediately produced what his mother described as 'masterpieces'. Indeed, his father and the latter's friend Princeteau, a fairly well-known artist, were also 'literally sent into transports of joy'. Shortly thereafter Lautrec went to Paris to take up in earnest the career of an artist. There he met John Lewis Brown, a reputable painter of equestrian subjects whom he found to be 'very likeable'. Yet he hardly commented in his letters on Léon Bonnat, the successful portrait-painter and teacher with whom he began to study in March 1882. When Bonnat closed his studio and dismissed his pupils in September of the same year, Lautrec consulted his father—an unusual action, to which he resorted only in times of crisis—about entering the studio of Fernand Cormon, 'an original and austere talent'. His letters also indicate that he had considered studying with the fashionable Carolus-Duran, but had decided that 'this prince of colour' turned out only 'mediocre draughtsmen, which would be the death of me', thus placing a premium on drawing that would remain characteristic of his entire career.

Cormon, a painter largely forgotten today, was at that time enjoying a triumph at the Luxembourg Museum (the museum of contemporary art) with his prize-winning picture of *Cain*, and was considered a good teacher. His letters show Lautrec as a beginner in the studio, anxiously waiting over a month for the master to hand down an opinion of his works, and then rejoicing when it turned out to be a favourable one. In 1883 he approved of one of Lautrec's 'big daubs', and even congratulated him on some works of 'an impressionistic bent'. In the spring of 1884, by which time they were on closer terms, Cormon chose Lautrec, alone among the younger students—'the only one in the whole studio', he reported proudly—to assist him in illustrating the Imprimerie Nationale's definitive edition of the works of Victor Hugo. Lautrec's drawings for *La Légende des Siècles* were not used after all, but they earned him the considerable sum of 500 francs. Yet he already realized that his grandmothers would understand little of what he was doing, which was 'so much outside the rule', and his father, too, considered him an 'outsider' for attempting to be more than the typical, social-minded amateur painters who were his friends.

How much more Lautrec was attempting emerges clearly from his letters to his mother. Passionately dedicating himself to mastering his art, he found that 'café life bores me', that all he could do was to sleep and paint. Indeed, around

1883 and 1884 his letters are filled with statements to the effect that he was 'working too much,' working 'like a madman', 'like a horse', 'killing himself with work', and was rarely 'taking it easy or even going out for a walk'. 'I'm an art student up to my ears', he wrote, and his mother declared in amazement to her own mother that he was 'the busiest man in the world'. To consecrate this new attitude he rented his own studio, after having worked in one belonging to Rachou, and from his correspondence we learn that he decorated it with Oriental rugs, like the studios of the painters on the Avenue de Villiers with whom he associated. Unfortunately, we have little information on his works themselves. In November 1884, he announced: 'I'm back in the old routine that will last until spring, and then maybe I'll do some really bizarre things', but he experienced difficulties, and on several occasions cursed 'this art which eludes me' and his dependence on a model who 'threatens to leave'. 'What a miserable calling this painting is', he grumbled. Yet his ambition was unlimited: he wanted to 'go everywhere to get impressions', wore himself out going to bed at two in the morning and rising at eight 'by candlelight—and for what?' The word 'everywhere' is important, since it indicates that he was giving up the conventional studio subjects and turning instead to contemporary urban scenes. In fact, following Whistler's precept in the famous 'Ten O'Clock' lecture, Lautrec now began to draw in the evenings 'in a bar'. One of his drawings, entitled *Gin-Cocktail*, was published in the Montmartre newspaper *Le Courrier Français*; and he prepared another one for *Le Figaro Illustré*, but did not submit it when his friend Rachou pointed out some mistakes in it.

In the years 1885 and 1886, Lautrec's letters show him moving out of the world of the art student and into that of the professional artist with a strong attraction to the bohemian life of Montmartre. His closest friends were Anquetin and Grenier, both of whom were very *Montmartrois*, and he enjoyed himself freely with them, even living for some time with the latter in his studio in Paris and his house at Villiers-sur-Morin. When the famous Chat Noir café opened, Lautrec and his companions immediately became habitués; on one occasion he described having made 'the people dance at the Chat Noir' and then going to bed at six in the morning. Thanks to Roques, publisher of *Le Courrier Français*, he had free access to the Eden music hall. At the same time, however, he tried to 'charm' the musicians of the Opera, so as 'to insinuate myself into the temple of art'—not, as he maintained, 'out of boredom', but because he already liked music and the spectacle of the opera, as he would continue to do for a long time. Hence his friendship with the Dihaus, who were musicians at the Opera, and with their sister, who was a music teacher. During these years, Lautrec also drew in the studio of Carrier-Belleuse, a distinguished sculptor, and even undertook sculpture himself, a fact that was not previously known.

From his letters of 1887, we learn of Lautrec's move to a larger studio, on the rue Caulaincourt in Montmartre, a studio whose colourful furnishings have been described by some of his contemporaries. But the letters of this year are otherwise rather meagre in information. In 1888, on the other hand, they are far more numerous, and give several indications that Lautrec's art was beginning to be

16

appreciated. He reports exhibiting 'right and left', notably in Belgium, where he was invited by the avant-garde group 'Les Vingt', two of whose members visited him in Paris and were 'charming and lavish with, alas, unmerited praise'. At the request of one of them, Théo van Rysselberghe, he tried to persuade Forain to exhibit there as well, and with characteristic generosity also tried to obtain an invitation for his friend Albert. He announced at the same time that his works were beginning to sell, as a result of which he had ceased to be an amateur and had become the kind of professional artist his father disliked thoroughly, since it meant, for him, that Lautrec would no longer be a 'gentleman'. From the year 1889 we have only three letters, in one of which he again asserted, with a familiar mixture of modesty and pride, 'I'm going to carry the good word, or rather the good paintings, to Belgium—poor Belgians!' Looking for viable subjects, he contemplated painting the female ward attendants at the hospital where his friend Bourges was an intern, since the 'old women wearing white bonnets' looked 'a little like milkmaids'. After giving up this project, he must have begun the well-known series of women sitting in the garden of Monsieur Forest, on the rue Ganneron, works marked by a new intensity of colour and freedom of execution. Yet he felt that 'my work still isn't very brilliant.'

By 1890, however, Lautrec was beginning to experience real success. In January he attended the opening of the Exposition des Vingt at the Musée Moderne in Brussels, where he showed five works; and in March he was at the opening of the Salon des Indépendants in Paris, where he showed two works. Returning from the latter, he wrote to his mother in a mood of exaltation: 'I'm still reeling from the second exhibition opening. What a day! But what a success. The Salon [that is, the older, conservative one] got a slap in the face from which it will recover perhaps, but which will give many people something to think about.' Significantly, the earliest of his letters to a picture dealer to be preserved dates from this year: he gives the price (300 francs) for each of two paintings he had shown in Brussels, neither of which is listed in the catalogue of his œuvre. During the summer, Lautrec made his first trip to Spain, although he went only as far as San Sebastian to see the bullfights; during the summers of 1894 and 1896 he would return to this country and visit the great museums of Madrid and Toledo.

The extant letters of 1891 are much more numerous than those of 1890, and provide some interesting information. At the beginning of the year, there were the exhibitions at the Cercle Volney in Paris and, almost inevitably, at the Exposition des Vingt in Brussels. To the former Lautrec sent two pictures, one of which he sold later in the year; always anxious to establish his success in his family's eyes, he informed his mother that it 'was sold for 300 francs, a little boost in the scale.' And what was equally significant for him, he could add that 'Degas has encouraged me by saying that my work this summer wasn't too bad.' In another letter he mentioned three portraits on which he was working, whose dates can thus be established more accurately than heretofore; they are the portraits of Gaston Bonnefoy, Henri Bourges, and Louis Pascal. More important, he noted in another letter, datable October 1891, that 'my poster is pasted today on the walls of Paris'; it is *La Goulue au Moulin Rouge*, his first effort in this medium and an almost instantaneous source of renown; indeed, in December he could state, 'My poster has been a success on the walls, despite some boners by the printer which spoiled my product a little.' In the same letter he referred to another historic event, the opening of Le Barc de Boutteville's gallery on the rue Lepeletier, in which his works and those of other avant-garde artists were displayed permanently. 'The newspapers have been very kind to your offspring', he informed his mother.

Through his correspondence, we can follow Lautrec's movements on two trips in 1892: one to Brussels, in February, where he attended the opening of the Exposition des Vingt, and reported it to be excellent, 'having (as it does) the benefit of my immense talent'; and another to London, in May, where he visited the National Gallery with his friend Ricci, and in the streets quickly found himself 'in the grip of the spell arising from the London hustle and bustle'. It was in 1892 that Lautrec became acquainted with the critic Roger Marx, who not only defended him in his articles, but bought his works for his collection. During most of this year, however, the financial troubles of the Pascal family preoccupied him, and no less than 21 of his letters are concerned with them. Lautrec felt particularly indebted to the Pascals since he had found with them at Respide 'what we vainly sought elsewhere, a home', yet his mother, who had shared that pleasure with him, remained indifferent to his repeated pleas that she cooperate in helping them. Exasperated by this, he finally told her: 'Please come and take care of all this business, because I've had *enough* of it.' The 'business' ended with the ruin of the Pascals, the sale of Respide, and the placement of his aunt in a sanatorium.

In so far as his personal life was concerned, the year 1893 was also not a happy one for Lautrec, since his good friend Bourges, with whom he had shared an apartment since 1887, was planning to marry, and Lautrec, who hated to live alone, would be obliged to do so. The references to this prospect in his letters indicate clearly enough how much it upset him, and not least because he felt unqualified to maintain a household: 'I shall have the ineffable pleasure of keeping my own household accounts and knowing the exact price of butter.' In his professional life, however, Lautrec was succeeding brilliantly, producing such outstanding posters as *Babylone d'Allemagne* and *Jane Avril au Jardin de Paris*, for the reproduction rights to which the editors of newspapers competed, and also beginning the series of lithographs illustrating Gustave Geffroy's text on Yvette Guilbert. At the end of December, he explained to his mother that he would remain in Paris for the holiday season, since 'I have an enormous lot to do. Two posters to deliver before January 15, which are still not started.' He also announced that he had 'just invented a new process that can bring me in not a little money', referring no doubt to the spatter technique of lithography that he was undertaking with Charles Maurin.

At the beginning of 1894, Lautrec went once again to Brussels, but this time he also visited Holland, where he appreciated greatly both the art and the landscape. 'It's useless to list for you the beautiful things I've seen', he explained to his mother, 'I've had a fine eight-day lesson with professors Rembrandt, Hals, etc.' Characteristically, however, he found 'the wonders of the Dutch masters a mere nothing compared with nature, which is unbelievable'. Towards the end of the year, he also planned to visit London for the opening of a poster exhibition to which he had contributed; and during the summer he made his second trip to Spain, this time visiting Burgos, Madrid, and Toledo, and discovering that 'they are even going to sing my praises in the newspapers of the country, such being fame and journalism.' At the same time, the album *Yvette Guilbert* appeared, and as Lautrec informed its publisher, André Marty, 'the book could not be better. Yvette has written a very nice note.' This seems to dispose of the legend that she wanted to take legal action against him for depicting her in an unattractive and offensive manner; nor is there any serious proof of a dispute between them at that time or later. At the end of the year, Lautrec was commissioned by André Antoine to design the stage scenery and programme for a production at the Théâtre de l'Œuvre, and announced to his mother, 'I have even made my debut in a new line, that of stage designer.'

Whereas Lautrec's correspondence of earlier years had often been dominated by letters to his mother and other members of his family, that of 1895, in so far as it has survived, contains almost exclusively letters to professional acquaintances and friends. There are notes to Edward Bella, the London paper-manufacturer who sponsored exhibitions of avant-garde posters; to Edouard Dujardin, the Symbolist writer and art critic; to Arsène Alexandre, the editor of the newspaper *Le Rire*; and several to Léon Deschamps, the editor of *La Plume*, a leading literary magazine, which published an extremely favourable article on Lautrec in November of that year. As for his friends, it was at about this time that he was acquainted with the brothers Natanson, directors of the periodical *La Revue Blanche*, with the youthful Francis Jourdain and his father Frantz, an influential architect. Of course, he continued to see, and to mention in his letters, such older friends as Dr. Bourges and the two from whom he was inseparable, yet whose divergent influences counterbalanced each other: Maurice Joyant, an old school-mate and man of taste and distinction, and Maurice Guibert, a chance acquaintance and inveterate pleasure-seeker.

The extant letters of 1896 deal with two subjects: Lautrec's one-man exhibitions and his fishing expeditions. As for the former, there were two exhibitions, which have sometimes been confused because they were both held at Joyant's gallery on the rue Forest: one of January 12, consisting of paintings and drawings, the other on April 20, consisting of lithographs. Although Gustave Geffroy, with whom Lautrec had collaborated on the *Yvette Guilbert* album, urged the dean of Naturalist writers, Edmond de Goncourt, to attend the first exhibition, he evidently did not do so. When, however, Lautrec wrote to him personally, he did attend the second one, and even met the artist there: 'A ridiculous little man', he remarked afterward in his journal, 'whose caricatural deformity is reflected in every one of his drawings.' Quite undaunted by Goncourt's opinion (whatever he had sensed of it), Lautrec continued to work energetically. 'I have two or three big deals with bicycle companies, all right, all right', he boasted to his mother in May; and indeed, early the following month he accompanied a French bicycle team to London to attend a meet and make sketches for use in 'a poster advertising "Simpson's Lever Chain", which may be destined to be a sensational success'. With equal energy he devoted himself to deep-sea fishing on a commercial fishing boat—a privilege rarely accorded, of which he was particularly proud—and to 'a magnificent and lively trip' by boat over an inland waterway through the lakes of the Landes region near Bordeaux, which he undertook with several friends.

Less information can be gleaned from the letters of 1897, which are fewer in number, but they do inform us of Lautrec's move to a larger, more comfortable apartment on the Avenue Frochot: 'an extraordinary apartment', he wrote, 'I hope to end my days in peace there.' And they do provide a certain number of facts about his illustrations for Clemenceau's book *Au Pied du Sinaï*, published in this year, and his plans for a large one-man exhibition at the Goupil Galleries in London, which took place in the spring of the following year. The few surviving letters of 1898 are also disappointing when compared with the earlier ones, although we learn from them of Lautrec's break with the print publisher Gustave Pellet, and of the limited public interest in his fine lithographs, as a result of which he had to reclaim most of the impressions he had left for sale with Pellet. Probably the most significant letter of this year was the one to his mother in which he stated: 'I'm relishing my Avenue-Frochot tranquillity so much that the least effort is impossible for me. My painting itself is suffering.' For this is a sign of the lethargy, the dissipation of energy that accompanied Lautrec's approaching breakdown, the tragic event of the following year.

On the confinement in a private mental hospital which followed Lautrec's breakdown early in 1899, the documents published here provide entirely new clarifications. Up until now, the only information available was a notice that appeared in various newspapers on March 18 and 19, to the effect that he had been 'overcome by a sudden illness in an "establishment" near the Opera', meaning perhaps in a brothel in the rue des Moulins. Lautrec must have been taken directly to the hospital. But this description of his illness as 'sudden' has surprised some writers, who have noted that as early as February 8 he had produced a bizarre, apparently incoherent lithograph, *The Parakeet with a Pipe*, and that at least two other prints characterized by infantile details and shaky lines date from about the same time. Other writers have retorted that these works should be viewed as audaciously modern, rather than as psychotic in origin. But Joyant, one of the most reliable witnesses, speaks of Lautrec's profound derangement in 1899, while prudently indicating that his own remedy would have been close care, detoxification and a trip, instead of institutional confinement. At this crucial moment, what part did Lautrec's mother play? The question is all the more pertinent since she had spent much of her life helping her son, and has always been considered a saintly individual who was endlessly attentive to his needs. What the new documents, only recently discovered, indicate is that in January-February 1899 Lautrec's mother, acting independently and against the advice of her intimates, decided to commit her son to an asylum. Perhaps to justify her action in the future, she preserved the letters which are published here; but whether they do so is another matter.

Forsaking Paris, as she often did when her family in the Midi needed her, Lautrec's mother, with her brother Amédée, who had come to fetch her, departed quite suddenly on January 3. Unable to understand her action—she left without informing even her closest relatives—Lautrec was infuriated and deeply confused. Indeed, he seems to have burned his hand on a stove deliberately, so as to have a reason for calling her. She had, however, left behind a faithful and intelligent servant, Berthe Sarrazin, to keep watch over her son and the contents of her apartment; and this servant's daily letters to her or, when the news was too bad, to another maid in Albi, Adeline Cromont, are documents of vital importance for understanding the tragic events that followed.

On January 3, when he learned of his mother's departure, Lautrec seems to have gone out of his mind; his system, already weakened by the excesses of the preceding years, could not withstand the shock. He sent a wire to his aunt Pascal, and went to see his cousin Gabriel, who handed over a thousand francs that his mother had apparently left for him. Nevertheless, he felt abandoned by his family and friends, and what is worse, he fell into the hands of several unsavoury characters: Calmèse, the owner of a livery stable and, it now appears, an alcoholic who encouraged Lautrec to drink; Stern, the printer of his lithographs at the time and an equally bad influence; and Big Gabrielle, a prostitute who hoped to take advantage of the situation. Whereas he had always been kept in short supply of money, Lautrec suddenly found himself rich, and succeeded in spending the thousand francs in one night, largely on knicknacks, dolls, spoons, and other objects which he felt had been fashioned with a perfect 'technik'. He then had his mother wire him more money.

On January 6, Lautrec received a somewhat reassuring letter from her; but he continued to buy foolishly, spending 400 francs at a time, and even worse, he began to 'varnish' his pictures with glycerine. 'I'm very much afraid he's going to ruin them all', wrote Berthe Sarrazin. On the 9th, however, Lautrec appeared more calm and began to see more trustworthy friends, such as Sescau and Albert; on the 12th, he had lunch with Séré de Rivières. Yet he remained troubled and uneasy, had someone search his studio for hidden intruders, and feared that his family intended to have him committed. Unfortunately, too, Calmèse was always present, encouraging him to drink, even spending the night with him, and as a result, Berthe reported on the 13th that he was 'in a state' again. He even tried to obtain money from his friends for Calmèse and Gabrielle, who constantly wheedled him for it, but was unsuccessful; pleased by this, Berthe expressed the hope that now 'perhaps they would leave him alone'. This was not what happened, however, and Lautrec was ready to borrow money anywhere, at any interest rate, for his 'friends'. All day long he drank at the shop of Père Francois, a wine merchant, and had his mother's wine brought there as well. Berthe painted a vivid picture of him sitting there with 'two dirty tramps' and 'that pig Calmèse', to whom he gave away all his possessions, 'even his bed-pillow', when he had no more money. His reliable friends urged that his mother return to Paris, and one of them, his neighbour Robin-Langlois, assured him that she was wrong in remaining aloof. Indeed, Lautrec was 'absolutely hostile' toward her, as was only too evident to Berthe.

Still unwilling to return, the Countess asked Berthe to consult Dr. Bourges, and he in turn sent her to Gabriel Tapié de Céleyran, but with the latter Lautrec wanted nothing to do. His mother also wrote to him directly: what she said is not known, but on January 24, some time after receiving this letter, Lautrec threatened to file a complaint at the Palais de Justice. In fact, he had already announced on the 16th that he had proposed to Mlle Séré de Rivières, so that her father, a judge, could support him. Meanwhile, his mother had Berthe ask Calmèse to return the things her son had given him, and when he finally did so on February 20, Calmèse asserted that 'Monsieur disgusted him'. The Countess herself remained away, despite Berthe's express calls for help on January 17, 18, 27, and 30, and her reports that Lautrec was extremely ill, his skin yellowing and his hands becoming covered with scales. Yet Dr. Mallet, who seems to have been observing him at this time, maintained that after about January 23 he was considerably improved. He was, it is true, no longer involved with Gabrielle, but he continued to associate with 'that demon Calmèse', and to estrange himself from his family, whom he accused of turning his mother against him. He even prepared to go away with his friend Joyant to Le Crotoy, on the Channel.

On February 3, however, Lautrec had another disastrous fit of rage. After spending a night in a hotel on the rue Pigalle, he was unable to come to terms about his bill, and in the ensuing argument declared, 'I am the Comte de Toulouse', momentarily adopting a social attitude which he had normally disdained. At this time his mother finally decided to return, and perhaps to celebrate the event, Lautrec ceremoniously invited Calmèse, together with *his* mother, to dinner at the Countess' apartment in the rue de Douai, where he now lived. This was on February 10; yet thereafter his condition did not improve; for there is preserved a bill dated the 13th (Schimmel Collection, New York) which indicates that she had engaged a male nurse to watch over her son, and she herself moved to the Cité du Rétiro. Moreover, this was evidently not the first such attendant; a letter of February 14 shows that there had been another one, named Andrieux, and a letter of the following day refers to yet another.

There now took place a medical examination, which 'settled nothing', but as a result the Countess began to think of having her son interned. In a letter of February 27, her brother Amédée warned her: 'Think it over well before making this confinement decision, because it is terribly serious.' Her husband, very much disturbed, did not share her views at all. By March 12, however, Lautrec was already in the asylum at Neuilly, for his mother reported to Joyant that 'he is reading and amusing himself by drawing.' On the following day, her brother wrote again, assuring her that she 'had acted as well as anyone could wish' by having her son taken into 'Dr. X's place'. According to this letter, Lautrec accepted a guardian and resigned himself to being locked up, so that 'it was all done quite painlessly'. Thereupon the newspapers, acting on information furnished by Joyant, announced on March 18 and 19 that Lautrec had been hospitalized, placing the date of confinement incorrectly on the 17th (in fact it was in late February or early March).

The formal confinement lasted until March 31, on which date two psychiatrists advised that he remain some weeks longer at Neuilly, 'in the establishment where he has recovered his health', In fact, he remained until May 17, making daily excursions to the Jardin d'Acclimatation, where he was fascinated by the spectacle of the animals in their cages, and also working on the series of drawings *Le Cirque* and attending the printing of his lithographs for Jules Renard's *Histoires Naturelles*. Several of the letters he wrote from Neuilly are published here, but are largely concerned with practical matters and give little insight into his state of mind. However, there are hints in a letter of April 16, telling his mother, 'Worried. Give me news of Grandma [who was ill] and orders for Berthe', and in one written at the end of the month, signed 'the prisoner'. In the same letter, he asks his mother to learn 'where you can buy fruit-flavoured "Eau Moscovite". It's harmless and very refreshing. I'll drink it *gladly*', which suggests what the strain of the detoxification treatment must have been. During this period, the loyal Berthe visited him several times, and reported to Lautrec's mother, who had returned to Albi to take care of her own mother. From these reports we learn, too, that Lautrec, now very 'rational', was allowed to go out with Séré de Rivières. Finally, after another medical examination on May 17, during which his production of the circus drawings without notes or models undoubtedly helped to convince the psychiatrists of his lucidity, he was released.

The two extant letters written by Lautrec later in 1899 inform us of the loss of his cormorant at Taussat, an event whose significance Joyant has underscored and more important, of his attitude toward exhibiting his works: declining an invitation from Frantz Jourdain to send some of them to the Exposition Universelle of 1900, he stated emphatically, 'if there is a jury, I *refuse categorically*. I will never deviate from this decision.' However, these letters can be supplemented by others, also in the Schimmel Collection, written about him by members of his family. One from his aunt Emilie, dated May 20, announced his arrival in Albi, described his father's great satisfaction at this, and asserted that 'all those who have seen Henry find him very well. One would not assume that he had been through such a crisis.' Three letters from his grandmother Gabrielle, dated May 20, 21, and 22, revealed how completely she was now out of sympathy with him; even urging that he leave soon, so that he would not be a disturbing influence; she was clearly more concerned with the problems of Raymond Tapié de Céleyran than with the graver ones of Lautrec. She did not have to see his 'horrible lips' for long because her grandson was on his way to Paris, le Crotoy, le Havre and Bordeaux. It is therefore ironic that the last of his letters to be published here was addressed to her; written from Bordeaux in December 1900, it informed her that he was 'working all day long', 'showing four pictures at the Bordeaux Exposition', and 'having success'. 'I hope that will please you a little', he added significantly. There were no letters to his mother, since she remained with him constantly; and as for the short ones addressed to Joyant from Le Havre, Bordeaux, and the other places where he spent his last months, they have been published in Joyant's monograph.

One last letter, although not written by Lautrec, is included here in an appendix. It is the one that his father sent to Michel Manzi, his former dealer, thanking him for the funeral wreath he had sent after Lautrec's death on September 9, 1901. It is perhaps too warm in tone, since the father knew that Manzi had not battled for Lautrec's success in the same manner as his associate Joyant. But it reveals that the father was beginning to realize that Lautrec had been 'deprived of his just heritage, even if he did not despair on that account', and that he had been 'matured by so many trials, native to him and accidental as well'. Nevertheless, he still refers to his son's works as merely 'rough sketches', betraying the same artistic prejudices that had prevented him from appreciating them when Lautrec was alive.

Lautrec's correspondence provides exceptionally valuable information about him both as an artist and as a human being. Concerning the events in his life, it confirms and enriches with greater detail the facts that were previously known, providing more precise dates and surprising indications about his accidents and illnesses, which physicians will perhaps now explain in a somewhat different manner. On his internment in a mental hospital in 1899, it throws a rather strange light, revealing that his mother, alone among his family and friends, favoured this action, probably because she hoped to avoid a scandal. The threat of one emerges clearly from the gripping sequence of letters by Berthe Sarrazin, published here to supplement those of Lautrec.

The image of Lautrec which emerges from his correspondence is that of a sensitive, tender, deeply affectionate man, conscious of his infirmity but wearing a mask of joviality and irony, and asserting himself in a forthright manner that is quite impressive. Around 1880 we see him in his letters as an emerging artist dominated by a family, a social group which would prefer to see him own vineyards and hunting estates, deal with farm managers, and maintain influential friendships, rather than attempt to make his living from the creation of art. His family does not object to painting as such, since his father, his uncle, and his cousins are amateur painters and sculptors, and it is a sign of good taste. But they do reproach him for seeking in art his exclusive enjoyment and means of support, and consequently Lautrec takes pride throughout his correspondence in proving to them that his works are being exhibited and sold, that he has dealers and collectors, that his posters are attracting wide attention. For that very reason, however, he is obliged to give up the joys of conventional family life and its reunions, although he remains in contact with his numerous family, travelling south several times a year to see his grandmothers, and—at least up to a point—keeping his mother as his confidant. More surprisingly, the letters to and by his father suggest that they, too, tried repeatedly to meet, to find one another, and that their affinities as well as their differences prevented them from doing so. In the letter to Manzi written after his son's death, the father even displays timidity regarding the former's talents.

Will these letters one day find a place in the anthologies? Surely in those devoted to artists' correspondence, because it would be difficult to find others that are more lively, informative, and authentic in tone. As to the literary anthologies, the answer is less obvious, but the vibrant style, the colourful language, and the sheer power of verbal expression in Lautrec's letters will always remain admirable qualities.

Note. In translating Lautrec's letters, we have attempted to render them as accurately as possible and in a style as close to his own vivid style as possible. The only changes made were those in punctuation and paragraphing, which are frequently quite confusing in the original manuscripts. Lautrec's occasional use of Provençal and Gascon words and phrases and his invention of expressive phrases have been noted, but his frequent use of English words such as 'fuss' and 'yours' has not. As for the difficult problem of dating the letters, rather few of which contain explicit dates, we have relied on a careful correlation of internal evidence, comparison of letters with each other, and information derived from biographies of the artist and similar sources. When a date has been determined by these means, it is of course indicated within brackets, to distinguish it from the dates actually inscribed by the writer; but it has not been possible in each of these cases to summarize our lengthy, frequently tedious, reasons for deciding on a given date. Finally, it should be noted that the references in the footnotes cite only the author of a publication, and that for full bibliographical information one must consult the Bibliography placed at the end. In the same way, and also in order to avoid unnecessary repetition, biographical information on the individuals mentioned in the letters is given only when a name first occurs, so that one must consult the Index to discover where this first occurrence, and the accompanying note, are to be found.

J.A.   T.R.

The Correspondence

Genealogical Note

Henri-Marie-Raymond de Toulouse-Lautrec-Monfa was born at Albi on November 24, 1864. His mother, née Adèle-Zoë Tapié de Céleyran, was born at Narbonne on November 23, 1841. His father, Count Alphonse-Charles de Toulouse-Lautrec-Monfa, was born on August 10, 1838. They were first cousins and were married on May 9, 1863. In addition to the future artist, they had one other child, Richard-Constantin, who was born in 1867 and died in 1868. (See the genealogical chart on page 304.)

1   TO MME L. TAPIÉ DE CÉLEYRAN

1   *Château de Céleyran, April 28, [18]71*

2   *My dear Godmother,*

      I kiss you with all my heart, and tell me please if Mlle Julie is well, if
3   *Annou, Justine and Antoine are well. Another kiss for you, and that is*
      all for now.

                            henri

2   TO MME L. TAPIÉ DE CÉLEYRAN   *[December, 1871]*

1   *My dear Godmother,*

      I am very happy to be writing you for New Year's Day. I wish you a
      happy New Year. I wish one, too, to everyone I know, uncles, aunts,
2   *cousins, etc. . . . . Tell Madeleine I would like to see her again very much.*
      A kiss for everybody, and for Godmama most of all.

                     Your grandson,

                     Henry de Lautrec

1. The property of Madame Tapié de Céleyran; near Narbonne, Department of Aude. See Ills. 4, 6.
2. Louise d'Imbert du Bosc (1815–1907), the wife of Léonce Tapié de Céleyran; Lautrec's maternal grandmother and also godmother, and the sister of his paternal grandmother. Lautrec uses the word 'Marraine'. Cf. Letter 3, note 3 and Ill. 18.
3. Annou is probably an affectionate name for Annette, who had been his nurse, and whose name recurs frequently in this correspondence. Antoine was the gardener at the Château du Bosc. Justine was undoubtedly a servant there.

Letter 2
1. This letter occupies one page of four. The other three, written by Lautrec's mother, concern the accidental death while hunting, on December 23, 1871, of Count Raymond-Casimir de Toulouse-Lautrec, the 'Black Prince', Lautrec's grandfather.
2. Madeleine Tapié de Céleyran (1865–1882), daughter of Amédée and Alix Tapié de Céleyran. A favourite cousin of Lautrec's, she often appears in his correspondence. She died at the age of seventeen.

1   *Paris, December 30, 1872*

2, 3   *My dear Grandma,*

    I am awfully glad to be sending you this letter, for it is to wish you a
4   *happy and prosperous New Year. I am anxious to be back at Bosc for*
my holiday, although I don't mind it here in Paris. We are on holiday
right now, and I am trying to have as much fun out of it as I can. Too
bad I have pimples that make me lose a lot of time scratching. Please
5   *tell Aunt Emilie that my little canary Lolo sings very well, he is*
awfully nice. I have bought him a very pretty cage with my New Year's
gift.
    Goodbye, dear Grandma. I kiss you with all my heart, my Aunt
6, 7   *Emilie, my Uncle Charles and my Uncle Odon as well, and please*
accept, all of you, my best wishes for a happy New Year.

Your respectful grandson

Henry

1. Lautrec was now living with his parents in Paris, at the Hôtel Pérey, an aristocratic lodging house at 5, Cité du Rétiro, near the rue du Faubourg Saint-Honoré and the rue Boissy d'Anglas. He was attending the Lycée Fontanes (now the Lycée Condorcet), which he had entered in October, 1872, and was in the eighth preparatory class, a class between the normal ninth and eighth forms.
2. Gabrielle d'Imbert du Bosc (1813–1902), the widow of Raymond-Casimir de Toulouse-Lautrec; Lautrec's paternal grandmother, and the sister of his maternal grandmother. See Ill. 18.
3. Lautrec uses the words 'Bonne Maman', as he always did in addressing her. Cf. Letter 1, note 2.
4. The property of Madame Raymond-Casimir de Toulouse-Lautrec; at Naucelle near Rodez, in the Department of Aveyron. See Ills. 5, 8.
5. Emilie d'Andoque de Seriège, the wife of Lautrec's paternal uncle, Charles. She should not be confused with Emilie le Melorel de la Haichois, the wife of another uncle, Odon.
6. Charles de Toulouse-Lautrec, Lautrec's paternal uncle. A gifted draughtsman and a man very much interested in art, he was Lautrec's favourite uncle, to whom he wrote letters reporting artistic events in Paris. See Ill. 12.
7. Odon de Toulouse-Lautrec (1842–1937), another of Lautrec's paternal uncles.

[*Paris, c. December 1872*]

My dear Grandma,

*I am sending you my best wishes for the New Year a little early because
I have something to ask you. Papa would like me to translate a chapter
in a big, red English book, easy to recognize because it's so heavy and*

1 *from the pictures about sports in it. It looks like a Bouillet dictionary.
Please be good enough to send it right away. Mama thinks it is in her
linen closet, but perhaps it's in her desk or in the chest at the foot of my
bed. Papa is asking me to do this translation as my New Year's gift
to him, and you will understand my desire to please him. We were
disappointed at not having him here for Christmas, but he will be here for*

2 *New Year's. I am very happy to be working at Mr. Mantoy's with*

3, 4 *Louis Pascal. Paul is grown up, now, and Joseph is a big young man. I
have a good time in Paris, however I am looking forward to going back
to Bosc. Goodbye, dear Grandma. I kiss you with all my heart, wishing
you a prosperous and happy New Year.*

*Mama asks me to send you her fondest regards. I suspect my birds are
asking me to send something nice to you, for they are singing their very
best.*

Your respectful grandson

Henry de T. Lautrec

5 *P.S. Please be kind enough to wish Urbain and the other servants a
happy New Year for me.*

1. Since Joyant identifies the author as Salvin, the book was either *Falconry: its
Claims, History, and Practice*, by Frances Henry Salvin and Gage Earle Freeman,
London, 1859, or *Falconry in the British Isles*, by Salvin and William Brodrick,
London, 1855 (2nd edition, 1873). Most biographers state that Lautrec translated
the entire book.
2. Lautrec's first teacher at the Lycée Fontanes.
3. One of Lautrec's maternal cousins; his father Ernest was the Prefect of the Department of the Gironde, and his mother, Cécile, was a first cousin of Lautrec's mother.
In 1878 Louis Pascal founded a small newspaper, *l'Echo Français*, which printed
Lautrec's story, *L'Histoire du Pélican et de l'Anguille*.
4. Paul and Joseph Pascal were Louis's brothers.
5. A groom on the estate of Madame de Toulouse-Lautrec.

My dear Godmother,

Thank you for your nice gift, for which I'm not thanking you soon enough. Oh! how happy I was when Mama opened the letter and gave me . . . 50 francs! I never had so much money all at once before. I am as happy as Cinderella, who also had a very generous godmother. We have been to see this beautiful story played by puppets at the Miniature
1   *Theatre. I now have a very nice cousin staying at the Hotel Pérey: it's*
2   *Jeanne d'Armagnac. She is 15 years old, but she plays with me. Goodbye, my dear little Godmother: give a kiss for me to Bébé and to Doudou, Bibel and Poulette as well. You are right in thinking my biggest hug is for you and that I am not forgetting my aunt and uncle.*
3   *I would ask you to kiss M. l'Abbé for me, only I know you wouldn't do it.*

Your respectful grandson

Henry

6   TO HIS MOTHER   *[Château du Bosc, c. 1873–74]*

Dear Mama,

Your nice letter made everybody so happy. I am going for walks the same as always, and this morning I went along hunting with Papa and
1   *Grésigue, who flew up into the top of a tree and didn't want to come*

1. A popular puppet theatre, located at 12, boulevard Montmartre in Paris.
2. One of Lautrec's cousins, and later Madame de Castellane.
3. The Abbot Peyre, chaplain of Céleyran and Lautrec's former tutor, to whom he later referred as 'my uncle the Abbot'.
   Letter 6
1. The name of one of the falcons kept by Lautrec's father for hunting. See Ill. 11.

down. Aunt Alix asks me to tell you that Laroque will be sure to be
waiting for you at the 8 o'clock train Wednesday morning. She would
very much like you to come and see her for a little while on Tuesday
evening. Poor Doudou died last night. Beatrix has lost a little of her
wobbliness. I have been having fun building a hippopotamus trap and I
am going to make one to catch the mouse. On Thursday I went to the
head of Vergnasse Brook (I think that's what they call it).

> *Goodbye, dear Mama. I kiss you with all my heart, and ask you to*
do as much for me to Aunt Joséphine.

2

3

4

5

Your son, who wants to see you soon.

Henri de Toulouse Lautrec

P.S. Please bring me four drawing board pins for spares.

7 TO MME L. TAPIÉ DE CÉLEYRAN   *Céleyran, August 23, 1873*

My dear Godmother,

I am writing to wish you a happy birthday, since it is Monday and the
feast day of St. Louis. As I am the only one of the little children in the
house who knows how to write, I am doing it for all. We leave on Monday
for Bosc and I am hoping you will soon be coming to meet us there again.

2. Alix Tapié de Céleyran, the wife of Amédée Tapié de Céleyran (1844–1925);
   Lautrec's paternal aunt. Amédée was in turn his maternal uncle.
3. Béatrix Tapié de Céleyran (1875–1913), one of the daughters of Alix and Amédée
   Tapié de Céleyran, and Lautrec's god-daughter. He usually calls her 'Kiki'.
4. Lautrec uses the word 'guincharderie', translated as 'wobbliness'. It is evidently an
   invention of his based on the slang word 'guinchard', or 'dance hall'.
5. Lautrec's great-aunt; known as Mademoiselle du Bosc, she owned the Hôtel du
   Bosc in Albi, where he was born.

1 *At the moment I am writing (9 o'clock) Gabriel is being naughty and Aunt Alix is saying she has a good mind to put him in prison with the*

2 *frogs. Yesterday we saw Mr. Vié, who found all the sick cured, Aunt Marie Delmas came on Thursday with Bébé Lamothe and we played*

3 *hide-and-seek. Yesterday we went up to the top of le Pech, and saw François and Augustin Renaud, the latter was scared of us. The storm made an awful racket last night, but Annou and Madeleine didn't even hear it. The lightning struck near Marie Bouisson's house, but no one was hurt. Goodbye, dear Godmother. Mama hopes you have a nice name day, also Aunt Alix, who hasn't had time to write, she has been so busy. Goodbye, and a thousand, thousand kisses.*

Your respectful godson,

Henry

4 *P.S. Hello to Miss Rosette.*

8 TO MADELEINE TAPIÉ DE CÉLEYRAN *[Paris, January 1874]*

My dear Madeleine,

I hasten to answer your very well written letter. You made me think about myself and I am ashamed of scribbling as I do. I am anxious to

1 *be having a good time with you all in the Gravasse or the big driveway at*

1. Gabriel Tapié de Céleyran (1869–1930), son of Amédée and Alix Tapié de Céleyran; Lautrec's cousin and later his faithful friend and companion, who often appears in his paintings.
2. Evidently a family doctor. He is mentioned again in 1881: cf. Letter 34.
3. Le Pech Ricardelle, a wine-growing estate, had been the property of Lautrec's great-grandfather in the eighteenth century, like the estate of Céleyran which it adjoins. Around 1882, it was acquired by his parents: cf. Letter 38, note 1.
4. A servant in the household of Madame Tapié de Céleyran.

Letter 8
1. A forest near the Château du Bosc.

Céleyran. Do you remember Mme. de Béon, at whose house at Arcachon I skinned my nose? She has made me a present of two pretty little canaries, which are getting along famously with the others. During my holidays I went to an American circus, where I saw eight elephants who walked on their heads. There was a cage full of lions who would have scared Raoul very much. I would like very much to go walking with you on the boulevards, where there are so many dolls you wouldn't know which one to pick. Please thank my godmother and Aunt Alix for me for their nice letters.

Goodbye, dear cousin. I wish you a happy New Year, sending you all my love, and ask you to do as much for me with all the others.

Your cousin, who likes you very much

Henri de T. Lautrec

9   TO MADELEINE TAPIÉ DE CÉLEYRAN   *Paris, March 29, 1874*

My dear Madeleine,

They tell me you would like to have a letter from me. There's nothing I'd like better than write to you, providing you write back. I think you would have an awfully good time seeing all the dolls here dressed in blue, white, pink, etc. . . . . I'd be glad to pick one out for you, but they cost too much for my purse. Raoul would rather watch all the thousands of omnibuses and carriages rolling along. Gabriel would prefer the sweet shops with barley sugar in all different colours and the Punch and Judy shows; I think Remi would like that, too; as for Emmanuel, we'll find out later what he'd like. I have a French teacher who puffs like a grampus, *and an English teacher who takes* snuff *and gives us exercises to do with stories about* cotton *and* thistles, *but in spite of that I like*

2. A summer resort in the Department of Gironde, near Bordeaux. Lautrec later spent many holidays there.
3. Raoul Tapié de Céleyran (1868–1937), son of Amédée and Alix Tapié de Céleyran.
   Letter 9
1. Emmanuel Tapié de Céleyran (1873–1931), son of Amédée and Alix Tapié de Céleyran; Lautrec's cousin.

2   *them very much. I must tell you that Aunt Pérey has let her little bird
be eaten by her cat. At first she scolded her precious* Moumoune, *but*

3   *pretty soon they made it up.* Lolotte *has grown tame and will perch on
your finger; when she's out of the cage* Lolot *sings like mad wanting her
to come back, and when* Lolotte *gets back he greets her with big pecks.
Adine has had nine babies, now reduced to two, the others having taken a
bath in the Seine from which they will never return.*

    Goodbye, my dear Madeleine. Give my best to Grandma Louise,

4   *your Papa, your Mama, Mlle Albanie, Aunt Armandine, Doudou,
Gabriel, Odon and to Emmanuel, who will hardly understand anyway. A
thousand, thousand kisses.*

Your loving cousin

H. de T. Lautrec

10   TO MME L. TAPIÉ DE CÉLEYRAN   *Paris, December 31, 1874*

My dear Godmother,

*I am sending you a quail as messenger of my best wishes for a happy
New Year. I am instructing him to tell you that your godson still loves
you very much and hopes to spend a good part of this coming year with
you. Raoul is very lucky to be with you all the time.*

1   *Last night Brick went to the Vaudeville with Papa, his impressions
of the theatre amuse us very much, but they would be too long to put* · ·

2. The owner of the Hôtel Pérey, on which cf. Letter 3, note 1.
3. Lolotte and Lolot are obviously the canaries mentioned in Letter 8. Cf. also Letter
3, where a canary is called Lolo.
4. Armandine d'Alichoux de Sénégra (d. 1893) was the sister of Julie de Sénégra, the
first wife of Léonce Tapié de Céleyran; her nickname was 'Tata'. She helped to
supervise Lautrec's early education.
    Letter 10
1. The steward of Lautrec's father, whose death is mentioned in 1881: cf. Letter 37.

*down here, he'll tell you all about them himself. I am having a few
days' holiday, which I don't mind at all. I have bought a very amusing
toy called an American Circus. There is a little Polish boy here who
has a room just filled with toys.*

*Goodbye, my dear Godmother, and please pass along my best wishes
for a happy New Year to my aunt and uncle, not forgetting M. l'Abbé
and Mlle Albanie. A kiss for all my cousins in a line, starting with the
last and ending with the first. Wish a happy New Year for me to
Annou and Rosette. I kiss you with all my heart, dear Godmother,
begging you to accept the fondest wishes of*

Your godson,

H. de T. Lautrec

11   TO HIS MOTHER   *[Neuilly, 1875. In English]*
1

My dear Mama,

I have received Marraine's [Godmother's] letter yesterday. We could not
2   *go out today because it rained very much. Miss Braine brings me*
3   *decalcomanies, and I do them well. M. Verrier does all he can for you
may be satisfied on your arrival. I am very happy. I will do all I can for*
4   *you may be satisfied. We have just taken a little groom for the pony.
Goodbye my dear mamma, I kiss you very much, and everybody too.*

Your loving son

H. de T. Lautrec

my kiss

1. In a letter to his mother, also written in English, and dated Neuilly, September 22,
   1875 (published in Huisman and Dortu, p. 20), much of the same material is found.
2. An Irish governess who remained with the family for many years. Lautrec still
   refers to her in 1885: cf. Letter 67.
3. Verrier was a physician who prescribed a treatment for Lautrec's legs.
4. See Ill. 15.

12 TO MME L. TAPIÉ DE CÉLEYRAN

[*Paris*] *November 2, 1875*

My dear Godmother,

It's not very long since I last wrote to you, but I must thank you for the nice gift you had Mama bring me. I know just what you would want me to do with it, that is, have as much fun as possible with it. On Thursday I go to be examined and hope to be admitted to the Catechism of the

1   *First Communion. The director's name is M. l'Abbé Paradis; he has promised me he'll put me in the first row. I shall do the best I can to be well prepared for my First Communion and I hope you will come to watch me take it. Goodbye, my dear Godmother. I kiss you with all my heart and beg you to give my warmest respects to my Aunt Joséphine; also please give all my relatives at Albi all my regards.*

Your affectionate godson

Henry de T. Lautrec

13 TO MME R. C. DE TOULOUSE-LAUTREC

[*Paris, January 1876*]

My dear Grandma,

I regret very much not being able to wish you a happy New Year in person. I haven't been as lucky as my cousins in spending vacations at Bosc. I haven't any idea when I shall be able to see you again; I hope it will be as soon as possible. I have been having a good time during the Christmas holiday and hope the same for the New Year's. I have been

1   *with Mama to see M. Princeteau's big picture showing Washington on*

---

1. Lautrec's first communion took place on June 12, 1876, at the church of St. Louis d'Antin in Paris.

Letter 13

1. René Princeteau (1844–1914), a deaf-mute, was the teacher and good friend of Lautrec's father; a specialist in horse and hunting scenes, he influenced Lautrec's early pictures of these subjects. See Ill. 2.

horseback. He is going to send it to the big exhibition in America. For
Christmas I have bought a beautiful book, drawn by Crafty, *on the*
Zoological Gardens. The falconer whom Papa admires so much is in
Ireland just now and I am consoling myself with my friend Toby.

Goodbye, my dear Grandma. I'm not very good at letter-writing,
but I love you very much and kiss you with all my heart, wishing you
a happy and prosperous New Year.

Your respectful
grandson

Henry de T. Lautrec

14 TO MME L. TAPIÉ DE CÉLEYRAN   *[Paris, December 1876]*

My dear Godmother,

I would very much like to be at Céleyran with all the cousins to wish
you a happy New Year. I can better say what I feel by talking than by
writing. Which means I must be satisfied with wishing you a happy New
Year and the best of health. I won't add 'and a numerous posterity' as
they do in stories, for the reason you already have them, with me having

---

2. I.e., *The 19th of October, 1781, Washington,* which was later shown at the International
   Exhibition in Philadelphia from May 10 to November 10, 1876. Cf. United States
   Centennial Commission, *International Exhibition 1876: Official Catalogue,* Philadelphia, 1876, Department of Art, p. 38. No. 193.
3. I.e., the *Jardin d'Acclimatation,* by J. C. Fulbert-Dumonteil, Paris, 1874, illustrated
   with drawings by Crafty. The latter, whose real name was Victor Géruzez (ca.
   1840–1906), specialized in drawing horses for publications such as *Paris à Cheval,*
   La Province à Cheval, etc. See also Ill. 11.

the honour of being No. 1. My mouth is just watering to try the chocolate

1 *and the* crottins. *Thank you very much for remembering my sweet tooth.*
Would you kindly tell M. l'Abbé that thanks to him my professor is

2 *very pleased with my Greek verbs. Louis Pascal is big and strong and*
your godson is a handsome fellow with a beautiful moustache. Joseph is a
young man who hates school now that he's getting ready for his

3 *baccalaureate. Unfortunately Louis is one class behind me in school.*

Goodbye, my dear Godmother. I send you a great big package of good
wishes for the New Year, and am asking you to divide up a part of
them among everybody while keeping the biggest part for yourself. I kiss
you with all my heart.

Your godson, who loves you very much,

Henry de T. L.

P.S. My birds are singing you their best wishes for a happy New Year.

4 *Kiss my goddaughter for me, meanwhile hoping she will do as much for*

5 *her godpapa. M. Willie Matheson sent me this pretty little picture for*
her.

The chocolate has just come. Thank you!

1. A kind of pastry, a speciality of Albi.
2. Having left the Lycée Fontanes in January 1875, because of ill health, Lautrec was now in another school or perhaps being tutored.
3. Most biographers state that Louis and Lautrec were in the same class, but that was no doubt at the Lycée Fontanes, his first school.
4. Béatrix Tapié de Céleyran.
5. Probably an English groom employed by Lautrec's father.

1, 2   Henri de Toulouse-Lautrec was born in 1864. His family was descended from the famous Comte de Toulouse who halted the invading Saracens. The photograph, right, shows young Henri at about the age of two, it was taken at Albi. The whole family was artistically inclined (cf. Ills. 12, 15) and Henri started to develop this trait, as the page of scribblings below, dating from about 1871, the time of Letter 1, shows.

3–5, 8   The Lautrec family houses: Top, the Château de Malromé, which belonged to his mother, where Lautrec often returned on holidays and where he died in September 1901. Centre, the Château de Céleyran, which belonged to his maternal Grandmother. Here he spent many of his childhood years. The Château du Bosc, bottom left, belonged to his paternal Grandmother and is still owned by a relative, Mary, Comtesse Attems. The house has become a Lautrec Museum. The photograph bottom right shows the farm of the Château du Bosc, with Lautrec, his mother, other relatives and servants.

Château de Céleyran le 28 Avril 71

Ma chère Marraine

Je vous embrasse ~~une lettre~~ de tout mon cœur, et dites-moi si Mlle Julie va bien, si Amou Justine et Antoine vont bien. Je vous embrasse encore une fois, et c'est qui...

henri

Céleyran Xe 8e

Toc Toc !!! — qui est là — C'est moi. — Ah c'est vous monsieur Henri — Comment va ma tante? Bien mieux — Puis-je la voir? Oui, mais ne la fatiguez pas trop vous êtes si bavard. Sans écouter le reste je bouscule Mélanie

6, 7   Two early letters (Nos. 1, 32). His drawing style at the age of sixteen is maturing. He was a compulsive doodler and his letters, envelopes and notebooks abound with dashed off sketches (cf. Ill. 10).

9, 10 Above left, photograph taken at Nice, at the age of 15 or 16 after breaking his legs. Above right, the half-title page of his Latin-French dictionary, covered with doodles as are the title page and margins.

11–13 Lautrec's family was interested in outdoor pursuits—Lautrec speaks of his father's interest in falconry (letters 4, 13) and hunting with ferrets (letter 27). They also hunted on horseback. The photograph, left, shows Lautrec with a pointer while one of his uncles sits watching the Comte Alphonse, who is holding a falcon. The drawing above by the Comte Alphonse shows him and his two brothers, Charles and Odon, hunting. Right, this early (1881) oil painting of Lautrec shows his cousin, Raoul Tapié de Céleyran, riding a donkey.

14   The Comte Alphonse, like many of his contemporaries, loved to dress up and is seen here in a suit of chain mail, standing, bow in hand, on his horse's saddle. The note in his own hand, roughly translated, reads: 'This acrobat is dead scared in spite of the supporting post'.

15–17   Horses played a great role in the life of the Comte de Toulouse and his family, as can be seen from these drawings. Below, a sketch of Lautrec on a fiery charger, allegedly by his father. After his accidents, Lautrec spent a lot of time immobilised and he used this enforced leisure sketching. Top right, the Comte Alphonse on the box of a four in hand (1880), a study for 'The Comte de Toulouse driving the mail coach to Nice' (1881) and an envelope on which Lautrec drew a coach and four and a dogcart (bottom right).

18, 19   In spite of his family's disapproval
of his way of life as a professional painter,
Lautrec, as his correspondence shows,
remained very close to his family. The photo-
graph above (probably taken in the 1880s or
1890s) shows, left to right, back row standing: Emmanuel Tapié de Céleyran (with hat),
Mme Cécile Pascal, Adèle Tapié de Céleyran,
de Toulouse-Lautrec, his mother, Amedée
Tapié de Céleyran (hat and beard), Louis Pas-
cal, the Comte de Cordes (hat and moustache),
Raoul Tapié de Céleyran, Mme Amedée
Tapié de Céleyran. Middle Row: Mme Raoul
Tapié de Céleyran, Germaine Tapié de
Céleyran, Geneviève Tapié de Céleyran,
Gabrielle d'Imbert du Bosc, Toulouse-
Lautrec, his paternal grandmother, Louise
d'Imbert du Bosc, Tapié de Céleyran, his
maternal grandmother, Béatrix Tapié de
Céleyran (Kiki), Mme Emmanuel Tapié de
Céleyran, Bébé Tapié de Céleyran. Front
Row: Henri de Toulouse-Lautrec, Marie
Tapié de Céleyran (hand behind dog), 'Tuck',
bulldog; Alexis Tapié de Céleyran, Oliver
Tapié de Céleyran. Right, a charcoal sketch
of his mother (1885). She was his confidante
throughout his life and she was with him
when he died at Malromé.

15 TO MME R. C. DE TOULOUSE-LAUTREC

Paris, March 1st, [18]77

My dear Grandma,

1   I should have thanked you long before this for the book by Stonehenge, but
    I haven't much time for correspondence. I have more free time just now
2   because Mama has taken me out of the professor's classes so they can
3   give me the electric brush treatment that once cured my Uncle Charles.
    I am awfully tired of limping with my left foot now that the right one
4   is cured. Hopefully it's only a reaction after my treatment, so Dr.
    Raymond says; I already feel better. We are definitely going to take the
    waters in the Pyrénées this year, won't you come there with us? ... My
    Uncle Charles left us the day before yesterday and I am very sorry
    that he has gone. Papa is still here. The day my Uncle Charles left,
5   Mama and I had dinner at my uncle de Rivières' house. My uncle de
6   Castellane and his wife and Monsieur and Madame de Bonne were there.
7   Hélène is awfully sweet and polite. Monsieur de Bonne advised her to
    marry anyone at all rather than stay an old maid. My Uncle Odon and
    his family are having fine sunny weather since they moved. Raymond is

1. The pseudonym of John Henry Walsh (1810–1888), an English writer who specialized in books on sports and physical fitness. The most popular one was the *Manual of British Rural Sports*, published in 1856 and in many subsequent editions until 1878.
2. See Letter 14, note 2.
3. Evidently a kind of massage intended to stimulate the circulation in his legs. Cf. Letters 48 and 87.
4. This shows that, contrary to what is usually stated, Lautrec had persistent trouble with his legs even before breaking them.
5. Georges Séré, Baron de Rivières (b. 1849), grandson of a namesake who had married Adelaide d'Imbert du Bosc (of the family of Lautrec's grandmothers). The younger Georges was the Procureur de la République in Fontainebleau, and was known as 'le bon juge' because of his leniency.
6. Distant relatives of Lautrec; listed as such in the obituary notice of Raymond-Jean-Bernard de Toulouse-Lautrec, December 23, 1888 (collection Herbert Schimmel, New York). Cf. Letter 5, note 2.
7. Hélène Séré de Rivières, the sister of Georges. She married Philippe Guinau de Mussy in 1881.

8 *starting to speak English and Odette to understand it. Raymond can*
sing a lot of songs and continues to like me very much. Odette has
become more pleasant, but still persists in not wanting to talk, although
she understands two languages.

Goodbye, my dear Grandma. I kiss you with all my heart, likewise
Aunt Joséphine. Please don't forget to give my fondest regards to all the
family and above all to my Uncle l'Abbé. Mama wants me to tell
you she is thinking of you, as is Papa.

Your respectful grandson

Henry de T. Lautrec

16 TO MME R. C. DE TOULOUSE-LAUTREC
[Paris] April 17 [1878]

My dear Grandma,

I am writing to have a little chat with you today. I think a lot about
1 *Adèle now that she is married and must admit it strikes me as very*
extraordinary. Awfully comical, isn't it, having a new cousin who wasn't
so at 8 o'clock, but is so at noon. Too bad I couldn't have been with my
Uncle Charles to stop him from having indigestion from so many
truffles!!!!!! I have been feeling much better the past four days and am
able to be up and around the house. But I haven't got back to going
outdoors yet and Mama still hasn't made up her mind about it. Papa is
waiting for M. Ramier and still hasn't come back, which has been a
disappointment to M. de Chantérac, who had been stopping over at the
Hotel Pérey, hoping to see him. He is going to leave for Orléans

8. Raymond and Odette were the children of Odon and Emilie de Toulouse-Lautrec,
the former being a younger brother of Lautrec's father. Odette was also called
'Dédette'.

Letter 16

1. Adèle Bouscher, the daughter of Adolphe de Gualy de St. Rome and Zoë, sister of
Lautrec's grandmothers. She married Joseph de Bouscher de Bernard.

because his grandmother is ill. Uncle Odon is posing on a horse for M.
2   *Princeteau. Aunt Odette is feeling very well. Raymond is hardly*
coughing at all any more; Odette is the one worst off now, but it's not
serious. I have started a theatre with Louis Pascal which has 60
(puppet) actors. My Béon canary is hatching 3 eggs, promising additions
to the family.

    Goodbye, my dear Grandma. I kiss you with all my heart and ask you
to give my fondest regards to Aunt Joséphine and to my uncle and aunt.
Please pass along my congratulations to Adèle when she is not so busy;
and don't forget to remember me to my Uncle l'Abbé.

               Your respectful grandson,

                  Henry de TL

17   TO MADELEINE TAPIÉ DE CÉLEYRAN   *[Paris, April 1878]*

My dear Madeleine,

1   *Thank you for your letter and for the portrait of our god-daughter. I*
like it very much, especially the eyes, though the rest could be improved
on; she stretches out her fingers like a little stamp-licker, although it
would be nice if she did have them that long so as to play the piano well
and charm me in my old age. The others are very good likenesses and I
take great pleasure in seeing them again; but I would like to have yours,
too, and also Raoul's. Tell Raoul that his friend Bébelle is sitting on
2   *three eggs; I hope to have some little ones out of them. I am hoping to*
see you all again and have some fun. I feel all right, but I'm still not
very nimble. I have a good time playing comedies with Louis Pascal. We
have 60 puppets about 10 centimetres tall. They are worked from the end
of wires. Tell me what happened to my chrysalides. Tell M. l'Abbé that

2. I.e., Aunt 'Odon', his uncle Odon's wife. Cf. Letter 46, where Lautrec also refers to her in this way.

Letter 17
1. Béatrix Tapié de Céleyran.
2. Lautrec writes 'cagonits', a Gascon term for 'little ones', in this case, little birds.

my Greek Grammar is having a rest and to the great joy of all the students they have done away with Greek Roots. *Be so kind as to remember me to him; I hope soon to serve Mass for him.*

Goodbye, my dear Delon. I kiss you on both cheeks, also all your brothers and sisters and especially my goddaughter: Also kiss your Papa and Mama for me, and don't forget to give my best to Mlle Albanie and everybody.

Your cousin

H. de T. Lautrec

P.S. Raymond was very happy to see his friend Toto again.

18 TO MADELEINE TAPIÉ DE CÉLEYRAN *[Albi, May 1878]*

1 *My dear Madeleine,*

2 *I'd like to know whether Raoul has received my letter asking him to find out at Augé's, through you, the address where you send for the sledge and the brougham. Write to me as soon as you find out. I'm not having too bad a time and I kiss you*

Henry

3 *(this is my first letter)*

1. This letter is written on a folded sheet of paper; the first page is addressed to Madeleine, while the third page contains the facetious letter published below.
2. A shopkeeper in Narbonne who was at this time ordering from Paris a child's dog cart and brougham for Lautrec and his cousins. Lautrec himself laid out miniature roads, like those in the Bois de Bologne, on the lawn at the Château du Bosc, on which he planned to play with his cousins.
3. Lautrec broke his left thigh bone toward the end of May 1878, when he slipped from a chair onto the floor. Cf. his letter to Charles Castelbon dated May 30, 1878; published in Huisman and Dortu, pp. 19–20. Hence he means his first letter since the accident, or rather his first handwritten one, since he had dictated to his mother a letter for his cousin Raoul on May 22 (cf. Attems, pp. 180–1).

Mother Superior,

4 *Emery is feeling better. We have bought a donkey and made a carriage like the dog cart. Tell Moujik that his daughters will be going out riding in the donkey cart, a picture of which follows* [*a pen sketch*].

5 *Tell Monsieur Tapié to write to me, or write to me yourself.*

Your devoted

6 *Philéas Fogg*

19 TO MME L. TAPIÉ DE CÉLEYRAN   [*Albi, c. July 15, 1878*]

My dear Godmother,

Thank you for your unanimous good wishes relative to the name day of my great patron, the famous Saint Henry (whose name day, parenthetically, is also my own). But if you would like to fill my cup of joy to overflowing, which to my over-excited imagination is already brimming to the ears from seeing I have not dropped as much as a single rung in your affec-tionate esteem, please see to it that the following carefully weighed request is passed along to M. l'Abbé Peyre, namely, that I would very
1 *much like him to intimate to my bony cousin a strict order to be kind enough to send me at once a little epistle giving me news about the whole personnel at Céleyran and of the children's vehicles that Augé, the*
2 *shopkeeper at Narbonne, has been told to have sent to me from the*

4. The Russian word for 'peasant', familiarly used in France. It probably refers to Lautrec's uncle, Amédée Tapié de Céleyran. The daughters mentioned would be Geneviève, Béatrix, and Madeleine herself.
5. Probably Lautrec's cousin, Raoul Tapié de Céleyran. A letter to him concerning the same dog-cart and also signed 'Philéas Fogg', is published in Huisman and Dortu, p. 17, but incorrectly dated ca. 1874. See Ill. 17.
6. Lautrec was enamoured of Jules Verne's *Tour du Monde en 80 Jours*, whose hero was Philéas Fogg. It was first published in 1872 and performed as a play in 1874.

Letter 19
1. Either Raoul or Gabriel Tapié de Céleyran.
2. Cf. Letter 18, note 2.

Capital of France. Now I have the honour of informing you that, in person no less, flesh and bone, I delivered myself in a chariot drawn by fiery horses to the Metropolitan church of this Albigensian city, there to consummate an audition of the Divine Office. And now, having given you this patibulary information forasmuch as it has to do with the improvement of my locomotor system, I will proceed to inform you about the mild constipation suffered by my person from the furious manducation of a certain paste made from the fruit of the quince. Having no more to relate, I shall take the liberty of pressing a tender kiss on your right cheek, begging you to do the same for me to everybody.

3   *Your crutch-walking godson,*

                                        Henry de Toulouse

20   TO MME L. TAPIÉ DE CÉLEYRAN   [c. *August 20, 1878*]

My dear Godmother,

I regret very much not being able to wish you a happy name day in person as in the two previous years. But although the personage who had the inopportune idea of breaking his leg cannot be with you to express his best wishes in his big ugly voice (but not big enough just the same to wish

1 *you a happy name day so that you'll hear it in Lamalou), his heart will*

2 *be with you on the Day of St. Louis. Happy name day! happy name day!*
     I kiss you ninety-two times

                                  your godson

                                  Henri TL

3. His leg was in plaster for forty days; he used a crutch for some time after.
Letter 20
1. Lamalou-les-Bains, a spa in south-west France, in the Department of Hérault, between Albi and Céleyran. Lautrec spent the summer of 1881 there.
2. The feast-day of St. Louis, August 25th; his grandmother's first name was Louise.

[Barèges, 1878]

My dear little creature who catches rabbits,

You are a very sensible girl and never do a thing without first knowing why. If you had been born in Solon's time, you certainly would have been named to the Areopagus; you would have looked very comical indeed in a pointed hat carrying a lot of big old books, and since you are so nice I'm going to give you a praise-ent; I'll give it to you at Bosc. First, the best part of it will be . . . my godfatherly blessing, followed by a collection of little kisses, and then something yellow wrapped in paper . . . try to guess. There's only one fault I have to find with you and that's your choice of a spelling teacher, for he is a person with very little brains, and if you don't believe it, run your little rabbit-catching paw over your brother's head and see if you don't feel a great big hole; it's so deep you'll be afraid of falling to the bottom; and now you ask me what connection there is between this big hole and your spelling teacher's brains. Here is the answer: the brain is a kind of gut that produces intelligence, it's in the head; there should be this brain I'm talking about instead of the enormous hole that scares you so, and that's why your dear spelling master isn't smart!!!! . . . We go riding on donkey-back and if you want to pretend to do the same get up on your spelling teacher's back; don't be afraid if you hear sounds like firecrackers going off, donkeys do it all the time; to correct this defect you just look brave and hold your nose. That's the rub.

There's a Prussian king here and I'm sure that if you were at Barèges you'd quickly wring his neck, even if he weren't a rabbit. Goodbye, my dear little dear, and give my fondest regards to Grandma, my uncle, your brother, M. l'Abbé, Aunt Armandine, Mademoiselle Rose and everybody, including my canaries.

I kiss you on both cheeks and on your pretty *little phiz (not the other!).*

Your Godfather

Henry de T.L.

1. Barèges, a spa in the heart of the Pyrenees, south-east of Lourdes.
2. Lautrec uses the Gascon 'poutous', a little kiss. Later he uses 'poutounégeade': cf. Letter 41, note 1.

1   *Pension Internationale, Nice (Alpes Maritimes)[January–February 1879]*

2   *My dear Déloux,*

*After a fine trip in the company of a bishop we are installed in the
Pension Internationale. It's a pretty hotel, surrounded by a fair-sized
garden planted with palms and aloes. Coming on the train we saw Cannes
and the sea. It is excessively pretty. Made me think of the Villa des
Cactus, the Pearl, etc. Arriving at Nice I saw a little boy who looked
exactly like David Louzéma except for the way he was dressed. We are
going to take a walk on the Promenade des Anglais, which is magnificent.
It runs along by the sea and you can watch tartans, cutters, etc., etc.
The harbour is splendid compared with anything I've seen up to now.
There are quite a few merchant vessels and an English yacht that is a
veritable jewel. They rent boats for sightseeing, but Mama is afraid to get*
3   *in them. Monsieur Lévi and his sister have welcomed us with open
arms, but we haven't yet seen Mme Peragallo. Monsieur Lévi goes to
Monaco twice a week to play. There's a little nine-year-old Russian girl
here who speaks French and German. The food is all right but dinner
is too long, even though there are five waiters in tails lined up to serve it.
One of them is very funny, and skips all the time. They are going to give
a ball next week. We are eating excellent tangerines, but the Nice
oranges are as bad as the ones with which I used to play 'Pretty Baby'.*
*   Goodbye, my ideal cousin. I respect and admire you and ask you give
my regards to Grandma, Tata, your Mother, your Papa, Uncle Odon,
Aunt Odette, Mademoiselle Maurin, Odon, Toto, Bibou, Kiki (kiss her*

1. Lautrec was in Nice, accompanied by his mother, to recuperate from his leg
injury. Two of his letters to his friend Etienne Devismes (published in Joyant, I,
pp. 42–4) are dated Nice, 1879, and Nice, January 1879.
2. Madeleine Tapié de Céleyran.
3. A friend who is also mentioned in Letter 23.

4   *fifty-three times), little Ermaine, Raymond and Odette. Once again*
    please be assured of my most complete admiration.

Your graceful cousin

Henry de Toulouse Lautrec

P.S. Give my compliments to all the servants.

23   TO MME L. TAPIÉ DE CÉLEYRAN

[Nice, January–February 1879]

My dear Godmother,

*I am writing to ask you if you will tell Grandma Gabrielle to save me
all the Egyptian stamps my Uncle Odon may send her. I have a fine
professor, twenty years old who has a boat and hunts sea gulls. He is
going to sail at the regattas. We are very sorry that Uncle Amédée didn't
come. We went to Monte Carlo. M. Lévi played for me and doubled*
1   *my money. I thank Madeleine for her letter. Could you send me some
more cancelled Napoleon stamps.*

Your godson, who loves you very much

HTL

4. Ermaine is Germaine Tapié de Céleyran (b. 1878), daughter of Alix and Amédée
   Tapié de Céleyran and Lautrec's cousin.
   Letter 23
1. His mother recounts the same incident in an undated letter from Nice: cf. Attems,
   pp. 174–5.

24 TO MME R. C. DE TOULOUSE-LAUTREC

Nice, Pension Internationale [January–February 1879]

My dear Grandma,

I am writing to see, knowing that Uncle Odon used French stamps when he wrote you, whether you would mind asking him in your next letter to buy me the Egyptian collection for five or six francs and send it to you; I would also like you to ask him to try and get me some Turkish and Suez Canal stamps through M. de Blignières.

I hope that you'll soon be able to give us some better news about fat
1 *Raymond, which regrettably is not as good as that about the Béon family, including Lolo. Once again, would you be so kind as to ask Aunt*
2 *Joséphine to send me some old Napoleon stamps (all of them are good) because there are stamp-lovers here who'll want them.*

Goodbye, dear Grandma. Be so good as to give my fondest regards to Aunt Joséphine, and to remember me most warmly to Uncle Charles,
3 *Aunt Emilie, Raymond and Dédette.*

Your grandson (collector) who loves
you very much

HTL

1. Either Raymond-Bertrand de Toulouse-Lautrec (b. 1870) or Raymond de Toulouse-Lautrec (b. 1874), both of whom were Lautrec's cousins.
2. Cf. Letter 6, note 5.
3. Odette de Toulouse-Lautrec.

1   *[Barèges, August–September 1879]*

My dear Godmother,

2 *I am sure you will be pleased to hear that I am as well as can be expected and that I have no pain. I'm not bored too much either, and hope you won't fret too much about my case because a clumsy fellow like me just isn't worth it. I suppose out here they will call Miss Fides my*
3 *very honourable* cuisine *(I mean cousin!) Fidèle or Fidèlou, and that at home they'll give her the name Fifi. Excuse this playing on words, but I don't have many things to keep my brain working. The doctor is delighted*
4 *at the prospect of a cure. The Andoques have just arrived and are very well; they will stay the afternoon.*

Goodbye, my dear Godmother. I kiss you as best I can and please give my best to everybody.

We have just received Monsieur l'Abbé's letter and are expecting Grandma and Papa.

5 *Kindly give my regards to Tata, Uncle Amédée, Aunt Alix, all the*
6, 7 *cousins, the Soréziens, Kiki and Gordon.*

My regrets to M. l'Abbé and Mlle Maurin.

Your clumsy godson

Henri de Toulouse

1. Lautrec was at the Maison Gradet, in Barèges, to recuperate from his leg injury.
2. Lautrec had fallen and broken his other leg. He assumes that it was due to his clumsiness, not realizing the physiological causes. In a letter of September 2, 1879 (Collection Herbert Schimmel), his grandmother Louise indicated that an apparatus that had been holding his right leg in place was removed the day before and that they hoped to leave shortly thereafter. According to the same letter, the doctor recommended that Lautrec refrain from walking for fifty days.
3. Fides Tapié de Céleyran (1879–1900), a daughter of Alix and Amédée Tapié de Céleyran; Lautrec's cousin. He puns here on the words 'cousine' (cousin) and 'cuisine' (kitchen), and also on her name 'Fides' and the word 'fidèle' (faithful).
4. Evidently relatives of his Aunt Emilie d'Andoque de Seriège. Cf. Letter 3, note 5.
5. Tata is his nickname for his aunt Armandine d'Alichoux de Sénégra.
6. Lautrec's nickname for some of his cousins who went to school at Sorèze, a small town south-east of Toulouse.
7. Gordon was a setter dog that belonged to Lautrec.

My dear Raoul,

We got here the day before yesterday and my first letter is for you. I was telling myself, pleased as Punch, how we would soon be having a nice New Year's vacation together again. I took it for granted you'd try as hard as you promised me!!! And now here they tell me your marks have been so unsatisfactory that if you didn't do any better during the time you had left, you would not be coming at New Year's at all!!! You can appreciate how painful that is to me and I am writing to urge you to do your very best so this punishment doesn't happen. And then how glad we

1 *would be. You would see the little Gordons born this morning. We would have all kinds of fun, play trains and make train signals, I don't know myself what all we wouldn't do!!! But if you keep on fooling*

2 *around, if you continue to do nothing but a poor job as they say, they'll keep you in school until you're bored to death, and your Mama will be unhappy, and me, too!!! And if you get into the habit of just loafing along, where will it all end? Do you think people are going to come to see you at Mardi Gras, on St. Cecilia's Day, at Easter, and even during the long vacation!!! I don't think you'll settle for anything like that once you've seen that with a few trips to the dictionary everything will go just fine, as wanted by your cousin*

Henri

Your mother asks me to tell you that she thanks you for your letter. She will write to you tomorrow and isn't at all satisfied with your marks.

1. Cf. Letter 25, note 7.
2. Lautrec uses the colloquial expression, 'acagnardir.

27 TO MME R. C. DE TOULOUSE-LAUTREC

[*Céleyran, December 1879*]

My dear Grandma,

Every letter that comes reports snow, snow . . . !!! Papa wrote just this
1 *morning that there's been snow for twenty days . . . !!! Here, on the*
contrary, Winter's Down has only briefly whitened the roofs. Uncle
Amédée has killed four woodcocks, and a wounded one gave him a brave
fight. It was nice weather for Midnight Mass and they sang Christmas
2 *carols in the dialect, but we had to bypass the* Minuit Chrétien *when*
3 *Uncle Albert failed to show up. Kiki is very changeable and as wilful*
4 *as can be. We are impatiently waiting for the Soréziens on Tuesday. I*
5 *was very happy to learn that Zibeline did so well hunting rabbits,*
please give her my congratulations and encouragement. I will write to
Papa about her exploits.

Goodbye, dear Grandma. My most sincere wishes for a happy New
Year to you, Uncle Charles and Aunt Emilie, whom I ask you to give a
hug for me.

Your respectful grandson,

Henry de Toulouse Lautrec

P.S. My best, if you please, to Lolo.

1. The winter of 1879–80 was one of the coldest on record throughout northern
Europe.
2. A Christmas carol, known in English by the French name *Cantique de Noël*.
3. An uncle whom Lautrec mentions again in the 'Cahier de Zig-Zags' (cf. Letter 30,
note 3) and again as being late for a rendezvous.
4. Cf. Letter 25, note 6.
5. A ferret which belonged to Lautrec.

My dear Godmother,

I am late in writing and this letter, intended to arrive before New Year's Day, will probably get there afterwards. I wrote what little I had to tell
1 *to Grandma Gabrielle, and she will pass it on. I send you a big hug, too, which is not a mere repetition, and please wish Aunt Alix—to whom I shall write soon—a happy New Year for me, also my uncle, and not forgetting M. l'Abbé, who, I believe, is with you. Thank you for your lovely presents and with that another kiss and a happy New Year!!!*

Your grandson and godson,

Henri

29 TO A DOG   *Le Bosc [1880]*

1 *Dear Madam,*

As your nice letter yesterday announced, maternity's joys are yours once again. There you are, once again the head of a family; grave responsibilities weighing down your curly little head. What care you will have to lavish on these warm and rosy little creatures, feebly stirring their tiny little paws at the bottom of your basket. I'm sure your nice Mistress
2 *and Mélanie will help you with this difficult task and that they will make as much and even more fuss over your children as you yourself. I also know you must have a crazy urge to eat the aforesaid Mélanie*

1. This was probably in the preceding letter.
   Letter 29
1. The dog belonged to Lautrec's Aunt Joséphine, Mademoiselle du Bosc.
2. Mademoiselle du Bosc's housekeeper.

when she wants to touch your progeny and that the echoes of your G-r-r-r-
G-r-r-rs will resound in the living room.

So, first of all, I implore you not to eat all of the above-mentioned
Mélanie and to leave at least a little piece of her to care for your nice
Mistress; second, to lick your babies very thoroughly, so that the good
3 *people of Castelnau will be able to raise their hands to heaven and say,*
4 *amid tears of emotion, 'Oh God, they're just like their Mother!'*

In closing I send you my heartfelt congratulations, and pray you to lick
your Mistress' hand for me.

I squeeze your little paw,

Henri de Toulouse Lautrec

P.S. Remember to give my best to Flavie, Mélanie and Benjamin.

30 TO MME R. C. DE TOULOUSE-LAUTREC
1 *Nice, January 13, 1880*

My dear Grandma,

I'm getting down to sending you best wishes for the New Year not a little,
nor a lot, but enormously late. I hope to make up for it by giving you
some news hot off the griddle. On Saturday we had a lovely day at Cannes;
the city is very pretty and my uncle's place superb. It's a very swanky
2 *villa on the shore, near the Villa of the Dunes, the Empress' residence.*
Uncle Odon goes riding on horseback and has rented a landau for after-
noons to go on drives up the mountain. We went with them there and
climbed up to a place where you can see Nice and the coast of Italy, and
then the sea so blue . . . !!! The Babies are very well and are taking

3. Castelnau de Montmiral, a town near Albi in the Department of Tarn.
4. Lautrec uses the Gascon phrase: 'Chés, semblo sa mairé'.
   Letter 30
1. Lautrec was in Nice, accompanied by some of his family, to recuperate from his leg
   injuries. One of his letters to his friend Etienne Devismes (published in Joyant, I,
   p. 46) is dated Nice, February 11, 1880. See Ills. 9, 16.
2. Probably the former Empress Eugénie, wife of Napoleon III.

long walks with Soué, who is delighted. Raymond is taking lessons from a priest. A detail for Uncle Charles: Uncle Odon has bought a collection of pictures from an estate and the way it looks there are lots of them. As for us, we are quite well. The pension isn't as gay as last year. But on the whole the winter is more sunny and we go for a lot of walks. We

haven't come across the Villeforts.

Goodbye, dear Grandma. I wish you a belated happy New Year, thanking you again for your presents. Mama joins me in sending you love and in asking you not to forget to remember us to everybody.

Your grandson,

Henri de Toulouse-Lautrec

We ran into the pride of Amélie-les-Bains. That's for Aunt Emilie.

31 TO MME R. C. DE TOULOUSE-LAUTREC

Céleyran, Dec[ember] 30, [18]80

My dear Grandma,

It's awfully hard to write something different, above all in the case of New Year's letters. But these commonplace letters with their commonplace compliments still have their value, more so indeed than the too interesting ones you were writing to us these days. We were shaking, watching the postman come, but, thank God, this morning's letter came

just in time to revive our hopes. Poor Aunty!!! How we thought of her!!!

3. Probably Lautrec's nickname for Mademoiselle Suermond, the daughter of a German family then staying in Nice, with whom he was friendly. She is mentioned in Lautrec's 'Cahier de Zig-Zags', a journal he kept in 1881 (published in *L'Amour de l'Art*, April 1931), and again in a letter to his Uncle Charles written from Nice (published in Huisman and Dortu, p. 23; cf. the drawings on p. 25).

4. Raymond de Toulouse-Lautrec, son of the Uncle Odon who is also mentioned here.

5. A Michel de Vignaud de Villefort later married Jacquette Tapié de Céleyran, the daughter of Gabriel Tapié de Céleyran and Anne-Marie de Toulouse-Lautrec.

Letter 31

1. His Aunt Joséphine, Mademoiselle du Bosc, was ill this winter.

Hopefully the new turn she has taken will continue, and this run of bad luck will be no more, at least for her. Here everybody is just fine, except 2 *for Suzanne, who's a little ailing and sick in her stomach. Aunt* 3 *Armandine is leaving in an hour or two to go and meet Madelon. As* 4 *for me, I'm just fooling around with 'St. Palette' and the dogs. How is Uncle and his foot? The uncles here are at Carcassone and Toulouse.*

Goodbye, dear Grandma, for to begin with it's getting dark and then there isn't much room left to tell you how much I love you and how genuinely I wish you a prosperous and happy New Year, also Uncle and Aunt Emilie. Goodbye for now. Happy New Year . . . happy New Year.

Your grandson, who loves you enormously

Henri

5 *P.S. I am going to write to Aunt Joséphine.*

32 TO HIS GREAT-AUNT JOSÉPHINE [MLLE DU BOSC]
Céleyran, Dec[ember 18]80

Knock, knock!!! Who's there?—It's me.—Ah, so it's you, Monsieur Henry.—How is my Aunt?—Much better.—Could I see her?—Yes, but don't tire her, you're such a chatterbox: Without listening to the rest, I brush by Mélanie, almost knocking her down, and greeted by the barks 1 *in G minor of Miss and Follette, I throw my arms around your neck, shouting from the bottom of my heart, happy New Year!!!*

2. Probably Suzanne Gonthier, who is mentioned in Letter 145.
3. I.e., Madeleine Tapié de Céleyran.
4. This is Lautrec's first reference to his painting; he playfully makes his palette his patron saint.
5. See the following letter.

Letter 32
1. Two dogs which belonged to Mademoiselle du Bosc. Lautrec's painting of Follette is reproduced in Joyant I, p. 35 (but is incorrectly dated 1888). See Ill. 7.

*That's what I would have done, if I'd stayed at Albi. But even
though the distance between us make it impossible to give you a real hug,
the emotion I feel is just as great.*

*But it is useless to say any more, since you know very well I love you
and all the paper and all the ink in the world would add nothing to that.
That's why, my dear Aunt, I am asking you to accept the most sincere
wishes for a speedy recovery, as well as for your happiness from your
respectful great-nephew*

Henri

P.S. Please remember me to Flavie, Mélanie and Benjamin.

33 TO MME L. TAPIÉ DE CÉLEYRAN
1   *Lamalou-les-Bains [August 1881]*

My dear Godmother,

*I don't know what broken-down hurdy-gurdy, what clumsy sermon, or
what nose——take your pick between mine and Madeleine's——could begin
to give you an idea of how long and dull our trip down was. However, just
as on noses there are some coloured warts, so there were some little
incidents en route to break the monotony. A big man, who looked like*
2, 3 *Gambetta, joked politely with Bibou and Kiki. Two conductors rolled in
the dust trying to tear each other's eyes out, an enormous nun almost sat
right down in Madeleine's lap, threatening to smother her, and Mama
left her suitcase on the train. Luckily they found and returned it. But
finally here we are with two baths taken, three and a half glasses of the
waters drunk, and me with an eye that looks like a tomato. With that,*

1. I.e., the Hôtel des Bains at Lamalou; cf. Letter 20, note 1.
2. Léon Gambetta (1838–1882), the famous statesman who was Premier of the
   Republic at this time.
3. Kiki: Béatrix Tapié de Céleyran.

dear Godmother, I give you a big hug, and ask you to accept my best
wishes for your name day.

Your grandson and godson

H. de Toulouse Lautrec

34 TO MME L. TAPIÉ DE CÉLEYRAN
Lamalou[-les-Bains, August-October 1881]

Dear Godmother,

I am writing just to have a little chat, since as far as real news goes, it's
quite impossible for me to give you any; in fact, there isn't anything
interesting here, unless you'd care to know the temperature of my bath and
1   *the number of minutes I shower.*
  I have the good luck to have a bath-man called Jacqrou, who has a face
like a bulldog. The other day coming out of the shower he wanted to rub
2   *my back with a horsehair glove 'that would smooth the hide of a donkey'.*
I soon had enough of that stuff, probably because I am one—an ass, that
is. We also have the boundless pleasure of the company of this dear
Doctor Salagade (Bedène) and on top of that of the sticky Bélugon. He
has introduced us to Mme and Mlle de Beaufort and M. du Bernard
3   *or Dubernard or D'Ubernart, or whatever, who, I may report, is*
feeling very well. Aunt Joséphine's illness failed to hold up his departure
(the dear Doctor's*). He only came here because of the little stratagem*
of making him believe he was going into the country to pick violets and
dandelions. Miss Capus, looking like a Sphinx, is by her fountain; it is
certainly a great pity she doesn't know how to draw, because if she did she

1. Lautrec does not mention one interesting project: the 23 drawings he was making
   to illustrate his friend Etienne Devismes' story *Cocotte*. Cf. the facsimile edition,
   Paris, 1953, and Lautrec's letters to Devismes from Lamalou, dated August 1881
   and October 1881 (published first in Joyant, I, pp. 48–50).
2. Lautrec uses the Gascon expression, 'qué lébario la pel dé sus un azé'.
3. Probably guests at the hotel.

could fill a whole album with all the grimaces of guests drinking the waters. We also have the company of cousin, or uncle (take your pick) Georges

4 *Foissac, with his better half. We discovered them at the* Temptation; *Cousin Félicie has quadrupled in size since last year. A testimonial*

5 *indeed to the kitchen at Castelnaudar-r-rys-s-s!!! Monsieur Bour-r-rges is as gloomy as always and is still wearing that bristly moustache of his like the ar-r-rse of a sick chicken. At our table there's a pastry-shop owner from Narbonne from the ancient house of Hortala, who's half-cracked. She bursts out laughing without rhyme or reason, and during one of these spells Madeleine claims to have heard a little . . . well, a certain funny sound. Bathing-hour is drawing near and so I give you a great big hug, Tata as well. Please be so kind as to pass along all the celestialities of the occasion to Mlle Maurin, Uncle Amédée, Uncle Albert, Monsieur le Vicaire and all the brats.*

Your sticky and clean-as-a-whistle godson, thanks to all the water used up in his honour.

Henri

6 *P.S. We also have M. Vié, and what a Vié!!! An adorable Vié so elegant, so amusing that if I were Mme Vié I'd put him under lock and key for fear someone would steal him.*

35 TO HIS MOTHER *Albi, Wednesday [late November, 1881]*

My dear Mama,

1 *Little new here. Uncle Ernest persists in remaining silent. Telegraph him within the hour to wring this authorization from him that is needed so much! . . . Ad. Montey has invited us to lunch on Thursday or Friday with a preacher. Spiritual as well as other delicacies. What luxury!*

4. The Foissac (Foyssac) family was related to the Séré de Rivières.
5. Possibly the father of the Dr. Bourges who was later Lautrec's close friend.
6. Cf. Letter 7, note 2.
   Letter 35
1. Ernest Pascal, the father of Louis Pascal; cf. Letter 4, note 3. The 'authorization' is for Louis to visit Lautrec in Albi.

Aunt Joséphine keeps picking at me to go to her doctor. I'll just have to
2 *resign myself to it. Saint Edme has written to me.* Carissime tibi totus.
What a card!!!

Goodbye for now. My letter is as dull as my thoughts, which are
3 *absolutely in a state of collapse after the tension of the exams. Give*
hugs, lots of little smacks and kiss everyone there for me, and try to get
Louis to come whatever the cost.

Your son, back from the grandeurs of this world and above all from
those of the baccalaureate.

H.

36 TO MME L. TAPIÉ DE CÉLEYRAN   [*Paris, December 1881*]

My dear Godmother,

Just got Mama's letter and will answer it right away. Papa came the
day before yesterday and was satisfied with my legs. *Also with my*
health.

On Thursday we had a big dinner party and I made the place-cards.
Well, dear Godmother, just had a silly notion that if I could leave my
legs here and go off in an envelope (just to kiss Mama and you), I'd
do it.

Today I'm going to the Zoological Gardens with Miss Braine. I'm
1 *afraid poor Brick won't be coming to Paris for a long, long time. Tell*
2, 3 *Mama we have to go to Rueil on Thursday. Raoul must be a big boy*
now and Gabriel, too. When you see Mlle Ronron again, say hello to
her for me.

2. 'I'm all yours my dear.' See Ill. 10.
3. Lautrec passed his baccalaureate examinations in Toulouse in November 1881,
after having failed them the previous July. Cf. his letter to Etienne Devismes, dated
November 22, 1881 (published in Joyant, I, pp. 51–2), describing the examinations.

Letter 36
1. In the following letter Lautrec mentions Brick's death.
2. A town near Versailles, where Lautrec's uncle, Georges Séré de Rivières, presumably lived. Cf. Letter 15, note 5.
3. Lautrec painted his cousin Raoul on a donkey this year. See Ill. 13.

I'm feeling marvellous and would like to lose weight but I don't think I'll be able to do anything about it. Goodbye now, dear Godmother. I kiss you with all my heart and Mama as well.

Your respectful godson,

H. de T. Lautrec

37 TO MME R. C. DE TOULOUSE-LAUTREC

Céleyran, December 29, 1881

My dear Grandma,

We're right in the middle of all the New Year's uproar. Uncle Amédée is leaving for Bordeaux, Aunt Alix is getting the bedrooms ready; and so everything's at sixes and sevens. It would be a fine day but for the fact that there are two sides to every coin. Poor Brick died last night and poor old Anna is on the way out, too. She couldn't be stopped from going to Midnight Mass and caught cold. The result, congestion of the lungs, and they've already given her the last rites. No doubt about it, the race of 1 *good servants is dying out. Uncle Jules is very low, all his daughters are with him. Hardly any hope for him left. Beatrix keeps on having attacks which are very trying for so small an object. The rest of the family just lives from one day to the next, all bawling and squawling. Have you any more Spanish letters? If so, I hope they won't be quite so animated as the other ones. Papa is limping and goes out with Uncle Amédée on the back of a bike. It's freezing here but the sun is so warm and bright that we don't mind it at all. How true it is that in a way you feel the cold much more through your eyes than your back. But I am losing sight of the real reason for my letter, which is to send you my tender if clumsy wishes for a happy New Year, gracefulness not being my strong point. Therefore, I send them to you and those around you as*

1. Jules de Gualy de St. Rome; married to Blanche, the sister of Lautrec's grandmothers.

sincerely as can be, but from myself only (since the others here at Céleyran will be writing to you on their own), and beg you to accept a thousand and one embraces from your respectful grandson

H. de Toulouse Lautrec

P.S. I would like Uncle Charles to write and tell me what Le Figaro
2   *said about Cabanel.*

38   TO HIS MOTHER   [*Paris, Spring 1882*]

My dear Mama,

I hardly ever see Papa these days and am waiting, feet firm on the ground, for my cousins. Papa finally told me that Le Bosc belongs to my
1   *aunt and that we were out in the cold. You know my opinion of that. Useless to rehash the subject.*

    You ask about my journals. I'm still keeping one, with no great enthusiasm however. They'll all be published at once with a text written
2   *for this purpose. Happy man of letters. Happy public and happy me if, as I hope, it proves worth my while. Paris continues to be warm and muggy with a few rays of sunlight every once in a while. I have finally*
3   *met Lewis Brown, who was very obliging to me. What's going to*

2. Alexandre Cabanel (1823–1889), a very successful painter and a teacher at the École des Beaux-Arts. Uncle Charles was regarded as an art expert within Lautrec's family: cf. Letter 3, note 6.

Letter 38
1. There was apparently a settlement of family properties, whereby the Tapié de Céleyrans acquired Le Bosc and the Toulouse-Lautrecs acquired Ricardelle, an estate of some 10,000 hectares. Cf. Letter 7, note 3, and Attems, p. 102.
2. Evidently a series of drawings illustrating incidents in his life, such as he had already made in 1881 for the 'Cahier de Zig-Zags' (cf. Letter 30, note 2).
3. John Lewis Brown (1829–1890), a painter of hunting and military scenes, who had influenced his early work. Brown's studio was in the same building as Princeteau's.

63

become of my cousins, give me your opinion. I'm very much afraid it
won't be a glowing one.

Tell Louis the enclosed note will give him all the information he needs.

As for the cash, I need all I can get, that is to say, 500 francs at
once. Of course you will have it by the first of July.

And now let's go and have lunch.

4   *Yours*

                                         Henri

39 TO HIS FATHER   *Monday, [April] 17 [1882]*

My dear Papa,

1   *I was taken in this morning by the students of the Bonnat studio.*
2, 3 *Thanks to the recommendation of Rachou, a friend of Ferréol, I had a*
      good reception. By chance a young American from the hotel went in with
      me. They had us talk and pay for a toddy. That's all there was to it.
      Not so terrible. They made enough racket, but not too much actual
      fighting. There are a lot of English and Americans.
          So, there I am, one of the boys, absolutely. Draw, draw, that's the
4   *rub. Mr. Moore, the deaf-mute American painter, has brought a lot of*
5   *splendid Japanese* bibelots *here. This young man is his friend. He has*
      set up his studio in one of the large rooms at the Pérey.

4. Lautrec uses the English word, as he will often do in signing letters.

Letter 39
1. Léon Bonnat (1833–1922), a very successful painter of portraits and historical subjects, who was at this time at the height of his fame. In a letter to his Uncle Charles, dated March 22, 1882 (published in Joyant, I, pp. 56–7), Lautrec mentions that he is about to meet Bonnat. See Ill. 23.
2. Henri Rachou (1855–1944), a painter who was at this time a student of Bonnat and who later became Director of the museum at Toulouse. See Ill. 21.
3. Ferréol Roudat, a goldsmith in Albi who was a friend of Rachou's brother.
4. Harry Humphrey Moore (1844–1936), an American painter who had studied art and had travelled extensively. He had just returned from a trip to Japan.
5. Lautrec's interest in Japanese art seems to date from this time. See Ills. 35–37.

5   *Yesterday I saw Du Passage, who asked me how things were with you.*

6   *Yesterday, for* La Vie Moderne, *he drew the different ways a horse jumps.*

    Princeteau is still at the hotel. He is charming to me and encouraging. Now to work!!

    Goodbye, dear Papa. Be so kind as to remember me to everyone.

Your son,
H. de Toulouse Lautrec

40   TO HIS MOTHER   *[Paris, Spring 1882]*

My dear Mama,

    It's I who am going to be a little hard on you for your silence. I've been on the point of sending you a wire to find out what had become of you. I'm lunching tomorrow with my father and Rachou. He ran into

1   *M. Verrier, who would like to have me to lunch. (He can whistle for it.) I've written to Grandma Louise to wish her a happy birthday. It was only by luck I remembered. I've been a little balked by the weather,*

2   *because of working out of doors. My meal at the Nababs on Sunday was so copious that I lay down to snore after dinner. Fine thing indeed!! On that, I kiss you and Tata and everybody, while put out with you for leaving me without news.*

    Perhaps your letter got lost.

Henri

5. The Vicomte Charles-Marie du Passage (b. 1843), a painter and sculptor, and an acquaintance of Lautrec's father.
6. A magazine of art and literature founded in 1879.

Letter 40
1. Cf. Letter 11, note 3.
2. A general name for wealthy people: nabobs.

My dear Mama,

Have you broken your arm, or have you forgotten that your offspring exists? A brief word, if you will, to bring me up on what's going on.

Everything's fine here. I'm working hard. All the best and a thousand
1 *small kisses.*

Yours,

H.

My dear Grandma,

I didn't want to let your name day go by without coming, my roll of congratulations in hand, with my best wishes (that classic image). So I do it as well as I can!!! There it is done, awkwardly enough, maybe, but gracefulness not being the key to my character, I am hoping to be pardoned, if not thanked, for it.

You may not be displeased to know how we've been living here in the
1 *fog or rather the mud of the Aveyron, since it's raining hard. Take my word it's raining cats and dogs (choice expression indicating a serious study of slang on my part). Grandma . . ., what is Grandma doing? She is putting up curtains and feels the clouds going by. Aunt Emilie is sewing*

1. Lautrec uses here 'poutounégeade', an invention based on the Gascon words 'poutou' (a little kiss) and 'négade' (a drowning). Cf. Letter 21, note 2.
   Letter 42
1. The Department of Aveyron, in south-western France, in which the Château du Bosc is situated. Lautrec uses the Gascon word 'bouillaque', i.e., 'boulhacas' meaning mud.

the aforesaid curtains on the machine. Uncle Amédée is off massacring all he can and Uncle Charles is looking for excuses (oh, diplomatic refinement) for his laziness, which shows through despite his protests. Mama, I think, is doing cut-out work on some moleskin, known by the fancy name of altar cloth. I am dividing my leisure time between painting and the toothache, an inexhaustible source of diverse enjoyments. Kiki

2   *sulks at anything not called a blanquette, a floury christening. Mariette is curling her hair and Doctor Farguent has just come to give her her pills. And that's all there is. We all send you our love, and I a great big kiss.*

Your godson,

Henri

43   TO HIS FATHER   *Le Bosc, this Thursday [September 1882]*

My dear Papa,

1   *Bonnat has let all his pupils go. Before making up my mind I wanted to have the consensus of my friends and by unanimous agreement I have just accepted an easel in the atelier of* Cormon, *a young and celebrated painter, the one who did the famous* Cain Fleeing with His Family *at*

2   *the Luxembourg. A powerful, austere and original talent. Rachou sent a telegram to ask if I would agree to study there along with some of my friends, and I have accepted. Princeteau praised my choice. I would very*

3   *much have liked to try Carolus, but this prince of colour produces only mediocre draughtsmen, which would be fatal for me.*

2. A white sauce that accompanies a veal stew.

Letter 43

1. Bonnat, having been appointed a professor at the Ecole des Beaux-Arts, had closed his private studio.
2. It had been exhibited at the Salon of 1880; cf. Bénédite, p. 22, no. 127. Fernand Piestre, called Cormon (1845–1924), was famous for this painting and for his teaching, many of his pupils having later achieved success. His studio was at 10, rue Constance. See Ills. 20, 23.
3. Emile Auguste Carolus-Duran (1838–1917), a fashionable portrait painter.

After all, I won't be married to the situation, will I? And the choice of teachers is by no means exhausted.

4   *We are leaving for Respide, where we are expecting to stay only briefly in order to get the indispensable work going again. Hoping to make a go of it, I shall be happy to have your approval of an un-prejudiced choice based on serious argument. Everything is fine here and Aunt Blanche is with us. We all send you our love.*

Your respectful son,

Henri

44   TO HIS MOTHER   *[Paris] October 9 [1882]*

My dear Mama,

I've received your not very cheerful letter, but please give me details on the incidents that occurred. Are you officially ruled out of a share in the family spoils, or have you retired into absolute silence? Or has there been

1   *an arrangement, and in what terms? Write me all the details because I'm completely at sea and wouldn't want to drop a brick. Everything here is as well as can be expected. I'm going to try to find a place to live but it isn't easy.*
      I kiss you.

Yours,

H.

2   *Where is Jalabert? Give me his address, please.*

4. The Pascals' country home, near Bordeaux.
   Letter 44
1. Cf. Letter 38, note 1.
2. The superintendent of his parents' property at Ricardelle.

My dear Mama,

1   *My life is dull. I drudge along sadly, and haven't talked to Cormon yet.*
2   *In all events, I'll be at your feet on the first, with my friend Claudon, a charming fellow. That will give us a lift.*

    Dora looks to me as if she's all loused up. You find that Louis is getting big and fat. More power to him. I wrote to him to explain why I didn't see him before he left. Papa is going to leave??? Let's hope so.

    I kiss you,

Henri

46 TO AMÉDÉE TAPIÉ DE CÉLEYRAN

[*Paris*] *Friday, December 1* [*1882*]

My dear Uncle,

Well, here we are at it again. You with your gadgets and me with my plumb line. Things are jogging along pretty well with me. Cormon gave me a warm welcome. He liked my drawings, particularly (beg your
1   *pardon) the one of Uncle Odon with his hands stuck in his pockets, in*
2   *other words: hip! hip! hurrah. Princeteau preferred the bat and Rachou the one of Uncle Charles leaning on the table. We had a restful stay at Respide, a truly pretty place, where you can really go boating. Louis is grinding away for his baccalaureate on the 6th. Poor little fellow: they*
3   *tell me Toto made up his mind to put on a little pressure. I can't get*

1. No doubt partly because his favourite cousin, Madeleine Tapié de Céleyran, died that autumn.
2. A fellow student at Cormon's studio.
   Letter 46
1. For this and the other drawings mentioned, cf. Joyant, II, pp. 183–4.
2. Lautrec uses here an invented onomatopoeic expression, 'raou, plaou, plaou'.
3. Probably one of Lautrec's Tapié de Céleyran cousins. Cf. Letter 84.

over it. Tell him not to carry the thing too far. My new boss is the
thinnest man in Paris. He often drops in on us and wants us to have as

4   *much fun as we can painting outside the studio. I haven't seen Bonnat yet.*
Will I ever!!! I knew all my fellow-students, so there's been no break.

5   *Uncle Odon and Aunt O. are here. Their kids have gone to Albi.*
The parents leave tomorrow for Florida. They are going to have things
planted and built. They look down in the mouth already. What will they
be like by the time they get back!

      I've heard about Uncle Bébert's marriage. Man overboard . . .
another one!!! Is he delighted! May these two experiments succeed, and
mine along with them!

6   *My most friendly regards and endearments to Dowager ladies and*
young ladies as well, meanwhile I shake your hand majestically by the
forefinger.

      Your nephew,

        H. Monfa

47   TO MME L. TAPIÉ DE CÉLEYRAN   *[Paris, December 1882]*

My dear Grandma,

I wish you a very happy New Year and beg you to pass along my best
1   *wishes to everyone. Mama must have told you about my small doings, so I*
won't repeat myself, because whatever she tells you, we tell you

4. In a letter to his Uncle Charles, dated February 10, 1883 (published in Joyant, I, p. 60), Lautrec complains that Cormon is a more indulgent teacher than Bonnat, and that he misses the latter's severity.
5. Actually Lautrec's Aunt Emilie, to whom he occasionally refers in this way. Cf. Letter 16, note 2. Florida is the name of their country villa.
6. Endearments: cf. Letter 41, note 1.

Letter 47
1. In a letter to his other grandmother, dated December 28, 1882 (collection Mme Privat, Paris), Lautrec mentions that he is working hard 'morning and afternoon', and wonders whether he has lost ground by shifting from Bonnat's studio to Cormon's.

together. I would have hoped really to kiss you, but I hadn't reckoned on
2 *emergencies. If the beard isn't there, the heart is. And a happy New Year.*

Your respectful godson and grandson,

Henri

48   TO HIS MOTHER   *[Paris, 1882]*

My dear Mama,

*I'm a little late but I know, first, that the fuss of getting ready to leave
must have kept you terribly on the hop and, second, that Louis must have*
1 *told you about my plans. I have definitely resumed my treatment. Gabriel
has left with the Abbé who was taking him to Lille (?), without
stopping by to see us. Papa, hot-tempered as always, gave an artillery-*
2 *man a dressing down for shouting at his horse. The sunshine is simply
beautiful today and I am sending you a kiss in the hope of making it a
real one next time.*

Your

Henri

P.S. We will have to have a serious talk about the proposal to sell
3 *Ricardelle. Papa having asked my opinion, I prudently kept it to myself.
Did I do right?*

2. Lautrec now wears a beard, a traditional part of the artist's appearance.
   Letter 48
1. Probably the one with an electric brush mentioned in Letter 15. Cf. also Letter 87.
2. The story is told in fuller detail in Mack, p. 16.
3. Cf. Letter 38, note 1.

My dear Mama,

1   *I've been happy about the good news you've been giving to Aunt Cécile,*
showing that you approve completely of my decantation. While regretting
your return should be delayed, I can't blame you for making the most of
your trip. I am continuing to eat with Princeteau every now and then,
2   *since at Lucas' they've cut out the table d'hôte owing to a shortage of*
3   *customers. I've been to Longchamps with P. to browse on the green*
4   *grass. My work is progressing. I'm finishing the portrait of d'Ennery,*
5   *who very obligingly posed for me. Cormon is a little worn out by the jury*
work which wound up only last Saturday.

     It's as warm as summer and an overcoat is becoming superfluous. I'm
calling a halt, for I'm just writing words, and with this send you a kiss,
6   *and ask you to distribute salaams and many small kisses to whom it*
may concern.

HTL

1. Cécile Pascal, wife of Ernest Pascal, was a first cousin and close friend of Lautrec's mother.
2. A fashionable restaurant where Lautrec, like his father, often dined.
3. Probably the painter Princeteau. Longchamps is a race track in the Bois de Boulogne.
4. Gustave Dennery or d'Ennery (b. 1863), a fellow student at Cormon's studio. In addition to the oil portrait that Lautrec mentions, he did one in charcoal that is dated November 1883. See Ill. 24.
5. By this time Lautrec felt that he had begun to know Cormon better; cf. his letter to Uncle Charles, dated February 10, 1883 (published in Huisman and Dortu, p. 45).
6. Cf. Letter 41, note 1.

20, 21   Portrait of Lautrec by Henri Rachou, above, 1883. This portrait was painted at the time Lautrec was in Cormon's atelier in Paris and is referred to in letter 92. Rachou was a compatriot of Lautrec's who introduced him to Bonnat, cf. Letter 39; they later moved to Cormon's atelier together. Lautrec shared Rachou's studio at 22 Rue Ganneron, cf. Letter 50, until he found his own. Lautrec, however, kept in touch with Rachou and, when the latter married, was a frequent guest at Rue Ganneron. Rachou later became curator of the Toulouse Museum, where he had a painting by Lautrec hung. The photograph right, was taken in 1938 at Rachou's studio in Toulouse.

22, 23, 25   In 1882, Lautrec took an easel at Léon Bonnat's atelier to which he had been
introduced by Rachou. When Bonnat (above right) was appointed Professor at the École
des Beaux-Arts in 1883, Rachou and Lautrec moved to Cormon (above left), 'a young and
celebrated painter, the one who did the famous 'Cain fleeing with his family' at the
Luxembourg' (far right), cf. letter 43.

24, 26 Cormon's atelier. The photograph on the left shows Lautrec (far left foreground), Grenier holding a dog, and Anquetin (centre) holding a stick. The others are, back row, left to right: Fauconnier, Bidault, Armand de Terratz, Gustave Dennery, Rabache, Henri Folley, Emile Bernard, Gaston Pujol, Granchi Taylor. Front row, left to right: Descamps, Tampiers, Dufour (a friend of Cormon's) Raphael Collin and Louis Muraton. Right, another photograph showing, from left to right, Grenier, Rabache, Métivet and Lautrec with Lily Grenier (cf. letter 86).

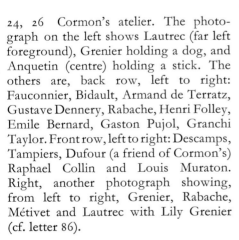

Château de Celeyran
par Courran (Aude)

Cher vieux.

Ne tremble pas devant
la perspective noire de mes
papiers. Je vais tâcher d'être
court……

Devant arriver a paris le 1er
Octobre, je désirerais savoir
si Cormon n'a pas de projets
voyageurs pour ce moment là —
Si l'atelier est terminé

[envelope]

Monsieur E. Boch
pleinairiste
22 rue Ganneron
pavillon A
Paris

27 Letter to his friend Eugène Boch (letter 50) whom he addresses on the envelope as 'pleinairiste', 'open air painter'; in the text he refers in slang to his summer's 'daubings' and signs himself 'young rotter'.

prêt à abriter nos jeunes
crânes frémissant du bouillonnement
de l'inspiration. Si les
camarades sont rentrés et
lesquels.
tu peux dire ouf. Voilà
qui est fini. Je te dispense
du récit de mes vachages
au soleil avec un pinceau
à la main et de taches
plus ou moins épinard,
pistache, olive ou merde
sur ma toile, Nous aurons
le temps d'en parler.

Je te la serre cordialement
et j'espère revoir quelques
mois precis de toi pour
m'esquisser la situation

La jeune pourriture

H. de Toulouse Lautrec

Château de Céleyran near Coursan (Aude) [September 1, 1883]

1   *Dear Old Fellow,*

Don't be frightened by the black prospect of my sheet of paper. I'll try to keep it short . . .
    Before I get to Paris on October 1st I'd like to know whether Cormon has any sketching trips planned for then. Also, whether the studio is finished and ready to shelter our young brains all simmering with
2   *the ferments of inspiration. And whether the fellows are back, and which ones.*
    I don't blame you for sighing with relief. Well, so much for that. I'll spare you the recital of my ruminations in the sun with a brush in hand and spots of a more or less spinachy green, pistachio, olive or shit colour on my canvas. We'll talk about that later.
    All the best, hoping for a few concise words from you to give me the lowdown on the situation.

                                           The young rotter,

                                H. de Toulouse Lautrec

1. Eugène Boch (1855–1941), a Belgian painter who was a fellow student at Cormon's studio. He was later acquainted with and portrayed by van Gogh. Lautrec's letter is addressed to him at 22, rue Ganneron, which was also Rachou's address. Four other letters to Boch are cited in the catalogue of the exhibition, 'Retrospective Anna et Eugène Boch', Musée des Arts et Métiers, La Louvière (Belgium), 11–31 October 1958. See Ill. 27.
2. Cormon had been looking for a new studio when Lautrec left Paris for the summer. He found one at 104 boulevard de Clichy.

Château Respide near Langon (Gironde) Saturday, September 8 [1883]

Dear Mama,

*I have just received your letter, so filled with solicitude and affection, but
devilishly worked up. I find it odd, having carried out your instructions
to the letter, that you should reproach me for not sacrificing my afternoon
chasing after a busy, will-o'-the-wisp uncle. The trip went off perfectly in
spite of my light clothing, which I had reinforced with one of Paul's
waistcoats and a shawl from Madame Méjean. We took a carriage and I
rode all by myself till I arrived, after leaving Paul and my aunt at
Toulouse.*

*They are at Lourdes today. Joseph is over the measles, they didn't
amount to anything. Yesterday I went to Malromé with Louis and an old*
1 *priest, who was delightfully bucolic. I've seen the shy Balade fellow, who
told me about your strange projects, which I'm falling in with, to be
agreeable. I shall probably come to have a quite different idea of*
2 *Malromé, living there in pleasant and cheerful quarters . . .*

The collar fits the horse we're trying out, Louis, Philippe and I.
Please send along the other instructions that you forgot.
A hug for all and a kiss for you.

Henri de Toulouse Lautrec

P.S. Have seen Rachou, who'll be in Paris on Tuesday. I've taken it on
3 *myself to send a groom to Malromé to tidy up our Bucephalus' hair.*
Goodbye—and please forward my mail . . . HTL

1. The Lautrecs' steward at Malromé. His name recurs in many later letters in which
Lautrec requests shipments of wine to Paris.
2. An old château set within a park, near St. Macaire in the Department of Gironde,
about ten miles from Respide, which Lautrec's mother had bought in May 1883.
In a letter to her mother, dated May 20, 1883 (published in Attems, pp. 211–13 and
incorrectly dated 1889), she explained her reasons for doing so and outlined her
plan for planting vines on part of the land, which is probably the 'strange project'
that Lautrec refers to. See Ill. 3.
3. The famous horse tamed and then ridden into many battles by Alexander the Great.
Here used simply to mean a horse.

My dear Mama,

I saw my sweet Papa last night and he was in very good spirits. Prince-
teau left abruptly without saying where he was going. It's odd. We went
1 *to the station at 10 o'clock to wait for the Odons, who didn't arrive*
until the 11 o'clock train, which being the case I took off.

Your news pleased me in the sense that you give me the impression of
feeling at home at Malromé. That means a lot and I imagine Tata must
2 *be busy impressing an odor* sui generis *on M. de Forcade's bedroom:*

Eau d' Addison	*7/14*
Little farts	*8 30*
Aq. dist.	*1 1/2*
Aunt Armandine	

3

There you have the formula.
On this I kiss you.

Yours,

Henri

My dear Grandma,

I'm availing myself of the impending New Year to give you some
news of our daily routine. Uncle Odon's arrival with his numerous
family has made things brighter for us, for we, or Mama, I should say,
have been rather lonely. Not being caught in the toils of the studio, she

1. I.e., his Uncle Odon de Toulouse-Lautrec and his family.
2. The former owner of Malromé, whose widow sold it to the Lautrecs.
3. Tata and Aunt Armandine are of course the same person.

has plenty of time to become highbrow. She is assiduously following the
I *metaphysical lectures of our dear master Caro (of the French Academy)*
and enjoying the perfumed prose of the old codger, who's just as affected
as ever.

Papa has left us to go and see his groom, who, in my opinion, was
spending a lot more money than he should have.

2 *As for myself, I'm working and am about to quit my little makeshift*
studio and move into a larger place which I intend to furnish. And here
is just the point to send the thanks I owe you for the money that Mama
sent me on your behalf and which will come in very handy. It will
probably go into rugs. I'm told you enjoyed my handsome friend Louis'
charming ways and patent leather shoes. You ought to find him an heiress
and throw her into his arms. He's not much good, I'd say, for anything
else. And now I'm going to make up for this meanness by wishing you a
happy New Year, so momentous that you can distribute slices of it
among the whole family, Uncle, Aunt, cousins of both sexes and abbés . . .
And I kiss you

Your respectful grandson and godson

H. de Toulouse Lautrec

Imitation artist

54 TO MME L. TAPIÉ DE CÉLEYRAN *[Paris, January 1884]*

My dear Grandma,

I am absolutely to blame for having put off sending you my good wishes for
the New Year till now, and Pater will now be able to distil the most

1. At the Sorbonne, Lautrec's mother followed the course of the fashionable and
conservative philosopher, Elme Caro (1826–1888), who had been a professor there
since 1864 and a member of the Académie Française since 1875.
2. Lautrec had just rented a larger studio in the rue Lepic, which he was furnishing.
Cf. his mother's letter of January 14, 1884, published in Attems, pp. 201–2; also
ibid., p. 204.

acid reproofs without fear of appearing unjust. Therefore, I bow my dauber's head in shame, because dauber I am right up to the ears. I'm working like a horse and don't even have the heart left to go for a walk in the evening, a pleasant habit I had acquired. Mama seems not to be unendurably bored. I'm very happy about that for I was afraid of her being more or less alone all the time. At least it's better than to condemn her to roost, as I do, in a quarter that continues to have its cut-throat character. Practical jokers set upon women walking alone and empty ink on their . . . necks. A fine idea of fun that is. I've had sad news of the death at sea of my poor friend Doctor Rouilat. Feeling he was done for, he wanted to come back to Paris to die, but was taken on the way. Louis Pascal is going to work in the Comptoir d'Escompte. A good place for this likeable old fool to end up in. Promise me you'll congratulate him.

Goodbye for now, dear Grandma, and please remember me to my uncle and aunt and to Tata. And lavish equitably floods of affectionate regards on all my cousins, but especially on Kiki.

I kiss you.

Your respectful godson and grandson,

Henri

P.S. Please tell my Uncle I haven't forgotten him. I haven't made up my mind yet about the hats. But for that I would already have done what he asked me.

HTL

1. I.e., the Comptoir National d'Escompte, a large commercial bank in Paris.
2. His Aunt Armandine.
3. Béatrix Tapié de Céleyran.

My dear Mama,

Just as I wrote to you, as soon as I found out, the board declared me unfit for military service, without having to show any kind of medical certificate. M. Mullin was as kind to me as he could be and had me taken first with some Auvergnat fellows with smelly feet.

1   *That evening I went to a party given by Mayet in his studio. We all went to bed at six in the morning, rather tired. Not a sign of the handsome Louis. However, I have seen Bourges, who told me he is well. A new oculist has found his eyes to be in very good shape and since then he has gone back to the Comptoir d'Escompte.*

As for Paul, it appears that the lizards have taken over his room and, the rebellion having cut his supplies, he had to eat meat without bread. All this put together so delighted him that he has packed his

2   *trunks . . . his father, I believe, plans to send him to Tonkin.*

There you have all the news. I don't know whether you read about the

3   *Count and Countess de Nattes' accident, thrown with their carriage and runaway horses against the Seine parapet and hurled through the windows of the said carriage, just like Uncle Odon, whom, by the way, I have yet to see. With this a kiss for you all, thanking you, my Aunt, my Uncle and Tata (specially reserved places) for all the nice things you have all done for me, who has done so little for you.*

All my love,

Your

Henri

1. Léon Mayet (b. 1858), another fellow student, had a studio at 15, Villa des Artistes, Impasse Hélène, where Bonnat's studio was, too.
2. Tonkin (North Vietnam) was then a part of French Indo-China.
3. The Count de Nattes had studied at Sorèze (cf. Letter 25, note 6) before going on to St.-Cyr and a military career, hence was probably known to the Lautrecs.

P.S. My money is running low and pretty soon I'm going to find myself dead broke. I'm letting you know ahead of time so you can forward me something, and I can wait for you without touching my friends.
Princeteau: no news of him.

56 TO HIS MOTHER   [*Paris, Spring 1884*]

My dear Mama,

1   I have received your far from reassuring letter. I've seen Papa, who had good news, about Ricardelle, and Louis, who had bad news about Respide. Anyway we are all right.

There has been a revolution at the studio. Cormon has fired the student in charge and plans to appoint another one. All this has stirred up more excitement than you could imagine. Rachou is our boss. I think
2   I mentioned that before. No wonder I'm writing nonsense, for I haven't been down from Montmartre for five days. I'm painting a woman whose
3   hair is all gold. My drawing for Le Figaro isn't completely finished, but it's getting along. Phew!—Have just eaten very quickly and am going to work.

I kiss you and Tata, too.

Yours,

Henri

P.S. I'll do your errand when I can.

1. I.e., concerning the expected yields of the vineyards at Ricardelle, the Lautrecs' estate, and at Respide, the Pascals' estate.
2. Apparently Rachou had been authorized by Cormon to correct the students' work when he was not present. Cf. Letter 39, note 2.
3. I.e., *Le Figaro Illustré*. His drawings were, however, not published there until July 1893. Cf. Letter 58.

My dear Mama,

1   *I got your letter, which gives me hopes as to Pérey. You can come to the*
2, 3   *Métropolitain and I'll join you there, or I'll stay on at Grenier's, who's*
    a peach of a pal, and even better, a friend. We've received Balade's
    multiple shipments, but unfortunately he sent very little red wine, which
    prompts me to ask for a second shipment, all red. You tell me you have
    a sore throat. Hope you're over it by this time. Aunt Armandine made a
    mistake moving. I would have been around to give her a hand in
    January and would have scrounged as much out of it as I could. The
    atelier is up in arms, they want to name a 'student in charge'. They'd like
    to give me this tiresome job, but I'm stubbornly refusing.
4   *I'm happy that you're satisfied with what I'm doing.*
    I haven't replied to Louis and won't.
    I find it terribly provoking the stubborn way most of the family insist
on making fun of me. Luckily you have several votes on that ballot.
    I kiss you, and, other than you, Aunt Armandine.

Your son,

H

Wire if I'm to meet you.

1. I.e., the Hôtel Pérey, where Lautrec apparently hoped his mother would stay.
2. The Hôtel Métropolitain, on the rue Cambon, where Lautrec's mother stayed. In a letter to her mother, dated 1885 (published in Attems, pp. 208–9), she expresses the hope that he will live there too, for she considers Montmartre 'a bad neighbourhood'.
3. René Grenier (1861–1917), a friend and fellow student of Lautrec's at both the Bonnat and the Cormon studios. During the summer of 1884, Lautrec went to live with Grenier and his wife Lily (who also posed for some of Lautrec's paintings) at 19 bis, rue Fontaine. According to some biographers, he lived there for two years; according to others, for only a few months. See Ill. 24.
4. This was particularly important, since he was discouraged, and in a letter to his godmother, written in June 1884 (collection Madame Privat), he referred to 'art which shuns me' and announced his decision not to enter the competition at the École des Beaux-Arts.

1   [*Restaurant*] *Lucas* [*Paris*] *Noon, August 15* [*1884*]

My dear Mama,

If I haven't written to you sooner it's because I've been snowed under by
2   *work. I've worked as much as I could on my drawing for* Le Figaro *but,*
Rachou not being satisfied with it, I haven't sent it off. He pointed out
to me that only the very best one can do should be submitted to the
public. Well, my drawing really could have been better. I'm sure you
won't mind my following this sensible advice. Since I'd had my nose to the
3   *grindstone right up to the deadline I went to work at night at the Bar.*
After all. Deuce take it!!!
I've seen nothing of Papa and don't know whether he has done your
errands. I still haven't been able to do any of mine.
I kiss you, and Tata as well. Shall swallow a quick Mass and then
reclimb the heights, where my model is waiting for me.

                         Yours,

                         Henri

59   TO MME L. TAPIÉ DE CÉLEYRAN   [*Paris, late August, 1884*]

1   *My dear Grandma,*

In all the confusion of my poor existence my correspondence has fallen into
arrears. I hope you'll forgive me so I may wish you a happy and prosperous

1. Exceptionally, Lautrec spent this summer in Paris, Cormon having asked him, as
well as Rachou, to collaborate on an illustrated edition of Victor Hugo's works.
Lautrec worked on drawings for *La Légende des Siècles*, which have recently been
found. However, the publisher did not approve of Lautrec's drawings. Cf. his
mother's letter to her mother, published in Attems, pp. 206–7.
2. Cf. Letter 56, note 3.
3. This is the first indication that Lautrec is frequenting the Montmartre cafes.
Letter 59
1. Lautrec addresses his godmother as 'Bonne Maman' rather than 'Marraine'.

name-day. I don't know whether you're at Malromé, busy tasting our pigeons. But if this is the case, please tell Mama that Papa hasn't left yet. In case you're at Bosc, please give everybody a kiss, and particularly Grandma Gabrielle for poor old me.

I'd like to talk to you a little about what I'm doing, but it's so special!!! I prefer simply to wish you the best of the season and to kiss you twice, as grandson and as godson.

Your respectful grandson,

H. de Toulouse Lautrec

60   TO HIS MOTHER   [*Paris*] *Wednesday* [*1884*]

My dear Mama,

I've just received your letter from Albi. Undoubtedly you'll find Joseph, who leaves tomorrow, at Respide. Laura Pérey is waiting for you to have a housewarming at the hotel, which has several new paying guests.

I haven't sent you the photograph and think for the time being I may wait for you to get back. Papa doesn't at all look as if he's going to follow you to Malromé. Sorry about it. I kiss you.

H.

P.S. please send the money to pay the landlord. *It would be better not to make him wait. Send it to Aunt Emilie's.*

61   TO HIS MOTHER   [*Paris*] *Sunday* [*October 1884*]

My dear Mama,

I haven't written to you sooner because I had several things to straighten out. Papa wrote me a very friendly letter asking me to pick up his packages from Pérey's where he'd left them. You can see that the break

1 *between us having petered out it may not be as hard to make up as we had feared. Be calm and don't drop any bricks. I still haven't shown*

2 *anything to Cormon, but I've seen him and he was very nice.*

3 *I am very much settled down in my kind friend's place, so much so indeed that I would be in danger of becoming an intruder were your arrival not in the offing.*

4, 5 *No more cholera, as far as I can see. Bourges gave me an awful going over when I told him how scared I was.*

6 *Poor Rabache is having tooth trouble. They took out half his jaw teasing him free of one of his molars. He's drinking milk and is terribly down in the dumps and welcomed me like a long-lost brother. Rachou is at Toulouse.*

There you have my little chronicle, short and sweet.

I kiss you ferociously and tomorrow am going to get down to work.

Your Son

62 TO HIS MOTHER *[Paris, October 1884]*

My dear Mama,

I've just come out of one o'clock Mass after having had lunch at Lucas'. That has civilized me a little, because these days I hardly ever budge

1 *from my heights. I saw Cormon this morning. He rather congratulated*

1. The first mention of any disagreement between Lautrec and his father, with whom he was in general on less close terms than with his mother.
2. Cf. Letters 62 and 63.
3. René Grenier's studio. Cf. Letter 57, note 3.
4. A cholera epidemic had started in southern France in the summer of 1884 and had soon spread through the rest of the country. Lautrec refers to it again in a letter to his mother written in July 1884 (published in Joyant, I, pp. 75–76).
5. Henri Bourges, a childhood friend of Lautrec's and later a well-known doctor, with whom Lautrec shared an apartment for several years after 1887. See Ill. 33.
6. A fellow student at Cormon's studio; he appears in a photograph of the students there, reproduced in Huisman and Dortu, p. 41. See Ills. 24, 26.

Letter 62
1. Cf. Letters 61 and 63.

me, at the same time making me conscious of my ignorance. Anyway, it bucked me up a little. In a word, we haven't been wasting our time.

Rachou was bitten on the hand by a dog and that kept him from working. He's in Toulouse, where he has just started a new series of horse studies.

Rabache is up and about and my concierge is going to leave me to go into the oyster business, which I find very annoying. Your letter made me regret not having gone along with you, but I'm definitely counting on coming to see you by the end of the year. Keep on reminding me of it.

You seem very happy to be home, and I'm glad of that. I haven't seen anyone, except Cousin Cupelet's blonde moustache from a distance. And there you have all my empty head can conjure up by way of news. Lots of kisses for both Grandmas and remember me to all. When will Papa be coming back? I suppose he doesn't know himself.

I kiss you and would like to see you (but well settled).

2   P.S. It was the big daub that Cormon preferred. That amazed me.

H.

P.P.S. Not a sound from our gang. I'm going to bed at 9. And deuce
3   take the Cholera!!

63 TO HIS MOTHER   [*Paris, November 1884*]

My dear Mama,

I thought I'd spoken about my poor daubs at Cormon's in my last two
1, 2   letters. It appears I was mistaken. He thought my cattle was bad,

2. Probably the landscape to which Lautrec refers in the following letter.
3. Cf. Letter 61, note 4.
   Letter 63
1. Cf. Letters 61 and 62.
2. Probably the *Boeufs Attelés* (Céleyran, 1882) reproduced in Joyant, I, p. 15.

the little Laffittes pretty good and the landscape really good. In sum, it's

3 *all very feeble stuff compared with the landscapes Anquetin produced.*

4 *Everyone is amazed. They're in an impressionist style that does him*
proud. One feels like a little boy indeed beside workers of this calibre.
I saw Papa on Sunday and couldn't tell you whether Uncle Odon is still
in Paris.

I'm back in the old routine that will last until spring and then maybe
I'll do some really bizarre things. All vague yet.

I haven't had the energy to go to the shirt-maker's. Too pooped even
to think of going out. It's so nice in the evenings at Grenier's in the
warm studio. A good thing if you were to knit me a stocking cap and
slippers. The café bores me, going downstairs is a nuisance, painting and
sleeping, that's all there is. I'll stop because I'm getting mumbly-
wumbly.

And a kiss for the grandmas, aunts and you.

Yours

HTL

I've seen Uncle Ernest.

64 TO HIS MOTHER *[Paris, Autumn 1884]*

My dear Mama,

1 *Your letter made me happy. I see you acting Juno Lucina with conviction.*

2 *Papa has moved on to Orléans and I didn't see him. He quarrelled with*

3 *Raymond's teachers, who wouldn't hand him over.*

3. Louis Anquetin (1861–1932), entered Cormon's studio in 1882. Although a daring painter in his youth, he later rejected Impressionism and became an imitator of Rubens. See Ill. 24.

4. In another letter to his mother, also of this period (published in Carco, p. 160, and incorrectly dated 1879), Lautrec speaks of the 'winds of Impressionism' blowing through Cormon's studio.

Letter 64

1. The Roman goddess of childbirth; he refers to a delivery at which his mother was present.

2. His hunting lodge at Loury-aux-Bois, near Orléans.

3. Raymond de Toulouse-Lautrec.

There's a terrible fog here, streetcars are misty and noses red. It's pretty sad.

We're in the competition up to our necks—there are so many people it's a nuisance. In short, it's simply more of a bore than other weeks.

*It would be very nice of you to send me 4 tins of goose-livers. That ought to be easy and I'll send 2 of them to Mme Dennery and two to Grenier, who very much enjoyed the other. That would be a sensible way of acknowledging their kindness. Two more wouldn't hurt. I'm very serious about this—(I under*line*). I'd like to go everywhere to get pictorial impressions, but at night it's terrible to go to bed at 2 o'clock knowing you'll have to get up at 8 by candlelight. And Why??? . . .*

After all, we'll talk better . . . cheeks reddened by the open fire—and soon, I hope.

I feel pretty well and have a desire to work. The deuce with everything else.

I kiss you,
a disillusioned old man,

Yours,

Henri

65 TO HIS MOTHER [*Paris, 1884*]

My dear Mama,

Nothing important to report. I keep jogging along per usual. Studio in the morning with Rachou correcting, and he's not easy, the brute. After-noons outdoors at Rachou's and evenings the bar where I wind up my

4. This may be the mother of Gustave Dennery; cf. Letter 49, note 4.
Letter 65
1. I.e., in a little garden of Rachou's studio at 22, rue Ganneron, where Lautrec painted figures seated outdoors. Rachou's memoir of this period (published in Huis-man and Dortu, p. 44) gives the same information, as well as an interesting picture of Lautrec.

little day. I've seen Papa very occasionally. He has managed to quarrel
with Lucas!!! I'm going there just the same. What a comical fellow he
is. I missed Odon's family. Wouldn't put it past them to cut me off.
I'm cutting this short because I was just about to go out
    and send you a kiss, and Tata and Grandma as well.
    but you especially
    your offspring, darling of the Graces

                              Henri

66   TO HIS MOTHER   *[Paris, January 1885]*

My dear Mama,

I intended to write you only a simple postcard, but M. Dufour having
this morning collected (from the verb collect) the payment for the first of
the year, that is, the three months in advance, the result has been a
considerable diminution of my finances. I'm not broke, but would be if I
paid what I owe. Except for this I'm on top of the world and the work
1 *is progressing. I've seen Bourges, who's beginning his two-month exam*
and who's bored stiff. And there you have it.
    I send a kiss to all of you and beg you to excuse the financial character
of my letter. I have been sensibly working away at a fellow-student's
place, on a female pierrot powdered white. I've been advised to start

1. I.e., the first part of the Concours d'Externat, a major medical examination. Cf.
Lautrec's letter to his mother (incorrectly dated July 1884) in Joyant, I, pp. 75–76:
'Bourges a passé heureusement, brillamment même, la première partie du concours
d'externat.'

something for the Salon: I am waiting for Cormon to speak to me about it himself, but I'm not going to start anything for fear of getting slapped down.

All this is very ambitious and needs some thinking over. I kiss you.

Yours,

HTL

P.S. Send money.

2   Jeannette Hathaway

67 TO HIS MOTHER   *[Paris, January 1885]*

My dear Mama,

I've got everything straightened out, or nearly, and can send you some news. I've seen Papa just once. He was very pleasant and gave me some cash and his blessing. We went together to see Uncle Odon. I've been to 1 *see my Aunt, Raymond, and Odette. That visit was a very sad affair. Really harrowing. I've yet to see Louis who wrote me a curt note. I did not hurry to reply, then an angry note arrived. I'm answering it with an invitation to dinner. Can hardly be more obliging than that.*

Bourges is passing his exams, his grades up to now have been brilliant Cormon hasn't seen my splotches yet. He's going to tomorrow morning. He has postponed the competition because there are people still away in the country.

2   *Oh, what fun Dayot made of us! We took up stations at the Café de Bordeaux. We had our dinner there Dutch treat and Deforges arrived very late, telling us that . . . anyway, making perfectly inadequate*

2. Presumably an invention, since no such person or fictional character is known.
   Letter 67
1. His Aunt Emilie le Melorel de la Haichois, the mother of Raymond and Odette.
2. Armand Dayot (1856–1934), a journalist and art critic who published reviews of the Salons of 1882 (under the pseudonym of Jean Merien), 1884, and 1890.

excuses. *As for Joseph, he could have found us easily enough, since we stayed within the same ten square metres the whole evening. So much the worse for us.*

There you have it. Mama, my little tale complete. You will excuse me for not having overdone with a lot of trifling messages that would never have caught up with you.

When I see Papa I'll give him your messages.

I kiss you and please hug my grandmas, too.

Do your best to purify kisses as soiled as mine are as you pass them on. Keep some for yourself.

Yours,

H.

I've seen Miss Braine, who's a bit off, I think.

68   TO HIS MOTHER   [*Paris, c. March 1885*]

My dear Mama,

I got your news through Grandma. There is indeed a canine epidemic. Two of Rachou's little ones are dead. The third is in the hospital. It's a kind of cholera or puppy diarrhoea.

The weather has turned fine which allows me to work hard. I took a physic this morning. Aah . . . Just about everybody is making an energetic effort for the Salon. Bordes, Rachou, etc. The latter has just had a portrait commissioned and at a very nice price. I'm telling you all this because I hope to interest you. Perhaps I'll bring you two guests

1. A continuation of the cholera epidemic first mentioned in Letters 61 and 62.
2. Ernest Bordes, a native of Pau and a fellow student of Lautrec's in the studios of Bonnat and Cormon. He began as a genre painter and later specialized in portraiture.

instead of one. You should gather together the girls of the neighbourhood
and teach them to pose a little so that all we would have to do is get
down to work. There you are, my little chronicle ended. I kiss you and
the grandmas ditto, if they are there.

Your
H.

Haven't seen Papa!

69   TO HIS MOTHER   [*Paris, April 1885*]

My dear Mama,

I must be wicked indeed to have you write such cruel things to me. I'm
not angry with you about it. I think the rain has a lot to do with your
bad temper. What you say to me about the subject of my friends leads
me to believe that you think I'm downright stupid, if you really think I'm
capable of letting wolves into your chicken-run. I simply wanted to
oblige a charming, very well-bred fellow and one whom you will certainly
have nothing to complain about. We will work to the best of our ability
and do justice to your wine. What more do you want?

Let's get on to the second matter. You don't see, then, that I didn't
want to let myself be influenced by an old memory. I have a definite
appointment this very day with my expert and won't have lost anything
by waiting. Calm Tata, I beg you. Hasn't she rubbed off on you a little
1 *and aren't you getting rather ticklish. If that's it, I'll lock myself up*
in the North Tower with my friend and the old St. Arnaud. We'll
2 *play bézique with two dummies, rare sight. I'd very much like to bring*
Grenier, but he doesn't seem to be too anxious about it. However, all is
not lost.

1. He writes 'trébadizez', derived from the Gascon word 'trebauda', to agitate
   violently.
2. A complicated game which can be played with several packs of cards. In 1895,
   Lautrec represented people playing bézique in an oil sketch and a lithograph; cf.
   Joyant, II, p. 264, and Delteil 115.

I've seen Papa, who is supposed to send you some precious stones from the Caucasus.

There you have it, you dreadful old bogey, all I had to say.

3   *I'm eagerly looking forward to the date of the Langon fair, and kiss you, or rather offer you my infant brow, adorned with what very little stuffing you've left there.*

Your unworthy son,

Henri

Kiss Tata for me, please.

70   TO HIS MOTHER   *[Paris, Spring 1885]*

My dear Mama,

1   *Your letter is friendly though ironic as regards my still legitimate request. I don't insist. I've seen all the family. Uncle Charles, etc., etc.*

2   *Except Uncle Amédée, who's spending all his time at Puteaux. But I haven't got the time to chase after him. I'm spending all my time at work, which leaves me hardly any opportunity to have new things to recount to you. Tell me if you're going to Bosc at the beginning of August. I would join you there and, about the 20th of the same month we would*

3   *get back home. Unless I do something with my cousins. Think it over and let me know.*

     I kiss your hands.

Yours,

Harry

3. A town in the Gironde, near Malromé. The fair took place in May and September.

Letter 70

1. I.e., to bring his friends to Malromé. Cf. Letters 68 and 69.
2. A city near Paris, now part of its suburbs.
3. Nothing seems to have come of this idea.

My dear Mama,

Your belated letter amused me very much. A madly merry one. I'm so knocked out by the heat that I'm leading a spa sort of life, shower, tub, plus work, which is tiring. I'm not giving in to Grenier and Anquetin who are taking turns at trying to drag me off to the country, for I know only too well I'd never get anything done there.

1   *We presented Cormon with a ridiculous silver palm which he received with much emotion.*

What are your plans and, with all the brood at Le Bosc, won't you soon be drawn there? If you were there, what lovely walks we'd take in the evening. . . . and enjoy each other's company much more than in the wintertime. Now just say that I have a heart of stone. But right now we'll have to settle for enjoying Papa, who persists in not giving me any appointments for a meeting, which in any case he wouldn't keep if he did.

I kiss you, perspiring profusely.

Yours,

Harry

My dear Mama,

Your horse question is hard to solve. As long as you entrust your animals to fools, *it's useless to look for anything but nags. In which case there's no point in my getting mixed up in it.*

1. At the Salon of 1885 Cormon's entry was awarded a silver medal. His students gave him a present in honour of the occasion.

However, if you've made up your mind to forbid anyone but the
coachman *from using the horses, I'm willing to look into the matter.*
M. Anquetin would like nothing better. With this restriction, I'm at
your command. Louis must have come to see you because he's at Respide.
So you must have had a chance to have it out with him. For my part

1 *I'm busy moving and the work is suffering from it. Besides, the weather*
is so sultry that the models sleep on their feet. I've sold some studies and
am about to sell some others. Papa hardly stirs. But I'm very much
afraid that the heat will drive us out of Paris before long. Where will I

2 *go? For the time being I sometimes go boating at Asnières. It smells*
awfully bad and bears only the faintest resemblance to the sea . . . much
sooner to sh . . .

Write to me and tell me your plans—pure or otherwise. And I kiss
you warmly.

Yours,

Henri

73 TO HIS MOTHER   [*Paris*] *Friday* [*July 1885*]

My dear Mama,

1 *My interview was relatively successful and I hope not to have to appeal*
to your generosity. I'm still ready to leave on the 20th or 22nd. About the
30th we'll move on to Malromé and after a short stay will go to spend

2 *a fortnight at* Taussat *or* Caussat. *I don't know the spelling but*

1. His new address is uncertain, but may have been Henri Rachou's studio at 22 rue
   Ganneron. Cf. Mack, p. 71.
2. A town on the Seine, now part of the suburbs of Paris, where Lautrec went boating
   with the Greniers.
   Letter 73
1. With his father, to ask for money.
2. Taussat-les-Bains, a resort town in the Department of Gironde, near Arcachon and
   Malromé, where Lautrec often went during the summer from this year until 1900.

3 *it seems to be very wild. At Robert Wurst's. It's settled. I'll
undoubtedly see my uncles and aunts tomorrow. The weather continues
to grate on my nerves but the approaching departure cheers me up. As*
4 *if I'd pulled a fast one on St. Médard. I'm glad your trip was a success*
5 *and here are little kisses for you.*

Your son,

Harry

74 TO HIS MOTHER *[Paris] Monday evening [Autumn 1885]*

My dear Mama,

*I've had a very good trip and was lucky enough to find Grenier at home.
He was leaving again for the country and wanted to take me along with
him. Naturally I held out against that. He has left me in charge of his
keys and his bed, which will permit me to look around. I'm thinking of*
1 *going to Ottoz's as the good fellow I spoke to you about is still there.
That would be company for me. I found everything in order—but it
appears I'm a quarter's rent behind (!) and I had miscalculated, sure
enough. The only thing to do is groan and pay. I'll write to you if it
becomes urgent, but I'll have to wait until Papa has forwarded me some
money.*
      I kiss you all and you above all.

Yours,

Henri

3. Probably the doctor, and later professor of medicine at the Sorbonne, whom
   Lautrec portrayed conducting a medical examination of Gabriel Tapié de Céleyran.
4. According to a popular belief, if it rains on June 8th, the feast day of St. Médard,
   it will rain for forty days thereafter. St. Médard was the patron of the corn-harvest
   and the vintage. Cf. Letter 95.
5. Cf, Letter 41, note 1.
   Letter 74
1. Emile Ottoz, a fellow student at Cormon's studio.

My dear Mama,

Your letter is short and has nothing really new to tell. I've been to see
1 *Grenier at Villiers. It's very cool down that way. Paris is dark and*
muddy, which doesn't prevent me from trotting in the streets after the
2 *musicians of the Opéra, whom I'm trying to charm so as to sneak into*
the temple of the arts and of boredom. Which is not at all easy.
Haven't seen Papa for a long time. Grenier is due to go deer-hunting
3 *in the Sologne this winter, or . . . to warm himself by the fireside.*
4 *I'm doing the portrait of one of my friends' beautiful sister, which is a*
lot of fun. I'm going there right now and am writing to you while
sipping my coffee (otherwise known as 'java').
I kiss you and am waiting for you.

Your boy,

Harry

1. Villiers-sur-Morin, a village in the Department of Seine-et-Marne, east of Paris, where the Greniers had a house. During one of his sojourns there with Grenier in 1885, Lautrec painted four murals in the public room of the Inn. Two are reproduced in Joyant, I, pp. 45 and 47.
2. Probably Désiré and Henri Dihau. Désiré Dihau (1835–1909) was first bassoonist at the Opera, and was portrayed by Degas as well as by Lautrec.
3. A region in the Loire Valley.
4. Probably Jeanne Wenz, sister of Frédéric Wenz, a fellow student at Cormon's studio. Cf. the photograph and Lautrec's portrait of her, reproduced in Huisman and Dortu, pp. 58 and 60.

My dear Mama,

I *I'm writing to tell you that my ears are cold and that I'm drinking a lot of cider. The countryside is quite white with hoar-frost but still has its charms. M. and Madame Anquetin are delightful as always. We're hunting crows with enthusiasm but no success. I hope you've sent my daub to the big newspaper. Apart from this, nothing new, except that I kiss you and beg you to do the same to this scrap of paper representing me.*

Your son,

Henri

Till tomorrow (Wednesday) evening,
Midnight.

My dear Mama,

I *I've come back from Normandy, where I've been hunting crows. A lovely day. I'm going to come back to Le Crotoy with Bourges to hunt seal. The country is terribly pretty and I can well understand that you are sorry to leave it. I'll tell you the details at Rivaude.*

Papa is in a very good mood because Princeteau is here. He has become hypochondriacal, but is very kind just the same. Try to get hold of Kiki if you can. Use all your diplomacy and think how nice it would be for me to have fresh air and work both together.

I kiss you.

Yours,

Harry

1. The parents of Louis Anquetin; they lived at Etrepagny in Normandy.
  Letter 77
1. A port in the Department of Somme, on the English Channel, where Lautrec, Bourges and their friends often went as late as 1900.

Château du Bosc [*December 1885*]

My dear Grandma,

I'm writing to you from Château Bosc, which at the moment is far from resembling the one where Sleeping Beauty lived, in view of all the young males frolicking up and down the long corridors. We are all sorry you aren't here to preside at this family reunion, the first I've been to for a long while. We are passing the time photographing the animals and

1 *people to the great delight of the cook, who seems to fancy himself a knockout, the way he poses in front of the lens.*

The weather (to imitate the eloquence of Monsieur Alary) is a little chilly but very clear. When we stick our noses outdoors they start to run right away, and it is the pipe, the horrible pipe, seducer that it is, that lures us round the hearth, where we smoke away all in a line, like

2 *so many Shoubersky portable stoves (only stove with castors found in the Place de l'Opéra for one hundred francs). Rereading my letter I see that I have forgotten the main thing I had in mind, that is, to send you, dear Grandma, my most sincere wishes for the New Year. I hope they will be as agreeable to you coming from my now bearded lips as they have always been heretofore. Please be so kind as to give my uncle and aunt, all snugged in their nest, my fondest regards, and thanks for all the good things you have showered on Mama on my account.*

With a hug,

your respectful grandson

Henri

1. See Ill. 8.
2. According to the Bottin, 'a portable stove invented by De Choubersky' was being sold at 6, place de l'Opéra.

My dear Mama,

My tonsillar troubles are ended, but my model is threatening to leave me. What a rotten business painting is. If she doesn't respond to my ultimatum the only thing I can do is bang out a few illustrations and join you in August. I shall go to Arcachon for a dip. Papa has given me some money, but I don't know whether I'm going to have enough to pay my rent and live on it, too. In which case you will help me, if it pleases Your Ladyship. Seeing we'll spend quite some time in the country, that will even things up. Perhaps I shall come to spend the month of September in Paris and return in October to see the grannies. Papa has spoken to me again about a studio quite near the Arc de Triomphe and I have explained to him clearly that that would never be anything but a salon. Perhaps he'll take it and leave me mine. There you are, a brand new combination, opening up the prospect of five o'clock teas. Think about all that, and about your boy, who slaves away as best he can and

1 *kisses you through his Auvergnat whiskers.*

Yours,

Henri

2 *Papa is going to shoot ducks at Rivaude.*
Uncle Charles and his wife are well.

---

1. Lautrec generally uses this term to describe something coarse, since the Auvergne was a somewhat primitive region. Cf. Letter 55.
2. The hunting estate of Amédée Tapié Céleyran, in the Department of the Loiret.

My dear Mama,

*I don't understand your postcard. I'd written to you two days before. The person I gave my letter to post must have forgotten! I've seen Papa, who claims to be broke and by the same token would have me the same. I tell you this frankly though I'm not hard up enough to call on you for help. We'll talk about all that again another*time, right now let it go. I've seen Uncle Odon and Aunt Odette who are bored and talking (don't spread it around) of going to Cannes.*

1   *I'm going to make some sketches for the* Courrier Français.—
Papa still has a quaint notion of going to the Arc de Triomphe
2 *section of town. We've even been to look at studios. Still no change.*
    They tell me you'll be coming with Uncle Amédée. Is that true? Nothing new apart from that. Cormon was satisfied with my work on Sunday. The competition will be judged on Wednesday. I kiss you hard.

Yours,

Henri

My dear Mama,

I've finally seen Louis, and he was very nice. I've seen Papa, who has a little white topcoat that's a knockout. Beyond this nothing to report. I've had dinner with Claudon's family, his mother and brother. They were

---

1. A newspaper founded in 1884 by Jules Roques. The first drawing by Lautrec to be published in it was *Gin-Cocktail*, which appeared in the issue of September 26, 1886. When Roques refused to pay Lautrec for his drawings, and moreover sold them at auction, Lautrec took legal action (cf. letter in collection of Madame Privat). Some of the unused drawings were published in 1888: cf. Letter 93, note 1.
2. A fashionable quarter near the Champs Elysées. Cf. Letter 79.

extremely pleasant. Everybody's looking forward to seeing you with a certain impatience and we shall be having some merry dinners together, I hope. Seems to me the heir-apparent is putting on airs and keeping people waiting on purpose. Anquetin is going to leave for the south, somewhere near Nice. Now, that really annoys me and if I felt strong enough I swear I'd follow him. It's dismal here.

Cormon is down in the dumps and doesn't have a penny.

1   *My publisher, M. Richard, is in all kinds of lawsuits. All to the good.*

2   *As for the Frayssinet affair, here's what it was: M. Gervex, having painted Mme de F.'s portrait, boasted, so some say, of having shared in the conjugal bliss of the handsome Jacques. Whereupon the latter is supposed to have given him a couple of slaps, which were answered by a sword-thrust. There are other versions, which I shall tell you about personally.*

There you have it, my chronicle.

A kiss for you and the Grandmas,

H.

82   TO HIS MOTHER   *[Paris, July 1886]*

My dear Mama,

I received your package in good shape. Unfortunately I wasn't able to come up with the 30 additional francs needed to pay the rent without completely emptying my purse. I'll pay up the first day I get my monthly

1. Probably Jules Richard (Maillot) (b. 1825), a journalist and writer. A 'M. Richard' is identified by Joyant (I. p, 261) among the spectators in Lautrec's painting, *Le Refrain de la Chaise Louis XIII au Cabaret d'Aristide Bruant*, 1886.
2. Henri Gervex (1852–1929), a successful artist at the time. He had painted a female nude, the face covered by a mask. In his 'Souvenirs' he affirmed that he had portrayed a professional model, but various rumours contradicted this explanation. The artist had to meet an irate husband in a duel, and later a lawsuit was brought against him.

allowance. Papa has been at Rivaude and then disappeared. I've been
having a very good time lately here at the Chat Noir. We organized
an orchestra and got the people dancing. It was great fun, only we didn't
get to bed until five in the morning, which made my work suffer a little
that morning. Right now I'm making a drawing at a sculptor's on the
Avenue de Villiers, who's a very handsome fellow and irreproachably
correct. It's very pleasant, but that won't prevent me from going to the
country to vegetate with no regrets and at Arcachon a good soaking is
very much indicated.

I'm a little knocked out because it's very hot and stormy as well (ah,
the clouds that pass by), I still haven't found the photograph which
Mgr. Guibert wants. I . . . but I feel I'm going to repeat what you
wrote in your last letter—which is useless. So, I kiss you warmly.

Yours,

Henry

83 TO HIS MOTHER   [*Paris, Autumn 1886*]

My dear Mama,

I just received your letter as I got back from Villiers, where I spent half
a day. Robby is a real jewel, he looks like a big rat and is beginning to
growl. Grenier will keep him all winter. I still haven't heard from
Papa, and seen hide nor hair of Bourges. I have an appointment with

1. The name of a 'cabaret artistique' founded in 1881 by Rodolphe Salis in his former
   studio at 84, boulevard Rochechouart in Montmartre. It was the first of its kind.
2. Probably Albert Carrier Belleuse (1824–1887), since Lautrec mentions in a letter
   written at the end of 1885 (Collection Madame Privat) that he is planning to do
   some work there.
3. Lautrec writes 'trempadou', which is apparently derived from the Provençal word
   'trempade', a wetting.
4. Monseigneur Joseph-Hippolyte Guibert (1802–1886), the Archbishop of Paris.

1, 2 *Roques and have nearly got an entrée to the Eden. Things are indeed picking up. Which makes me kiss you gaily, even though I have a cold which is stuffing up my nose. Kiss the grandmas.*

Yours,

Henri

84   TO HIS MOTHER   *[Albi] Monday [1886]*

My dear Mama,

I'm forwarding a bulletin from Albi which, as you can well imagine, has little in it. Your mother is sprightly and Grandmama Gabrielle is being very kind to me. Papa is hawking up phlegm and rubbing himself
1   *with oil of terebinth. We were invited today to Vigan, but he lost his nerve at the last moment and I am going alone with Grandma.*
   Yesterday, I attended all the archepiscopal and papal benedictions. It
2   *was very beautiful. Fat Raoul has arrived with his wife, whose girth is also growing, but for other reasons.*
   The sewing machine has done marvels. The only one missing on parade is Toto, his leave having been postponed till later. No *significant exchange yet between Papa and me.*
   I kiss you,

Your

HTL

3   La Vie Parisienne *came. Thanks.*

1. Cf. Letter 80, note 1.
2. A 'café-concert' on the boulevard de Sébastopol which catered to the 'family' trade. The purpose of Lautrec's entrée was probably to draw or paint there.
   Letter 84
1. A town in the Department of Gard, on the road from Albi to Nîmes.
2. Raoul Tapié de Céleyran, who had married Elizabeth de Lavalette. Their daughter Mary, later the Countess d'Attems, is the author of *Notre Oncle Lautrec* (cf. Bibliography).
3. A periodical of 'mœurs élégantes et choses du jour', founded in 1863.

My dear Mama,

Nothing of any importance to tell you. I often see Papa and Gabriel. I've begun to work again!!! However, it's very hard to keep oneself shut up indoors. It's beautifully sunny and despite a sharpness in the air I enjoy taking a walk in the morning. My friend Lesclide came close to going down on a trip from Le Havre to Cherbourg. The men were terrified and sick and he had to steer and manoeuvre alone in a frightful sea. It's a miracle he came out of it alive.

I've had lunch with Gaston Bonnefoy and his very pleasant wife. However, he's beginning to find that it's no sinecure. He gets up at 6 o'clock. Raoul off looking for discoveries, has two properties under consideration. Still under the seal of secrecy. I kiss you. And thank you for your grapes, which we enjoyed very much.

Yours,

H.

Duchess,

I want to remind you that tomorrow we are eating together. The waiters at the Ermitage told me that the other day you were there waiting for us, with an old man. Kindly forget him in some cupboard.
I kiss your little hands

HTLautrec.

1. Richard Lesclide (1825–1892), a writer and journalist. He was Victor Hugo's secretary in 1876–1881, and the director of *Le Petit Journal*. Lautrec had probably met him in working on the projected illustrated edition of Victor Hugo's works in 1884; cf. Letter 58, note 1. In 1875, Lesclide had published Mallarmé's translation of *The Raven*, with illustrations by Manet.
2. A doctor friend who was also known to Lautrec's family.

Letter 86
1. No café or restaurant with this name is listed in the Bottins or guide books of the period.

My dear Mama,

I'm glad to be able to tell you that Papa has been able to go hunting and kill pheasants and woodcocks. It's given him a lot of courage and he has
1 *come without complaint to resume the electric treatment that Bourges is having him take every day. He's having himself massaged by his coachman and is doing his arm rotation exercises several hours a day. These pursuits, if hardly very amusing, are keeping him busy and preventing him from dying of boredom.*

As for me, the lack of a model has me out of a job. I'm making up by eating a lot, my appetite not having run out yet. As for the apartment, we've been to look at it together but even he seems to feel that it has some
2 *shortcomings. So, everything's all right more or less, which is just what I wish for you, and kiss you.*

Yours,

Henri

My dear Mama,

This time it's you who let your inkwell run dry, in such a fashion that, Papa having gone away (for a day or two, I think, to Orléans), here I am, absolutely an orphan. I am working as much as I can outdoors. As for going to Grenier's, I think I might be off there in a week or two,

---

1. A treatment with brushes that was popular at the time. Cf. Letters 15 and 48.
2. Lautrec's father was still considering living with his son in Paris (cf. Letter 80). But in March 1887 Lautrec and Bourges took an apartment at 19, rue Fontaine, where they lived for almost four years. See Ill. 28, 34.

subject to leaving if I can't work. That is, if I don't decide to hire a
model with Claudon and go to Cernay. All very complicated. Claudon
himself is due back from the country, where he had started to work with
a model from Paris. They argued immediately.

A serious question. If Papa doesn't come across with my rent (which
it doesn't look like he will) I am counting on you. I'll telegraph you
'Send Money', but only in case of emergency, which will mean send the
necessary 335 francs, 33 centimes by telegraph (to 27 rue Caulaincourt).
My illustrations are yet to be finished, thanks to the stereotyper who
made them as black as my hat.

Everything is fine apart from that and I kiss you like the faithful old
campaigner that I am,

Henri

89 TO HIS MOTHER
[*Château du Bosc or Céleyran*] *January 1, [18]88*

My dear Mama,

New Year's is going off very well, everybody's just fine and congratulating
each other right and left. Really too bad that circumstance hastened your
departure, for you would have cut a fine figure at the family table, where
I am the oldest male. (The Abbé not being counted as such.) This dear has
invented a long evening prayer with a preamble he made up by himself
which gives Gabriel fits of uncontrollable laughter. Godmama sends you
all sorts of greetings. Grandma Gabrielle is looking absolutely tops. It

1. A small town in the Department of Seine-et-Oise, near Rambouillet.
2. One of the addresses of the large studio in Montmartre (the other address was 7, rue
   Tourlaque) that Lautrec used from 1887 to 1897. Cf. Arsène Alexandre's description of it, quoted in Mack, pp. 71–2. See Ill. 29.

appears that the move to Albi is going to take place, all the workmen
having left the apartment. My goddaughter is showering me with kind
1   *attentions!—Hosanna!!! Marie de Rivières is entering the Sacred Heart*
(not having found a husband). This is my own idea of it and I think it's
right. And that's it.

2   *We're going to climb Miramont this afternoon, and as I look out at it*
I kiss you. Nothing from Papa.

Yours,

Harry

90   TO HIS MOTHER   *[Paris, January 1888]*

My dear Mama,

For two days I've been in a ghastly mood and don't know what's going
to come of it. The sky is unsettled and is sprinkling us with an unconcern
that proves how little feeling the Eternal Father has with regard to
outdoor painters. Other than this, business is all right. I'm going to
1   *exhibit in Belgium in February and two avant-garde Belgian painters*
who came to see me were charming and lavish with, alas, unmerited
2   *praise. Besides, I have sales in prospect though don't count your chickens*
before they are hatched.
I am feeling wonderfully well. And give you a kiss
Gaudeamus.

Yours,

Harry.

1. A cousin of his.
2. Miramont, a hill in the Department of Lot-and-Garonne, west of Albi.
   Letter 90
1. I.e., Théo van Rysselberghe (1862–1926) and another member of the avant-garde group called 'Les Vingt', who were among the first to appreciate Lautrec's art. In 1888 he exhibited for the first time with them, sending five works.
2. Lautrec uses the Gascon expression, 'Canta abaud d'avé fa l'iovu'.

My dear Théo,

I'm writing to thank you for the invitation which obviously I owe more to your recommendation than to my personal merit. I've made some overtures
1 *to Forain, who will very probably send something. and I do hope he does, for his works are a real treat. Now, may I ask you a favour without*
2 *abusing your good nature? One of my good friends, Albert, who has shown with the Intransigeants this year in Paris, wants me to ask you to think of him if there are any more invitations to go out. He would be very happy to show his paintings with yours and ours. Forwarding this request I beg you to do for him what you have so kindly done for us. Thanking you in advance, believe me to be most cordially yours,*

H. de T. Lautrec

27 rue Caulaincourt

My dear Mama,

I've spent the day with Papa, who is very amiable, and to me appears little disposed to flee from the enchanting precincts of the Capital, though the weather is thundery-muggy, that is, somewhat enervating. My work is getting along pretty well and I'm busy enough to exhibit right and left, which is the only way to get your work seen. I'm going to take care of

1. Jean-Louis Forain (1852–1931), a painter, draughtsman, and printmaker, whom Lautrec admired.
2. Adolphe Albert, a fellow student at Cormon's studio, who later specialized in print making and became Secretary of the Société des Peintres-Graveurs Français. He remained a good friend of Lautrec's until the end.

1, 2   *sending you the portrait by Rachou. . . . As for Miss J. Matheson, the*
3   *best would be to go to Mlle A. Dubos, 56 rue du Rocher. I think*
       it's 10 francs a lesson, but that isn't bad. (Just between us, she's a
4   *friend of Juliette's.) Did I tell you I am going to have a showing in*
5   *Brussels in the month of February? Invited by the Vingtistes.—On*
       which note I kiss you and Grandma and Tata as well.

Yours,

Harry

93   TO HIS MOTHER   *[Paris, February–March 1888]*

My dear Mama,

My letter had to catch up with you, which explains your telegram. Since
my letter on Sunday, have nothing new to report. I am delivering some
1   *photos of my Mirliton panels to Roques. What will become of them*
     is hard to tell, my other drawing was declared bad after being reduced.
     A nuisance.
        I think I wrote to you what Papa told me and what I thought about
     it.—Miss Matheson hasn't written yet. It's not surprising that Grandma
     should have lots to do. But it's not so funny, her not sending you what I
     wrote, because you get into a tizzy so easily and full of protective worry

---

1. I.e., the portrait of Lautrec that Rachou painted in 1883. It is now in the Musée des Augustins in Toulouse. Cf. Letter 96. See Ill. 20.
2. Probably a relative of Willie Matheson: cf. Letter 14, note 5.
3. Angèle Dubos, an art teacher.
4. This is the first mention of Joseph Pascal's future wife. Cf. Letter 111, note 1.
5. Cf. Letter 90, note 1.

Letter 93
1. I.e., *Le Refrain de la Chaise Louis XIII au Cabaret d'Aristide Bruant* and *Le Quadrille de la Chaise Louis XIII, à l'Élysée-Montmartre*, both painted in 1886 to decorate Bruant's cabaret, 'Le Mirliton'. Neither was finally reproduced in *Le Courrier Français*.

*about what your duckling is up to. We had a snowy day and it melted
so fast I was dumbfounded. Besides this I've had an attack of indigestion
from eating some pâté, as did two of my fellow-students who were equally
sick. We assume that some sort of poison or other was the cause. Verdigris*

2   *or bad meat? That is the question. Well, it's over. Let's not talk about
it. I was running both ways copiously, with perfumes as varied as they
were delicate.*

    *I keep on with my regular routine and kiss you and the whole clan
of Albi to boot.*

               Yours,

               Henri

94   TO HIS MOTHER   *[Paris, Summer 1888]*

My dear Mama,

*I haven't any word about you from anywhere, though I've often seen my
uncle and aunt and Papa as well. Anything new? No doubt you have
more news than I, who am leading a dull life and if I didn't have the
showers to take and work to do I'd be bored to death. Bourges, who's not*

1   *feeling well, is probably going to go to Mont Dore? And I'll be alone
with my disgrace. That's cheerful. Too bad?*

    *If you were here we'd have the use of the carriage in the evenings on the
Champs Elysées. There's an idea to think over. You'd see more of me,
everybody having skipped off.*

               Your boy,

               Harry

2. Lautrec writes this allusion to Hamlet's famous soliloquy in English.

   Letter 94

1. A popular health resort in Auvergne, in the Department of Puy-de-Dôme.

My dear Mama,

*The rotten weather got me down to the point where I've come here to
Grenier's in the country to cheer myself up a bit. Aunt Emilie must have*
1   *told you my drawings have appeared. I'll send them to you on Monday.*
2   *We're still leaving on the 20th or 22nd. May the devil take St. Médard
and his watering can. As for me, I'm feeling better since I got away
from Paris and my models. For that matter it's raining just as much
in the country as in Paris, but I sleep and digest my food without any
trouble.*

Your boy,

Henri

Write to me in Paris, I'm going back there.

My dear Mama,

*It's frightful weather, which makes me groan all the more since I lost
two days going to see Grenier in the country. You really should send him
some wine. You should really keep your promise to this fellow. I hope
you will send him good quality, and to me a list so as to know how he can
go about getting hold of what he wants, and some samples if possible. I*

1. These are four of the drawings that Lautrec had made for Roques in 1886, now
used as illustrations of Émile Michelet's article, 'L'Été à Paris,' published in *Paris
Illustré*, No. 27, July 7, 1888. Cf. Joyant, I, p. 265; Adhémar, p. IX; and Letter 80,
note 1.
2. Cf. Letter 73, note 4.

1   *am having a packing case made for the portrait by Rachou. As for my plans, I have hardly any. Do what you like and I'll manage as best I can. I will send you Brédif's bill (a mystery), which comes to 114 francs, if you want to send me the money directly. Or send it to him.*

Bourges is at Mont Dore for his lungs. He's going to come back here. No doubt you heard about the death of his aunt, murdered in Bordeaux.

I kiss you, Tata and Grandma and you.

Yours,

Henri

97   TO HIS MOTHER   *[Paris], Saturday, [November 24, 1888]*

I'm writing to you on my 24th birthday, dear Mama, first of all thanking you for all your presents, which arrived safe and sound. Smallpox is the fly in the ointment and I'm wondering whether I should expose myself—not having seen Bourges for the last two times. He has settled in at the hospital.

Gabriel comes to see me often and seems to be interested in what he's doing. All to the good. Beside this, I'm in fine fettle, doing three studies at the same time, with a will. Besides the sky is bright, a rarity this time of year, and here it lets me give free rein to my fine plans.

I shall see Papa tomorrow, and haven't seen him at all for several days, leading the life of a recluse as I do, and in the evenings only going out just enough to get a little exercise. Not very exciting, but it is very satisfying. So, no news, unless it's my old age, which has just marked up another notch, which does not prevent me from giving you a big hug and kiss

Your son,

Harry

1. Cf. Letter 92, note 1.

My dear Mama,

I am afraid as I take pen in hand (to write you this little letter, as the
soldiers say) to make you feel the backlash of the evil humour I'm
1   *in, thanks to the torrents of rain that haven't let up for the past 3 days.*
Nothing to do but look out at the rain coming down. Saw the family
yesterday. Uncle Charles is buying daggers, windlass crossbows and other
assorted little toys to clutter up his hostel.

Your plans strike me as based on vague assumptions. You'll not be
2   *having to push on to Coursan if you think it's urgent until towards the*
end of September. I doubt very much that the tribe will still be there
3   *then, or at any rate still be in Palavas. I'd like to make some sort of*
Arcachon arrangement, but there are a lot of buts.
I end with a kiss soaked to the skin.

Your boy,

Henri

I'm rereading my letter, it's not too much out of sorts. So much the
better.

My dear Mama,

We have been all wrapped up in the great pleasure of exhibition opening
1   *day, which was quite gay despite the pouring rain. Uncle Odon and*

1. In another letter written in the summer of 1889 (Collection Madame Privat),
   Lautrec describes himself as 'dejected', because the rain prevents him from working.
2. A town in the Department of Aude, near Narbonne.
3. Palavas-les-Flots, a resort town on the Mediterranean, near Montpellier.
   Letter 99
1. The Salon des Indépéndants, where he exhibited three works in September.

Auntie were there and asked me when and how you were going to come.
I've also left word with Laura Pérey. Paul and Joseph have gone to
Panguiers and we are expecting them back tomorrow. I also have an
appointment with Charles du Passage to go and see some painting. Not a
sign of life from Princeteau. Bourges is being unfaithful to me. He has to
stay at the hospital, all the others being off in the country. Though for that
matter his hospital is quite cheerful, little gardens everywhere. Perhaps
I'll go there and do some studies of old women wearing white bonnets that
2 *make them look a little like milkmaids.*

 Hoping to see you soon, I kiss you.

    Yours,

    Harry

3 *and Tata, don't forget her.*

100 TO HIS MOTHER   *[Paris, September 1889]*

My dear Mama,

I was very much distressed to learn about the unhappy state of your
stomach, because I'm afraid the cold won't do it a bit of good and that
Paris and above all Rivaude will only mean more of the same only worse.
Luckily I am out of danger, as is Uncle Odon, who has left again for La
1 *Haichois cleansed from head to toe. I had lunch with Papa today. We*
went to call on du Passage, who dribbled his healing spittle on my young
brow. So, I'm saved, by the laying on of hands by that fat giant. I paid
my respects to his ailing wife. And that is all I have new to tell.

2. Nothing seems to have come of this project.
3. His Aunt Armandine.
 Letter 100
1. The family estate of Uncle Odon's wife, Emilie le Melorel de la Haichois.

*My work still isn't very brilliant, it's so hard to buckle down again.
Enough to take all the pleasure out of rest, the reaction afterwards being
truly painful. We've received the wine, for which many thanks. And
now, dear little Mama, pay heed to your old son, take good care of
yourself and above all do take it easy.*

Yours,

Harry.

101 TO MME R. C. DE TOULOUSE-LAUTREC   [*Paris, January 1890*]

My dear Grandma,

*No doubt you're up on all our small affairs through Papa, who must be
nearby keeping busy poking up the fire (if I'm not mistaken) and I am
writing simply to kiss you and to wish you a happy 1890. Doing this I
hope you won't catch my influenza, which I've had twice and which is
still hanging on. I can barely open my eyes and for four days I've hardly
worked at all, because when I get all set and look at my model I begin
to cry like a baby. Without good reason, though Mama didn't escape it,
either, but managed to throw it off quickly. We really are full of
lamentations, aren't we!*

    At the end of January I'm going to carry the good work, or rather the

1   *good paintings(?) to Belgium—poor Belgians!*

    *I'm devoting what is left of my paper to send you a kiss and to ask
you to remember me to everyone in your entourage who is the least bit
interested in the efforts of your respectful grandson,*

HT Lautrec

1. I.e., at the Seventh Exposition des Vingt, at which Lautrec exhibited five works.
He attended the opening at the Musée Moderne in Brussels, which he described
in a letter to his mother dated February 6, 1890 (published in Dortu, Grillaert and
Adhémar, pl. 12).

My dear Mama,

1   *I'm still reeling from the second exhibition opening. What a day!!
But what a success. The Salon got a slap in the face from which it will
recover perhaps, but which will give many people something to think
about.*

    *You must be completely Albigensified just now and in a pleasant
torpor induced by eating and boredom. I regret it's too early yet to go
down and brave the dangers of the bay of Arcachon. Here not much to
do—models are scarce and serious models very scarce. Nothing interesting
in all that.*

    *Yesterday I saw Doctor Bonnefoy, very much worn out by eight days
of Paris, who tells me he has a little mare to sell you. Louis appears to
be a little down on his luck. Papa and Princeteau, presided over by*

2 *Nabarroy-Bey, shed the lustre of their presence on Lucas. My servant
is decidedly odious, and, as for myself, I kiss you,*

Yours,

Henry

My dear Mama,

*Your unexpected change is a problem I shall not even try to understand.
Why this sudden detour to Rivaude? One wonders. I'm going to ask you
to do me a favour. Could you say for sure whether I will be able to work*

1. Of the sixth Salon des Indépéndants, where Lautrec showed two works. The first
opening would have been that of the seventh Exposition des Vingt; cf. Letter 101,
note 1.
2. Nabarroy-Bey was a friend of his father's.

1 *with Juliette unencumbered. And whether you think I might get on steadily with the work without interruption.*

To change the subject, where are Uncle Amédée's family going to spend their holiday? If need be, you could bring Kiki to Malromé for a while. I might be able to do something interesting of her. I'll need a reply about this right away because I'll decide on that basis whether to leave Paris at the beginning or end of July. Which will definitely get me back to Paris by the end of October. These are fine plans. What to tell about myself? Well I'm all alone, not a friend in sight except my neighbour

2 *Gauzi. Bourges is staying at the hospital. He intends to go to Scotland in the middle of August. Princeteau has made reservations at the Hôtel Pérey.*

Goodbye for now, dear Mama, and try to cut short your unexpected detour, the more quickly to be face to face with this horribly abject being, who is your despair and who signs himself

Yours,

Harry.

3 *Kiss Tata for me. She'll probably stay near her aunt. You are wrong to let her leave.*

1. Lautrec was planning to paint a portrait of Juliette, who evidently married Joseph Pascal later in the year (cf. Letter 111). Joyant (I, p. 262) dates this portrait 1887, but stylistically it appears to be later. See Ill. 40.
2. François Gauzi (1861–1933), a fellow student at Cormon's atelier, and a good friend of Lautrec's. He too had a studio on the Rue Tourlaque.
3. His Aunt Armandine.

104 TO AN ART DEALER

1   *[Paris, August 1890]*

My dear Sir,

The other day I forgot two pictures, one showing a 'seated woman in pink, full-face, leaning forward a little', the other 'a red-haired woman seated on the floor, seen from the back, nude'. These two pictures were shown
2   *this year in Brussels at the Vingtiste exhibit. Be so kind, I beg you, to confirm the fact that you have them. I am asking 300 francs for each.*

Cordially yours,

H. de Toulouse Lautrec

27 rue Caulaincourt

105 TO HIS MOTHER   *Taussat, Wednesday, September 3 [1890]*

My dear Mama,

I'm back in the fold after a very amusing but somewhat tiring excursion. On Saturday I left Taussat by train at 5 in the morning, arriving at
1   *Boucau, the station before Bayonne. At noon lunched with one of my*
2   *friends who's painting a picture of toreadors. Left for Biarritz to get tickets for the bullfight. Dinner and to bed after the Casino. Next*

---

1. The recipient noted on the letter that he answered it on August 24, 1890.
2. Two of the paintings shown there were entitled *La Liseuse* and *La Rousse*. The latter is probably the second work that Lautrec mentions. Cf. Dortu, Grillaert and Adhémar, p. 29.

Letter 105
1. Bayonne, a town in the Department of Basses-Pyrénées, on the Gulf of Gascony. Boucau, a town in the same region.
2. A town in the Department of Basses-Pyrénées, on the Gulf of Gascony, famous as a resort.

3 *morning I left for St. Sébastien with some very nice people who are*
natives of the place (thanks to Bordes' *being along everyone went out of*
his way to be nice to me). Spanish lunch and at 4 o'clock the bullfight
with six 5-year-old bulls. Roaring crowd, eviscerations, smells, nothing
was missing, and then back that evening by excursion train to Biarritz.
We waited at the railway station for two *hours jammed in a third-class*
4 *coach and what heat!!! Next morning I went to Fontarabie (having*
slept in Biarritz) with a Parisian journalist and returned the
following morning to Taussat. I saw your town from a distance, it's
perched up very high. I went bathing several times in the sea, with waves
that roll you around rather briskly, but agreeably. I shall doubtless go
back to Biarritz in a couple of weeks. We'll let you know. I kiss you
warmly, because here the sun is beating down hotly, too. Kiss my god-
mother for me.

Yours,

H.

106 TO HIS MOTHER *Taussat, Friday, 11th [September 1890]*

My dear Mama,

I received your letter from Biarritz just as I was beginning to worry
1 *about you. Didn't you get my letter in Lourdes describing the bullfight,*
and sent from Taussat where I am settled now, enjoying the last beautiful
days and the swimming. My plan would be to go to Biarritz two days
2 *before you leave and to visit the Boucau factories, then to go with you*
to Bosc *for a week. Think about it, and plan. I would then leave for*
Paris. If your plans work out, I think this will take place at the end of

3. I.e., San Sebastian, a port and seaside resort in Spain, on the Gulf of Gascony.
4. I.e., Fuenterrabia, a town on the Gulf of Gascony, near Biarritz, but in Spain.

Letter 106

1. A town in the Department of Hautes-Pyrénées, which became a pilgrimage centre.
2. There was an important metallurgical industry there.

the month. Otherwise I would go to Biarritz anyway and from there directly to Paris. I went fishing with my birds in the ponds where they were quite splendid. I close in kissing you and asking you for a detailed answer. Princeteau is coming to Arcachon on Sunday and I'll go to see him.

Kiss my godmother and tell her that I sympathize with her, knowing how unpleasant it is to be tied to one's bed without moving. Tell her also how much I wish for her recovery.

Your boy,

Henri

I have heard from no-one.

107 TO HIS MOTHER   [*Paris, December 1890*]

My dear Mama,

I was very glad to get your socks. I have enough for the time being. Now have 3 more pairs of them made, which you can bring along when you come back. I've passed on your news to Papa, who's having troubles with his tapestries being held as security by the landlords of Altamoura, from whom Papa had sublet the studio . . . There he is, delayed once again. I'm continuing to work despite the poor light. We had thick ice, and just when the skaters' festival opened a thaw set in. So much the better, but what a mess.

I wish you a merry Christmas, meanwhile looking forward to the New Year. Lots of kisses to all.

Your boy,

Henri

1. Probably the Altamura, peintre-artiste, who is listed in the Bottin as living at 13 rue Washington, i.e., near the Champs-Elysées.

[*Paris, December 1890*]

My dear Mama,

I have received your best wishes for a happy New Year and can only return them in kind. As for the mirror you offer me, first of all I thank you and then would like to ask you to please keep it under your wing for me until further orders.

I   *Both of us, Bourges and I, have been celebrating the wine sent by his brother from Bergerac. On the other hand the truffles didn't agree at all with me, and whether because of quality or quantity, I had to throw up what I owed to the turkey, without sufferings nor interruption of good spirits. You see how I'm upholding family tradition.*

I've had it out quite calmly with Papa about why I'm in no hurry to go see my uncle and he fully approved. The whole thing very diplomatically, moreover. There you have it, a point made—let it be known—

It remains cold here, so much so that Bourges goes skating every day with a great deal of enthusiasm. He's very anxious to have some of the goose-livers you spoil me with and is impatiently awaiting their arrival— will you remember?

At this point, I am going to work, and I still kiss you in 90, as I'll do in 91.

I am going to write to my grandmas. Please send me Aunt Armandine's address.

2   *Lots of little kisses, etc., etc.*

Happy New Year,

Yours,

Henri

1. A town in the Department of Dordogne, famous for its wine and truffles.
2. Cf. Letter 41, note 1.

28–32 In Paris, Lautrec occupied several apartments and studios, all in the same district around the Boulevard de Clichy at the foot of Montmartre. Top left, Rue Fontaine, where he lived with Dr. Bourges at Nos. 19 and 21 from 1884 to 1891. Calmèse, the evil genius of his last years, had a livery stable at No. 10. Top right, 21, Rue Caulincourt, at the corner of the Rue Tourlaque, where Lautrec lived in 1886. In 1897, he moved his studio to the Avenue Frochot (below right), near the Dihaus, friends of Degas and musicians to whom they introduced him in 1889. Lautrec painted Mlle Dihau at the piano in 1890 (below left). Centre right, Lautrec sleeping in his studio.

33, 34 Dr. Henri Bourges (left), whose portrait Lautrec painted in 1891, was a childhood friend. They shared apartments on the Rue Fontaine from 1887 until Bourges' marriage. It is worth noting that Lautrec did not always live and work at the same address though he twice moved to apartments in the same or neighbouring buildings as his studios. Below, a page from Bourges' and Lautrec's household account from January to May 1893. They kept separate accounts. Lautrec's expenses for January include the purchase of Kakémonos (Japanese hanging scrolls) for 37.50 francs.

35–37 Lautrec's interest in oriental, and particularly Japanese, art
started early. In 1882 (letter 39), he
mentions that the American painter
Harry Humphrey Moore, who lived
at the Hôtel Pérey and had be-
friended Lautrec, had shown him
some 'splendid Japanese bibelots'.
The statuette, top right, is from
Lautrec's collection and the photograph, right, of Mme Ymart-
Rachou, taken about 1890 at her
home Rue Ganneron where Lautrec
often came for meals, shows a screen
decorated with Japanese prints
bought by Lautrec and Rachou and
pasted up by them. The photograph
above shows Lautrec wearing
Japanese ceremonial costume.

38   Portrait of Paul Sescau,
1891. This portrait was sold to
Roger Marx, cf. letter 216, for
400 francs, Lautrec acting as an
intermediary for Sescau. Paul
Sescau, the photographer, was
one of the first to photograph
Lautrec's work and Lautrec in
return drew a poster for his
studio at 9, Place Pigalle.
Sescau himself appears in
several lithographs and drawings.

19 rue Fontaine [*Paris, January 1891*]

1   *Dear Sir,*

2   *My friend Desmet has assured me that by writing to you I can get an*
3   *invitation to the* bal des Incohérents.
         I thank you in advance, asking you to believe me most sincerely yours,

                              H. de Toulouse Lautrec

[*Paris, January 1891*]

     My dear Mama,

     Out of paper and I'm obliged to make do with the notebook kind. I've
     received Grandma Louise's presents and her pâté, which made for a
     pleasant quarter-hour. Tell her that for me, thanking her most kindly.
         We are having a cold spell, very dry, but which continues to skin our
     hides. Bourges is skating like fury and hopes it lasts forever. However,
     he just almost left for the Congo with two intrepid explorers for five
     months. The deal fell through and he's going to console himself by going
     to Beirut to make a report on the cholera. Every man to his poison!
     Papa is always saying he's going to go somewhere, sometimes to Albi,
     sometimes to establish himself in a studio in the Cité du Rétiro? I'm still

1. Jules Lévy (b. 1857), a popular playwright.
2. Probably Henri De Smeth (1865–1940), a Belgian painter and illustrator.
3. I.e., the revue *Vive la Liberté! Revue libre, rapide, incohérente et aristophanesque autant*
   que possible, by Lévy, the one production of which was at the Folies-Bergère during
   the night of January 17–18, 1891. Five thousand guests had been asked to bring
   their own tufts of grass for a rustic collation.

1 *thinking of going to Belgium and Holland in February as my exhibition*
2 *at Volney's opens on the 26th.*

*Give me an idea for a present for Kiki, who has asked me to get her a
mechanical ostrich which I haven't got the time to go looking for. I'll
send you whatever you think will be best and you can forward it to her or
deliver it to her mother.*

*I kiss you and ask you to do the same for me to all whom it may
concern.*

Yours,

Henri

*Gaston Bonnefoy, back from Saigon, has chalked up two new carriage
accidents with no one hurt. 1. The Vathoins and the Massapins,
overturned in the same break. 2. The Lanures' carriage with only the
coachman aboard.*

I think that your idea of a coachman is good.

III TO HIS MOTHER   *[Paris, January 1891]*

My dear Mama,

*I'm glad to see that food and wine are helping you to bear valiantly with
the bad weather and that far from being down in the dumps you're
bright, well and eating like a house on fire.*

*Last night I just missed being roasted, a beam under my bedroom having
caught fire. Fortunately the firemen put the fire out in a quarter of an
hour. Besides, the thing happened last night at 11 o'clock and when I came
home to go to bed all I found was a lot of smoke.*

1. There is no evidence that he did make such a trip in 1891.
2. In January–February 1891, Lautrec showed two works at the Cercle Volney: an
Etude de Jeune Fille and *Le Jovial Monsieur Dihau.*

122

Is it Joseph Pascal who's getting married? Bourges got a letter signed
1 *Joseph with no last name and the writing vaguely resembles his. I was*
amazed to learn I had forgotten the text of the card addressed to Papa.
2 *Excuse me. Please answer the question about Béatrix. Here everyone's*
freezing—no let-up in sight. Who knows when I'll be able to go to
Belgium! Lots of kisses for grandmas and uncles and aunts and nephews.
Best of everything to Papa. I kiss you.

Your son

Henri

Can you send us a good-looking Albi capon? I hope you can and am
counting on it, also on the goose-livers.

yours H

112 TO HIS MOTHER   *[Paris, January 1891]*

My dear Mama,

Looks to me as if the Albi carnival cannot have disturbed your family
effusions to any serious extent. Here little excitement except for a traffic
jam, such that I crossed the Boulevards with an officer of police pulling
my horse, or rather the horse of my carriage by the nose between the two
lines of policemen, holding back a roaring, red-faced crowd that
reminded me a little of a riot. Very amusing, too.
1   *I saw Gérard de Naurois, very lively, at the Moulin Rouge. We are*

---

1. He evidently married Juliette at this time.
2. I.e., concerning a Christmas present for her: cf. the preceding letter.

Letter 112
1. A popular dance hall at 90, boulevard de Clichy, in Montmartre, and Lautrec's favourite pleasure spot. Cf. Mack, Chap. XVI.

2   *definitely going to rent the apartment at 21 rue de Fontaine—it having*

3   *been judged ideal. Emile Pérey is not yet getting married, so there need be*
no concern about that. Louis hasn't said a thing about Respide, though he

4   *sees me all the time, since I'm doing his portrait. No other news, not*
even on the horizon. A kiss for you all, and for you more than anyone,

Your boy,

Henri

I'm sending you the flattering clipping I forgot the last time.

---

113 TO HIS MOTHER   *[Paris, February 1891]*

My dear Mama,

The whole family gathered here, and there you have it, the news of the day.
I'm very much afraid my esteemed personage will be missing at this little
party. We are enjoying splendid weather here. So good I had the buggy
hitched up and with Gaston we've been out to breathe in the Bois de
Boulogne air two or three times. I don't think Papa will have any
objection, quite the opposite, since horse and carriage have had an airing
—and me, too.

*   I'm busy with my exhibition, with 3 portraits in the works: Gaston,*

1   *Louis and Bourges. Louis has two sure positions lined up, thanks to*

2   *Mgr. Richard, either in insurance or with the Transatlantique. So much*

---

2. In 1891 he and Bourges moved to this address from the one they had had at 19, rue Fontaine.

3. Probably the son of Laura Pérey, on whom cf. Letter 9, note 2.

4. Joyant lists no such portrait painted earlier than 1893. But cf. Letter 113, note 1.

Letter 113

1. Lautrec evidently exhibited these, together with five other works, at the seventh Salon des Indépéndants in March 1891. They are not listed in the Salon catalogue, but Coquiot mentions them (1921 edition, p. 208). In a letter to his mother (published in Huisman and Dortu, p. 71) Lautrec states that he has 'just finished the portrait of Gaston Bonnefoy and started one of Louis'. Cf. also Letter 112.

2. François-Marie Benjamin Richard (1819–1908), Archbishop of Paris from 1886 on.

the better. Come back quickly because I'm going to be on my own, with
3   *Bourges going to Africa early in March, a month on horseback all the*
way south with a promise of gazelle-hunting. What a pity I can't go
with him. Perhaps Papa might be able to go. Bourges often speaks about
him and asks me to send him his best.

   Kisses to all and to you,

                              Your boy,

                              Henri

114 TO HIS MOTHER   [*Paris, Spring 1891*]

My dear Mama,

For once the newspapers have come close to telling the truth. The
exanthematous typhus we're having is a disease that only attacks badly
nourished people shut up in prisons or boarding schools. We luckier
ones are safe from this highly limited epidemic. I'm still in a lazy
mood and waiting for inspiration. Every day I go to the Bois and
absorb as much oxygen as possible. I almost took the train to go and
spend a week or so at Taussat, but I was afraid of not being able to
come back. I shall be delighted to see if I can think of something to
1   *decorate the Rochegude Museum and it would be comical to appear*
there as a painter where I used to go barelegged as an altar-boy.
2   *Calm yourself, then, fear nothing, and salaams to all around you.*

                         I kiss you.

                         Yours

                         Henri

3. Cf. Letter 110.
   Letter 114
1. The home of Henry Paschal de Rochegude (1741–1834) in Albi, and now the home
   of its municipal library. He had been a naval officer, writer, and political leader.
   Lautrec had presumably served mass there in a private chapel, before 1880.
2. An Arabic expression of politeness, meaning 'peace be with you'.

My dear Uncle,

1   *Everything steadily improving. Appetite has more than come back, it's ravenous. The doctor says not to get up yet to be on the very safe side. But probably he will allow it tomorrow. Mama is very cheerful and has a good time reading and talking. Fondest regards to all,*

Your nephew

Henri.

116 TO HIS MOTHER   *[Paris] Sunday [May 31, 1891]*

My dear Mama,

1   *I received your note—and have had lunch with Papa and Aunt de Gualy, very cordially, moreover, and with a good appetite whetted by the cold which has gripped Paris since yesterday. I was glad to put on my winter overcoat again and have relit my studio fire. What do you think of that?*

2   *Thursday, a brilliant opening with too many people but some painter friends. In all a good day. Except for this, nothing new. Our furnishing is coming along little by little and sometimes a very little. And I kiss you on your cheeks, stuffed with asparagus, at least as I suppose. You should send us a nice bunch.*

Yours,

Henri

1. His illness had probably been jaundice. Cf. Letter 117.
   Letter 116
1. I.e., the Baroness de Gualy de St. Rome. Cf. Letter 37, note 1.
2. At the Salon du Palais des Arts Libéraux, which opened on May 28th. Lautrec exhibited a portrait of Sescau and *Au Moulin de la Galette* there. See Ill. 38.

My dear Mama,

Your letter has made a most painful impression on all of us. But Bourges would like to have details as to the kind of paralysis, that is if it's localized about the mouth, the eye, or the face in general. This last
1   *case being much less dangerous. I've known several painters who suffered attacks of this kind and who are living with it. Besides, all those who work* outdoors *are doomed to it. Be getting as much myself no doubt in in the future.*

   Aunt Emilie, her husband and her brother have arrived, I haven't seen them at all yet. I've seen Gabriel again, who told me of having worked hard and having profited by his experience. His father is going to come. My jaundice is all over *and you will be able to count on seeing me by the end of July or the beginning of August. It would be very kind of you if you could see your way to send me, about July 14, that memorable*
2   *date, a few sesterces to distribute among various merchants. If you can, you will make me very happy, because M. Roques is keeping me waiting indefinitely for his payments and not having any contracts in writing I'm very much afraid I may be stuck. Trust in people's honesty!!!*

   I kiss your hands, so dear, and remember me to Louis and my aunt.

Yours,

Harry

1. Probably an attack suffered by his mother: cf. the following letter.
2. Literally, a kind of Roman coin. Here used simply to mean money.

[Paris] Monday [June 1891]

My dear Mama,

I'm happy to learn your improvement is becoming more marked and hope you'll carry out your plan to leave. What more can I say.
   I am impatiently waiting for you and kiss you.

Yours,

H

I've received the book by Jalby, so there's no need for you to bother about it.
1 *Is it true the Abbé is going to be a canon, or is it just a story?*

[Paris, early July 1891]

My dear Mama,

I thank you in advance for sending the 500 francs earmarked for the tradesmen. We are not neglecting you either, for tomorrow morning
1 *with Gaston Bonnefoy I'm going to take Musotte's 4 puppies to Maison*
2 *Alfort to have their ears cropped. She will be a regular little dog. Your future bow-wow is dappled, that is, iron grey with black spots. Madame Bonnefoy had invited us over to make us acquainted with this little family. Here we have a Nice-like sun and Bourges has bought a horse. Those are the only events that stand out. My maid is improving*

1. Abbé Peyre.
   Letter 119
1. I.e., the four puppies of his mother's dog.
2. A town outside Paris, which has a veterinary school.

a little. Perhaps she has got it into her head I was going to sack her.
Madame de Montecuculli strikes me as being a little in the clouds. I'm
writing to Papa in this vein.

I kiss you and would like you to send me some news about Emmanuel's
trial as soon as there is something new. Guibert feels he'll never
be able to get rid of his faithful (?) companion and laughs about it in a
forced sort of way. He shouldn't have got involved in the first place.

Yours,

H.

120 TO HIS MOTHER   *[Paris, early July 1891]*

My dear Mama,

Bourges, who left yesterday for Respide, will tell you I'm fit as a fiddle.
A couple of weeks from now, or sooner I'll be breathing the fresh air
of Malromé. I'm not counting on staying more than one month in all in the
country. We'll go to the Narbonne area, to Bosc, etc. . . . rapido,
presto, subito.
Try to coax Aunt Cécile to let us take Louis with us on this Cook's
tour. I kiss you.

Your Harry

3. Maurice Guibert (1856–1913), a salesman for a champagne company and a *bon vivant* who appears in several of Lautrec's paintings, including *A la Mie* of 1891. His mistress was Mariette Berthaud.

My dear Mama,

1 *You must have received your long-eared daughter. I had to pay the postage. That makes 34.50 francs, you owe me. She has a very gay and lively air. I hope she'll get along well with the other little dogs but at all events she's of a breed that knows how to take care of themselves. All of us are counting on going to Nîmes and I shall even bring my friend Guibert along, who will follow like the Doctor in* L'Histoire de M.
2 Cryptogame.

I'll take advantage of the occasion to see Marseilles and will go by way of Ricardelle. I hope very shortly to be announcing my arrival, for I'm thirsting for the salt water. On Sunday I went to see Grenier, who has broken his leg falling out of a carriage. He's getting on as well as possible and was very nice. Claudon is not so hot, crippled with rheumatism.

Send me word about the young lady and I kiss you,

Yours,

H.

P.S. I'll probably need to dip into the big sum to pay some bills. We'll talk about this again later.

1. Lautrec writes 'esperpil', which is a Gascon word for 'bright-eyed'.
2. A book by the Swiss author Rodolphe Töpffer (1799-1846) illustrated with humorous drawings; published in 1846.

My dear Mama,

*Everything's fine. I'm out boating all the time and have received a long
letter from Papa, who seems to want me to take charge of Ricardelle*
1 *directly, in case Jalabert should happen to die. It's a big subject and needs
to be discussed by us together. I'll have you look at the letter and we'll
see what's to be done. I'll come to Malromé on Tuesday or Wednesday.*
I kiss you.

Your

H.

My dear Mama,

*I think it's useless for me to go to Narbonne. Therefore, I'll wait for you
at Respide, or I'll come for you on* Monday *if you really think I ought.
Everything here's in a state of confusion. No doubt it's just the moment
Papa will pick to come, though I'm not really counting on it. So, I'll
be at Arcachon until Saturday.*
Write to me.

Your boy,

Henri.

1. Cf. Letter 44, note 2.

My dear Mama,

1   *I had a magnificent crossing, but when I arrived at Paris I found my*
maid in bed with a typhoid fever that will deprive me of her services, I'm
afraid, for nearly a month. I shall probably have her taken to the hospital,
to a room that will cost me pretty nearly 4 francs a day and she will
have everything there that she needs. It will also keep neighbours out of
my apartment—devoted, true enough—but whose presence I can nicely do
without.

    I wasn't expecting this piece of bad luck. The poor girl is a sad sight
to behold. Anyway, I'm going to try to manage the best I can. I hope my
next letter will be less fussy, in all events, I kiss you.

              Yours,

               H.

125 TO HIS MOTHER *[Paris, September 1891]*

1   *My dear Mama,*

    Your letter got here just as I was about to write to you. I've seen
Uncle A., Gabriel and Papa, who's in a charming mood. He has
opened his cash register without any trouble. As for my uncle and Gabriel,
they've gone back to Rivaude until the 5th, at which time the courses are
2   *to begin. Gabriel will live in a hotel, in the Latin Quarter. Which one*

1. In returning to Paris from the South, Lautrec usually went by boat from Bordeaux
to Le Havre and then proceeded to Paris.

   Letter 125

1. This letter is published in Huisman and Dortu, p. 88, but with important omissions.
2. Gabriel began to work under Dr. Péan at the Hôpital St. Louis in Paris in 1891.
He had been living in Paris at various times before this.

*hasn't yet been decided. He looks happy and as for Papa he's always
getting ready to go somewhere. Bourges has had the jaundice and is
horribly thin, practically unrecognizable.*

3   *I've seen my dealers. I am to get 200 francs for one study, which
means it was sold for 300 francs, a little boost in the scale. Outside of
this, business is slack. Grenier, who came back to Paris yesterday, is
more distraught than ever and Anquetin almost had another rheumatic
attack. My piles are better thanks to the* populeum *ointment. My
studio is being swept and cleaned, and I haven't really made up my mind*

4   *yet what I'm going to do. Degas has encouraged me by saying my work this
summer wasn't too bad. I'd like to believe it.*

       *I end with a kiss for Tata and you, and by asking to be remembered
to all at Respide, where I'd like you to tell Paul that I've been*

5   *introduced to M.* Jouard. *Kiss you.*

                              Yours,

                              Harry

126 TO HIS MOTHER   *[Paris, October 1891]*

       My dear Mama, ·

       I begin by reassuring you about Papa's condition, he has had a touch of

1   *influenza and treated it at the Turkish bath. The steam room suffocated
him and after a brief fainting spell he was quickly up on his feet thanks
to a few glasses of kümmel. He's still watching himself but looks well
enough.*

3. Probably the *Étude de Jeune Fille* mentioned in Letters 127 and 129.
4. Lautrec had been introduced to Edgar Degas (1834–1917), who was already recognized as a great artist, by their mutual friend Désiré Dihau in 1889. Lautrec
   admired the older artist immensely.
5. Probably the Jouard who is listed in the Bottin as an office manager of 'La Nationale'
   Insurance Company, since Louis Pascal had worked for such a company (cf.
   Letter 113).

Letter 126
1. This is the first indication of what will later become an epidemic of influenza. Cf.
   Letters 131, 132 and 133.

What you tell me concerning Louis doesn't surprise me at all. You know my views on that subject. For a long time I've felt there's nothing better you could do than help him. I thank you for the prospective truffles. If you send me a fowl stuffed with truffles, write on the address the weight: Fowl so much

                    Truffles so much

because the excise charges are exorbitant when this precaution isn't taken.

Another thing. Towards the end of next week and towards the end of the one after have a fowl—capon or chicken—sent to me. Bourges' brother, who usually supplies the poultry, is off on a two-week trip.

Has the goose-liver season started? If it has, remember to have a dozen tins sent to me. I am re-reading my letter and find it to have a

2 *gastronomic character. My poster is pasted today on the walls of Paris*

3 *and I'm going to do another one.*

Affectionate regards to everyone around you whom it may concern I kiss you,

                                  Yours,

                                  Henri

127 TO HIS MOTHER   *[Paris, October 1891]*

My dear Mama,

I'm again asking you for a little time to make up my mind. Because I've just had a very bad attack of dental neuralgia, which is obliging me

1 *to take a course of treatment at a famous dentist's, Cruet, a friend of Bourges'. (I'll have to touch you for some money to pay this man, who is charming, but expensive.) If all goes well, as I hope, I will come, if not*

2. I.e., *La Goulue au Moulin Rouge* (Delteil 339), Lautrec's first poster, and an immediate source of renown for him. In a slightly earlier letter to his mother (published in Huisman and Dortu, pp. 90–1), Lautrec states that this poster 'has been fun to do. I had a feeling of authority over the whole studio, a new feeling for me.'
3. Perhaps *Le Pendu* (Delteil 340), which was published in April 1892.

Letter 127

1. His practice was at 2 rue de la Paix. Lautrec continued to consult him as late as 1899.

I'll let you know by the 15th at the latest and you will take Louis.
Other side of the coin, I've sold the young girl which was on exhibition at
2 *the Volney.*

*I haven't seen Papa because I hardly ever go out on account of the
humidity. Goodbye and don't worry. All this is only a matter of patience.
My only mistake was not taking care of it sooner.*

Your boy

Henri

128 TO HIS MOTHER   [*Paris, October 1891*]

My dear Mama,

I had sent *you an acknowledgement of the receipt of the 150 francs. Did
my letter go astray perhaps? I'm very glad your life-saving operation was
carried out without a hitch and I hope you're not going to delay coming
here, leaving Tata in good company, to see your son for a little, whom you
leave in the lurch as casually as you please, thanks, it's true, to numerous
unexpected impediments; but it seems to me the hour for making
amends has come and I hope you're not going to wait for New Year's to
transport yourself here bag and baggage. Nothing new apart from that.
The weather is gloomy and everything's just carrying on along as usual.
Papa talks about going away, without conviction. The exhibitions are
getting under way.*

And I close with a kiss for you,

Yours,

H.

Come soon.

2. I.e., the *Étude de Jeune Fille* that Lautrec showed there in January–February 1891.
Cf. Letter 110, note 2; also Letters 125 and 129 on its sale.

My dear Mama,

I'm happy to report that my jaw repairs are going much better, although I still have quite a bit to be done. I will certainly *be able to come and pick you up and Papa has* almost *offered to do it, or at least to come along with me. What you tell me about Respide is more serious. It's useless to rehash this so painful subject. We've done it enough.*

   My treatment consists of pulling out doubtful ones and fixing up the ones that are fairly good. Thanks to injections of cocaine, *there's no pain at all. As for being confined to the house, luckily there's none of that.*

   Bourges is taking care of a little girl with the croup and has just successfully performed a tracheotomy *on her.*

   Papa is playing with the idea of spending some time at M. Pothain's. It's dark and rainy. I've sold my thing for 200 francs over and above the
1 *dealer's commission. . . . Which means I'm not losing on it, but I'm not gaining either.*

   I kiss you.

Yours,

Harry

My dear Mama,

I'm a little late but for an excuse I have my new models, who have been making me blow my top. This lot is decidedly a menace to the painter's peace of mind, who unfortunately can't get along without them. Papa looks

1. Cf. Letter 127, note 2.

as if he really *is of a mind to go and pick you up. He has ideas of going
hunting with M. Pothain. Will he succeed in making a move? In all
events he's in a good mood. My dentist continues to work on me very
expertly. Look out for the bill.*

1

*It's beginning to rain hard, which isn't exactly cheerful.
Nothing more to tell you, except that I kiss you.*

Your boy,

Henri

131 TO HIS MOTHER   *[Paris, December 1891]*

My dear Mama,

*Why don't you come here? There is influenza, but it is not dangerous
yet. So come as soon as possible, ready to go to Albi later.*

1

*I've seen Papa, who has been hunting!!! With the Prince de Bourbon.
Everything is fine here. Everyone's working, myself included. Thank
you for the jam. Arrived in good shape. Apart from that, nothing
new. I've just sent a horrible Infant Jesus in wax to Kiki, bought
according to her directions. I hope she'll be satisfied with it. I kiss you
and hope to see you put in an appearance one of these days.*

2

Yours,

Henri

1. In another letter of this period (published in Huisman and Dortu, p. 123), Lautrec mentions that 'Papa is going hunting with a Monsieur Potain, Pothain, or Pothin'.

Letter 131
1. An influenza epidemic began in Paris in early December 1891. There had been signs of it coming earlier: cf. Letter 126.
2. Louis Philippe Albert d'Orléans (1838–1894), the Comte de Paris, a member of the royal family.

My dear Mama,

I have had *the influenza. Thanks to my vigorous medication (Bourges had me running from both ends). I have my sight, appetite and good spirits back after being sick for only 24 hours. It didn't amount to much and by being a little careful I got out of it easy, whereas Gabriel has had it for quite a few days. Not serious, to be sure, but painful; we've just*
1   *opened a shop, a sort of permanent exhibit, in the rue Le Peletier. The newspapers have been very kind to your offspring. I'm sending you a*
2   *clipping written in honey ground in incense. My poster has been a success*
3   *on the walls despite some mistakes by the printer which spoiled my product a little.*

The sun is beautiful today. Bourges is skating like mad. Thanks for your capon which arrived safe and sound. I'm happy to be able to celebrate it with fitting respect. When do you think you'll come?! The sheltered life at Albi no doubt has its charms, but just see, it will soon be 3 months since we parted and I call for a little maternal sustenance.

I wish you a Merry Christmas and New Year. I promise I'll write to the grandmas tomorrow or later.

I kiss you.

Yours,

Henri

---

1. I.e., Le Barc de Bouteville's gallery, where many of the younger avant-garde artists exhibited as 'Les Peintres Impressionnistes et Symbolistes.' Cf. J. Darnelle's interviews with Lautrec and his colleagues in *L'Echo de Paris*, December 28, 1891, quoted in Rewald, pp. 497–8.
2. Cf. Letter 126, note 2.
3. 'Charles Lévy (Affiches Americaines) 10, rue Martel, Paris', is the printer's name that appears on the poster itself.

My dear Mama,

1   *I've just come back from the opening of the Cercle exposition, where my*
daubs, although hung about as badly a possible, have had favourable
mention in the press.

Besides this they're being very nice to me in the newspapers since my
2   *poster. The 'Paris', a very republican paper (don't breathe a word to the*
3   *family) has even seen fit to devote two columns to me, in which they tell all*
4   *about me down to the last detail. I am leaving for Brussels on February 3*
and will be back on the 7th or 8th at the latest. So, pack your trunks
accordingly. You'll still have time to get some digestive upsets. Papa is
5   *back from Chambord with a little recurrence of the influenza, and very*
much affected by the death of his friend.

Adieu, my dear Mama. I hope this letter will be, if not the last, the
next to last, and that it won't be long before we see each other in the
flesh.

Give my love to all whom it may concern.

Your son,

Henri

1. I.e., the Cercle Artistique et Littéraire, rue Volney, where Lautrec exhibited one
version of the painting *Celle qui se Peigne* and, apparently, other works. This was his
last participation in the exhibitions there. In January 1893 the jury rejected his
entries. An unpublished letter to Roger Marx, in Paris, contains his reaction, 'I did
not know that although I am paying for part of the rental, they had, or arrogated the
right to show the artists to the door'.
2. Cf. Letter 126, note 2.
3. Cf. Arsène Alexandre's article in *Le Paris*, January 8, 1892, the most perceptive
review this far devoted to Lautrec.
4. Cf. the letter Lautrec wrote to his mother from Brussels, some time between
February 3rd and 8th (published in Huisman and Dortu p. 160, but not dated
there).
5. Cf. Letter 126, note 1.

1   *Dear Maître,*

Can you send me the periodicals (Art Moderne) *and* (Mouvement
2   Littéraire) *where they refer to the Vingtistes? I would be very glad if*
3, 4 *you would and happy to see what Picard and Verhaeren say about us. I
hope this chore won't be too much of a bother.*
Thank you, and please remember me to Mme Van Rysselberghe.

Sincerely yours,

H. T. Lautrec

135 TO ROGER MARX   *[Paris, May 25, 1892]*

1   *Dear Sir,*

*The posters will only go up on the first, please let it be known and
bear it in mind in the notice you were kind enough to promise me.*

Yours,

HT Lautrec

1. Addressed to him at 422, avenue Louise, Brussels.
2. In January 1892 Lautrec exhibited with Les Vingt in Brussels eight works: the poster *La Goulue* and seven paintings.
3. Edmond Picard (1836–1924) a Belgian lawyer, art critic, poet, playwright and editor of the magazine *L'Art Moderne*. He had cordially received Lautrec during the latter's visit to Brussels in 1890.
4. Émile Verhaeren (1855–1916), a Belgian poet, dramatist, and critic. He had praised the works that Lautrec exhibited with 'Les Vingt' in 1891. One of the few books surviving from Lautrec's library is an inscribed copy of Verhaeren's *Poèmes*, 1894.

Letter 135
1. Roger Marx (1859–1913), a writer and art critic who helped to gain public acceptance for many painters. He was co-editor of *L'Image*, artistic editor of *Le Voltaire*, etc. His relations with Lautrec stretch from 1892 to 1899.

My dear Mama,

1   *Here I am, installed at Charing Cross after a perfect trip, the sea
like a lake and a sky like Nice. I'm already in the grip of the spell
arising from the London hustle and bustle. Everybody wrapped up in his
business and neither man nor beast letting out a useless cry or word. The
hansom cabs here have an air that would put plenty of private carriages*

2   *to shame. With me is my friend Ricci, who, moreover, is a perfectly
restful and goodhumoured travelling companion. Tell Papa that his
letter of recommendation probably won't be able to do me much good, the*

3   *Sackvilles being on the Continent and, above all, our stay being very
'limited'. We ought to be back in Paris on the 10th. Bourges had got
your letter before I left and must have replied to it. Goodbye, dear
Mama. I am going to play at 'breakfasting' and start my campaign with
the National Gallery. I'm not going to mention the names of the*

4   *paintings so as not to be like Adèle Bouscher.*
      I kiss you.

                        Yours,

                        Henri

1. Probably on May 23rd: cf. Pissarro's letter to Lucien, May 17, 1892, informing him
   that he might take the same train as Lautrec on that date: Pissarro, p. 286.
2. Guiseppe Ricci (1853–1901), an Italian painter who was a student of Bonnat and
   was influenced by Carrière and Besnard. In another unpublished letter to Roger
   Marx, Lautrec describes him as the artist of *La Mariée Piémontaise*.
3. A well-known English family, one of whose most prominent members was Sir
   Lionel Sackville (1827–1908), who for a time was ambassador to France.
4. Cf. Letter 16, note 1.

My dear Mama,

I've been so knocked out by the muggy weather since I got back from London that I've been sleeping day and night, which explains my silence. Woke up only yesterday and am making the most of it by writing you. In case it shouldn't last—I'm sending my portrait aboard the boat from Dover to Calais. Anyway it's a first instalment. I have no news from Respide except for the mediocre prices we'll have to accept in the end.
1 *Hardly 320,000 francs of which 280 are owed by my aunt. I don't*
2 *know what the story is with those ladies at St. Médard.*
   Let's talk about something else. Jalabert to me has the look of the
3 *heron with the gudgeon. I would like a frank reply so as to know what I'm going to have to settle for, being at the end of my money, and certainly having the right to know where I stand since I've lived two years on one. Tell me what you think of all this. It may prove necessary to sell at any price. I haven't made up my mind on this and don't know what to do about it. I'm counting on going to Taussat about July 14, unless my presence is needed here since I have a deal on the fire.*
   I kiss you.

                         Yours,

                         H.

My dear Mama,

I have indeed received your letter. My uneasiness came from the fact that I was broke and was impatiently awaiting your letter in order to tap

1. I.e., his aunt Cécile Pascal, who lost the family estate of Respide as a result of the financial disaster mentioned here and in many of the following letters.
2. St.-Médard-de-Guizières, a small town in the Gironde, close to Respide.
3. An allusion to La Fontaine's *Fables*, Book VII, No. 4. Jalabert seems to hold out for a better offer and, like the heron in the fable, might be forced to settle for less.

Jalabert and you showed hardly any sign of understanding my impatience.
Charity begins at home.

    *What you tell me about Respide was in the cards, but you know my
way of looking at that situation. There's nothing to be done about it.
Be guided by your own feelings and write to me. Unfortunately I'm too
sceptical to believe in gratitude, but it mustn't be forgotten that in
Respide we've found what we looked for in vain elsewhere, a home.*

    *I struggle against rain and models without bitterness, but also without
enthusiasm.*

    *We're going to move nearby, rue Mansart probably, into a larger
apartment. Bourges is opening a surgery in Paris. I'll have to pay a little
more rent, but nothing to speak of (200–300 francs), which will be more
than made up by the lack of the servants' pilfering that I would have
being alone. All this makes for grey hairs.*

    Goodbye, my dear Mama.

    Write to me with plenty of details.

Yours,

H.

139 TO HIS MOTHER   *[Paris, June 1892]*

My dear Mama,

*I didn't want to write you until after I'd seen Uncle Charles but he was
so tired out I was only able to say a quick good evening to him. I've seen
Louis, who showed me your letter. He has sunken into a state of
indifference, unfortunately justifiable. Short of acting like a tyrant, he
cannot do a thing. (At the risk of regretting it afterwards?). This
completely personal opinion is well grounded.*

    *Let's get back to our own affairs. Jalabert is keeping 11,000 francs
at my disposal, with a contingent additional sum which, with those*

---

1. This move was never made.

143

already advanced, gives me a share of 20,000 francs. Which will allow me to live a good part of next year. Your 25,000-franc share, therefore, is larger than mine. All this by way of the record. We shall always see eye to eye, I have no doubt of that. I have preferred to let the money stay in Jalabert's hands, first not wanting to look too greedy and in the second place wanting to have an understanding with you about investing it, or depositing it in a safe place. If you believe, however, I should convert it into cash (prudently perhaps), write to me specifying what I ought to do.

I kiss you affectionately.

Yours,

Harry.

140 TO HIS MOTHER   [*Paris, June 1892*]

My dear Mama,

What you say about Jalabert is definitely a nuisance, because I'm afraid he's a little fed up. This state of mind is especially terrible for the future, for if he's rebuked, he will send the whole business packing. Try to promote a cordial meeting between you and him and try to make him see things a little less pessimistically. As soon as you're at Malromé I think I'll make a quick run down there and back and we'll be able talk at greater length about it, although wait is what we have to do now. I am up to my neck in drawings and am fairly well satisfied. Juliette, as you must know, has given birth to a boy by the name of Marc. This mark of courtesy no doubt will cost the family several pounds sterling.

I kiss you.

Yours,

Henri

1. Marc Pascal, son of Joseph and Juliette, died in 1916 at Verdun.

39 Lautrec and a man—who has variously been identified as Tremolada or Zidler, the proprietors of the Moulin Rouge—standing in front of Chéret's poster. It has been suggested that Lautrec posed with his hat off in mock deference to the superior work of his competitor.

40–42   In 1887 Lautrec painted the portrait of Juliette Pascal, his cousin Louis' sister-in-law (above), and in a letter of 1890 he asks his mother (letter 103) whether he will be able to portray Juliette again. In the summer of 1892, Mme Cécile Pascal, Louis' mother, above right, lost the family estate at Respide as the result of a financial disaster (letter 131). Lautrec interceded with his mother for the Pascals who had been left penniless and continued to help his aunt and cousins in every way he could. They spent some time at Soulac at a hotel where Bourges reports that 'they will only leave if they are kicked out' (letter 151). Lautrec's letter of October 1892 (letter 152) below, shows how desperate the situation was.

My dear Mama,

I am in receipt of a joyful note from Jalabert. He says that Papa has replied satisfactorily, and the work has been resumed.
    Hosanna (*for the moment*)
    I kiss you.

Yours,

H.

My dear Mama,

I was counting, in fact, on indirect news, of which, moreover, there has been no dearth, and was expecting what happened more than you, who are directly concerned. Bourges has briefed me on everything. It is useless, isn't it, to rehash the sad event and feel blue about it. I'll only tell you that I've been completely out of joint the whole week, having lost the feeling of time and place a little. In what a state Joseph must be!
    Papa continues to talk about his fancied departure. Tell Louis I'll send him the document as soon as it is given to me. Probably tomorrow.
    Tell me when Paul and Jo are to come and whether they intend to avail themselves of our more Scottish than comfortable hospitality.
    And now tell everybody again what you must already have told them, and what, I hope, there was no need of spelling out, my great concern over everything that has happened . . . and will happen.

Your boy

Harry

P.S. Forgive me for bringing up a financial matter, but I would be grateful if you would send me 500 francs, if you can, repayable by me on the 1st of July.

H.

I'll explain why when you come and I hope this will be soon.

143 TO HIS MOTHER   [*Paris, June-July 1892*]

My dear Mama,

I am indeed a model of rudeness, not to have answered your letter. I was thinking, a little mistakenly, that Paul and Joseph, having written a lot to Respide, would have given you my news. They are here and exposed to all the lawyers' chicaneries. Papa had us for lunch on Sunday and for dinner on Monday. He was very nice. I've seen Uncle Odon, who had nothing of importance to tell me. As for the way Papa spoke to me about Bosc, it was in a rather waggish tone. I know that Aunt Armandine is at Malromé. Do you know that Papa has informed me Uncle Charles was

1 *decorated with the Order of Gregory the Great? And Albi is in a*
2 *tumult of joy. Mgr Fonteneau is a marvellously clever man. Aunt Alix has also written to Papa, probably to sweeten the bitter pill. What a lot of diplomacy!*

I'm looking forward impatiently to good weather. It's warm but stormy. Try to send us the sun as soon as possible and ask Tata to intercede with St. Michael, who, I believe, is very good to her.

3 *Kiss her for me, and to you my Auvergnat kisses.*

Yours,

Henri

1. A pontifical order created by Pope Gregory XVI in 1831.
2. Jean-Émile Fonteneau (1825–1899) had become Bishop of Albi in 1884.
3. Cf. Letter 79, note 1.

My dear Mama,

1   *Your not very cheerful letter reached me this morning. It highlights the fact that the imminent catastrophe is going to spoil our season (sad). I've seen Louis who doesn't seem to be too down in the dumps. For that matter Gaston must have given you the news. Papa is complaining, not knowing where to dispose of his assorted belongings.*

2   *As for my plans, they are absolutely vague, but all adding up to going, no matter where, to breathe sea air! As for my excursion in the Tarn, that's still pretty much set for about August 10. Couldn't you keep the new sheets and send me some of the old ones immediately. Thanks for the wine. I shall be looking for it.*

In sum, the result of these rains is a great fidgetiness, which I shall try to overcome as best I can, but it won't be easy.

I kiss you.

Yours,

Harry.

My dear Mama,

1   *According to latest reports, very vague ones, the Pascals are at Soulac at the seashore. In what circumstances? I'm totally in the dark about it. I'd like to leave myself but it's hardly possible for a couple of weeks.*

1. The loss of Respide. Cf. the preceding letters.
2. A department near Albi made from the old Languedoc and the southern part of the Massif Central.
   Letter 145
1. Soulac-sur-mer, a seaside resort in the Department of Gironde, near Royan.

My little efforts have turned out perfectly and I've caught onto some-

2 *thing which can lead me quite far—so I hope. I understand how, in spite of your pleasure at being at Bosc, you should want to go back to your nest. I want to go by Palavas to look at the deep-blue sea before going on to the Atlantic. But, who knows. I'll be very grateful if you send me the money you have at my disposal by return. Louis is very philosophical and no longer makes useless complaints. I'm going to have lunch with*

3 *Georges de Rivières and Suzanne Gonthier.*

I kiss you.

Yours,

Henri

4 *The photos will be sent to you.*

146 TO HIS MOTHER   *[Paris], July 26 [1892]*

My dear Mama,

I've received your package and thank you for it. Your letter, as far as it concerns my aunt, shows that the end is near and I'm very much afraid the

1 *medicine isn't doing any good at all. Only Louis, although not very cheerful is able to get something done. What good is it anyway talking about it, since even if you tried to help it would look as if you were interfering. I*

2 *saw George yesterday, sentencing my victims, who copped 15 days to a month in jail.*

There it is, all the news. I don't run into Papa very often, who in

2. I.e., his experiments in the colour lithography of posters, which had begun in 1891 and greatly absorbed him in 1892. Cf. Adhémar, pp. ix–xi.

3. Probably the Suzanne who is first mentioned in Letter 31.

4. Cf. Letter 185, note 3.

Letter 146

1. Cf. Letter 153, note 1.

2. Probably the forgers of Lautrec's works who were arrested, tried, and convicted after he discovered their activities. One of them was a notorious forger who ended his career in exile in New Caledonia. Cf. Mack, p. 351.

the summertime deserts Lucas for outdoor restaurants that don't
appeal to me.

I kiss you.

Yours,

Henri

147 TO HIS MOTHER   *[Paris], Saturday [July 31, 1892]*

My dear Mama,

I'm writing to you at the height of the excitement of leaving. The
Pascals have nothing *at all any more. Do therefore write and offer*
my Aunt temporary lodgings at Pérey's, whatever it costs you, as that is
what seems the most practical to me. The sons and daughter-in-law
1   *would stay at M. Niguet's. Joseph will arrange something with Bourges*
2   *as has been agreed. (Where will they find money for the trip?) I hope to*
give you some clarifications when I arrive in the Gironde towards the
middle of next week, but write to my Aunt on your own accord.

Because, unfortunately, the people we are talking to are now absolutely
down and out, *please don't forget it and put aside all susceptibilities,*
however justified they might be. Be charitable, absolutely.

I kiss you.

Yours,

Henri

3   *After Monday I'll be at Taussat near Audenge (Gironde), at*
M. Fabre's.

1. The father-in-law of Paul Pascal; he lived in Neuilly, a suburb of Paris.
2. Bourges arranged for him to stay at a hotel on the rue de Constantinople, corner of
   the rue de Naples, according to another letter from Lautrec to his mother, written
   in this month (collection Herman W. Liebert, New Haven).
3. Louis Fabre, a friend who owned the Villa Bagatelle in Taussat, where Lautrec
   liked to stay. An unpublished letter to him (Bibliothèque Nationale) is addressed
   to 63, rue Lepic, Paris.

My dear Mama,

Your letter had nothing to tell me. But I believe you are exaggerating in thinking you shouldn't come to the country. I *think you should come to Malromé, on the chance of getting together with Bourges, and see how we can* switch *my aunt's situation at the critical moment. Writing wouldn't do any good. Everything has been said and re-said over and over again. Try to break through and* come to the Gironde. *I'm taking advantage of the good weather to constantly soak in the bay. Other than this, nothing new.*

Yours,

Henri.

Jalabert has received a little money. He must have told you.

My dear Mama,

I've spent 4 days at Soulac with my cousins, who were charming, and my poor aunt, who is doing her best not to appear crushed. I've told her I would try to get you to come here, because the exchange of stern but fair letters has made her very sad. In case it wouldn't suit you to see Juliette, I think my aunt would come to see you, either at Malromé or wherever you like, where you could (I think) make her swallow the bitter pill of separation, an idea which so far hasn't entered her head. As for my lodging, your categorical reply gives me no room to insist. However, see what might be done—and send me a reply—or come to Malromé. We will talk. After all I'm there to back you up and I have had justice done to you. They recognize you are the only one who has shown any heart. As for the rest of the family, they're not Simon Pure. I left them in the presence of Suzanne Gonthier, who is giving the beach a lift with the éclat of her presence. They are, incidentally, settled at Soulac for a more than modest sum. 4 adults, a maid and 3 children for 35 francs a day. I don't think they could live more economically and the rumours of exaggerated luxury are false indeed. Bourges thinks that for the time being the best thing for them to do is to stay where they are and wait for the winter to look for work.

So, come to Malromé, that will be best.

Yours,

Henri

150 TO HIS MOTHER   *[Taussat] 20 [August, 1892]*

My dear Mama,

I've little news to tell you since yesterday and I'm writing simply to lend support to Bourges' letter, which brought you up to date on Louis' sad situation, with figures to back it up. We'll really have to give him a hand if you don't want him to be ruined for good and lose everything that has been done up to the present. He's doing the best he can to live on the little money he has, but for all practical purposes it's impossible for him to pay off his back debts if you and my uncle (to whom Gabriel is writing on his own) don't help him out. So, for your part, send 200 francs and we won't ask you for any more for him before the month of December. You will only have to concern yourself with my aunt when
1 *Mme Niguet will have gone, which will inevitably happen if the plan to*
2 *settle down in Neuilly is carried out.*

Yours,

Henri.

1. The mother-in-law of Paul Pascal.
2. Cf. Letter 147, note 1.

My dear Mama,

Your doubts about the future don't make too disastrous an impression on me considering the current miseries I see. The Pascals (this just between us) will only leave Soulac if they are kicked out. They owe their hotel and board. I have all this from Bourges, who has been to Soulac, which has let me off from going there again. I think in a case like this the family won't have the cynicism to let them be sued and sentenced and that they will spare my poor aunt the shame of the police court. There you have it, a frank impression. Admit that it would ill become us to complain. To crown it all, Louis has fallen sick with nervous cramps and after a

1   *month's rest at St. Gratien with good old Gaston the company will be obliged to buy him a typewriter. All this is no joke. Bourges has had a check made by experts and I'm very much afraid the poor chap may become completely impotent, making you a lady-companion. In short, it's better not to paint the future too black, when it's already black enough naturally without any additional colouring. I'll tell you all about it around the 27th. Kindly write to me and to Balade, because I intend to*

2   *go to Malromé for a day or two about the 25th with Viaud and Fabre, to have lodgings prepared for us. Tell me how to go about it, also about food and drink. Fabre would like to see the country and is a friend of the purchaser of Respide. I can't refuse him that, he's too nice. Adieu, my dear Mama, and see you soon.*

Yours,

H.

Regards to people who remember me.

---

1. A town in the Department of Seine-et-Oise, near Pontoise.
2. Paul Viaud, a native of Bordeaux, who was appointed by Lautrec's mother to be his constant companion and watchdog during the last two years of his life.

My dear Mama,

My aunt's balance must *be sent right away, directly to the hotel-keeper, with the request for a receipt specifying that it's my aunt's personal account you're paying.*

Paul and Juliette are in Paris. *And Joseph and my aunt are only waiting for the payment of the aforementioned bill and the money for my aunt's trip, 100 francs, a hundred francs that you'll send immediately with the address of whatever convent you like, into which she's ready to*
1 *move. I'll take her there myself. So, everything's going the way you want. Hurry up and get the matter straightened out and give me orders.*

Your son,

Henri

I have had a very good trip.

My dear Mama,

I understand your alarm and unfortunately there is little hope. If poor Tata pulls through this adventure, overworked as she is, she will indeed have St. Michael to thank. I suppose you haven't yet got my letter in which I gave an accounting of the expenditures to be made for Aunt Cécile whose situation fades into the background, given the regrettable
1 *precedence of Tata's illness.*

1. In another letter of this month (Collection Herman W. Liebert, New Haven), Lautrec announced placing his aunt in a convent with the help of Juliette and Joseph Pascal. See Ill. 42.

Letter 153
1. His aunt Armandine had been ill for some time, and in 1893 she died. Cf. Letter 146.

In case my letter should have gone astray. I am repeating my reckoning. Paid out by me, 70 francs, plus 100 francs I'll need to redeem the wreckage of Respide, my aunt's linen and winter clothing, which are being held at the station.

I regret insisting, but it's an emergency and we'll have to put up with it, unless she's to be fitted out anew.

I'm distressed that your arrival in Paris should be postponed until doomsday, and beg you to take care of yourself so you don't fall sick in your turn.

Kiss Tata for me, and a kiss for you.

Yours,

H.

Reply by return.

154 TO HIS MOTHER   [*Paris*] *October 19* [*1892*]

My dear Mama,

Your presence in Paris is urgently needed. Your intentions are good, but results are negative. My aunt is being refused hot water after 6 o'clock in the morning, firewood not being included in the board and payable separately. Moreover, the food isn't clean and the toilets are like those in a barracks. Either you didn't get across what you wanted to the management or there's a better way out and, in spite of the fact my aunt is willing, it's impossible to leave her in this home, which doesn't provide

1 *even elementary comforts, however it may look on the outside. You*

1. In a letter to the Mother Superior, written about October 23, 1892 (Collection Ferdinand de Goldschmidt-Rothschild, Basel), Lautrec asked for improvements in his aunt's room.

must *come yourself to take care of all this, something which I'm just not up to. There are a lot of things a character of my type just can't handle. Therefore, I'm counting on you for next week and kiss you.*

Yours,

H.

155 TO HIS MOTHER   [*Paris, October–November 1892*]

My dear Mama,

I have no choice but to bow to the motives keeping you at Bosc. But I beg you to re-read my letters and see if your presence in Paris wasn't clearly indicated, for you can't indefinitely remain a spectator of a truly
1 *grave situation when your presence here is urgently needed. I've had to advance my aunt 100 francs to pay for mending jobs that were absolutely necessary, in Bourges' and my opinion. Please reimburse me by return. Moreover, I've authorized my aunt and her son to find a convent or a family hotel in the 300-franc range, where the poor woman won't be tortured quite so much (they've even gone so far as to make her polish*
2 *her own shoes). And I think that I was not wrong to do this.*
  Please come and take care of all this business, because I've had enough *of it and can't keep on covering up for a line of conduct that I see as too rigid. The Convent is fine as long as one doesn't overdo it. Come and see for yourself.*
  I kiss you.

Yours,

Henri

If necessary I'll go and get you myself, if you don't come.

1. The grave situation is Aunt Armandine's illness.
2. Eventually, his mother invited his aunt Cécile to live with her. See Ill. 41.

My dear Mama,

I'm feeling well and have got back into circulation, but poor Aunt Pascal is in bed with an attack of asthma and can't sleep without morphine. My friend Fabre from Taussat, having come to Paris on a pleasure trip, is also confined in the Grand Hotel with an acute rheumatic attack. Bourges is doing what he can for him, but can't give him much relief. There's a fellow who has no luck at all.

Come, everyone's anxious to see you, and I kiss you.

Yours,

Henri

157 TO HIS MOTHER   *[Paris, December 1892]*

My dear Mama,

Guibert is forwarding you by freight a banana plant that was going to be thrown on to the rubbish pile. You will have to follow his instructions concerning this delicate tree. If it dies, well, too bad.

I'm working a little. Very hard to get going again. It's so nice doing nothing. I think that temporarily Bourges will keep the apartment where we are, while waiting for a position near or far from Paris. But in any case outside Paris. He hates terribly to leave me alone, but a change had to be expected, sooner or later. It was too good. I'm going to take a
1 *little apartment in the neighbourhood, and try not to be too bored. For*

1. In fact, however, Lautrec did not move until January 1894, after Bourges married.

the time being I'm keeping the maid, who's perfect. Mum's the word about the secret.

I kiss you.

Yours,

H.

Herewith a product of Guibert's

158 TO HIS MOTHER   [*Paris, December 1892*]

My dear Mama,

1 *Let us start with a merry (relatively) Christmas and happy New Year, in other words best wishes of the season. Gabriel must have given you the news about me, good news, moreover. It's too bad I can't go to Albi, because you will have to rush your Paris trip or not see me. Which would be unpleasant for you and especially for me, since other than Gabriel, I don't see many people except for those who don't matter.*

Now another theme—I've just made my year-end count, with the meagre Ricardelle harvest, I'll hardly make it till April and then only by keeping to the straight and narrow. So, you will have to put the famous reserve, already dented, at my disposal. Best thing will be to deposit it, at the Credit Lyonnais, for instance. Tell me what you think of all this and kiss the grandmas for me, to whom I'm going to write.

Your boy

Henri

159 TO HIS MOTHER   [*Paris*] *Tuesday, 20th* [*December 1892*]

My dear Mama,

I hope to see you on Friday. But (please forgive the financial side of this letter) Louis has a payment due on the 23, and I beg you, in case you

---

1. Lautrec writes these phrases in English.

would postpone your trip, to send me 200 francs *as soon as possible by registered post. We will consider this the last payment for this poor fellow who is really to be pitied, since he is still the only one to earn a fixed salary courageously. Paul is struggling with the newspaper directors with much energy, but without much result. I think you will not*

1 *find this settlement inconvenient; besides, I did mention it to you before.*

2 *My aunt is better and sleeps a little. I am cured now and am waiting for you. Meanwhile I kiss you.*

Yours

160 TO AN UNIDENTIFIED MAN   [*Paris, June 2, 1893*]

1 *Cher Maître,*

Here are some addresses of friends of Bourges and myself who would be
2 *glad to enhance with their presence the brilliance of your performance. I hope I will not arrive too late and beg you to receive, with my thanks, my most cordial handshake.*

H. de Toulouse Lautrec

1. Cf. Letter 150, where Lautrec also asked his mother (on the 20th of the month) to send 200 francs for Louis Pascal, promising not to ask again until December.
2. Cf. Letter 156, where Lautrec mentions his Aunt Pascal's attack of asthma.

Letter 160
1. The lack of letters written earlier in this year is partly compensated by several letters to René Wiener, now in the Musée Lorrain; cf. T. Charpentier, 'Quelques lettres et un dessin inédits de Toulouse-Lautrec conservés au Musée Lorrain', *Annales de l'Est*, 5ᵉ sér., XIII, 1962, pp. 215–16. In an unpublished letter to Marty written shortly before the opening of the Salon des Indépendants on 17 March, 1893 (private collection, France) he announces that the critics will be admitted on 16 March and asks Marty to give special mention to Mme Ymart and Gauzi. Victorine Henriette Imart Rachou (1864–1954), the wife of Henri Rachou, specialized in painting flower subjects. See Ill. 37. The same letter also praises Vallotton's painting *La Valse*.
2. Evidently an actor, perhaps André Antoine. Cf. Letter 234, note 2.

1   *Dear Sir,*

2   *I received a request from M. Roques, editor of the* Courrier Français,
     *asking me for permission to reproduce my Jane Avril poster. As you
     are the first one I authorized to make this reproduction, I have let him
     know he should come to an agreement with you to the end that your copies*
3   *will come out simultaneously so as not to make the thing stale.*
       This letter gives you full power so that if the Courrier *should pull a
     fast one on you, we would be able to give the editor a rap on the knuckles,*
4   *you, I and Kleinmann.*
       Please accept my sincerest regards,

                              H. T. Lautrec

        27 rue Caulaincourt

162 TO HIS MOTHER   *[Paris] Monday [July 17 or 24, 1893]*

     My dear Mama,

     *Long live Russia!! And curious thing, there's such a patriotic or inter-
     national fervour that this 8-day July 14 hasn't been tiring. Of course, I
     had to put up with being kept waiting here and there a half-hour at a*

1. Firmin Javal (b. 1842), a playwright and journalist, and the director of the magazine *L'Art Français*, which was published from 1887 to 1901.
2. *Jane Avril au Jardin de Paris* (Delteil 345). In a letter to his friend and publisher
   André Marty, dated June 2, 1893 (private collection, France), Lautrec states that his
   poster will appear the following day.
3. In fact, a reproduction of it appeared in *Le Courrier Français* on July 2, 1892, and
   in *L'Art Français* only on July 29.
4. Edouard Kleinmann, a print dealer and publisher whose shop was at 8, rue de la
   Victoire. Between about November 1893 and 1896, he served as publisher of, and
   repository for, Lautrec's prints, as is suggested by Letters 175 and 179.

1   *time, but it was a question of the European balance of power and I put
a good face on it. The policemen themselves tried to be decent and that's
not saying a little. Anyway, they're leaving tomorrow, probably tired out.
Now let us talk seriously. At a price of 800 francs I've rented the*

2   *ground-floor apartment in the house next to my studio, same owner. This
way I can look ahead, either to renting the ground-floor of my studio, to
move in completely , or finding another studio with an apartment. I
doubt I could get the same space for the same price. The advantage is that
I know the tenants, the concierge, the owner, etc. . . . For the time being*

3   *Bourges will occupy our present apartment with his wife, waiting for the
probable position at Suez (20,000 francs), which is not to be sneezed
at. He has plenty of pull and hopes to get it.*

    *If you could make me a present of 6 small-size tablecloths and some
table napkins you would oblige me very much, because I'm going to have
to stock up. I'm keeping my old maid and find that with an outlay of
40 francs a month I have all the advantage of having my clothes mended
and lunching at home. I'm counting on taking possession of my quarters at
the end of January, because they're going to renovate them under my
direction.*

    I am working as much as possible under these conditions and I have a

4   *poster to make for the newspaper* Le Matin*—I've glad that Mlle the
Cat is nice and amuses you a little.*

    I kiss you.

                   Your

                   H.

Mum's the word on the secret, of course.
    P.S. Some very ordinary table knives would also be a great help.
    *In sum, I'm getting married without a wife. The package has arrived
in good shape.*

1. In July 1893, two Russian grand-dukes visited Paris, and subsequently an alliance
between the two countries was formed. Cf. Lautrec's lithograph *Union Franco-Russe*
(Delteil 50) of this month.
2. Hence at 27 rue Caulaincourt, where Lautrec finally moved in January 1894.
3. Cf. Letter 157, note 1.
4. *Au Pied de l'Echafaud* (Delteil 347), made to advertise the serialization in *Le Matin*
in autumn 1893 of the Abbé Faure's book of that title.

43 Lautrec loved the sea, often travelled from Le Havre to Bordeaux by boat, sailed with deep sea fishermen (letter 204) and often went boating at Taussat and with Joyant. He is seen above with Viaud, a friend from Bordeaux, and Languerre, the sailor. The former poses with a gun. This pose may also be seen in the sketch of 1899, *Maurice Joyant à la chasse en baie de Somme*.

44, 45 *La Visite du Docteur*, 1893, is a caricature of Lautrec's cousin, Gabriel Tapié de Céleyran, but Lautrec was as ready to laugh at himself as at others, as the caricature below shows.

46–48 Lautrec frequented the fashionable cabarets and music-halls as well as the performers, a field which provided a background and the subjects for his paintings. Yvette Guilbert, a cabaret singer, figures largely in Lautrec's graphic works both in posters and in a collection of lithographs. A unique copy on Japan paper of the song *Dans la rue*, was jointly inscribed to Lautrec by Steinlen and Bruant, the former did the watercolour and Bruant wrote the poem. In 1897 (letter 211), Lautrec illustrated and drew the cover for Clemenceau's book about the Jews, *Au pied du Sinaï*.

My dear Mama,

1 *Here I am back in Taussat, having had a magnificent and lively trip.*
The last day was hard, the men had to steer the boat through regular
rapids over the rocks. We covered the whole distance from Cazaux to
2 *Mimizan on our own, camping out and preparing our own grub ourselves.*
The lazier ones slept at the hotel (?), but paid for their relative comfort
3 *with bedbugs and other nasty things. As for me, I divided my pleasures.*
Bourges was with us. It was intensely hot but with two or three baths a
day we were able to put up with it. I'm going to go back down there in a
4 *couple of weeks with some cormorants.*
  I'll come to Malromé on Tuesday or Wednesday, perhaps Thursday.
I kiss you.

Yours,

H.

The wine has arrived safely.

1. Together with Bourges, Fabre, Viaud, and Guibert, Lautrec travelled by train to
   Cazaux and thence by boat to Mimizan.
2. Towns in the Department of Landes, near the Atlantic coast of France.
3. Lautrec uses the word 'babaous', perhaps derived from 'babou' a child's expression
   for an ugly black insect. He often used the related words 'ouax rababaou', which
   he had invented: cf. Joyant, I, p. 212.
4. He went to Sainte Eulalie, in the same region: Cf. Letter 207.

1   *My dear Geffroy,*

Pardon my delay in replying, but I would like to talk with you tomorrow,
Tuesday, at 6 o'clock. I will come and look you up at the Justice
2   *offices. And I hope not to have lost anything by having waited.*

Yours,

H. T. Lautrec

My dear Geffroy,

I've just seen Joyant, who told me he would come with you and that he
was at our service. You'll only have to pick him up on the way. I will
be home tomorrow Wednesday, Thursday and Friday between 4 and
5 o'clock. I hope that you will be able to come because the case is pressing
1   *and Valadon would think me very much overdue.*

Cordially yours,

HT Lautrec

1. Gustave Geffroy (1855–1926), a noted art critic of the Naturalist school, who championed Impressionism. Other letters to him from Lautrec are in the Bibliothèque Nationale and in the collection of Lessing J. Rosenwald.
2. *La Justice*, a liberal newspaper directed by Georges Clemenceau (1841–1929), for which Geffroy wrote regularly. Lautrec's letter is addressed to him at the offices of *La Justice*, at 10, faubourg Montmartre.

Letter 165
1. Probably the Valadon who was the editor of *Le Figaro Illustré* and a partner in the firm of Boussod, Valadon et Cie., the art dealers and publishers, for whom Joyant served as gallery director. Lautrec had his first drawings published in *Le Figaro Illustré* in No. 40, July 1893; others were published in No. 47, February 1894, and in subsequent issues.

166 TO ROGER MARX   *[Paris] Thursday [October 19, 1893]*

1   *My dear Marx,*

2   *Maurin my accomplice and myself will have the honour of presenting
     tomorrow, Friday morning at 9 a.m., a brand new creation. Please
     give orders to let us in. The work is Maurin's and will interest you
     considerably.*

                         Sincerely yours,

                         HT Lautrec

167 TO GUSTAVE GEFFROY   *[Paris] Wednesday, November 29, 1893*

1   *My dear Geffroy,*

2   *My designs are too big to carry, but I'll be at my studio at 4 o'clock—
     today. Tomorrow, all afternoon. Come and see them, please.*

                         Cordially yours

                         H.T. Lautrec

     We must be ready on December 2

1. Addressed to him at 24, rue St. Lazare.
2. About Charles Maurin, cf. Letter 168, note 1.
   Letter 167
1. Addressed to his home at 133, rue de Belleville, Paris.
2. These are seven paintings made to be reproduced in colour to illustrate Geffroy's
   article, 'Le plaisir à Paris. Les restaurants et les cafés-concerts des Champs-Élysées',
   published in *Le Figaro Illustré*, No. 40, July 1893.

My dear Mama,

I'm very happy about your last letter, which shows we have done well not to show our hand. I'm very busy and printing with might and main.

1   *I have just invented a new process that can bring me quite a bit of money. Only I have to do it all myself. . . . My experiments are going*

2   *awfully well. We have just founded a periodical. In short, you can see all is well. There's only the bother of moving and getting settled in again, which is the cloud, not black but grey, on my horizon. Keep on not saying a word to anybody about all that business, and I kiss you*

Yours,

H.

My dear Mama,

I think I'll wait till the end of January to go to the lovely town of Albi. I have an enormous lot to do. Two posters to deliver before

1   *January 15 and which are still not started. I will also go to Brussels in*

2   *February about the 4th or 5th, almost upon returning from Albi—That will allow you to stay a little longer with the family. Louis is as well as*

1. Shooting paint from a pistol at a canvas or more often at a lithographic stone, thus producing a spatter effect (the so-called 'crachis'). Lautrec worked on it with the painter and etcher Charles Maurin (1856–1914), and Geffroy brought it to Edmond de Goncourt's attention: cf. the Goncourts' *Journal*, September 2, 1894.
2. The newspaper *L'Escarmouche*, founded with Lautrec's encouragement by Georges Darien (1862–1921), a journalist and writer, on November 12, 1893. Lautrec published 12 lithographs in it in 1893 and 1894 (Delteil 40–51).

Letter 169
1. Probably *Babylone d'Allemagne* (Delteil 351), which was issued in February 1894, and *L'Artisan moderne* (Delteil 350).
2. Lautrec was in Brussels from about February 12 to February 21, 1894: cf. Letters 171 and 174; also Dortu, Grillaert and Adhémar, pp. 15–16.

3 *can be expected. As for the rest of the family, I see only J. from time*
  to time. He is very much improved and is less of a Quixote.

  Gabriel is working steadily. We have dinner together once or twice a
4 *week. I'm doing his portrait on Sundays. We haven't had any snow yet*
  here. At the printer's, I am meeting Prouho, the widower, who has also
5 *turned to doing lithography and is a very nice fellow. M. de Mathan has*
6 *also paid me a call and introduced me to his son, a painter. Other than*
  that, I am doing nothing for him.

  I kiss you and would like you to tell me what Kiki needs—have it
  sent if you have an address. You can do that better than I.

Your

H

170 TO MME R. C. DE TOULOUSE-LAUTREC
  [Paris] Friday, December 29 [1893]

My dear Grandma,

I intended to go and spend New Year's with you, but it's impossible to
leave Paris before the 15th, at which time I'm counting on coming to my
home town to warm my feet by the fire for a little, a smile on my lips.
Which again leaves me obliged to wish you a happy New Year by letter.
You will be seeing, or have seen, the celebrated Doctor Gabriel, who will
have told you about our numerous labours, he bloodthirsty, I a printer.
He may have told you, perhaps, that because my friend Bourges is getting
married I'm forced to change my apartment, which is not very amusing.
But I have found very suitable quarters in the same house where my
1 *studio is. I shall have the ineffable pleasure of keeping my own household*

3. Presumably Joseph Pascal.
4. It shows him standing in a corridor of the Comédie Française, and was completed in 1894. It is now in the Albi Museum. See also Ill. 44.
5. Prouho was related to Louis Séré de Rivières, who was a relative of Lautrec's.
6. Raoul de Mathan, an artist born in Albi, who specialized in Provençal landscapes.

Letter 170
1. Cf. Letter 162, notes 2 and 3.

accounts and knowing the exact(?) price of butter. It's charming. Please remember me to all and I kiss you, and count on me to see you soon.
Happy New Year.

Your respectful grandson

H. de Toulouse Lautrec

21 rue Fontaine and, after January 15, 27 rue Caulaincourt

171 TO HIS MOTHER *[Paris] Friday [January 1894]*

My dear Mama,

We're having a bone-chilling cold. 12° below zero. So I stayed in bed this morning like a marmot, not having the spunk to go to work. I've had your news through Gabriel, but I'm afraid you'll be as weatherbound in Bosc as in the Land of Furs. I still don't know a thing as regards my trip. It would be the last of January or the first of February that
1   *I'd come to Albi, and take off from there to spend a week in Belgium. So, you can take it easy and not arrive in Paris until about the 15th of February. By merest chance I ran into the son of Mme Bourgaux, maiden-name Piedevache, who was so nice at Barèges of baneful memory. She can't have changed much. She's at Monte Carlo, to get over the death of her daughter. He paints.*
  I give you a chilly kiss and am going to have lunch.

Yours,

H.

Bourges ought to be back on the 15th.

1. Cf. Letter 169, note 2.

My dear Mama,

It's not your son but an icicle that's writing to you. It snows, snows, snows, and in spite of all modern conveniences the cold pierces just the same. I hope that as soon as the thaw comes you'll come too, but it would be really risky to budge in weather like this. The merry Fabre is here and battling the cold with not a few brandies. I keep working happily, stamping my feet, but getting up in the morning is hard. I have friends who come to pose, and so I wait like a coward for them to be here to get me up.

Nothing new apart from that. I hope your patient is on the mend and am counting a little on the famous 'no news is good news'.

1   *See you soon, I hope, and little kisses, as befits*

Your son

Henri

My dear Mama,

It's raining and too much. So, I'm going to Brussels to spend a day
1   *making inquiries about furniture. My setting up house is progressing slowly, and so I'll try to finish soon so as to come and give you a hug. I'll come, according to what time is available, by boat or train. Every-*
2   *thing's fine here. Papa looks to me like a Fabius Cunctator. I've seen*

1. Cf. Letter 41, note 1.

   Letter 173
1. In Brussels, Lautrec met Henry Van de Velde (1863–1957), an architect and a leading designer of furniture and decorative objects in the current Art Nouveau style, and returned with some carpets and pottery.
2. A Roman general who employed prudent tactics; a temporiser or procrastinator.

*Louis but not Juliette yet. They've sent for Rosalie to nurse the little one.
I'm rushing off for time is pressing and I kiss you.*

Yours,

Henri

174 TO HIS MOTHER   [*Paris*] *Sunday* [*January 28 or February 4, 1894*]

My dear Mama,

*I've nearly finished moving out, the question of moving in remains. I'm
going to buy pots and pans, etc., etc., and when we see each other again
you'll let me use some of the money you have for me for these extra
expenses. I hope to get out of it for 500–600 francs. Maid's furniture,
kitchen utensils, crockery, wardrobe, etc. . . . As for my new quarters,
they are spacious enough. I'm still hopeful about the little dream town
house, but the owner is reluctant about making repairs. Another
subject: Tell Balade to send me some wine addressed to 7 rue Tourlaque
so I can have it bottled about the end of the month. Let him fix it so
I'll get it between the 10th and the 15th.*

1   *I'm going to Brussels around the 12th and will be back the 15th–20th.
I don't think it would be at all convenient for me to go to Albi at
present and I'll wait for you. I'd prefer you to come before February 10th,
because I won't be away long and I'd very much like to talk with you a
little and to see you.*

  *Try to arrange that. I'll go to see the grandmas at Easter with
Gabriel.*

1. Cf. Letter 169, note 2. At the exhibition of La Libre Esthétique, which succeeded
Les Vingt, Lautrec showed posters, lithographs and the album, *Le Café Concert*.

My poor head is full of numbers, although I've made some progress in that direction.

I'm expecting Bourges at the end of February.

Yours,

H.

Reply quickly.

175 TO ÉDOUARD KLEINMANN   *[Paris, February 9, 1894]*

Dear Sir,

1 *Madame Jane Avril will be at your place today at 1 o'clock. Will you*
2 *please give her two of her posters.*

Sincerely yours,

H.T. Lautrec

176 TO HIS MOTHER   *Amsterdam, Thursday [February 15, 1894]*

My dear Mama,

For three days we've been in the midst of Dutchmen who hardly under-
1 *stand a word you say. Fortunately the little English I know and*
pantomime gets us along. We're in Amsterdam, which is an extra-
ordinary city, the Venice of the North, *because it's built on piles.*

1. Jane Avril (1868–1943), a popular dancer at the Moulin Rouge and other cabarets in the 1890's, whom Lautrec portrayed in many paintings, prints, and posters.
2. I.e., *Jane Avril au Jardin de Paris* (Delteil 345), which Kleinmann had printed on heavier paper in November 1893 and sold for 10 francs. Cf. Letter 161, note 2.
Letter 176
1. From February 12 to 20, Lautrec travelled in Holland with the painter Anquetin.

*We're travelling, Baedeker in hand, among the wonders of the Dutch
masters, which are a mere nothing compared with nature, which is
unbelievable. The amount of beer we're drinking is incalculable, and no
less incalculable the kindness of Anquetin, whom I cramp with my small,*

2   *slow person by keeping him from walking at his own pace, but who
makes believe it doesn't bother him.*

      And soon all the details. Saturday or Sunday.

Yours

Harry

177 TO HIS MOTHER   *[Paris] Wednesday [February 21, 1894]*

1   *My dear Mama,*

*I found your letters when I reached Paris last night and got the last one
this morning. No comment, except that you know I'm with you in spirit
if not in the flesh, and if I thought my presence would serve any purpose
I'd be with you. Moreover, I am at your service when you want me—my
disillusion in not finding you here was great, as you can very well imagine.*

    So, my admirable *trip has had a sad ending. It's useless to list for
you the beautiful things I've seen, with an experience of art acquired little
by little, which means that I have had a fine eight-day lesson with
professors Rembrandt, Hals, etc. The Belgians, as usual, were always
nice. Anyway, we'll talk about all this again, a little more cheerfully,
I hope. And I kiss you for everybody and for yourself.*

Yours,

H.

    7 rue Tourlaque

2. One of the few allusions to his deformed legs. See also Ill. 45.
    Letter 177
1. Two sentences from this letter, undated and described as referring to a 'journey to
the north of Belgium', are published in Huisman and Dortu, p. 162.

1   *My dear friend,*

I'm just back from Brussels and Holland for the opening of 'La Libre
2   *Esthétique,' which has replaced the Vingtists. Maus, more pompous than*
3   *ever, was in charge of the thing. Tell MacKnight to come and see me in*
4   *Paris and perhaps we can organize something for him. The Indépendants*
have no gallery and are having no luck trying to find some place to leave
their daubs. Personally it's all the same to me because I'm wrapped up in
5.   *lithography. The Peintres-Graveurs have also been kicked out of*
6   *Durand Ruel's and the official salons so far don't have much to offer. . . .*
In sum, we'll try to muddle through, but I haven't much confidence.
Goodbye, my friend, and see you soon, I hope. Make the most of the
sun, what there is of it; here it's as cold as Greenland.

Yours,

HTLautrec

27 rue Caulaincourt

1. The letter is addressed to him at Pollensa on the island of Mallorca.
2. Octave Maus (1856–1919), founder of the Libre Esthétique group and one of the
   founders of the magazine *L'Art Moderne* in 1881. Some 25 letters from Lautrec to
   Maus are preserved at the 'Archives de l'Art Belge' in Brussels.
3. W. Dodge MacKnight (1860–1950), an American painter, and, like Boch himself, a
   friend of Van Gogh, in whose correspondence he is mentioned several times.
4. The Société des Artistes Indépendants, founded in 1884, with whom Lautrec had
   exhibited annually from 1889 on.
5. The Société des Peintres-Graveurs Français, founded in 1891. In 1893 Lautrec had
   exhibited two posters with them.
6. The picture gallery founded by Paul Durand-Ruel, which had championed the
   Barbizon painters and then the Impressionists.

179 TO ÉDOUARD KLEINMANN [*Paris, 1894*]

1   *M. Kleinmann*

    is requested to give to the bearer copies of the two Théâtre Libre
2   *programmes, proofs before letters.*

                H.T. Lautrec

180 TO GUSTAVE GEFFROY [*Paris, June 21, 1894*]

1   *My dear Geffroy,*

2   *As soon as you have the proofs of Yvette, be so kind as to let me know.
I'd very much like us to finish all that together. Truly yours*

                H.T. Lautrec

1. Written on the back of the card of P. Clauzel, art supply store, 33, rue Fontaine.
2. I.e., for Luguet's *Le Missionnaire* (Delteil 16) and Björnson's *Une Faillite* (Delteil 14). The Théâtre Libre was an avant-garde company founded by André Antoine in 1887. Cf. Letter 234, note 2.

Letter 180
1. Addressed to him at 133, rue de Belleville, Paris.
2. A series of lithographs illustrating and forming the cover of Geffroy's *Yvette Guilbert* (Delteil 79–95), which was evidently published in early July 1894, by their mutual friend André Marty. Lautrec's correspondence with Marty (private collection, France) permits us to follow the development of the project. One of the letters, dated January 30, 1893, indicates that Lautrec was already in contact with Yvette Guilbert at this time, contrary to what most biographers state. On Yvette Guilbert (1868–1944), a popular singer in the 1890's, see Mack, Chap. XXI. See Ill. 46.

My dear Mama,

Paul was astonishing last night, which confirms what I told you about him. It's doing him a lot of good. Louis is back, and is very busy. He has started to work on posters and circulars with a great deal of energy.

 I won't come until Monday. Come to lunch and take me. *I read in* the Courrier de Narbonne: *Ricardelle, 10,000 hectares sold, price not disclosed. I'll keep this issue for you. And there you are. . . .*

1

Yours,

Harry

My dear Mama,

I haven't much of importance to tell you. It's hot, hot, hot. I haven't had word from the Bertrand couple and am not asking for it. My upholsterers are working slowly.

 Madame Bourges has lost her dog, which swelled up and died. Our
1 *trip was wonderful, on a sea smooth as a pond. Which didn't prevent Fabre, who went with us, from puking his guts out. There's imagination for you!! Nothing of interest in sight.*

 I kiss you.

Yours

H.

1. Lautrec's parents had acquired this estate around 1882: Cf. Letter 38, note 1
Letter 182
1. Probably between Le Havre and Arcachon, by boat.

Grand Hôtel de la Paix,
Puerta del Sol, 11 & 12
Madrid Wednesday

My dear Mama,

1

I received your letter upon arrival. After having seen a very fine bull-
fight on Sunday, we went to Burgos, where we inspected the marvels of the
Cathedral and two monasteries. We travelled all night in a sleeping car
and here we are, in Madrid. I have letters of introduction and they're
even going to sing my praises in the newspapers of the country, such
being fame and journalism. I think we'll pull out on Saturday night or
Sunday after having been to Toledo. Send me everything here. *News-*
papers, etc. Letters. I kiss you

Yours,

H.

184 TO HIS MOTHER [*Paris, October 1894*]

My dear Mama,

1

You probably know about the death of poor Nini, died on Saturday at
the Hospital of the Infant Jesus after suffering terribly. I was told too
late and wasn't able to go to the funeral. I went with Bourges yesterday
to see Juliette and my aunt. These poor women are dejected and not at all
theatrical. The comic note is supplied by Joseph who pictures himself as
having had to bear it all and isn't far from imagining that it's he who's
dead.

1. In a letter to André Marty, datable July-August 1894 (private collection, France),
he states that he is leaving for Burgos and Madrid. This first trip to Spain, before
the one of 1896, has been mentioned by several biographers, but never dated.
Letter 184
1. Evidently the nickname of a member of the Pascal family, otherwise unidentified.

Bourges' wife has been hit hard by a bad case of pneumonia. She has
lost a lot of weight but is in very good spirits. In a word, cured. As
for my maid, the sickness was simply a stubborn constipation, so I had
her thoroughly cleaned out, and she's beginning to get about. I have a very
handy helper, the maid of one of my friends who lives in the house, and so
I'm rid of that problem, too. I'm thinking of going to London for the
2   *opening of the poster exhibition—at the end of the month, but for only*
3   *2 days. Gabriel is here, happy and content, although Péan as usual is*
replacing his staff in February. However, he has some very interesting
work in view. It appears (just between us) that Odon's marriage is in the
4   *offing, with plenty of money at stake; so much the better. I kiss you.*

Yours,

H.

Be so kind as to send me a hamper of Chasselas and Malaga grapes.
5   *I'd like to give some to Robin, who has put me up all this while.*

185 TO HIS MOTHER   *[Paris, early November 1894]*

My dear Mama,

1   *I didn't want to write you before Gabriel got back bringing E. with him;*
I hope that thanks to a very possible set of circumstances everything is

2. It was held at the Royal Aquarium in November 1894, and was organized by J. and
E. Bella, an English paper manufacturing company. Cf. Jules Roques, 'Une
Exposition d'affiches artistiques à l'Aquarium, à Londres', *Le Courrier Français*,
No. 45, November 11, 1894.
3. Jules-Emile Péan (1830–1898), a famous surgeon and teacher, and the founder of
the Hôpital International in the rue de la Santé, Paris. Gabriel did indeed leave his
service in 1895, after four years with him.
4. Odon Tapié de Céleyran later married Marguerite de la Portalière.
5. See Letter 215, note 1.
Letter 185
1. Probably Emmanuel Tapié de Céleyran.

*going to take on its proper proportion and turn into an escapade,
whereby neither country nor family need be ruined. I am still at my daily
routine, broken by words with my maid, who's hard pressed to take care
of my studio and my apartment.*

*I spent All Saints Day with Bourges and his wife in Normandy at
M. Anquetin's—my friend Anquetin is doing the sculptures for his*
2 *village church, just like people of the Middle Ages.*
3   *Guibert is going to send you the splendid photographs of Malromé, big*
4 *enough so that Philemon and Baucis can be appreciated by your Mama.
Besides this, nothing new to report. Tell my uncle and aunt how much I've
thought about them in all that. And try to instil a little optimism in them.*
   I kiss you.

Your very own son,

H.T.L.

186 TO HIS MOTHER   *[Paris, late 1894]*

1   *My dear Mama,*

*I beg your pardon for having been such a poor scribbler, but I'm up to
my ears in work and a little fagged out meanwhile. Nothing but marches,
counter-marches, appointments, etc., etc. I have even made my debut in a
new line, that of stage-designer. I have to do the stage scenery for a play*
2   *translated from the Hindustani called* Le Chariot de Terre Cuite.

2. At Etrépagny in the Department of Eure. The church, which dated from the
fifteenth century, was largely destroyed by fire in 1929.
3. The photos of Lautrec and the others, taken by Guibert at Malromé over a period
of several years, are in the Cabinet des Estampes, Bibliothèque Nationale.
4. In Greek mythology, an old couple rewarded by the gods for their kindness and
hospitality; the story is told in Ovid's *Metamorphoses*.
   Letter 186
1. Published in Huisman and Dortu, p. 126.
2. Lautrec designed the set for the first act of *Le Chariot de Terre Cuite*, an adaptation
by Victor Barrucand of a classical Hindu play, which opened at the Théâtre de
l'Oeuvre on January 22, 1895. Lautrec also designed the programme. Cf. Delteil 77
and 78.

*It's very interesting, but not easy—besides, no use counting one's chickens
before they're hatched. I'll try to come to Albi to say hello after the
Odons have left. Would you be game to come back with us??? Gabriel
would be with us. A thin coating of frozen rain punished Paris yesterday.
All you see is horses strewing the plain.*

    I kiss you.

Yours

H.T.L.

187 TO HIS MOTHER   *[Paris, late December 1894]*

My dear Mama,

    *I'm very much pushed at the moment by my new calling of stage designer.
I have to run all over the place, collecting information. And it's quite
absorbing. I think Papa must be moaning, if not officially, at least*

1   *inwardly, there being a possibility of building in the Cité. I believe the
Prince of Monaco's business manager has written to him in this vein. If
he hasn't mentioned it to you, don't bring up the risky subject, which is*

2   *sure to make him fly off the handle. Grandmaison looks very perky now
he has his pockets lined. I don't know whether I'll be able to get away for*

3   *New Year's because the play opens sometime in the first days of January.*
    *I have had a new photo made of myself and will send it to you soon.
It looks very true to life—Gabriel has a touch of the flu, but not me yet.*
    I kiss you.

Yours,

H.

4   *I'm sending you Y. Guilbert in* Le Rire.

1. The Cité du Rétiro.
2. Possibly Léonce Lorzeau de Grandmaison (1868-1927), a theologian who also
   wrote literary criticism under the pseudonym of Louis des Brandes.
3. Cf. Letter 186, note 2.
4. I.e., a drawing by Lautrec, published in *Le Rire*, no. 7, December 24, 1894, which
   shows Yvette Guilbert singing 'Linger Longer Loo.'

1, 2 *I beg M. Bella to be so very kind as to introduce M. Hartrick to M.*
3   *Bing, and I thank him for his kindness, past, present and future.*

H. de T. Lautrec

189 TO ÉDOUARD DUJARDIN   *[Paris, June 6, 1895]*

1   *My dear Dujardin,*

2   *Alex Natanson apologizes for not being able to come tomorrow. I am*
3   *replacing him, agreeably, with J. P. Sescau. I hope there'll be some ladies.*

Yours

HTLautrec,

1. Edward Bella was a partner in an English paper manufacturing concern that was interested in modern posters. Cf. Letter 184, note 2.
2. A. S. Hartrick (1864–1950), an English artist who was familiar with avant-garde circles in France. He wrote the preface for the second exhibition of posters organized by J. and E. Bella in London in 1896.
3. Samuel Bing (1838–1905), an art dealer who opened a gallery in Paris in 1895, where he showed Japanese prints, Art Nouveau decorative and fine art, and the work of younger painters such as Signac and Lautrec. Cf. Pissarro's letter to Lucien Pissarro, May 26, 1895, p. 381.

Letter 189
1. Edouard Dujardin (1861–1949), one of the leading writers of the Symbolist movement and editor of the *Revue Wagnérienne*. He appears in many paintings and drawings by Lautrec. This letter is addressed to Dujardin at 21, avenue Carnot.
2. Alexandre Natanson (1867–1936), brother of Thadée Natanson (1868–1951), and co-director with him of the *Revue Blanche*, one of the leading Symbolist journals of art and literature.
3. Paul Sescau, a photographer, with shops at 53, rue Rodier and 9, place Pigalle. He appears in several drawings, paintings and lithographs by Lautrec, and was one of the first to photograph the latter's works. See Ill. 38.

Cher Maître,

1   *It's for Saturday. See Sescau so that we have dinner together, at my house if you wish. Have a white dinner jacket and tint your face—if possible.*

Yours,

HT Lautrec

7 rue Tourlaque
27 rue Caulaincourt

191 TO HIS MOTHER   *[Paris, July 1895]*

My dear Mama,

I'm writing to ask your forgiveness for my silence, but this silence was due to a state of irritation that happily is beginning to go away. I was right
1   *in the middle of moving. Everything is almost finished, but I don't know anything more horrible than these moves in the heat, the dust and other disagreeable things. Everything is ugly and uncomfortable, it's been said a hotel becomes an ideal at moments like these. Well, let's get back*

1. Cf. Letter 189, note 3.
   Letter 191
1. I.e., from his apartment in the rue Caulaincourt to one at 30, rue Fontaine, where he remained until 1897. Cf. Astre, p. 147. This is the only biography to mention this address.

to the subject. *Everything's about to be finished and on Tuesday I shall leave Le Havre with the faithful Guibert, which will put us at Malromé on Thursday or Friday. We'll stay two days and return by boat to Le Havre to get Bourges, who will make the journey with his wife. Which will make three trips by sea, one on top of the other. If I don't smell of codfish I'll be lucky. In any case, see you soon and I kiss you.*

Yours

H.

I'll keep in touch by wire.
My address is now 30 rue Fontaine.

192 TO LÉON DESCHAMPS   [*Paris, July 12, 1895*]

1   *Dear Sir,*

Write to me at 30 rue Fontaine, my new address.

Cordially yours,

H.T. Lautrec

1. Léon Deschamps (ca. 1863–1899), editor of *La Plume*, a literary and artistic periodical, in which an article on Lautrec by Maindron was published on November 15, 1895. In addition to the five letters to Deschamps published here, there are eight others: one in New York (Collection Anahid Iskian) and seven in Paris (Collection Pierre Berès). This letter is addressed to him at the office of *La Plume*, 31, rue Bonaparte.

1   *Taussat [September 8 1895]*

2   *My dear Alexandre,*

3   *Henri Albert, Paris editor of the magazine* Pan, *which is publishing*
4   *one of my prints, will come to ask you for some facts on my paltry self.*
     Since you were the first one to speak well of me, I'm anxious that you
     should be the one to trumpet my great deeds the other side of the Rhine.

                              Cordially yours,

                              H.T. Lautrec

     Taussat near Audenge
     Gironde

5   *P.S. When is Tristan Bernard's story appearing in* Le Rire *?*
     Would you be so kind as to have the last 4 issues of this rag sent to this
     address? My family has mine and fails to forward them.

1. In an unpublished letter to Henri Albert, postmarked with the same date (Bibliothèque Nationale), Lautrec states that he will remain at Taussat until the 20th and then visit Malromé.
2. Arsène Alexandre (b. 1859), the editor-in-chief of the newspaper *Le Rire*, and a devoted friend of Lautrec's. The letter is addressed to him at 29, rue Gérando.
3. An avant-garde German magazine of literature and art, edited by Julius Meier-Graefe.
4. The lithograph *Marcelle Lender en Buste* (Delteil 102). In an unpublished letter (Bibliothèque Nationale) Lautrec advises Albert to offer Alexandre a proof of this lithograph.
5. Tristan Bernard (1865–1948), a journalist, author and sportsman who was one of the founders of *La Revue Blanche*, and the director of the Vélodrome Buffalo and Vélodrome de la Seine, where the bicycle races, so popular at the time, were held.

194 TO LÉON DESCHAMPS *[Paris, October 1895]*

My dear Deschamps,

I'll come on Tuesday or Wednesday to La Plume. Make me an
appointment for between 4 and 5 o'clock in the afternoon. Or bring me
1   *the thing yourself at 11 a.m. to Ancourt's. Please send me a note, at*
30 rue Fontaine *and not 27 rue Caulaincourt.*

Cordially yours,

HT Lautrec

195 TO LÉON DESCHAMPS *[Paris] Friday, 11th [October 1895]*

Could you stop by tomorrow at 9.30 at Ancourt's. I'll be there.
Order a grained stone.

Yours,

Lautrec

reply 30 rue Fontaine

196 TO LÉON DESCHAMPS *Paris, November 14, 1895*

Received from 'La Plume' the sum of two hundred francs for
1   *reproduction rights to a poster in folio size,* The Chap-Book.

Henri de Toulouse Lautrec

1. Edward Ancourt, an expert printer whose shop was at 83, rue du Faubourg Saint-
Denis. Lautrec relied on his technical experience in printing many of his posters.
Letter 196
1. The actual title is *Irish and American Bar, Rue Royale* (Delteil 362). It was published
by the 'Affiches artistiques de la Plume' to advertise the American magazine *The
Chap-Book.* See Ill. 49.

Paris, 30 rue Fontaine, Thursday [November-December 1895]

My dear Mama,

After a superb trip in all respects we arrived in Paris this morning. All is in order and my maid, though not forewarned of my coming, hadn't done anything at all unusual. I have a male kitten, weaned, from my cat. If you want it, it could be sent to you. Bourges is here with his wife, barely over a fall from a bicycle but dying to ride again. Paris is dark and muddy, but I'm going to work hard. They're waiting for me in a number of places. Aunt Alix has asked me to urge you to go to Albi,

1   *where you could help her in moving. I've been to Creissels and Roquebelle, where everybody was most kind—and inquired after you.*

Another matter. Tell Balade to get another barrel ready to send so that we can bottle it. I have the space. According to my calculation, I drink a barrel and a half a year. I kiss you.

Yours,

H.

2   *Papa really has been on the Montagne Noire, from where he wrote. No other details.*

1. Villages in the Department of Aveyron in south-western France.
2. A mountain range on the southern edge of the Massif Central in the centre of France.

198 TO MAXIME DETHOMAS

[Paris] 30 rue Fontaine [Autumn-Winter 1895]

1   *My dear Dethomas,*

2   *Miss Belfort is asking around for a husband for her cat. Is your
Siamese ready for this business? Drop me a line, if you please, and name
a date. We'll be going to Sescau's at 2 o'clock, or elsewhere if you wish.*

Yours,

HT Lautrec

199 TO ÉDOUARD KLEINMANN   *[Paris, 1895]*

My dear Kleinmann,

1   *Please give M. Rousselot a copy of each of my posters which belong to
me, and let him have a list of all those I have done.*

Yours,

H.T. Lautrec

1. Maxime Dethomas (1868–1928), a painter, print-maker, and theatre designer, and
   one of Lautrec's closest friends. See Ill. 51.
2. May Belfort, an Irish singer who at this time performed at the Café-concert 'Les
   Décadents' with a black cat in her arms; it is represented in Lautrec's lithograph
   of her (Delteil 117). See Ill. 52.

Letter 198
1. Probably a journalist.

1   *My dear Kleinmann*

2, 3   *Please entrust 'Polaire' to the employee of M. Moline.*
        See the latter for conditions of sale.

Yours,

H.T. Lautrec

201 TO MME R. C. DE TOULOUSE-LAUTREC [*Paris, January 1896*]

My dear Grandma,

I thank you for the appetizing pâtés that Mama brought me on your
behalf. We're going to feast on them as heartily as we know how, while
drinking to your health.
    I'm hard at work all day long and am very happy to have a schedule to
keep. Foreigners are definitely most kind to painters. I have just sold
1   *two paintings to King Milan of Serbia. I'll be able to put Painter to the*
Court of Sofia on my cards, which would be all the more absurd since
Milan has fallen. He seems to be taking it very well and is no longer in
2   *fear of the yataghans of the anarchists, who did get Stambulov. What*

1. Written on a correspondence card of the Galerie Laffitte, 20, rue Laffitte.
2. I.e., the lithograph *Polaire* (Delteil 227), which dates from 1894, not 1898 as Delteil
   states. Lautrec depicted her again in a drawing that was reproduced in *Le Rire* on
   February 23, 1895.
3. The director of the Galerie Laffitte.

Letter 201
1. The King of Serbia, Milan IV, lived in exile in France under the name of the Count
   of Takovo after his abdication in 1888. One of the paintings he bought is *Au Moulin
   Rouge, la Clownesse Cha-U-Kao.*
2. Stephan Stamboulov (1854–1895), a leading figure in Bulgarian politics, who was
   murdered in Sofia in 1895. Lautrec seems to have confused Serbia and Bulgaria.

news to tell you except that my Pascal cousins have embarked on an affair that doesn't seem to make sense to me and from which, as I see it, they'll have a hard time getting out of with a whole skin. Perhaps they thought they were making a clever deal? . . .

Please kiss Papa for me and I kiss you.

Your respectful grandson,

Henri

202 TO LÉON DESCHAMPS   [*Paris, April 20, 1896*]

My dear Deschamps,

1   The letter of invitation to come to rue Forest was indeed for you. We are counting on seeing you there.

Cordially,

H.T. Lautrec

203 TO HIS MOTHER   [*Paris, May 1896*]

My dear Mama,

I've delayed writing to you, but I did come close to buying you a splendid horse. Unfortunately I spotted it too late and I'm afraid it would have cost more than you'd have been willing to pay. I've had dinner twice with Mme Bourgaux, who is delightful. She'll be staying at Pérey's and is going to paint(?).

1. The address of Joyant's gallery, where Lautrec held an exhibition of his lithographs. A similar invitation to Edmond de Goncourt, dated April 20, 1896, is in the Bibliothèque Nationale. However, an invitation to an exhibition of ten colour lithographs, evidently *Elles* (Delteil 179–89), held in the Salon of *La Plume* on April 22, is published in Joyant, II, p. 255.

1   *I can finally go out in the morning and I'm taking a fresh-air cure.*

2   *I have two or three big deals with bicycle companies, all right, all
      right.*

*Tell me again the amount I'm to be reimbursed for the chair. Your
rug doesn't arrive till tomorrow.*

3   *I've chartered the Dutch boat for June 20–July 5. I think, consequently,
      we'll be seeing each other again at Malromé on the 14th of July.*

*The horse question is still on the agenda. I'm working on it. Little
kisses for all.*

Your boy

H.

204 TO HIS MOTHER   *Paris, Friday [early June 1896]*

My dear Mama,

*I thought I'd told you I'd be back from London in two days. I stayed
there from Thursday to Monday. I was with a team of bicyclists who've*
1   *gone to defend the flag the other side of the Channel. I spent 3 days
      outdoors and have come back here to make a poster advertising 'Simpson's*
2   *Lever Chain', which may be destined to be a sensational success.*

1. The exact nature of neither the illness nor the cure is known, but several biographers
   speak of Lautrec's growing nervousness and instability, evidently due to his
   alcoholism.
2. Lautrec was preparing posters for *Cycles Mickael* and *La Chaine Simpson* (Delteil
   359 and 360). The latter was printed in June 1896.
3. Probably to visit Walcheren and Antwerp.

   Letter 204
1. At a meet organized by Louis Bouglé (alias 'Spoke'), sales manager of a company
   that manufactured the Simpson bicycle chain. Lautrec made sketches of the racers
   from the Vélodrome Buffalo, whom he accompanied to London with Bouglé.
2. Cf. Delteil 360, which can now be dated June 1896. Ill. 50.

*After two days of rain, Paris has again become something of an oven.
I'd very much like to go and get a breath of fresh air. Another thing:
Guibert and I have rented a chalet for the Arcachon season. If you can
send us a half-barrel of wine, it would have to be to the address of
Mr. Brannen, real estate agent at Arcachon, who would have it bottled.
I'm taking my maid. Guibert may have his valet along, but I don't
think so. If you send the wine let me know about it so I can plan
accordingly. Another thing, you remind me of the properties you have put
at my disposal—a bundle of cash. If you can send me 500 francs, it will
put me in a position to pay off some debts before I leave, and the sooner,
the better. Another thing, I don't know when I'll be able to move in, but*

3   *I think it will not be until October. Another thing. No need to say
anything about my trip to London because, as you can well imagine, I*

4   *had no time to spend with Raymond, or any intention of doing so.
    I kiss you warmly.*

Yours,

Henri

205 TO HIS MOTHER   *[Paris] Wednesday [Summer 1896]*

My dear Mama,

1   *I've just spent two days on board the Johnston steamer and I've been
deep-sea fishing. It's extraordinary and I won't launch into trivial
descriptions. But think of it, they throw back into the sea by the shovel-
ful 400 francs worth of unwanted fish a day. They keep only the best.*

3. This move apparently did not take place, since he did not move to the avenue
Frochot until the following year.
4. One of Lautrec's cousins.
   Letter 205
1. A commercial fishing boat owned by Johnston.

The sailors are very nice and had us eating formidable fish chowders. Don't say a word about all this to a living soul, because we've given our word, Guibert and I, not to talk about it even to Fabre and Viaud. M. Johnston is overwhelmed by requests and wouldn't know where to begin if he once half-opened the door. What you tell me about the harvest isn't very cheerful. We'll talk about it in person. I kiss you.

Yours,

H.

206 TO HIS MOTHER [*Arcachon, August 1896*]

My dear Mama,

I received your letter this morning. No news here. Sail, sleep, eat. Fishing unsuccessful despite our united efforts. We shall come on Monday or Tuesday in a week or so, but at our leisure, because Guibert and his brother are keeping the chalet, and are having their cook come down. I would think that pulling a fast one on the cousin is part of this arrangement. She's at her father's and will stay there for the month of September. I am sending Marie back to her beloved studies. Louis has thanked me for the remittance, arrived safely.

As for me, have 2,000 francs to draw on for the 10th of September. It's all that's needed at this time.

Yours,

Henri

My dear Mama,

I've come back here and am getting ready to visit you with Guibert toward the end of the week. From there I'll leave for Paris by way of Toulouse. I'll let you know by letter or wire when we are to arrive. Be so kind as to send me 500 francs in 100-franc notes immediately by registered letter to pay my bills.

1 *We had a splendid time at Ste. Eulalie. The birds were very active but didn't catch many fish, though they even went for the pike, which is very creditable.*

I kiss you.

Yours,

Henri

208 TO AN UNIDENTIFIED CORRESPONDENT [*Paris, 1896*]

1 *My dear Sir,*

2 *I beg leave to inform you that I have some Aube posters at your disposal, stamped impressions, at M. Ancourt's, at a price of 50 francs for 50. I would appreciate it if you would send me the impression of my little*

3 *American poster. We can make an exchange on this one.*

By the way, I'll be at Ancourt's tomorrow, Wednesday, at 11 o'clock.

Very sincerely yours,

H. de T. Lautrec

1. A forest in the Department of Les Landes, near the Atlantic coast of France. Cf. Letter 163, note 4.

Letter 208
1. Evidently a collector of, or dealer in, posters.
2. Issued in 1896 to advertise *L'Aube*, an illustrated magazine (Delteil 363).
3. I.e., *Au Concert* (Delteil 365), which was commissioned by the Ault & Wiborg Co., a Chicago ink manufacturer, and issued in 1896.

1   *My dear Sir,*

2   *Thanks for the paper. I haven't tried it yet. I have had a Lender proof
     sent to you. For you 30 francs, for the public 50 francs. This vulgar
     detail is simply to make sure you don't let it go for less.*
        *Would you be in favour of exhibiting some drawings that have
     appeared in* Le Rire? *Or would you advise me to send this lot to the*
3   Libre Esthétique? *Let me know, please.*

                                    Cordially yours,

                                    H. T. Lautrec

Address: 30 rue Fontaine

     My dear Mama,

1   *I've been fooled again by the concierge of the new place, but I have
     finally found, for 1,600 francs, don't tell a soul, an extraordinary
     apartment. I hope to end my days in peace there. There's a country-sized
     kitchen, trees and nine windows giving out on gardens. It's the whole top
2   floor of a little town house next to Mlle Dihau's; we will be able to*

1. A publisher in Brussels who had printed works by Mallarmé, Gustave Kahn,
   Verhaeren, and other Symbolist writers.
2. Cf. Letter 193, note 4.
3. An avant-garde society of artists and writers founded in Brussels by Octave Maus.
   Cf. Letter 178, note 2.

Letter 210
1. At 15, avenue Frochot, where Lautrec now planned to live and work. It was very
   close to his mother's apartment on the rue de Douai, where he took his meals. See
   Ill. 32.
2. The sister of Désiré and Henri Dihau, and like them a musician and a friend of
   Lautrec's; cf. Letter 75, note 2. In an unpublished letter (Bibliothèque Nationale)
   He asks her for an appointment to hear 'some passages from *Sigurd*'. See Ill. 31.

3   *have musical evenings. It was Mlle Suermond, unmarried, I saw.*
Perhaps that's happiness. Chi lo sa. *In any case she's still a good and*
open friend without the least pretension of being something special like
that poor Suzanne. Her husband is indeed to be pitied for having a
treasure like that!
   I kiss you.

Yours,

H.

You must have received my Figaro.

211 TO HIS MOTHER   [*Paris, Summer 1897*]

1   *My dear Mama,*

Terrible heat, which has hit us all of a sudden. I'm winding everything
up and am going to face the move, or rather the moves. I had dinner the
day before yesterday at Bonnefoy's with Louis and Joseph who were
rather distant with each other.
2   *My friend Joyant has definitely bought the Goupil gallery. I'm finishing*
3   *a book with Clemenceau on the Jews. My publisher owes me 1,200*

3. Mlle Suermond is mentioned in a Letter of 1880: cf. Letter 30, note 3.
   Letter 211
1. Partly published in Huisman and Dortu, p. 178.
2. Goupil and Company, an art gallery and publisher of reproductions, had been
   succeeded by Boussod and Valadon in 1890, with Joyant serving as manager. In
   1893 the firm became Boussod, Manzi and Joyant; and in 1897, Manzi-Joyant.
   Maurice Joyant (1864–1930) was Lautrec's classmate at the Lycée Fontanes and
   after 1888 his closest friend. After Lautrec's death, he was asked to classify his
   works, and in 1926–7 published his important monograph (cf. Bibliography).
3. *Au Pied du Sinaï* by Georges Clemenceau, published in 1897. Lautrec contributed a
   lithographed wrapper and illustrations. (Delteil 235–49, etc.) Of the letters ex-
   changed between Clemenceau and Lautrec only one survives, at the Musée
   Clemenceau in Paris. See Ill. 48.

francs. He'll give me 300 of it tomorrow. Let me know if you can advance me 500 francs on the 900 balance. Repayable in six months. If you can't, I'll make other arrangements. I hope to place my maid in a good house. I'm sweating like a bull and kiss you.

Your boy

Henri

Forgive all the figures, but business is business.
P.S. I'm thinking of painting a portrait of a friend of mine at Malromé.
4 *I've naturally invited the model himself, Mr. Paul Leclercq. A young man of the world and of the best. This way you'll have the pleasure of my company. I shall go first to Burgundy.*

Yours,

H.

212 TO HIS MOTHER   *[Summer 1897]*

My dear Mama,

We're cooked. It's impossible to stay out of doors. It's roasting even in the boat. Which didn't prevent me from going out at high noon to chase the mullet that come in to spread out along the shore. In two casts of the net we took 150 of them. Fabre is staying in the country at his brother's, near Paris, which means we are reduced to saying painful things to each other, which doesn't really happen. I've received the socks in good shape. Thanks.

Be so kind as to send me 200 francs directly. And 100 francs to Louis at 32 rue des Mathurins, which he must be waiting for. I'd rather send the thing to the upholsterer myself, because I have to specify

4. Paul Leclercq (1871–1957), a writer and one of the founders of *La Revue Blanche*. Lautrec did indeed paint his portrait, but in Paris, not Malromé. Cf. Leclerq, pp. 43–4, for an account of this portrait.

certain details. So, that will make 300 francs in all. If you can send us some Chasselas grapes it would help us put up with the temperature. Goodbye, dear Mama, and see you soon, I hope, I kiss you.

Yours,

H.

213 TO HIS MOTHER   *[Paris, end of 1897]*

My dear Mama,

I sympathize with you about your neuralgia. I've been a little knocked out myself, but by too good a dinner. So, I only got what I deserved.
1   *I haven't completely moved in yet and am still sleeping at rue Fontaine. The wine arrived safe and sound. I'm busy organizing an exhibit in*
2   *London for the spring. Don't say anything about it on account of my more or less epileptic cousins, whom I don't care to take out. Bourges must have written you about poor Joseph's old clothes. I long more and more to see you in Paris, because the evenings are empty indeed for us old bachelors. In a word, see you soon, I hope; as for going to Albi, I can't dream of it for the moment. I kiss you.*

Yours,

H.

214 TO HIS MOTHER   *[Paris, early 1898]*

My dear Mama,

I haven't written to you sooner because I'm in a rare state of lethargy. I'm relishing my avenue Frochot quiet so much that the least effort is

1. On Lautrec's move from rue Fontaine to avenue Frochot, cf. Letters 210 and 211.
2. It was held at the Goupil Gallery—now owned by Manzi, Joyant, and Co.—in London, in May 1898.

*impossible for me. My painting itself is suffering, in spite of the works
I must get done, and in a hurry. Also no ideas and therefore no letters.*

1   *What is there to say to you about the death of Aunt Isaure? She's better
off having finished with the vegetative existence she'd been dragging out for
so long. The fowl and Co. were appreciated and I thank you for them,
again. Pass along my thanks to all concerned. Gabriel has told me that
Aunt Alix was sending me a present intended to enhance the beauty of
my home. Thank her in advance. I'll do it myself directly as soon as I'm
a bit more awake. There you are, my dear Mama, a very quiet accounting.
Will I become a stay-at-home? Anything can happen and I have only*

2   *one trip to London in April to make me budge.
    On that I kiss you.*

Yours,

Henri

215   TO ROBIN LANGLOIS   *[Paris, early 1898]*

1   *My dear Friend,*

2   *On Wednesday I'm coming by to pick you up at 11 o'clock. Jourdain
and I have an understanding on the matter.*

Cordially yours,

H.T. Lautrec

15 avenue Frochot

1. The sister of Alexandre Léonce Tapié de Céleyran, maternal grandfather of Lautrec, and the widow of Charles Séré de Rivières.
2. For the opening of his exhibition at the Goupil Gallery. Cf. Letter 211, note 2.

Letter 215

1. An engineer who was a friend and neighbour of Lautrec's, to whom he dedicated his first dry-point, *Bonjour Monsieur Robin* (Delteil 1).
2. ·Francis Jourdain (1876–1958) an architect, decorator, and painter, who later wrote several books on modern artists, including three on Lautrec (1948, 1951, 1952).

My dear Marx,

1   *I will have the portrait of Sescau collected for you tomorrow morning,
    Sunday. Give the necessary orders.*

Sincerely yours,

HT Lautrec

217 TO FRANTZ JOURDAIN   *[Paris] Saturday, March 12 [1898]*

1   *Dear Sir,*

*I thank you for your kind invitation, but I have caught some kind of flu
which completely prevents me from going out in the evening.*
    *Believe my regrets and present, please, all my excuses to Mme
Jourdain.*
2   *My cordial greetings to you and your son.*

H. T. Lautrec

1. The portrait executed in 1891 is referred to in 1895 in another unpublished letter to
Roger Marx, in Paris. He says, 'Sescau, much to his regret, wishes to part with the
portrait I have made of him. I consider it one of my best.' Roger Marx bought it for
400 francs. See Ill. 38.
   Letter 217
1. Frantz Jourdain (1847–1935), an architect, writer, and art critic, who also played an
active role in the organization of several exhibitions.
2. Francis Jourdain.

218 TO EMILE STRAUS   *[Paris] Tuesday [November 8, 1898]*

1   *Dear Sir,*

*I shall not be able to be at home tomorrow at 4.00 o'clock to show you
the Forains. I shall be there at 4.00 o'clock the day after tomorrow,
Thursday, and I hope to see you there, at 15 Avenue Frochot.*

2   *My respectful greetings to Mme Straus and to you.*

H. de T. Lautrec

219 TO GUSTAVE PELLET   *[Paris] November 15, 1898*

1   *Dear Sir,*

2   *On the 30th of this month my printer, Stern, will come to your place
and please have prepared for delivery to him all the unsold copies on
deposit with you. Also, please be good enough to pay him for those that
have been sold. He will give you a regular receipt signed by me.*

Believe me, sir, very sincerely yours,

H. de Toulouse Lautrec

15 avenue Frochot

1. Emile Straus, a lawyer. Addressed to him at 104, rue de Miromesnil.
2. Geneviève Straus, formerly married to Georges Bizet, and daughter of Fromental
   Halévy, had a salon frequented by leading figures in arts, literature, politics,
   finance. Cf. Degas, *Letters*, p. 147, note 1.

Letter 219
1. Gustave Pellet (1859–1919), a publisher and print-dealer whose shop was at 9,
   quai Voltaire. In 1896 he published Lautrec's series of lithographs entitled *Elles*
   (Delteil 179–89).
2. A printer of lithographs. At a time when he was becoming suspicious of everyone,
   Lautrec continued to admire Stern, to whom he dedicated many proofs of his
   lithographs.

[Paris, November 28, 1898]

1   *My dear friend,*

2   *Could you send me the name of the charming keeper of the Musée
Guimet who received us most kindly. I completely forgot to read it
when I had your introduction sent in to him, for which I thank you
again.*

Yours,

H de T-Lautrec

15 avenue Frochot

221 TO GUSTAVE PELLET *[Paris] November 30, 1898*

Dear Sir,

1
On July 8, 1897, you took 25 impressions in black (Intérieur de
Brasserie) *at a net price of 10 francs and 12 impressions of* Femmes
2
dans la Loge *at 20 francs net. You have sold 2 imp. of* Brasserie,
making 20 francs, and one impression of La Loge *at 20 francs. Making
a total of 40 francs.*
   *You advanced me 200 francs on the lot, 160 now outstanding.
Therefore I am leaving you 8 impressions of* La Loge *on deposit and
taking back the rest.*

Very truly yours,

H. de Toulouse Lautrec

---

1. Addressed to his home, 105, rue de la Pompe.
2. The Musée Guimet, 6, place d'Iéna, is the Asiatic art department of the Louvre.
   Letter 221
1. Probably the lithograph *A la Souris, Madame Palmyre* (Delteil 210), published in
   June 1897.
2. The lithograph *La Grande Loge* (Delteil 204), published in January 1897.

222 TO ROGER MARX

1   *Pavillon d'Armenonville [Paris] December 5, 1898*

My dear Marx,

2   *Could you receive Albert, my friend Bouglé and myself on Thursday
morning at 10. We will come to see your knick-knacks and to thank
you for your introductions. Albert intends to bring you some prints of
his own vintage to thank you for your kindness. My regards to
Madame Marx*

                 and to yourself,

                   HT Lautrec

A note 15 av. Frochot please.

223 TO ROBIN LANGLOIS   *[Paris, January 1899]*

My dear Robin,

1   *Come and see me at rue de Douai as soon as you can. I'll be waiting for
you there.*

                 Yours sincerely,

                   HTL

1. On stationery of a restaurant in the Bois de Boulogne.
2. Lautrec twice painted Bouglé in 1898. Cf. Letter 204, Note 1.
   Letter 223
1. The apartment of Lautrec's mother at 9, rue de Douai, which she had begun renting
   around 1893.

My dear Mama,

I have wired you to send me 100 francs so I won't be obliged to beg from the concierge, who is a rude man—by telegraph if possible. Everything is pretty much all right except for the weather. It's raining.

Kiss you,

Yours

Henri

225 TO EDMOND CALMÈSE   *9 rue de Douai* [*Paris, February 10, 1899*]

Monsieur de Toulouse Lautrec requests the pleasure of the company of
1, 2 *M. Calmèse and his mother at dinner tonight, Friday, February 10. Respects and kind regards.*

H. de Toulouse Lautrec

1. The proprietor of a livery stable in the rue Fontaine, who was one of Lautrec's constant drinking companions during this time.
2. Staying at the apartment of his mother, who returned to Paris early in February, Lautrec could see Calmèse only by inviting him formally to dinner.

49–50   In 1895, Lautrec produced a poster to advertise the American magazine, *The Chap Book*. The next year, see letter 203, Lautrec went to London for five days with a cycling team and produced a poster (below) advertising Simpson's Lever Chain, for Louis Bouglé (alias Spoke), the manufacturer's agent for the chain. The poster shown below is a second attempt as Bouglé was not satisfied with Lautrec's first rendering of the chain.

51–52 Dethomas, the addressee of this letter (197), a painter, scenic artist and man-about-town, was also a friend of Lautrec's. May Belfort, who is mentioned in the letter, is shown above with her cat.

53 Lautrec's mother, against the wishes of his father and family, hired a succession of male nurses to look after him. Berthe Sarrazin, in a letter dated 14 February 1899 (letter 269) complains about the conduct of one of these men and it seems, from the contract (left), that his mother hired a Monsieur Briens or Brieus on the 15th of February to replace him.

54–55   Lautrec was interned at 'La folie St. James', 16, Avenue de Madrid, at Neuilly in early March until May of 1899. His handwriting (above) shows considerable strain. He asks Berthe Sarrazin for rum and other provisions. Below is Berthe Sarrazin's letter to his mother, enclosing Lautrec's letter and explaining the ruse she used to avoid taking him the rum, letters 226, 270.

66 rue de Candiras
Bordeaux

Ma chère Bonne Maman,

je suis à Bordeaux

et vous souhaite une
bonne année. Je
suis en train de partager
votre opinion sur
les brouillards de la

Gironde mais
je suis tellement
occupé que je
n'ai guère le temps
de faire des réflexions.
Je travaille toute
la journée. Je
figure à l'Exposition
de Bordeaux avec
4 tableaux et
j'ai du succès. —

J'espère que cela
vous fera un
peu de plaisir.
Je vous souhaite
une bonne année
et de la part
d'un revenant
comme moi cela
compte double
comme qualité de
souhait.
Je vous embrasse
votre petit fils respectueux
Henri

56 Lautrec's affectionate concern for his
family continued until his death—here he sends
New Year's greetings and news to his Godmother, with a joking allusion to his poor state
of health: 'a ghost like me'. His ill health had
not prevented him working and he had exhibited at the Exposition d'Art Moderne in Bordeaux (letter 236).

226 TO BERTHE SARRAZIN

1
16 avenue de Madrid, Neuilly, [April 12 or 13, 1899]

2   *Dear Madam,*

I beg you to come to 16 avenue de Madrid, in the morning and bring a pound of good ground coffee. Also bring me a bottle of rum. Bring me the whole lot in a locked valise, and ask to speak to me.
    Very sincerely yours,

H. de Toulouse Lautrec

3   *Bring me all the mail. Newspapers, printed matter, etc.*

227 TO HIS MOTHER   *[Neuilly, April 16, 1899]*

Madame A. de Toulouse, rue du Manège, Albi

1   *Worried. Give me news of Grandma and orders for Berthe.*

H. de Toulouse Lautrec   Neuilly

16 avenue de Madrid

1. The sanatorium of Dr. Sémélaigne, in the Saint-James quarter of Neuilly, where Lautrec remained from March to May 1899. Cf. Lautrec's letters to Joyant and to Joseph Albert, written from there and dated March 17 and April 12, 1899, respectively (published in Joyant I, pp. 216 and 220). See Ill. 54.
2. A housekeeper sent by Lautrec's mother to take care of her apartment on the rue de Douai. Cf. the prefatory note to the publication of her letters, in Appendix II, p. 212.
3. Berthe Sarrazin forwarded this letter to Lautrec's mother: cf. Letter 270 and Ill. 55.
   Letter 227
1. Cf. Letter 271. His grandmother had been ill. This text was to be sent as a telegram.

My dear Mama,

I've just seen Georges who is to bring you here. Be so kind as to give the keys of my studio to my friend Robin, who will keep them for me, since only he knows every nook and cranny of my studio. Looking forward to your visit, I kiss you.

Yours,

Henri

229 TO HIS MOTHER [*Neuilly*] *Tuesday* [*late April or early May 1899*]

My dear Mama,

1   *On Thursday I won't be coming to rue de Douai because Georges is taking me to Rueil to have lunch. So try to come in the afternoon. We'll arrange our little affairs so as not to miss each other.*
   I kiss you.

Yours truly,

Henri

2   *I have an appointment at the printer's on Friday. Could you have me for lunch? Even if it is a snack?*

1. Where Georges Séré de Rivières had an estate. Cf. Letter 272.
2. Undoubtedly to supervise the printing of his lithographic illustrations for Jules Renard's *Histoires Naturelles*, published in 1899 by Floury (Delteil 297–323).

My dear Mama,

My workman Stern will come to rue de Douai to pick up the studio keys and bring me different things. Have Berthe go along with him. In the state we're in, alas, we couldn't be too careful. I continue to bear my misfortune patiently. Take care of all my errands and come often. The prisoner.

Yours,

Henri

Bonnefoy came with his whole family. The Dr. will come soon.
P.S. Don't forget my table-knives.

Have someone ask Robin where you can buy fruit flavoured Eau

I   Moscovite. *It's harmless and very refreshing. I'll drink it* gladly.

My dear Raoul,

I've had a small animal in bronze sent to you. I hope you'll like it.
   You ask me what I would like. Some wine. Moreover, we'll drink

1. Lautrec was forbidden to drink alcoholic beverages after his internment in the sanatorium.
   Letter 231
1. Cf. Lautrec's letter to Joyant, written from Taussat in July 1901 (published in Joyant, I, p. 230).

it together, I hope. Here's what I'll do. I'm going to look over some samples of red wine. I'll let you know what they cost and you'll send me the number of bottles you want. Few but good.

Cordially yours,

Henri

at M. Fabre's

232 TO FRANTZ JOURDAIN   *[Taussat, probably Summer 1899]*

Dear Sir,

1   *I find it very difficult to comply with your request. I have already refused to belong to the placement committee. On the other hand, if there is a jury, I refuse categorically. I'll never deviate from this decision. Send me the regulations anyhow to Villa Bagatelle at Taussat, Gironde.*
   I would very much like to cooperate with you, but after books on
2   *lithography such as the one by M. Bouchot of the Cabinet des Estampes, I have to be extremely cautious, especially in matters where the old clan has a say.*
   Cordially yours and a handshake for your son.

H. T. Lautrec

1. Evidently to send some of his prints to the Exposition Universelle of 1900, in the organization of which Jourdain played an active part.
2. I.e., Henri Bouchot (1849–1906), Conservator of the Cabinet des Estampes, Bibliothèque Nationale. In *La Lithographie*, Paris, 1895, pp. 209–10, he had written of the artists in the *Estampe Original* group, and of Lautrec himself, in derogatory terms.

My dear Mama,

1
We were glad to get the things you sent and we're getting ready to do them honour. We've been to Arcachon where Damrémont greeted us with an air of embarrassment. . .? . . . Yet another victim. Celibacy does have its charms. The poor fellow pained me. He had a look on his face like the gentleman who just shit in his pants as he forced himself to utter amenities that didn't come off.

2
I've lost one of my cormorants, who must have bitterly rued the day he left me, because the inhabitants of Audenge greeted him with gunshot and he bit the dust. Have you sent the straw wrapping? If not, do. A little package of keys will come to your address. Keep it. It will be the keys to my studio. I'll come to stay for 24 or 48 hours on Friday or Saturday, with Viaud. I'm beginning to get my skin back, but I've been cruelly peeled.

I kiss you.

Yours,

H.

1. The son of Charles Denys Damrémont (1783–1837), a well-known general, and the commodore of a yacht which Lautrec led to victory in a regatta at Arcachon. Cf. his father's letter to Joyant, quoted in Joyant, I, p. 88.
2. The story is told in greater detail in Joyant, I, pp. 87–8. Audenge, a town in the Department of Gironde, near Taussat.

234 TO ANDRÉ ANTOINE

1   *Bordeaux* [*June 1900*]

2   *Monsieur Antoine,*

3   *You are decorated, I'm told.*
          It is an honour for the house, and that always gives pleasure.
          Affectionately,

                              H. T. Lautrec

235 TO MICHEL MANZI   [*October 1900*]

1   *My dear Manzi,*

2   *Congratulations without commentary, and we will share in your success.*

                              Yours,

                         H. T. Lautrec

1. Lautrec and Viaud stopped at Bordeaux on their way to Taussat, where they spent the summer. Cf. his letter to Joyant, dated June 30, 1900 (published in Joyant, I, p. 231).
2. André Antoine (1857–1943), an actor and producer, who had formerly directed the Théâtre Libre (1887–97), and now directed the Théâtre Antoine (1897–1906). Another letter to Antoine, written between May 17 and 20, 1899 (Collection Kornfeld, Berne), begins rather ominously: 'Lautrec sorti de prison. . . .'
3. Antoine had been decorated with the Légion d'Honneur on January 15, 1900 (information from the Musée National de la Légion d'Honneur).

Letter 235
1. Michel Manzi (1849–1915), an art dealer, publisher of art journals, and specialist in the photographic reproduction of paintings. In 1893 he became Joyant's partner in Boussod, Valadon et Cie., and helped organize exhibitions of Lautrec's work. Cf. Letter 237.
2. Manzi was decorated with the Légion d'Honneur on October 14, 1900 (information from the Musée National de la Légion d'Honneur).

1 *66 rue de Caudéran, Bordeaux [December 1900]*

My dear Grandma,

I'm at Bordeaux and wish you a happy New Year. I share your opinion of the fogs of the Gironde, but I'm so busy that I've hardly any time to think about it. I'm working all day long. I'm showing 4 pictures at the
2 *Bordeaux Exposition and am having success.*

I hope that will please you a little. I wish you a prosperous year—and from a ghost like me that counts double—for what my wishes are worth.

I kiss you.

Your respectful grandson,

Henri

1. From December 1900 to May 1901, Lautrec and Viaud remained at Bordeaux. Cf. Lautrec's letters to Joyant, written between December 6, 1900 and April 16, 1901 (published in Joyant, I, pp. 233–7). See Ill. 56.
2. The Exposition d'Art Moderne at Imberti, which was reviewed by P. Berthelot in *La Petite Gironde*, December 1900.

Appendixes

APPENDIX I

FROM COUNT ALPHONSE DE TOULOUSE-LAUTREC
TO MICHEL MANZI   *Malromé, September 15, [19]01*

Dear Mr. Manzi,

1 *Your funeral wreath arrived exactly as if to say your heart was with us during the sorrowful interval before the final separation from the only one surviving of my two sons, a token as precious as it was ephemeral from both of you, because you are One with Joyant, united in the same tutelary sentiment towards him who was deprived of his just heritage, even if not on that account despairing.*

These flowers from Paris deserved a more prompt expression of thanks. Flowers from Paris, I say, conquering *flowers, it might be said, assuring artistic fame whatever form it may take among its many forms and revelations, displeasing perhaps to average idlers who may think that making money is all there is to an honest education.*

Sincerity, it means everything.

They may criticize the brief works of the deceased, not old in years, but matured by so many trials, native to him and accidental as well.

He believed in his rough sketches, and you with him.

Thanks to your support he has been recognized and he owes it to you for having suppressed the malevolent opposition.

Joyant said to his schoolmate: He's a sensitive soul . . . to which a father may be permitted to add, an inoffensive *one.*

Between us there was never one of those flashes of feeling in which rancour replaces sweetness in the father-son relationship.

There you have the intimate side. He is your *child for having fostered his art.*

LAUTREC

1. Lautrec had died on September 9, 1901.

APPENDIX II

The following letters are from Berthe Sarrazin, a housekeeper of Mme de Toulouse-Lautrec, the artist's mother. She had been sent to Paris to take care of her apartment on rue de Douai. Upon the departure of the Countess she was entrusted with the protection of Lautrec, to keep an eye on him, and to prevent him from distributing furniture, silver or wine belonging to his mother. She was to report to the Countess in Albi, and most of the letters are addressed to her. When the news appears too difficult to relate, Berthe writes to Adeline, the faithful chambermaid who had helped educate Lautrec.

The documentary importance and the human interest of these letters is truly exceptional. We possess no similar document about any other artist of that time outlining the painter's activities day after day. Berthe Sarrazin writes as she speaks, without striving for effect. For the benefit of the reader we have followed neither her unorthodox spelling nor her absence of punctuation. Passages of no relevance to Lautrec or his family have been omitted.

238 TO MADAME LA COMTESSE DE TOULOUSE-LAUTREC

7 rue du Manège
Albi, Tarn

Paris, January 4, 1899

Madame la Comtesse,

When I got back in the evening yesterday I went to Monsieur Henri's. He was getting himself ready for coming to dinner. I told him that Madame had left. He was very angry. He swore and pounded the floor with his cane. He took a carriage. He came to the house, he rang the bell so hard he almost broke it. The concierge told him there wasn't anyone there. He didn't even say a word. He left to look for Monsieur Gabriel. Stern told me he had sent a telegram to his aunt. I waited for Monsieur till 11 o'clock in his studio. Seeing he hadn't come home, I went back to go to bed. He returned at midnight. The concierge got him to go to bed this morning. I went over at 8 o'clock. He was a good deal calmer, though he keeps on saying things that aren't sensible. He again burned some newspapers in the toilet bowl, but he's much better just the same.

He made me look for the keys to the apartment. He thinks he has lost them. He's getting back his memory a little. I think that in a few days the trouble will have disappeared. He told me he didn't understand what kind of fast one they were pulling on him, why Madame hadn't warned him, that when there was something happening in the family he was always told first. . . .

. . . He hasn't come back yet. I am still going to have the turkey roasted. I think Monsieur Gabriel will come to dinner. . . . Madame should get some rest and calm herself. I think it will all turn out very well. I will do my best to justify Madame's confidence and will do the best I can to take care of Monsieur Henri. . . .

Berthe Sarrazin

239 TO MADEMOISELLE ADELINE CROMONT

at Madame la Comtesse de Toulouse's
7 rue du Manège
Albi, Tarn

[Paris], Wednesday, 9.30 [January 5, 1899]

My dear Adeline,

I'm very much of your opinion about this unfortunate turkey. It's still on my hands. Nobody came to dinner. It's a bad luck turkey. I haven't any desire to eat it, either. Monsieur has been gone since this morning. I don't know what's going on. He hasn't come back. He had given me his word to come for dinner. He had me set the table for four and no one showed up. I've just come from his studio and no sign of him. There's a telegram there for him and one here. I forgot to tell Madame that Mme Pascal has been here with her daughter-in-law. She was very much surprised that Madame had left without telling her. Cécile also came this evening and asked me questions. She would have very much liked to know but I didn't say a thing. She said she'd know tomorrow from Madame de Bernard. She made all kinds of guesses. I'll tell you about it when I get back.

My poor Adeline, Monsieur isn't any better. He had another litre of turpentine delivered. I took it back. All he does is buy a lot of things, old pastry-moulds, spoons for 20 francs at the paint shop; but I'm going to take them back and tell them not to deliver anything else. . . .

the 5th, 12.00 o'clock

I was very much worried again this morning. Monsieur hadn't come back by 10 o'clock. I took a carriage. I went to Monsieur Gabriel's, who told me he knew where he was. He gave him all the money in a lump sum and I don't think he's got any left now. This morning he came back at 10:30. I asked him for money for coal. He told me that tomorrow he'll get some. So, during his night out he spent a thousand francs. Don't tell Madame. . . .

Your friend,

Berthe Sarrazin

9 rue de Douai

240 TO MADAME LA COMTESSE DE TOULOUSE-LAUTREC

7 rue du Manège
Albi, Tarn

Paris, January 6, [1899]

Madame la Comtesse,

There's nothing new. Monsieur is still about the same, better if anything, although he's still not entirely in his right mind. He is still buying a lot of knick-knacks, even dolls. Tonight we are having people to dinner, 6 places. I don't think it will be like the night before last. I'm doing a fish, a rabbit and the cold turkey and a pineapple ice. Monsieur wanted lobster 'à l'américaine', bouillabaisse, goose-livers in sauce, but I made him understand that it was too complicated and that I was all by myself. Monsieur has received Madame's letter. He is very pleased. He read it to me. Everything's all right. As I hadn't any more money, Monsieur gave me 100 francs. I'm marking it all down. Madame will go over it when she gets back.

I'm very busy with Monsieur. Yesterday I went over eight times. This morning I stayed until noon. . . .

Berthe

241 TO MADAME LA COMTESSE DE TOULOUSE-LAUTREC

7 rue du Manège
Albi, Tarn

Paris, Saturday, [*January 7, 1899*]

Madame la Comtesse,

I received Madame's good letter this morning, which consoled me a little and at the same time saddened me, because I see that Madame is still as unhappy as ever. It would be the same if she was here. Monsieur is still about the same, except that he doesn't touch the fire any more, on the other hand, all he does is buy all sorts of knick-knacks. This morning, for 172 francs, a man brought him some little figures, made of painted plaster apparently, besides this he gave the masseur a present of 100 francs and paid the bill, which looked to me like 70 francs. In short, in an hour nearly 400 francs. He has a lot of money. He got plenty of it by telegraph money-order. It makes me very sad to see him throwing away so much money uselessly, not to mention that I'm not always there and can't see everything.

My dinner went off very well. Seven people came. I hadn't made much for so many, and so there wasn't anything left over, except a little turkey which I gave to the concierge. I had enough of it.

The gentlemen stayed until midnight to smoke and sing. While this was going on Monsieur Henri slept near the fire. When he woke up he wanted to lie down in Madame's bed. I got it ready for him. Afterwards he wanted me to get him 4 flannel shirts. Nothing would do but that I find them. Finally everyone left. Nobody stayed but Monsieur Albert, who offered to go along with Monsieur to his studio and they left. This morning I went over at 8 o'clock. Monsieur didn't want to let me in. I went back at 10 o'clock and the things happened that I have just told Madame about above. I shall go back at 5 o'clock. Monsieur asked me if I'd heard anything from Madame. I told him no. He told me he'd received good news from you. He no longer remembered having read me the letter. I asked Monsieur if he'd answered it, he told me: 'no, never, it would have to wait'. I think he's very much put out because Madame isn't here.

I'd like to do something, but I can't do more than I am doing. As for Calmèse, I went to see him the day Madame left and told him not to come. An hour afterwards he was at Monsieur's. As for Gabrielle, she hasn't shown up again, nor Stern, either. Until tomorrow, then, Madame, and have courage.

Berthe.

242 TO MADAME LA COMTESSE DE TOULOUSE-LAUTREC

7 rue du Manège
Albi, Tarn

Paris, January 8, [1899]

Madame la Comtesse,

There's nothing new. Monsieur is still the same thing. He is still buying antiques, varnishing his pictures with glycerine and rubbing them down with a sock. This morning his face was red and swollen like the other day. He has his lunch at Boivin's with Monsieur Bouchef. . . .
. . . Stern came this morning. He stayed with Monsieur all morning. He didn't mention Madame at all. . . .

. . . He seems to be going on drinking. If it could only be kept away from him for a week or so he would be cured. He is quieter and doesn't touch the stove any more. He doesn't disinfect any more and the only irrational thing he does is buy old junk. He spends a lot of money. The shopkeepers take advantage by selling him all sorts of dirty old stuff. . . .

Monsieur Gabriel told me he had given him a thousand francs and the next morning, when I asked him for money for coal, Monsieur told me he was going to get some money by mail, that he didn't have any, and I know that Monsieur got money by a telegraph money order. I think I told Madame that Monsieur had given me 100 francs for expenses. . . .

243 TO MADEMOISELLE ADELINE CROMONT

7 rue due Manège
Albi, Tarn

[Paris, January 9, 1899]

My dear Adeline,

I got your short letter this morning. . . . Monsieur continues to be calmer. He talks less nonsense, too. He came to have lunch this morning with Monsieur Sescau. Monsieur Maurin was to have come, too, but he didn't. They waited for him until 1 o'clock. Yesterday Monsieur spent the day with Monsieur Albert. . . .

It is easy to see that Madame isn't here and they make themselves at home. Monsieur didn't buy anything yesterday. I don't think he has any more money. He keeps on rubbing his pictures with vaseline and glycerine. I'm very much afraid he's going to spoil them all. . . . Tell Madame that things are much better and that she can come back. I think Monsieur would be very glad. . . .

7 rue du Manège
Albi, Tarn

Paris, January 10, [1899]

Madame la Comtesse,

*I wish I could give Madame better news, but unfortunately it's the same
story. However, Monsieur is calmer at the moment. He talks very
sensibly at times but you mustn't go against him. For example, yesterday
at lunch he wanted to put rum into the dish of orange preserves. I wanted
to stop him and he put me in my place in no uncertain terms. He said
he was the master. You always have to approve, to say yes all the time,
otherwise he's not bad. All he talks about is giving presents to everybody.
Monsieur keeps on making a mess of his linen. He takes all of it out of
the chest, throws it all on the floor. This morning I gave him 8 pocket
handkerchiefs. At 10 o'clock when I returned he didn't have one of them
left. He puts vaseline on his pictures and wipes it off with his handkerchiefs. . . .*
*. . . (Monsieur Mallet) tells me that Monsieur is telling everybody to
buy things on his account and that for 2 years Monsieur hasn't paid his
bills, that he had a big bill which he didn't dare present for fear of
offending Monsieur. . . .*
*. . . At 11:30 (Calmèse) had his stable-boy come to get Monsieur. I
think they were to have lunch together. I'm going to go back a little later.
I am staying as long as possible at his place. He talks and talks and he
doesn't go out. He forgets to drink. If one could be with him all the time
to keep him busy perhaps he wouldn't think about drinking any more. . . .*
*. . . I only bring eggs which Monsieur eats raw mixed with rum. That
can't do him any harm. And coffee every morning. . . .*

7 rue du Manège
Albi, Tarn

Paris, January 11, 1899
6 p.m.

My dear Adeline,

I haven't written to you sooner, but Madame must have given you the news. It's not very good. It's still the same thing. What are we going to do about Monsieur Henri? He can't keep it up this way forever. However, nobody does anything about it. I never see Monsieur Gabriel or anybody. It's strangers, mostly Calmèse, who take care of him. They both drink, one as much as the other. Poor Monsieur is always the same. Every time he sees me he shows me his hand and tells me it's all right, it's well again. He doesn't remember anything at all. This morning he asked me if Madame knew he burned his hand. He doesn't touch the fire any more. He doesn't even light the newspapers any more. He didn't buy anything today or yesterday. . . .

. . . I've just been to Monsieur's place. Calmèse was sleeping on the couch with his dog. Monsieur Montcabrier was there, too, you know, the little young man who often comes. Monsieur kept pestering me for rum. I gave him the rest of the bottle that was in the cupboard. . . .

7 rue du Manège
Albi, Tarn

Paris, January 11, 1899

Madame la Comtesse,

I was glad to receive Madame's letter this morning with the 100-franc note, but I wasn't worried since Monsieur had given me some money. I

1. A young artist whom Lautrec advised at this time, warning him particularly against a career in art; cf. his letter, published in Beaute, *Il y a cent ans, Henri de Toulouse-Lautrec.*

haven't spent all of it yet. I thank Madame very much. Monsieur is much
better but he still can't remember a thing. For instance, I asked him if
he'd had any news. He told me he'd received a telegram, that things were
going better for him. This was the wire that Madame sent the day after
she left. He thinks that's today. He also found the envelope again of
the telegram which announced a money order. He sent me to the office to
tell them to bring the money to the house. I went there. I thought it was
another money order, but not at all. Monsieur had got the money on
January 6. They told me at the post office that Monsieur hasn't much of a
memory if he can't remember receiving a thousand francs; then he was
furious and sent me to fetch Monsieur Calmèse. I pretended to go there.
I said he wasn't there; he wanted to throw the telegraph girls into jail.

Monsieur is still angry with Madame. He told me this morning that
Madame had left him right in the middle of work, that he had done
everything to keep Madame but that she had wanted to go travelling, that
her leaving had upset him and made him sick, that he was going to write
an outspoken letter: he even wanted to send a telegram but a minute later
had forgotten all about it. That terrible Calmèse is always around and
never leaves Monsieur. They have lunch and dinner together.

The woman who sells wine across the way (at the Père François) told
me that Monsieur was afraid at night. He came to fetch their boy at
1 o'clock in the morning to have him search all the corners of his studio
to see whether anybody was hiding there. He told them he was at outs
with his family, that his family wanted to have him locked up and that
he was afraid they'd take him away while he was asleep. He never says
anything like that to me. . . .

247 TO MADAME LA COMTESSE DE TOULOUSE-LAUTREC

7 rue du Manège
Albi, Tarn

Paris, January 12, 1899

Madame la Comtesse

Monsieur hasn't paid his October rent. The concierge had me look at the
bill. It's for 409 francs, 85 centimes. She hasn't got the January bill

ready yet, but she thinks it's pretty much the same. The concierge at our house still hasn't been paid for postage costs. She told me she had sent 2 registered letters, which makes 80 centimes.

Monsieur is still the same as ever. He talks a lot. I again stayed the whole morning at the studio. Monsieur told me that he was having lunch with some cousins, magistrates. I think it's with Monsieur de Rivières. . .

I am reopening my letter. I have seen Monsieur de Rivières in the street. I talked to him. He told me that he thought Monsieur was much better, that they had had lunch together, that he had written to Madame under the dictation of Monsieur, so that Madame should set her mind at rest. I think that things are going to be better.

Berthe

248 TO MADEMOISELLE ADELINE CROMONT

7 rue du Manège
Albi, Tarn

Paris, January 13, 1899

Dear Adeline,

I don't know whether you have received your coffee glass, . . . Monsieur Henri, who was better yesterday, today is in a state. All he did all night was go in and out of the house. This morning he'd already left by 7 o'clock. I went looking for him. He was with Calmèse at the wine seller's in the rue Fontaine. He was furious with Madame over not having heard from her. He told me he'd never set foot in the apartment again, that he would rent smaller lodgings and would keep me in his service. He thinks that Madame will never come back again. He is very worried.

I have just come away from Monsieur, whom I left with Mr. Bouchef in his studio. I shall go back again by and by. . . .

7 rue du Manège
Albi, Tarn

Paris, January 13, 1899

My dear Adeline,

Still nothing good to report. I told you that Mr. Henri was in a sad state all day yesterday. I went back in the evening. Big Gabrielle was there. That dirty bag told him that I had sent her a telegram telling her not to come again on orders from Madame, and so Monsieur is even more angry with Madame. You see how much you can trust that dirty woman. She must be pestering Monsieur for money. He asked me if I had any. I replied that Madame hadn't left me any. Then he sent me with a letter to Monsieur Robin's. There wasn't anybody there. His concierge, Monsieur's concierge, told me that Monsieur had done nothing but come in and out all night. He wasn't happy about it because it kept him from his sleep. Monsieur stayed all morning at Calmèse's. They had lunch together at the tobacconist's across from the livery stable. Monsieur received two telegrams this morning which the concierge brought to him at Calmèse's. I went to take him a letter to Mr. Sescau's. I spoke to him. He told me he thought he was worse, that he didn't know what was going to happen. I came back to the studio with the answer. That Gabrielle was there, with Calmèse and, I think, Gabrielle's boy-friend. A fine lot, as you see. Monsieur is going to be worse than ever tonight, what a pity, my God!

I'm glad that Monsieur hasn't any more money, since those people only hang around him for that. When they see he hasn't any more they'll let him alone, perhaps. Madame shouldn't give him any for a while to see what they'll do. Monsieur told Mr. Sescau that he was going to call them to account, that he would get 3,000 francs tomorrow. . . .

Berthe Sarrazin

Give Madame whatever news you think fit.

7 rue du Manège
Albi, Tarn

Paris, January 15, 1899

Madame la Comtesse,

Monsieur hasn't paid his rent. When the concierge presented him the bills he said that he was not on good terms with his family, that a week from now it would be taken care of. All he did was send some telegrams. He ¹ *got one from Coursan. Monsieur told me he was going on a trip. He is going to go to Coursan with 2 detectives and get his due. He said that Madame doesn't understand it very well, that his father doesn't attend to things and that he's being robbed. Monsieur continues not to sleep at night. The other night he went to Monsieur Robin's at 3 o'clock in the morning. This morning at 4 o'clock he went out. He sent a girl selling newspapers to look for me at 6 o'clock. I was very scared. I thought that something had happened. But no such thing. Monsieur was busy drinking at the tobacconist's with a hackney coachman. Stern came this morning as he does every Sunday. I think they went to have lunch together. Tomorrow I'll go to Monsieur Bourges' as Madame told me.*

I'll write at greater length tomorrow. I'm afraid of missing the post. I hope that Madame is well and wish her courage.

Berthe Sarrazin

1. A town in the Department of Aude, near Céleyran.

7 rue du Manège
Albi, Tarn

Paris, January 16, 1899

Madame la Comtesse,

I've just come from Monsieur Bourges', whom I told what was going on. He told me he couldn't do a thing, that I'd have to go to Monsieur Gabriel's. So I went to Monsieur Gabriel's, but he had left. I'll go back tomorrow morning. Monsieur is somewhat better but is very much put out because of the money. He told me this morning that Calmèse had found him moneylenders at thirty per cent. There's a danger they'll get him to do something really foolish. I've just come from his place. There were 2 men there I didn't know. He sent me away. Gabrielle is waiting at Père François' until 4 o'clock. Monsieur is supposed to go and fetch her and I have to go back myself. So, Monsieur asked me if I had the keys to the yard. He wanted me to get some white muscat wine. I had to take 2 small bottles of muscat to the tobacconist's and a bottle of blue label. I am very much concerned. He promises wine to everybody, to Big Gabrielle, to the stable-boy. He says that it's his. I haven't given anything to anybody yet. Fortunately he forgets about it.

Now he doesn't want to see Monsieur Gabriel any more. He told me that if he came I should throw him out, that he was a spy. He also told me he had just asked Mademoiselle de Rivières to marry him, that he will have a magistrate for a father-in-law, that he will have them give an account of everything. But you mustn't pay any attention to what Monsieur says. He forgets about it a minute later. Madame mustn't worry about it. I will do my best to take care of her interests and Monsieur Henri's, although if I listened to him I'd be spending all of 500 francs a day. I'm going to try and find M. Gabriel tomorrow morning. Will Madame be so good as to give my regards to Adeline: until tomorrow, Madame.

Berthe

1. Interviewed by Robert Sadoul in 1964 (cf. *Nouvelles Littéraires*, October 8, 1964), Aline Séré de Rivières said she was not told of Lautrec's proposal at that time. She was portrayed by Lautrec in the 1899 lithograph *Au Bois* (Delteil 296), as indicated in the M. Loncle Sale Catalogue.

7 rue du Manège
Albi, Tarn

Paris, January 17, [1899]

My dear Adeline,

I'm still terribly bothered by all these goings-on. When will it all end?
Monsieur was much better last night. He asked me himself to come and
sleep in the studio last night. So I went. He came home at midnight.
He got up 2 or 3 times and finally at 5 o'clock he told me he was going
for a walk. You can imagine how much I slept. I've had a toothache come
on me and something's the matter with one of my eyes. . . .
. . . This morning Monsieur is still in an awful mess. He had me take
6 bottles of wine to Calmèse's. I went to the wine merchants; he was
sitting with 2 dirty sluts. That pig Calmèse, they should put him in jail.
He's going to be the death of poor Monsieur.

This morning I went to see Monsieur Gabriel. He said he was going
to write to Madame. Monsieur Bourges told me I didn't have to tell
Madame everything that happened, that I should tell her things were
improving because Madame would get all worked up. I really don't
know where all this will end. My poor Adeline, all of Monsieur's friends
blame Madame for having gone away, for having left her son in this
condition in the hands of strangers. Just between us, Adeline, I think
they're right. Madame's place should be here. Poor Monsieur isn't
bad. On the contrary, he has never been nicer than now. He's always
promising me something. This morning he told me he was going to
settle an income of 3,000 francs on me. I couldn't help laughing. I saw
in a minute that he was going to take offence.

Don't show my letter to Madame whatever you do. Say that Monsieur
is feeling better and I will write tomorrow. . . .

Berthe Sarrazin

7 rue du Manège
Albi, Tarn

[*January 18, 1899*]

Madame la Comtesse,

Nothing new, if anything for the better. Monsieur looks well. However, unfortunately he still drinks a little. As long as he goes to Calmèse's, it will always be the same. If there were some way of stopping him, if Madame would write. It's true that Monsieur hasn't anyone else. You never see any of his friends any more. There's only Calmèse and Gabrielle, who never leave him. Monsieur is giving everything in his studio, all the knick-knacks, to Calmèse and Gabrielle. He has even given them the pillow from his bed. I don't know where this new craze will end. Monsieur never comes to the rue de Douai. He says he'll never set foot there again; when I talk about Madame and say that she's going to come back, he says he doesn't want Madame to return. Another time he says that you have to be lenient, that Madame is sick. He changes ideas 20 times in 2 minutes. I don't pay any attention to what he says, but at the bottom he's very angry with Madame for not being here. He doesn't work at all any more. He doesn't even rub on glycerine. All he talks about is his money. He is going to force his uncle to make an accounting. He says that Madame has been favouring the steward, that the matter has been put in the hands of the public prosecutor. It's Monsieur de Rivières who's taking care of that. He tells all these things in the bars.

Monsieur always asks me if Madame has written to me. He asks to see the letters. If Madame would only write a letter that I could show Monsieur, to see what he'll say. Madame should feel easier in her mind. Things if anything are better rather than worse. If Madame could come back perhaps things might be entirely better.

Berthe

7 rue du Manège
Albi, Tarn

Paris, January 19, [1899]

My dear Adeline,

I didn't want to write today because there's nothing new, but I thought that Madame would be too unhappy if she didn't have some news. I saw Monsieur this morning for 5 minutes. He had just come home with Gabrielle, who had been waiting for him since 8 o'clock in the morning. Yesterday she waited all afternoon at Père François' but Monsieur didn't come back. She wasn't able to get any money out of him and that's why she was so bright and early this morning.

I saw Monsieur Albert last night. I talked to him. He told me he would put a stop to it. It's terrible just the same to have Monsieur in the clutches of that slut. She has walked off with all the small objects she was able to carry. I came back twice this afternoon to Monsieur's, but he wasn't there. I'm going to go there once more when I post my letter. I wanted to ask you, Adeline, where you've put the pongee silk to mend Monsieur Henri's overcoat. Tell me. . . .

Berthe

7 rue du Manège
Albi, Tarn

Paris, January 20, 1899

My dear Adeline,

As I told you I would last night, on the way back from posting my letter I went there again. He was at Père François' with Gabrielle and Stern, I wouldn't dare tell you how drunk. This morning I went at

8 o'clock. He didn't let me in. The wine seller's boy told me he had brought some shortbread (you know how he likes his shortbread!) and that he had two women in bed with him, Gabrielle and another one. I went back at 11 o'clock but he had bolted the door. I wasn't able to do the housework. I've just been to Calmèse's. He told me that he didn't want to be bothered with Monsieur any more, that he disgusted him, that he had done what he could but that he saw it was hopeless, that he had been very nasty to him yesterday morning. He told me he had been having lunch with these two women at the tobacconist's across the way since 11 o'clock and it was 2 o'clock now. He's going to make another mess of it tonight. He didn't have any money last night. Gabrielle said at the bar that all he had left was 22 sous. I don't know if Monsieur Robin lends him money or if Monsieur Henri has given him some to keep for him. However, the fact remains that he gave him 50 francs . . .

. . . Everybody is amazed that he can keep up such a life. It would be better if poor Madame doesn't know about it. Now then, Adeline, it's an act of charity to keep her in the dark. What can you do? There's nothing to do but wait till he drops, which perhaps will happen before long. You ask me if he's working. He doesn't do a stroke any more. . . .

. . . He doesn't talk about Madame, or if he does mention her, it's more often bad than good. His friends are tired of him. I never see anybody any more. I don't think Monsieur Gabriel has very much to do with him. . . .

Berthe

256 TO MADAME LA COMTESSE DE TOULOUSE-LAUTREC

7 rue du Manège
Albi, Tarn

Paris, January 21, 1899

Madame la Comtesse,

I wasn't able to do Monsieur's housework yesterday. He didn't let me in all day. I went there 6 times. He went to Monsieur Robin's to spend that night. I went this morning and saw Monsieur as he was going out. He told me to get some wine, which I did. Today Monsieur is fidgety and

*preoccupied. All he does is talk about putting somebody in gaol. I don't
know who. He is very reserved with me. I think that Gabrielle must have
got him worked up.*

*I should warn Madame that Monsieur Robin is completely hostile
towards her. He says that it's the family's fault if Monsieur is like this,
that he's been abandoned, that no one cares about him, that he's greatly
to be pitied and that he's sorry for him. I think that Monsieur is going
to stay with them, but I don't think that will last long. Monsieur will
change his mind quickly. I said yesterday to Adeline that Monsieur had
drunk a lot again. Today he looked better. If he can stay at Monsieur
Robin's he'll drink less, but as I just told Madame, that won't last for
long.*

Berthe Sarrazin

257 TO MADAME LA COMTESSE DE TOULOUSE-LAUTREC

7 rue du Manège
Albi, Tarn

[January 22, 1899]

Madame la Comtesse,

*Monsieur again spent the night at Monsieur Robin's. I was on the
lookout for him when he went out this morning. He's always in an angry
mood and has a restless look. He told me he was going to have a lot of
people put in gaol, that he would be out of debt in 3 weeks. It's his
family and the friends of his family that he's angry with. He doesn't go
to the studio much any more. I haven't been back since the other day. He
told me to go there this afternoon, that he would be there. I asked the
concierge for the rent bills, which I am putting in the letter. I'll go
tomorrow where Madame told me about the silver, although there's no
danger here. Monsieur never comes here and I wouldn't have let him take
it anyway, even though this will be safer.*

*I've just come from the livery stable. I think Monsieur is having
lunch with M. Calmèse at his mother's.*

As Madame sees, it's still the same old thing. There isn't much improvement. However, Monsieur is drinking less and, since he is spending the night at Monsieur Robin's, he doesn't get up again to drink. He still has a red face all the same. We'll have to be patient, poor Madame. May God have pity. I ask Him often enough. Eventually He will answer our prayers. Let's not lose courage. . . .

Berthe Sarrazin

258 TO MADAME LA COMTESSE DE TOULOUSE-LAUTREC

7 rue du Manège
Albi, Tarn

[January 23, 1899]

Madame la Comtesse,

1   *I have done what you told me. I took the silver this morning to Madame de Vismes'. Madame will find the list of what I took in the letter. Monsieur is still very much in an angry mood. This morning he came to the concierge's at the rue de Douai. He said he was going to have all the house locks changed. I was afraid he'd do it while I was gone and so I hurried to get back. I went to Monsieur's studio. He was there. He has*

2   *got hold of a tiny little dog at Père François'. He has bought a nursing bottle and has put the errand-boy in his studio to take care of the dog all day long. I've sent the errand-boy away and I am going to go there. That's why I'm in such a hurry to write a few words to Madame. Monsieur is still spending the night at Monsieur Robin's. He's always talking about putting everybody in gaol. I will write to Madame again tomorrow.*

Berthe Sarrazin

1. The mother of Étienne Devismes, Lautrec's childhood friend, whose story *Cocotte* he had illustrated in 1881. Lautrec's mother had hidden some of her silver in her rue de Douai apartment.
2. This is the dog Pamela that Joyant mentions (I, pp. 213–14).

7 rue du Manège
Albi, Tarn

[*January 24, 1899*]

Madame la Comtesse,

I was rushed yesterday when I was writing to Madame. I don't know whether I said that Monsieur finally let me into his place on Sunday evening. He is still sleeping at M. Robin's, but now that there's the little dog he wants me to stay in the studio all day to take care of it, but I'm taking it to the rue de Douai in the kitchen.

I saw Monsieur this morning. I waited until he came out of Monsieur Robin's. I asked if Monsieur had any news. He told me that Madame had written to him. He seemed angry. He told me he didn't want what Madame wanted, and ended by saying he was going to the Law Courts. I thought he looked bad, his skin yellow, his lips full of yellow crust, too, and a little thin. However, he seemed to me to be less overexcited than on Sunday and yesterday. It's true he was only just going out and hadn't had anything to drink. Monsieur stayed the whole day yesterday with Calmèse. He had his lunch and dinner with him. I told Madame how I took 6 bottles of white wine. Monsieur wanted me to take another 6 this morning. I didn't take them. I'm going to see if Monsieur remembers. I'll say that I forgot. Gabrielle has dropped out of sight. I think Monsieur Robin and Calmèse must have got him to drop her by telling him she was stealing. Good riddance. But on the other hand there's still this Calmèse. Monsieur never leaves him and they drink all day. Monsieur never thinks of anything else any more. He doesn't work at all either. He's always at Calmèse's place or at the tobacconist's. He doesn't get angry with me, on the contrary, he's very nice, but he got into an argument with his concierge at the avenue Frochot and he also came here to our concierge at the rue de Douai to make suggestions about his letters. . . .

Berthe

7 rue du Manège
Albi, Tarn

[January 25, 1899]

My dear Adeline,

I still haven't anything really good to tell you. Monsieur is still just the same, rather worse just lately. Yesterday, in the evening, he came to rue de Douai to see the dog. He looked all around the apartment. He opened the dining room sideboard. He made me make him a package of two tins of goose-liver, a little tin of truffles, the last of the German sausage. He also wanted a pot of jam, but that made it too big. He told me to take everything that was left to M. Robin's. I said I would, but I didn't take anything this morning. I have hidden everything. I'll say there isn't any more. I went to the studio this morning at 8 o'clock. I didn't think Monsieur would be there, but he was, although he had spent the night at M. Robin's. But you should have seen him! Good God, he really scared me. He had lain down on the bed with all his clothes on. He wasn't able to walk. I took off his shoes. I wanted to put him to bed, but he flew into a rage. Finally, little by little, things quietened down. He told me I had made him lose 30,000 francs, that Madame Bourges had commissioned a picture and that she didn't want it any more, that it was all my fault. I had to go out for a moment and when I came back he'd forgotten all about it. He spoke to me about M. Gabriel, with whom he's very angry, and his uncle. He told me all about them till I thought he'd never stop. Calmèse again sent his stable-boy to see what Monsieur was doing (he can't let him alone), although he had told me he didn't want any more to do with him. Now, you see! Monsieur told Batiste, the stable-boy, to get an errand-boy and come and take all the wine he wanted from the cellar, that it was his, that he was making a present of it because he was marrying his daughter, but you can imagine I don't want to let him get away with that. Perhaps I'll have to give him a basketful just the same. I'll try to do the best I can.

Monsieur hasn't got a sou left. Calmèse told me he had lent him 15 francs yesterday. I don't dare to ask him for money for the gas. There's 24 francs, 20 centimes owing for that and 22 to the laundress.

Tell it to Madame. My dear Adeline, I still have a little money of my own. If Madame wants me to, I'll advance some of it. I've spent everything that Madame sent me and what Monsieur has given me, too. . . .

Berthe

261 TO MADEMOISELLE ADELINE CROMONT

7 rue du Manège
Albi, Tarn

Paris, January 26, 1899

My dear Adeline,

I received your letter this morning. I see that you're not calm and that you must be worrying very much. But what can you do? You might be even unhappier here, although I wish with all my heart that you had come back. I assure you I find the days long. But nothing has improved. Yesterday Monsieur was drunk all day and couldn't stand on his feet. He spent the night at Monsieur Robin's and this morning he looked better. He's always with that Calmèse. He is lunching there. I'll go and take a look by-and-by. I still have the little dog. He's an awful bother to me, all he does is cry. When I'm not there he does his business all over the place. The concierge is afraid the other tenants will complain. I'm going to try to put him at Calmèse's, if Monsieur is willing. Cécile came last night. I wasn't there. I'm very glad she didn't find me in. She told the concierge she was leaving for Albi for several days. She came to see if Madame had come back so as to get some news. Maybe you're going to see her turn up one of these days. Tell Madame, Adeline, that Père François has demanded I pay 61 francs that Monsieur owes him. A paint-dealer has also been here with a bill for 19 francs, but that isn't urgent. He can wait. It's very cold. It has been freezing for two days. . . .

Berthe Sarrazin

7 rue du Manège
Albi, Tarn

Paris, January 27, 1899

Madame la Comtesse,

I think that Monsieur is feeling better. I wasn't able to see him this morning. It was Monsieur Robin who told me that Monsieur was to go to Crotoy yesterday evening with Monsieur Joyant. I got his valise packed but he didn't come back. I think he must have forgotten. I went to Monsieur Robin's this morning. Monsieur wasn't either there or at his studio.

I don't know where he must have spent the night. I was very worried. I went back several times. Finally I learned he was having lunch with Monsieur Calmèse. I must go back this evening to Monsieur Robin's. Other than this there's nothing new. I've managed to get rid of the dog. He is at Calmèse's place. Adeline was to have told Madame about Monsieur's gas bill. It's 24 francs, 40 centimes and the laundress', 22 francs. If I'm able to see Monsieur tonight, I'll ask him for some money, but I don't think he has any.

Monsieur told me about having heard from Madame, but said he'd give me the news later, that for the time being he couldn't say anything, it was too serious. He doesn't talk quite so much nonsense. I think it would go away if Monsieur could get back to work and if he weren't always with that Calmèse. But one can't do anything about that.

Berthe Sarrazin

7 rue du Manège
Albi, Tarn

Paris, January 28, [1899]

Madame la Comtesse,

I saw Monsieur last night at 9 o'clock at Monsieur Robin's. He hadn't drunk much. This morning, at 8 o'clock, he was better. He had had a good night. But at 11 o'clock he wasn't so good. I've just left him at the tobacconist's with a hackney coachman. They were just about to go into town with a gentleman with a red moustache whom I didn't know. I'd like to be able to tell Madame things are better, but I don't dare to yet. That is, Monsieur has changed. He doesn't talk about kerosene any more, he talks a little more sensibly. Despite this I don't think he's well. He looks sick. However, Monsieur Calmèse tells me he eats a lot. He has a boil on his neck, but it isn't serious. Monsieur Mallet has learned about it. Now all he talks about is his boil. He puts muslin with a poultice on his neck like a scarf. He has either lost or had stolen all his scarves.

Monsieur is still angry with his uncle, Monsieur Tapié. He says he's a scoundrel, that he turned Madame against him, that he has had a grudge against him for a long time, that Madame has given him a better deal, that he will make him pay. In short, a lot of stuff that I don't remember very well now since I don't pay any attention. He's always talking about taking a trip. I think he wants to go and be with Madame again. Madame asks me why Monsieur made a scene with his concierge for no reason. He imagines there are burglars and that they've been in his studio. He hasn't been there for two days. I think he's afraid and that's why he sleeps at Monsieur Robin's. I'm sending you a note that Monsieur has given me for his concierge.

As for the masseur, he hasn't been back since the day Monsieur paid him and gave him a present of 100 francs. I saw him in the street and told him Monsieur was out of his mind, that he shouldn't be taking his money. He told me he was a poor fellow, that he had six children, that the money would do him a lot of good, in short, he didn't want to give it back. . . .

Berthe Sarrazin

7 rue du Manège
Albi, Tarn

Paris, January 29, 1899

Madame la Comtesse,

I received your registered letter with 150 francs safely this morning. I will go and pay the insurance tomorrow morning, also Monsieur's gas. It's still the same old thing with Monsieur. He's still spending the night at Monsieur Robin's, but he wants to come to rue de Douai to sleep. This morning he wanted me to find a locksmith to have all the locks changed. I am going to have to give up the keys to stop him. Monsieur Robin is egging him on to do it. I took advantage of it being Sunday to say that I couldn't find one, whereupon he left to look for one himself. He can't have found one for he hasn't come back. It's two o'clock. I'm going to see where he is before finishing my letter.

I've just seen Monsieur. He was still eating lunch in rue Fontaine with Stern. He spoke to me about the locksmith. I said I was going to look and see if I could find the keys, and that he should wait a little. He wanted a tin of goose-livers. I said there weren't any left at all. . . .

Berthe Sarrazin

7 rue du Manège
Albi, Tarn

Paris, January 30, [1899]

Madame la Comtesse,

I have just received the telegram. I will go tomorrow morning to Monsieur Gabriel's to look for the keys. I was obliged to give the one I had to Monsieur last night. He absolutely wanted to have other locks installed. Monsieur came to spend the night at rue de Douai. That night poor Monsieur was like a child. He looked into every nook and cranny, he wanted to take everything to Monsieur Robin's. Each thing he found he tucked under his arm. He said 'just fits the pipe'. When he had too many things he gave them back to me. I put them back in place. He forgot all about them a minute later. I relit the gas heater to warm up a little although Monsieur made a roaring fire in Madame's bedroom. It's very cold, we have snow today for the first time. Monsieur Robin came to get Monsieur for lunch and I went to pay the gas and insurance. I'll keep a list of what I spend each day on a sheet of paper which I'll send to Madame tomorrow or later as Madame asks me to. Monsieur is still very much at outs with his uncle, M. Tapié. He says the inheritance is being illegally withheld which is reducing him to great poverty, that he has to live by loans and begging on account of him. But he is going to take a trip in the Midi and then he'll make them laugh on the other side of their faces. He has also got a grudge against Monsieur Gabriel. He told me that if he came, to drive him out with a broom, or lock him up in a bedroom and go and fetch him and he'd give M. Gabriel what was coming to him. Madame can see that Monsieur is still talking nonsense. However, there are times when he talks very well. Luckily he isn't down on me, on the contrary, he speaks well of me to everybody. I don't cross him, either. I do what I can for him, to be agreeable. I think that if Madame came back Monsieur would be very happy. He tells everybody that he hasn't a mother any more, nor any family, that he is in the deepest of poverty. People pity him, they believe it's true. . . .

Berthe Sarrazin

7 rue du Manège
Albi, Tarn

Paris, January 31, [1899]

My dear Adeline,

I was still very worried this morning. Monsieur didn't come back to spend the night at rue de Douai as he had promised me. I waited for him all night. This morning at 8 o'clock I went to Monsieur Gabriel's. I wanted to see him very much but they wouldn't let me come up, claiming it was too early. Nevertheless Monsieur Gabriel had brought down the key so it would be given to me. At 10 o'clock. Monsieur sent me a letter for a locksmith, telling me to go right away to his studio. Monsieur had had his bolts taken out. So I told the locksmith to just pretend to fix them (which he did). Reassure Madame about the burglars, Adeline. There aren't any at all. Right now Monsieur has persecution mania. He has been robbed just the same. He no longer has his watch nor his beautiful scarf. His tie-pin has disappeared, too. Tell Madame that nonetheless he has some money. He told me that some art dealers have lent it to him. It's Calmèse who is in charge of his wallet. He's in good hands, as you can see.

   I went to Monsieur Mallet's to ask how he felt about Monsieur. He told me that he was much better, that he judged him to have been very well for the last week, that to be sure he was still talking irrationally but that, in his view, he had always done that. Monsieur knows that Madame's brother came to get Madame. You could have knocked me down with a feather this morning. He asked me if I hadn't seen a tall gentleman with spectacles and a grey beard. I told him no. I don't know who is stirring him up against his relatives. He is still furious with Monsieur Gabriel. He told me he had dined facing him last night and didn't even smile at him. If he comes here to go and get Monsieur Calmèse to throw him out. He kept on repeating this to me . . .

1. I.e., Amédée Tapié de Céleyran.

Monsieur told me he was going to write to the Department of Public Health, that he didn't want to pay unless he could have his house repaired, that he had almost been asphyxiated by the toilets. . . .

Berthe

267 TO MADEMOISELLE ADELINE CROMONT

7 rue du Manège
Albi, Tarn

Paris, February 1st, 1899

My dear Adeline,

I don't know what to tell you. It's still the same old thing. Monsieur keeps on drinking and now and then becomes disagreeable. Monsieur Mallet says he thinks he's better, but as for me, I don't think so. For two nights now I don't know where he has been sleeping. He came this morning to rue du Douai with the dog. He calls her Pamela. Poor Monsieur went rummaging in all the drawers again, even among your things. He wanted to take your knife, my poor Adeline. I don't think he'll ever come out of it until he stops seeing that demon Calmèse. He sticks with him every minute. He never goes to his studio any more. He's at the tobacconist's all day long, where they eat. This morning he made me take 2 bottles of white wine, one muscat, the jar of English jam you had bought and even the last bit of ham that was in the kitchen cupboard. Luckily he didn't see the one wrapped up in cloths. He would have made me take that one, too. How will it all end, my poor Adeline? . . .

Berthe Sarrazin

7 rue du Manège
Albi, Tarn

Paris, February 3, [18]99

Madame la Comtesse,

As I told Madame yesterday, Monsieur stayed in the kitchen all after-noon, cooking the ham that was in the cloths. I thought he hadn't seen it, but he knew very well that it was there. He put in a bottle of white wine, one of red, some vinegar, some rum and so much pepper and salt and so on that it wasn't edible. He made me take it to Calmèse's with 3 bottles of wine. I've told Madame how Monsieur was bad at times. He came back like a wild man. I'd never seen him so violent. He wanted to hit the little concierge. He took him by the arm and shook him as hard as he could, meanwhile calling him all sorts of bad names. He accused him of not taking proper care of the house and to me he said all kinds of nonsense, that he would have me put in gaol with his family. I was so frightened that I'm still sick over it today. He says he's going to have all the furniture sold in the street. There are debts and they are going to seize the furniture. He does it on purpose. Finally he said such awful things that I couldn't help crying. When he saw I was crying that made him sorry. He begged my pardon, saying that it was his family he was angry with, but since none of his family was there it was I who had to bear the brunt, but that he bore me no grudge. Monsieur spent last night here. He didn't sleep. He kept the fire burning all night long. The wood won't last for long. He stayed until noon. He cleaned out the gas stove by running a lit candle over it. In sum, he did all sorts of crazy things that would take too long to tell.

The other night they almost took him to the police station. It was Guichard, the barkeeper, who told me that. He had just taken a room in the rue Pigalle. There was another gentleman and two loose women. The other gentleman left shortly after. Monsieur, however, stayed to pay, but didn't have any money. It did him no good to say that he was the Count of Toulouse. The landlord wouldn't listen. Then Monsieur came to wake up Guichard who lent him the 3 francs, 50 centimes that were owing.

Monsieur hasn't any money at all any more. I asked him for gas money.
He gave me 20 francs which makes 120 francs I have received from
Monsieur. . . .

Berthe

269 TO MADAME LA COMTESSE DE TOULOUSE-LAUTREC

Cité du Rétiro 5, Hotel Pérey
Paris

Paris, Tuesday, the 14th [February 1899]

Madame la Comtesse,

1   *I've had trouble this morning. This man is as stupid as a goose. I don't*
think he'll be able to keep on looking after Monsieur. He lets him
drink, he doesn't at all know how to handle him. Furthermore, I didn't
dare tell Madame by word of mouth that he wasn't decent to me, and
that's why I don't want to spend the night here any more. They went to
2   *the Brasserie de la Souris in the rue Bréda. Monsieur told the proprietress*
of this dirty dive to send for wine, I don't know how many bottles.
Two of them came with baskets, a man and a woman. I didn't want to
give them anything. She sent back a little boy with a letter that he wanted
to deliver to me personally. I didn't want to let him in, but I was afraid
she might watch out for Monsieur and that he might learn about it.
That would leave me in a fine kettle of fish. I miss Andrieux very much.
He wouldn't have let Monsieur go into that place. . . .
. . . Monsieur ate well at lunch but that fool of a man didn't bring him
home until 1:30. I had given up waiting. It's agreed that they'll come
back at 7 o'clock for dinner. They've left by carriage. . . .

Berthe

1. A guardian hired by Lautrec's mother to replace Andrieux. Ill. 53 shows that she
   must have fired the former as a result of this letter and hired a M. Briens, on
   February 15, instead.
2. Now the rue Henri Monnier. Lautrec had done a lithographic portrait of the
   proprietress, Mme Palmyre, in 1897 (Delteil 210).

7 rue du Manège
Albi, Tarn

Paris, April 13, [1899]

1   *Madame la Comtesse,*

I've just seen Monsieur Henri. He is still the same, if anything better, above all very calm. He received me nicely and was glad to see me. I had got a letter from Monsieur by post this morning. I am attaching it to my letter so that Madame may see it. I brought some coffee, the chocolate
2   *drops and the handkerchiefs. Pierre complains there still aren't enough of them, that Monsieur dirties a lot of them. I didn't bring the rum, as Madame can well imagine, but I told Monsieur that I had brought some but that the doorkeeper took it away from me when I came in. Whereupon he told me to take the bottle back on the way out because the doorkeeper would drink it, to his health. Monsieur was to have gone out yesterday for a walk but, I don't know why, they wanted to have the keeper go along with him, whereupon Monsieur flew into a rage and didn't want to go out. He wanted Pierre to go along with him. Monsieur told me that Madame was going to return soon, that he had got word that his grandmother was feeling better. . . .*

Berthe Sarrazin

7 rue du Manège
Albi, Tarn

Paris, April 17, [1899]

Madame la Comtesse,

I went to see Monsieur Henri this morning, since I received no letter from Madame. There are three letters that Monsieur Henri had sent me,

1. See Letter 226 and Ills. 54, 55.
2. One of the guardians at the asylum in Neuilly.

one by M. Joyant, another by M. Dihau and another by mail. He finds
that time hangs heavy. I have brought him what he asked for, namely,
lavender water, chocolate, coffee, biscuits, powdered cinnamon, lime juice,
the six handkerchiefs that were left and 4 prs. of socks. I found Monsieur
very well. He seemed to me to be very much more rational than before.
He spoke very well to me of Madame and his grandmother. He was
very much concerned to know that she was worse. He quickly wrote the
telegram that I sent yesterday. . . .

I went to Mlle Dihau's to give her the news, as Madame told me to.

Berthe S.

272 TO MADAME LA COMTESSE DE TOULOUSE-LAUTREC

7 rue du Manège
Albi, Tarn

[April 20, 1899]

Madame la Comtesse,

(. . .) I'm glad that Madame Tapié continues to improve and that
Madame is coming back on Monday. I have just seen Monsieur Henri.
I took him a little pot of orange jam from the grocery and different
things that I went to get from his studio. Monsieur continues to get
better and better. He is to go out this afternoon with Monsieur de
Rivières, who is taking him to visit a property that his father-in-law has
left him. Pierre told me that Monsieur no longer speaks ill of Madame
as he did at the beginning, which shows that he is becoming completely
rational. . . . He also told me that he had asked Madame de Vismes
and M. Joyant write to Madame. Léon took Pamela to Monsieur
Henri. He thought she was very pretty. She recognized him right away
and couldn't make enough fuss over him. . . .

Berthe Sarrazin

APPENDIX III

Paris, March 18, 1896

1   *Mr. Arnould,*

Monsieur de Toulouse-Lautrec asks me to tell you that he authorizes you to reproduce all the posters of your choice, on the condition that you show him the proofs before printing them.

Cordially,

Edw. Ancourt

Approved: T-Lautrec

1. A dealer in prints and posters. In his catalogue of June 1896, Lautrec was represented by three posters; *May Belfort* (Delteil 354), *La Revue Blanche* (Delteil 355), and *Troupe de Mlle Eglantine* (Delteil 361). In an unpublished letter to Arnould, dated May 22, 1896 (private collection), Lautrec asks him to 'make the hair of Eglantine a little greyer.'

*Transcriptions of
the Original Letters*

1 TO MME L. TAPIÉ DE CÉLEYRAN
Château de Céleyran, le 28 Avril [18]71

Ma chère Marraine,

Je vous embrasse de tout mon cœur, et dites-moi si Mlle Julie va bien, si Annou, Justine et Antoine vont bien. Je vous embrasse encore une fois, et c'est fini.

henri

2 TO MME L. TAPIÉ DE CÉLEYRAN
[December 1871]

Ma chère Marraine,

Je suis bien content de vous écrire pour le jour de l'An. Je vous souhaite une bonne année; je la souhaite aussi à toutes mes connaissances, oncles, tantes, cousins, cousines, etc. . . . Dites à Madeleine qu'il me tarde bien de la revoir. J'embrasse tout le monde, et Marraine principalement.
Votre petit-fils
Henry de Lautrec

3 TO MME R. C. DE TOULOUSE-LAUTREC
Paris, 30 Décembre 1872

Ma chère bonne maman,

Je vous envoie cette lettre avec grand plaisir, car c'est pour vous souhaiter une bonne et heureuse année. Il me tarde de revenir au Bosc au temps des vacances, quoique je ne m'ennuie pas à Paris. Nous sommes en vacances ces jours-ci, et je tâche d'en profiter de mon mieux; malheureusement j'ai des boutons qui me font perdre beaucoup de temps à les gratter. Je vous prie de dire à tante Emilie que mon petit serin Lolo chante très bien, il est fort aimable. Je lui ai acheté une très jolie cage sur mes étrennes.

Adieu, ma chère bonne maman, je vous embrasse de tout mon cœur ainsi que tante Emilie, mon oncle Charles et mon oncle Odon, et je vous prie tous de recevoir mes vœux de bonne année.
Votre respectueux petit-fils
Henry

4 TO MME R. C. DE TOULOUSE-LAUTREC
[Paris, c. Dec. 1872]

Ma chère bonne maman,

Je viens vous offrir mes vœux de bonne année un peu en avance, parce que j'ai une chose à vous demander. Papa désire que je lui traduise un chapitre d'un gros livre rouge anglais, facile à reconnaître à son épaisseur et à ses images de sport. Il ressemble à un dictionnaire de Bouillet. Soyez assez bonne pour me l'expédier tout de suite. Maman croit qu'il est dans son armoire à linge; mais il est peut-être dans son bureau ou dans l'armoire au pied de mon lit. Papa me demande cette traduction pour *ses étrennes*, et vous comprenez mon désir de la satisfaire. Nous l'avons attendu en vain pour Noël, mais il

viendra pour le premier de l'an. Je suis très content de travailler chez Mr. Mantoy avec Louis Pascal. Paul est devenu un homme, et Joseph un grand jeune homme. Je m'amuse beaucoup à Paris, et cependant j'aspire à revenir au Bosc. Adieu, me chère bonne maman, je vous embrasse de tout mon cœur en vous souhaitant une bonne et heureuse année.

Maman me charge de vous offrir ses tendresses. Je soupçonne mes oiseaux de me charger de quelque chose pour vous, car ils chantent de leur mieux.

Votre respectueux
petit-fils
Henry de T. Lautrec

P.S. Ayez la bonté de souhaiter le nouvel an de ma part à Urbain et aux autres domestiques.

5 TO MME L. TAPIÉ DE CÉLEYRAN
Paris, 19 Janvier 1873

Ma chère Marraine,

Je vous remercie de vos bonnes étrennes, et ce n'est pas trop tôt. Oh! que j'ai été content quand maman a ouvert la lettre, et qu'elle m'a donné . . . 50 f.! Jamais je n'ai reçu tant d'argent à la fois! Mille et mille fois merci, merci et encore merci. Je suis aussi heureux que Cendrillon qui avait une marraine très généreuse. Nous avons été voir cette belle histoire, jouée par des poupées, au théâtre Miniature. J'ai maintenant une aimable cousine à l'hôtel Pérey: c'est Jeanne d'Armagnac. Elle a 15 ans, mais elle s'amuse avec moi. Adieu ma chère petite marraine: faites un baiser pour moi à Bébé ainsi qu'à Doudou, Bibel et Poulette. Vous pensez bien que ma plus grosse caresse est pour vous, et que je n'oublie pas ma tante et mon oncle. Je vous chargerais bien d'embrasser M^{r.} l'abbé, mais vous ne le feriez pas.
Votre respecteux p.^{tit} fils,
Henry

6 TO HIS MOTHER
[Château du Bosc, c. 1873-74]

Ma chère Maman,

Votre bonne lettre a fait plaisir à tout le monde. Je me promène toujours de même et ce matin j'ai suivi Papa à la chasse [avec] Grésigue qui s'était juchée au haut d'un arbre, et ne voulait pas en descendre. Tante Alix me charge de vous dire que Laroque vous attendra pour sûr au train de 8 heures Mercredi matin. Vous lui feriez beaucoup de plaisir d'aller pour la voir un peu Mardi soir. La pauvre Doudou est morte cette nuit. Béatrix a perdu un peu de guincharderie. Je me suis amusé à construire un piège à hippopotame, et j'en fabriquerai un pour prendre la souris. Jeudi j'ai été jusqu'au fond du ruisseau du Vergnasse (je crois que c'est ce nom).

Adieu, ma chère Maman, je vous embrasse de tout cœur, et je vous prie d'en faire autant de ma part à Tante Joséphine.

Votre fils qui désire vous voir bientôt.

Henri de Toulouse Lautrec

P.S. Apportez moi s.v.p. quatre punaises acier de rechange.

7 TO MME L. TAPIÉ DE CÉLEYRAN
Céleyran, 23 Août 1873

Ma chère Marraine

Je vous écris pour vous souhaiter une bonne fête, puisque c'est Lundi la St. Louis. Comme je suis le seul des petits enfants de la maison qui sache écrire, je le fais au nom de tous. Nous partons lundi pour le Bosc et j'espère que vous viendrez bientôt nous y retrouver. Au moment où j'écris (9 hs) Gabriel est méchant, tante Alix le menace de le mettre à la prison des grenouilles. Hier nous avons vu M. Vié qui a trouvé tous les malades guéris. Tante Marie Delmas est venue jeudi et Bébé Lamothe et nous avons joué à cache-cache. Hier nous avons été sur le sommet du Pech, et nous avons vu François et Augustin Renaud; ce dernier a eu peur de nous. L'orage a été très-tapageur cette nuit, mais Annou et Madeleine ne l'ont point entendu. Le tonnerre a éclaté près de la maison de Marie Bouisson, mais personne n'a eu de mal. Adieu, chère marraine, maman vous souhaite une bonne fête ainsi que tante Alix, qui n'a pas eu le temps de vous écrire, tant elle était occupée. Adieu, je vous embrasse mille et mille fois.

Votre filleul respectueux
Henry

P.S. Bonjour à Miss Rosette.

8 TO MADELEINE TAPIÉ DE CÉLEYRAN
[Paris, Jan. 1874]

Ma chère Madeleine

Je m'empresse de répondre à ta lettre si bien écrite. Tu m'as fait rentrer en moi-même, et je suis honteux d'écrire comme un chat. Il me tarde bien de faire de bonnes parties avec vous tous dans la Gravasse ou dans la grande allée de Céleyran. Te souviens-tu de Mme de Béon, chez laquelle je me suis pelé le nez à Arcachon? tante m'a fait cadeau de deux jolis petits serins qui font très bon ménage avec les autres. Pendant mes vacances, j'ai été au cirque Américain, où j'ai vu huit éléphants qui marchaient sur la tête. Il y avait une cage pleine de lions qui auraient fait bien peur à Raoul. J'aurais un grand plaisir à me promener avec toi sur les boulevards, où il y a tant de poupées que tu ne saurais laquelle choisir. Je te prie de remercier pour moi marraine et tante Alix de leurs bonnes lettres.

Adieu, ma chère cousine, je te souhaite une bonne année, en t'embrassant de tout mon cœur, et te charge d'en faire autant de ma part à tout le monde.

Ton cousin qui t'aime bien,
Henri de T. Lautrec

9 TO MADELEINE TAPIÉ DE CÉLEYRAN
Paris, 29 Mars, 1874

Ma chère Madeleine,

On m'a dit que tu désirerais recevoir une de mes lettres. Je ne demande pas mieux que de t'écrire, à condition que tu me répondes. Je pense que tu aurais beaucoup de plaisir à voir toutes les poupées habillées en bleu, blanc, rose, etc. . . . Je t'en choisirais volontiers une, mais elles sont trop chères pour ma bourse. Raoul aimerait mieux voir rouler les innombrables omnibus et voitures. Gabriel préfèrerait les boutiques de sucres d'orges de toutes les couleurs et les Guignols; je pense que Rémi serait du même avis; quant à Emmanuel nous connaîtrons plus tard son opinion. J'ai un maître de Français qui souffle comme un *cachalot*, et un maître d'Anglais qui prend du *tabac* et qui nous donne des devoirs où il y a des histoires de *coton* et de *chardon*; malgré cela je les aime beaucoup tous les deux. Je te dirai que Tante Pérey a laissé manger son petit oiseau par sa chatte. Elle a commencé par gronder sa *Moumoune*, mais bientôt a eu lieu une réconciliation. *Lolotte* s'est apprivoisée et se tient facilement sur le doigt; dès qu'elle est hors de la cage, *Lolot* chante comme un fou pour l'appeler, et quand Lolotte revient, il la reçoit à grands coups de bec. Adine a eu neuf petits qui sont réduits à deux, et les autres ont été prendre un bain dans la Seine, d'où ils ne reviendront jamais. Adieu, ma chère Madeleine; sois mon interprète auprès de bonne maman Louise, de ton papa, de ta maman, de Mlle Albanie, de tante Armandine, d'Odon, et d'Emmanuel qui ne te comprendra guère. Je t'embrasse mille et mille fois.

Ton cher cousin
H de T Lautrec

10 TO MME L. TAPIÉ DE CÉLEYRAN
Paris, 31 Décbre 1874

Ma chère Marraine

Je prends une caille pour messagère de mes souhaits de bonne année. Je la charge de vous dire que votre filleul vous aime toujours beaucoup, et espère passer avec vous une bonne partie de l'année qui va commencer. Raoul est bien heureux de ne vous jamais quitter.

Brik a été hier soir au Vaudeville avec papa; ses impressions de théâtre nous amusent beaucoup, mais seraient trop longues à vous raconter, il vous les dira lui-même. Je suis en vacances pour quelques jours, ce qui ne me fait pas de peine. J'ai acheté un joujou très amusant, nommé Cirque Américain. Il y a ici un petit Polonais qui a une chambre toute pleine de joujoux. Adieu, ma chère marraine, je vous prie d'offrir mes vœux de bonne année à mon oncle et à ma tante sans oublier M. l'abbé et Mlle Albanie. J'embrasse tous mes cousins à la file, en commençant par la dernière et finissant par la première. Souhaitez la bonne année de ma part à Annou et à Rosette. Je vous embrasse de tout mon cœur, ma chère marraine, en vous priant d'agréer les meilleurs vœux de

Votre filleul
H de T Lautrec

[Neuilly, 1875]

The original of this letter was written in English.

12 TO MME L. TAPIÉ DE CÉLEYRAN
[Paris], 2 Novembre 1875

Ma chère Marraine

Il n'y a pas très longtemps que je vous ai écrit, mais je vous dois des remerciments pour les bonnes étrennes que vous avez chargé maman de m'apporter. Je saurai très bien en profiter selon vos intentions, c'est-à-dire en m'en amusant le plus possible. Jeudi je vais être examiné, et j'espère être admis au Catéchisme de première Communion, Le directeur s'appelle Mr. l'abbé Paradis: il m'a promis de me placer au premier rang. Je ferai mon possible pour me bien préparer à ma première communion, et j'espère que vous viendrez y assister. Adieu, ma chère marraine, je vous viendrez y assister. Adieu, ma chère marraine, je vous embrasse de tout mon cœur et vous prie d'offrir mes tendresses respectueuses à ma tante Joséphine; offrez aussi mes souvenirs à tous mes parents d'Albi.
Votre affectionné filleul
Henry de T Lautrec

13 TO MME R. C. DE TOULOUSE-LAUTREC
[Paris, Jan. 1876]

Ma chère bonne maman

Je regrette bien de ne pouvoir vous offrir de vive voix mes vœux de bonne année. Je n'ai pas été aussi heureux que mes cousins qui ont passé leurs vacances au Bosc. J'ignore même quand je pourrai vous revoir: je souhaite que ce soit le plus tôt possible. Je me suis bien amusé aux vacances de Noël, et j'espère en faire autant à celles du jour de l'an. J'ai été voir avec maman le grand tableau de M. Princeteau qui represente Washington à cheval. Il va l'envoyer en Amérique pour la grande exposition. J'ai acheté à Noël un beau livre dessiné par *Crafty* sur le Jardin d'Acclimatation. Le fauconnier, que papa admire tant, est en ce moment en Irlande. Je m'en console avec mon ami Toby.

Adieu, ma chère bonne maman, je ne suis pas très-éloquent, mais je vous aime bien et vous embrasse de tout mon cœur, en vous souhaitant une bonne et heureuse année.
Votre respectueux
petit fils
Henry de T-Lautrec

14 TO MME L. TAPIÉ DE CÉLEYRAN
[Paris, Dec. 1876]

Ma chère marraine,

Je voudrais bien être à Céleyran pour vous souhaiter la bonne année avec tous les cousins. Je sais bien mieux m'exprimer à coups de langue qu'à coups de plume. Il faut donc me contenter de vous souhaiter une heureuse année et une bonne santé. Je n'ajoute pas, comme dans les

contes, une nombreuse postérité, car vous l'avez déjà, et j'ai l'honneur d'en être le no 1. J'aiguise déjà mes dents dans l'attente du chocolat et des *crottins*. Je vous remercie de penser à ma gourmandise. Je vous prie de dire à M. l'Abbé que, grâce à lui, mon professeur est très content de mes verbes Grecs. Louis Pascal est grand et gros, et votre filleul est un bel homme à belles moustaches. Joseph est un grand jeune homme qui méprise le collège puisqu'il se prépare à son bachot. Par malheur Louis est en retard d'une classe sur moi.

Adieu, ma chère Marraine. je vous offre un gros paquet de souhaits de bonne année, en vous priant d'en distribuer une part à tout le monde, en réservant la plus grosse part pour vous. Je vous embrasse de tout mon cœur.
Votre filleul qui vous aime bien.
Henry de T L

P.S. Mes oiseaux vous souhaitent une bonne année par leurs chants. Embrassez bien ma filleule pour moi, en attendant qu'elle puisse s'acquitter de ses devoirs envers son parrain. M. Willie Matheson m'a envoyé pour elle cette jolie image.
Le chocolat arrive. Merci!

15 TO MME R. C. DE TOULOUSE-LAUTREC
Paris, 1er Mars 77

Ma chère bonne-maman,

Depuis longtemps j'aurais dû vous remercier de m'avoir envoyé le livre de Stonehenge; mais je n'ai pas beaucoup de temps pour ma correspondance. Je suis plus libre ces jours-ci parce que Maman m'a retiré de chez mon professeur, pour me faire suivre le traitement de la brosse électrique qui a jadis guéri mon oncle Charles. Je suis bien ennuyé d'être boiteux du pied gauche maintenant que le droit est guéri. Il faut espérer que ce n'est qu'une réaction après mon traitement comme dit le docteur Raymond; je me trouve déjà mieux. Nous irons certainement aux eaux des Pyrénées cette année-ci, n'y viendrez-vous pas avec nous? . . . Mon oncle Charles nous a quitté avant hier et je le regrette beaucoup. Papa est encore ici. Le jour où mon oncle Charles est parti, maman et moi avons été dîner chez mon oncle de Rivières. Il y avait mon oncle de Castellane et sa femme et Monsieur et Madame de Bonne. Hélène est très-gentille et Monsieur de Bonne lui a conseillé d'épouser un *chien coiffé* plutôt que de rester vieille fille. Mon oncle Odon et sa maisonnée ont un beau soleil depuis qu'ils ont déménagé. Raymond commence à parler l'Anglais et Odette à le comprendre. Raymond chante plusieurs chansons et m'aime toujours beaucoup. Odette est devenue plus aimable, mais s'obstine à ne pas vouloir parler tout en comprenant deux langues.

Adieu ma chère bonne maman, je vous embrasse de tout mon cœur ainsi que tante Joséphine. Ne m'oubliez pas auprès de la famille et surtout de mon oncle l'abbé. Maman veut que je vous offre ses souvenirs et ceux de Papa.
Votre respectueux petit-fils.
Henry de T. Lautrec.

Ma chère bonne-maman,

Je viens causer un peu avec vous aujourd'hui. Je pense beaucoup à Adèle qui devient *Madame*, et je vous avoue que cela me parait très extraordinaire. C'est très drôle, n'est ce pas, d'avoir un nouveau cousin qui ne l'était pas à 8 heures, et qui l'est à midi. Que ne suis-je à coté de mon oncle Charles pour l'empêcher d'avoir une indigestion de truffes!!!!!! Je vais beaucoup mieux depuis quatre jours, et je puis circuler dans la maison. Mais je n'ai pas encore repris mes habitudes de sortie, et maman n'a encore rien décidé. Papa attend M. Ramier, et n'est pas encore venu, ce qui a désappointé M. de Chantérac, qui était descendu à l'hotel Pérey pour le voir. Il va partir pour Orléans parce que sa grand'mère est malade. Mon oncle Odon pose à cheval chez M. Princeteau. Ma tante O. va très bien. Raymond ne tousse presque plus; Odette est maintenant la plus souffrante mais c'est sans gravité. J'ai fondé avec Louis Pascal un théâtre comprenant 60 acteurs. Cela nous amuse beaucoup. Ma serine de Béon couve 3 œufs qui nous promettent une augmentation de famille.

Adieu, ma chère bonne maman, Je vous embrasse de tout mon cœur, en vous priant d'être mon interprète auprès de tante Joséphine, de mon oncle et de ma tante. Je vous prie d'offrir mes félicitations à Adèle quand elle sera moins occupée; ne m'oubliez pas auprès de mon oncle l'abbé.

Votre respectueux petit fils,
Henry de TL

Ma chère Madeleine,

Je te remercie de ta lettre et du portrait de notre filleule. J'en suis très fier, surtout de ses yeux, car le reste laisse à désirer; elle allonge les doigts comme une *mouinette*, cependant je veux qu'elle les ait longs pour bien jouer du piano, et me charmer dans mes vieux jours. Les autres sont très ressemblants et j'ai grand'plaisir à les revoir; mais je voudrais t'avoir ainsi que Raoul. Dis à Raoul que son amie Bébelle couve trois œufs; j'espère avoir des *cagonits*. J'espère aller vous rejoindre et faire de bonnes parties. Je vais mieux, mais je ne suis pas encore bien leste. Je m'amuse avec Louis Pascal à jouer la comédie. Nous avons 60 poupées d'environ 10 centimètres. Elles sont emmanchées au bout d'un fil de fer. Fais-moi savoir ce que sont devenues mes chrysalides. Dis à M. l'abbé que ma Grammaire Grecque se repose et qu'à la grande joie de tous les écoliers on a aboli les *Racines Grecques*. Je te prie de lui offrir mes respectueux souvenirs: j'espère bientôt lui servir la Messe.

Adieu ma chère Delon, je t'embrasse sur les deux joues, ainsi que tous tes frères et sœurs et surtout ma filleule: Embrasse aussi de ma part

bonne-maman ton papa et ta maman, ne m'oublie pas auprès de Mlle Albanie et de tous.

Ton cousin,
H. de T. Lautrec

P.S. Raymond a été content de revoir son ami Toto.

Ma chère Madeleine,

Je ne sais pas si Raoul a reçu ma lettre dans laquelle je lui demandais de s'informer chez Augé, par ton intermédiaire, de l'adresse d'où il a fait venir le traîneau et le Brougham. Réponds moi dès que tu la sauras. Je ne m'ennuie pas énormément, et je t'embrasse

Henry
(c'est ma première lettre)

Mme la Supérieure

Emery va mieux. Nous avons acheté un âne et fabriqué une voiture comme le break des chiens. Dites au Moujik que ses filles se promèneront dans la voiture à âne dont voici le portrait.

Dites à Monsieur. Tapié de m'écrire ou écrivez-moi

Votre dévoué
Philéas Fogg

Ma chère Marraine,

Je vous remercie de vos souhaits unanimes, par rapport à la fête de mon grand patron, le grand saint Henri (qui par parenthèse est aussi la mienne). Mais, si vous vouliez faire déborder la coupe de joie, dont mon imagination surexcitée est remplie jusqu'aux oreilles en voyant que je n'ai pas baissé d'une ligne dans votre estime affectionnée, vous feriez parvenir jusqu'à M. l'abbé Peyre par le canal de votre parole la demande soupesée, de vouloir bien intimer à mon cousin osseux l'ordre rigide de vouloir avoir la complaisance de m'expédier par la poste une petite épitre dans laquelle il me donnerait des nouvelles du personnel de Céleyran et des véhicules enfantins qu'Augé, marchand Narbonnais, a reçu l'ordre de me faire venir de la Capitale de France. Maintenant, j'ai l'honneur de vous informer, qu'en personne et en chair et en os, je me suis rendu en char trainé par des chevaux fougueux à l'église métropolitaine de la ville albigeoise, afin d'y consommer l'audition de l'office divin. Pour lors, vous ayant donné cette nouvelle patibulaire, vu qu'elle traite de l'amélioration de mon système jambaire, je vous informerai de la constipation relative qu'a subi mon individu par la manducation acharnée d'une certaine pâte confectionnée avec le fruit du coignassier. N'ayant plus rien à vous relater, je prendrai la liberté de déposer un tendre baiser sur votre joue droite, tout en vous priant d'en faire autant de ma part à tout le monde.

Votre filleul béquillard,
Henry de Toulouse

20 TO MME L. TAPIÉ DE CÉLEYRAN

[*c.* August 20, 1878]

Ma chère Marraine,

Je regrette bien de ne pouvoir vous souhaiter de vive voix une bonne fête comme je l'ai fait les deux années précédentes. Mais, quoique le personnage qui a eu la malencontreuse idée de se casser la jambe ne puisse être auprès de vous pour formuler ses souhaits de sa vilaine grosse voix (pas assez grosse tout de même pour qu'il puisse vous souhaiter la fête de manière à ce que vous l'entendiez à Lamalou), son cœur sera auprès de vous le jour de la saint Louis. Bonne fête! bonne fête! . . .

Je vous embrasse quatre vingt douze fois
votre filleul
Henri TL

21 TO BEATRIX TAPIÉ DE CÉLEYRAN

[Barèges, 1878]

Ma chère petite bête qui prend des lapins,

Vous êtes une fille très-sensée, et jamais vous ne faites rien sans chercher préalablement le pourquoi. Si vous étiez née du temps de Solon, vous auriez certainement été nommée dans l'aréopage; vous auriez été fort drôle avec un bonnet pointu et de gros bouquins; puisque vous êtes sage, je vous ferai un *Kado*, je vous le donnerai au Bosc. D'abord, le plus précieux de l'histoire sera . . . ma bénédiction parrainale, ensuite une collection de *poutous*, et puis quelque chose de jaune enfermé dans du papier . . . , cherchez à deviner. Il n'y a qu'une chose que je blâme en vous, c'est votre choix de maître d'orthographe, car c'est un être qui a très peu de cervelle; pour vous en convaincre, passez votre lapinerde griffe sur la tête de votre illustre frère, et vous sentirez un abîme; il est si profond que vous aurez peur de tomber au fond; maintenant vous me demanderez quel rapport il y a entre cet abîme et la cervelle de votre maître orthographique, voici la raison; la cervelle est une tripe qui fait l'intelligence, elle est dans la tête; à la place du gouffre qui vous fait peur devrait être cette cervelle, et voila pourquoi il n'est pas intelligent ce cher magister!!! . . . Nous montons à âne, et, si vous voulez nous imiter, montez sur votre maître d'orthographe; n'ayez pas peur s'il fait des pétarades, les ânes en font très souvent; pour le corriger de ce vice, prenez l'air indomptable, et bouchez vous le nez. C'est là le *hic*.

Il y a ici un roi Prussien, et je suis sûr que si vous étiez à Barèges vous lui tordriez prestement le cou, quoique ce ne soit pas un lapin. Adieu, ma chère petite chérie, soyez mon interprète auprès de bonne maman, mon oncle, vos frères, M. l'abbé, Tante Armandine, Mademoiselle Rose et tout le monde, ainsi que mes canaris.

Je vous embrasse sur les deux joues et votre minois (pas l'autre) votre parrain.
Henry de T.L.

22 TO MADELEINE TAPIÉ DE CÉLEYRAN

Pension Internationale, Nice
(Alpes Maritimes)   [Jan.–Feb. 1879]

Ma chère Déloux,

Après un excellent voyage en compagnie d'un évêque, nous sommes installés dans la Pension Internationale. C'est un joli hotel, entouré d'un jardin assez grand qui est planté de palmiers et d'aloës. En chemin de fer, nous avons vu Cannes et la mer. C'etait excessivement joli. J'ai pensé à la villa des Cactus, à la Perle etc., et, en arrivant à Nice, j'ai vu un petit garçon qui ressemblait trait pour trait à David Louzéma, sauf le costume. Nous allons nous promener sur la Promenade des Anglais, qui est magnifique. On côtoie la mer, et on voit de tartanes, cutters, etc. etc. Le port est magnifique en comparaison de tous ceux que j'avais vus jusqu'ici. Il y a une assez grande quantité de vaisseaux marchands et un yacht anglais qui est un véritable bijou. On loue des bateaux pour promenade, mais Maman n'ose pas y monter. Monsieur Lévi et sa sœur nous ont reçus à bras ouverts, mais nous n'avons pas pu encore voir Mme Peragallo. Monsieur Lévi va deux fois par semaine jouer à Monaco. Il y a ici une petite fille Russe qui a neuf ans, et qui parle le français et l'allemand. On mange assez bien, mais le dîner est trop long, quoique *il y ait* cinq domestiques en habit à queue de morue pour le servir. Il y en a un qui est très drôle, et qui saute toujours. On va donner un bal ici la semaine prochaine. Nous mangeons d'excellentes mandarines, mais les oranges de Nice sont aussi mauvaises que celles qui me servaient à faire le Petit Bébé.

Adieu, mon idéale cousine, je te respecte, et je t'admire, en te priant d'être mon interprète auprès de bonne maman, Tata, ta maman, ton papa, oncle Odon, tante Odette, Mademoiselle Maurin, Odon, Toto, Bibou, Kiki (embrasse la cinquante trois fois), la petite Ermaine, Raymond et Odette. Je te renouvelle l'assurance de ma plus parfaite admiration.

ton cousin gracieux,
Henry de Toulouse Lautrec

P.S. Fais mes compliments à tous les domestiques.

23 TO MME L. TAPIÉ DE CÉLEYRAN

[Nice, Jan.–Feb. 1879]

Ma chère Marraine,

Je viens vous prier de dire à bonne maman Gabrielle de me réserver tous les timbres d'Egypte que mon oncle Odon pourra lui envoyer. J'ai un excellent professeur de vingt ans, qui a un bateau, et qui chasse les mouettes. Il courra aux régates. Nous regrettons bien qu'oncle Amédée ne soit pas venu. Nous sommes allés à Monte Carlo. M. Lévi a joué pour moi, et a doublé mon argent. Je remercie Madeleine de sa lettre. Pouvez vous m'envoyer d'autres timbres de Napoléon ayant servi.

votre petit fils qui vous aime beaucoup.
HTL

24 TO MME R. C. DE TOULOUSE-LAUTREC
Nice, Pension Internationale   [Jan.–Feb. 1879]

Ma chère bonne maman,

Je viens vous demander, sachant qu'oncle Odon vous a écrit avec des timbres français, de vouloir bien le prier dans votre prochaine lettre de m'acheter pour cinq ou six francs la collection égyptienne, et de vous l'envoyer; je voudrais que vous lui demandiez aussi de tâcher d'avoir par M. de Blignières quelques timbres turcs et du canal de Suez.

J'espère que vous nous donnerez bientôt de meilleures nouvelles du gros Raymond qui ne sont pas aussi bonnes malheureusement que celle de la famille de Béon y compris Lolo. Je vous prie encore de vouloir bien demander à tante Joséphine de m'envoyer quelques vieux timbres de Napoléon (tous sont bons), car il y a ici des amateurs pour ces timbres là.

Adieu, ma chère bonne maman. Je vous prie d'offrir mes respectueux baisers à tante Joséphine, et d'embrasser pour moi oncle Charles, tante Emilie, Raymond et Dédette.

votre petit-fils (collectionneur) qui vous aime bien

HTL

25 TO MME L. TAPIÉ DE CÉLEYRAN
[Barèges, Aug–Sept 1879]

Ma chère Marraine,

Je suis sûr de vous faire plaisir en vous disant que je vais aussi bien que possible, et que je ne souffre pas. Je ne m'ennuie pas trop non plus, et j'espère que vous ne vous tracassez pas trop à mon sujet, car j'en suis indigne par ma maladresse. Je pense que, dans le pays, on appellera Miss Fides ma très honorable *cuisine* Fidèle ou Fidèlou, et qu'à la maison on lui donnera le nom de Fifi. Excusez moi de cette philonomie, mais je n'ai pas beaucoup de sujets pour faire travailler mon cerveau. Le docteur est enchanté de la perspective d'une cure. Les Andocques viennent d'arriver, et vont très bien, ils restent l'après midi.

Adieu, ma chère Marraine, je vous embrasse tant que je le puis, et je vous prie d'être mon interprète auprès de tous.

Nous venons de recevoir la lettre de monsieur l'abbé, et attendons bonne maman et papa.

Je vous prie d'être mon interprète auprès de Tata, oncle Amédée, tante Alix, les cousines, les cousins, les Soréziens, Kiki et Gordon. Mes regrets à M. l'abbé et Mlle Maurin.

Votre filleul maladroit.

Henri de Toulouse

26 TO RAOUL TAPIÉ DE CÉLEYRAN
Céleyran X^{bre} [18]79

Mon cher Raoul,

Nous sommes arrivés avant hier, et ma prem-ière lettre est pour toi, je m'étais dit avec plaisir que nous recommencerions les agréables vacances du jour de l'an. Je tenais pour certains tous les efforts que tu m'avais promis de faire!!! Et voici que l'on m'a dit que vos notes étaient si peu satisfaisantes que si vous ne travailliez pas mieux pendant le temps qui vous reste, vous ne viendriez pas au Jour de l'an!!! Tu comprends ma peine, et je viens vous exhorter à faire votre possible pour que cette punition n'ait pas lieu et alors comme nous serions contents. Vous verriez les petits Gordon qui sont nés ce matin. Nous ferions des parties aussi amusantes que possible, nous jouerions au chemin de fer, nous aurions des signaux; est-ce que je sais Moi, tout ce que nous n'aurions pas!!! Tandis que si vous *acagnardissez*, si vous continuez à ne faire que de *la mauvaise ouvrage*, comme on dit, on vous laissera à l'école à vous ennuyer, et votre maman aura du chagrin, et moi donc!!! Et si vous prenez cette douce habitude, qu'arrivera t-il? Est-ce qu'on ira vous voir au Carnaval, à la sainte Cécile, à Pâques, et peut-être même aux grandes vacances!!! Je pense que tu n'en prendras pas ton parti comme cela quand tu auras vu qu'avec quelques tours de dictionnaire de plus tout marcherait à merveille, comme le désire ton cousin.

Henri

Votre Maman me charge de vous dire qu'elle vous remercie de votre lettre.

Elle vous écrira demain, et n'est pas très satisfaite de *vos notes.*

27 TO MME R. C. DE TOULOUSE-LAUTREC
[Céleyran, December 1879]

Ma chère bonne maman,

Toutes les lettres qui viennent annoncent la neige, la neige . . . !!!! Papa écrit ce matin même que depuis vingt jours il a la neige . . . !!! Ici au contraire la Veloutine Hivernale n'est venue que courtement blanchir les toits. Mon oncle Amédée a tué quatre bécasses dont une, blessée, lui a tenu tête avec bravoure. Il a fait beau temps pour la messe de minuit, et l'on a chanté des Noëls patois. Nous avons été obligés de nous passer de *Minuit Chrétien*, faute d'oncle Albert. Kiki est très capricieuse et volontaire au possible, les Soréziens sont attendus avec impatience pour Mardi. J'ai été très content d'apprendre que Zibeline avait bien chassé le lapin, je vous prie de lui faire mes félicitations et encouragements. J'écrirai ses exploits à Papa.

Adieu, ma chère bonne maman, recevez mes souhaits les plus sincères de bonne année pour vous, oncle Charles et tante Emilie que je vous prie d'embrasser pour moi.

Votre respectueux petit fils,
Henry de Toulouse Lautrec

P.S. Salutations, s'il vous plaît, à Lolo.

28 TO MME L. TAPIÉ DE CÉLEYRAN

[Céleyran, December 1879]

Ma chère Marraine,

Je suis en retard, et ceci qui est destiné à devancer le jour de l'an arrivera probablement après. J'écris mes petites nouvelles à Bonne maman Gabrielle qui vous les communiquera. Aussi je vous embrasse fort, ce qui n'est pas une redite, et vous prie de distribuer mes souhaits de bonne année à ma tante Alix, (*à qui j'ecrirai bientôt*) et à mon oncle, sans oublier M. l'Abbé, qui est avec vous je crois. Je vous remercie de vos bonnes étrennes, et vous embrasse encore, et Bonne Année!!!

  votre petit-fils et filleul,
  Henri

29 TO A DOG

Le Bosc [1880]

Chère Madame,

Comme votre jolie lettre d'hier me l'annonçait, les joies de la maternité se sont renouvelées pour vous. Vous voilà de nouveau à la tête d'une famille; de graves responsabilités se viennent abattre sur votre petite tête frisée. Que de soins ne vous faudra-t il pas prodiguer à ces petits êtres chauds et roses qui agitent mollement leurs petites pattes au fond de votre corbeille. Je sais bien que votre bonne maîtresse et Mélanie vous aideront dans cette tâche difficile, et qu'elles se tourmenteront au sujet de vos enfants, autant et plus que vous-même; je sais bien aussi que vous devez avoir une envie folle de manger ladite Mélanie quand elle veut vous toucher votre progéniture, et que les échos du petit salon doivent retentir de vos Gnaff Gnnaff. . . .

Je vous exhorte donc! primo à ne point manger toute entière la susdite Mélanie, et à en laisser au moins un petit morceau pour soigner votre bonne maîtresse; 2° a bien lécher vos enfants, de façon à ce que toutes les bonnes gens de Castelnau puissent venir lever les bras au ciel en disant au milieu de leurs larmes d'attendrissement '*Chès, semblo sa mairé*'.

Je termine en vous félicitant de tout mon cœur, et vous priant de lécher pour moi votre maîtresse.

Je vous serre la patte.

  Henri de Toulouse Lautrec

P.S. Ne m'oubliez pas auprès de Flavie, Mélanie et Benjamin.

30 TO MME R. C. DE TOULOUSE-LAUTREC

Nice, 13 Janvier 1880

Ma chère bonne maman,

Je m'y prends non pas un peu, ni beaucoup, mais incommensurablement trop tard pour vous offrir mes souhaits de bonne année. J'espère racheter ma faute en vous servant des nouvelles toutes chaudes. Nous avons passé une charmante journée à Cannes, Samedi; la ville est très-jolie, et l'installation de mon oncle est superbe.. C'est une villa très-gentille au bord de la mer, dans le voisinage de la Villa des Dunes, séjour de l'impératrice. Mon oncle Odon monte à cheval, et il a loué un landau pour les après-midi, pour faire des courses dans la montagne. Nous y sommes allés avec eux, et sommes montés à un endroit d'où l'on voyait Nice et les côtes d'Italie, et puis une mer bleue . . . !!!! Les Bebés vont très bien et vont faire de grandes promenades avec Soué qui est enchantée. Raymond prend des leçons d'un abbé. Détail pour mon oncle Charles: mon oncle Odon a acheté toute une collection de tableaux, et, à ce qu'il paraît, on en trouve des masses. Quant à nous, nous n'allons pas trop mal. La pension n'est pas aussi gaie que l'an passé. Mais l'hiver est généralement plus beau, et nous nous promenons beaucoup. Nous n'avons pas découvert les Villefort.

Adieu ma chère bonne maman, je vous souhaite une tardive bonne année en vous remerciant encore une fois de vos étrennes. Maman se joint à moi pour vous embrasser, en vous priant de ne pas nous oublier autour de vous.

  Votre petit fils,
  Henri de Toulouse Lautrec

Nous avons rencontré la gloire d'Amélie-les-Bains. Ceci est pour Tante Emilie.

31 TO MME R. C. DE TOULOUSE-LAUTREC

Céleyran, 30 Déc. 80

Ma chère bonne maman,

Il est bien difficile de varier, surtout quand il s'agit de lettres de jour de l'an. Mais ces lettres fades valent encore, avec leurs compliments fades, bien mieux que les lettres trop intéressantes, comme celles que vous nous écriviez ces jours-ci. Nous tremblions, en voyant arriver le facteur, mais grâce à Dieu, celle de ce matin nous est venu bien à point pour faire renaître l'espoir. Pauvre tante!!! Comme nous pensions à elle!!! Il faut espérer que la nouvelle voie dans laquelle elle s'est engagée sera bien suivie, et que cet escalier de malheur n'existera plus, du moins pour elle. Ici tout va bien, sauf Suzanne, qui est un peu molle, et a un peu mal à l'estomac. Tante Armandine va partir dans une heure ou deux pour aller chercher Madelon. Pour moi, je boulotte, avec sainte palette et les chiens. Comment va l'oncle et son pied? Ceux d'ici sont à Carcassone et à Toulouse.

Adieu, ma chère Bonne maman; d'abord il fait nuit, et puis la place n'est pas trop grande pour vous dire combien je vous aime, et avec quelle véracité je vous souhaite une bonne et heureuse année, ainsi qu'a mon oncle et tante Emilie. Adieu donc pour cette fois. Bonne année. Bonne année.

  Votre petit fils qui vous aime énormement.
  Henri

P.S. Je vais écrire à ma tante Joséphine.

32 TO HIS GREAT-AUNT JOSÉPHINE
(MLLE DU BOSC)

Céleyran, Déc. 80

Toc Toc!!!—qui est là—C'est moi.—Ah c'est vous monsieur Henri—Comment va ma tante? Bien mieux—Puis-je la voir? Oui, mais ne la fatiguez pas trop, vous êtes si bavard: Sans écouter le reste, je bouscule Mélanie, et, salué par des aboiements en la mineur de Miss et de Follette, je vous saute au cou, en criant du fond du cœur Bonne année!!!

Voila ce que j'aurais fait si j'étais resté à Albi. Mais, malgré la distance, je ne puis vous embrasser reellement, l'émoi que j'en ai n'en est pas moins immense.

Mais il est inutile de parler davantage, car vous savez bien combien je vous aime, et tout le papier et toute l'encre du monde n'y ajouteraient rien. C'est pourquoi, ma bonne tante, recevez les vœux les plus sincères pour votre prompt rétablissement, comme pour votre bonheur de votre petit neveu respectueux.

Henri

P.S. Ne m'oubliez pas auprès de Flavie, Mélanie et Benjamin.

33 TO MME L. TAPIÉ DE CÉLEYRAN
Lamalou-les-Bains, [August 1881]

Ma chère Marraine

Je ne sais quelle orgue de barbarie détraquée, quel sermon maladroit ou quel nez choisi entre le mien et celui de Madeleine pourrait vous donner l'idée incomplète de la longueur et de la fadeur de notre voyage. Cependant toujours, comme sur les nez, il y a eu quelques petits incidents qui, semblables à des verrues colorées, sont venus trancher sur l'uniformité du reste. Un gros Monsieur, qui ressemblait à Gambetta, a plaisanté galamment avec Bibou et Kiki. Deux conducteurs ont roulé dans la poussière en voulant s'arracher les yeux, une énorme sœur a failli s'asseoir sur les genoux de Madeleine, et par cela déterminer une asphyxie complète, et maman a laissé sa valise en route. Heureusement on la lui a rendue. Enfin, nous tenons deux bains, trois verres et demi, et j'ai un œil qui ressemble à une tomate. Sur ce, ma chère Marraine, je vous embrasse bien fort, en vous priant d'agréer à mes vœux les plus sincères pour la St. Louis.

votre petit fils et Filleul
H de Toulouse Lautrec

34 TO MME L. TAPIÉ DE CÉLEYRAN
Lamalou, [August–Oct 1881]

Chère Marraine

Je viens causer un peu avec vous, car en ce qui regarde les nouvelles, il m'est totalement impossible de vous en donner; en effet, qu'y a-t-il d'intéressant ici, à moins que vous ne vouliez connaître la température de mon bain et le nombre de minutes de ma douche.

J'ai le bonheur d'avoir un baigneur qui s'appelle Jacqrou, il a une figure de bull-dog. L'autre jour, au sortir de la douche, il a voulu me frotter le dos avec un gant de crin 'qué lébario la pèl dé sus un azé'. J'en ai eu bientôt assez, probablement parce que je suis 'un azé'. Nous avons aussi l'incommensurable félicité de jouir de ce cher *docteur* Salagade, (Bedène) en plus du poisseux Bélugon. Il nous a amené Mme et M^{lla} de Beaufort et M. du Bernard ou Dubernard ou D'Ubernart, ou etc. etc. qui se porte fort bien. Son départ (celui du cher *Docteur*) a failli rater par un malaise de Tante Joséphine. Il n'est venu ici que par le *pétit estratagème* consistant à lui faire croire qu'il allait à la campagne cueillir la violette et le pissenlit. Miss Capus, semblable à un Sphinx, est près de sa fontaine: c'est certes dommage qu'elle ne sache pas dessiner, car elle aurait pu remplir un bel album de toutes les grimaces des buveurs. Nous avons aussi le cousin d'oncle (comme vous voudrez) Georges Foissac avec sa moitié. Nous les avons dénichés à la *Tentation*; la cousine Félicie a quadruplé depuis l'année dernière. Gloire à la cuisine de Castelnaudarrrysss!!! Monsieur Bourrrges est mélancolique, et est toujours en possession de sa moustache hérissée comme le derr . . . d'une poule malade. Nous avons à table une patissière de Narbonne de l'ancienne maison Hortala qui est à moitié toquée.

Elle part d'éclats de rires sans rime, ni raison, dans un desquels Madeleine prétend avoir entendu un petit . . . certain bruit. L'heure du bain approchant, je vous embrasse de toutes mes forces, ainsi que Tata. Je vous prie d'offrir toutes les célestineries de circonstance à Mlle Maurin, oncle Amédée, Oncle Albert, Monsieur le Vicaire et toute la marmaille.

Votre filleul poisseux et bien propre grâce à toute l'eau dépensée en son honneur
Henri

P.S. Nous avons aussi M. Vié. Mais quel Vié!! Un petit amour de Vié, si élégant, si joli que, si j'étais Mme Vié, je le mettrais sous clef de peur qu'on me le vole.

35 TO HIS MOTHER
Albi, mercredi [late Nov. 1881]

Ma chère Maman,

Peu de chose de neuf ici. Oncle Ernest s'obstine à rester muet. Télégraphiez-lui à la dernière heure pour lui arracher cette autorisation si désirée! . . . Ad. Montey nous a invités pour jeudi ou vendredi à déjeuner avec un prédicateur. Des gourmandises spirituelles et des autres. . . .

Quel luxe. Tante Joséphine me pistonne pour aller voir son docteur, il faudra s'y résigner. Saint Edme m'a écrit. Carissime tibi totus. Quel lapin!!!

Adieu, ma lettre est fade comme mes idées, qui sont absolument dégonflées après la tension examinatoire. Embrassez, poutounégez, et sucez tout le monde autour de vous pour moi et, *tâchez d'amener Louis à n'importe quel prix.*

Votre fils revenu des grandeurs de ce monde, et surtout de celles du baccalauréat
H.

36 TO MME TAPIÉ DE CÉLEYRAN
[Paris, Dec. 1881]

Ma chère Marraine,
J'ai reçu la lettre de maman tout à l'heure, et je m'empresse d'y répondre. Papa est venu avant hier, et a été satisfait de *mes jambes* aussi bien que de ma santé.
Jeudi nous avons eu un grand dîner, et j'ai fait les cartes. Enfin, ma chère marraine, j'ai fait une réflexion assez naïve, c'est que si je pouvais laisser mes jambes ici et m'en aller dans une enveloppe (rien que pour vous embrasser maman et vous), je le ferais.
Aujourd'hui, j'irai au Jardin d'Acclimatation avec Miss Braine. Je crois que le pauvre Brick n'ira pas à Paris de longtemps. Dites à maman que nous devons aller Jeudi à Rueil. Raoul, je pense, doit être un grand garçon, et Gabriel aussi. Quand vous la reverrez, dites bien bonjour à Mlle Ronron pour moi. Je me porte à merveille, et j'ai envie de me faire maigrir, mais je peux assure que je n'en ferai rien. Adieu, ma chère Marraine, je vous embrasse de tout mon cœur, ainsi que maman.
Votre respectueux filleul,
H. de T Lautrec

37 TO MME R. C. DE TOULOUSE-LAUTREC
Céleyran, 29 déc. 1881

Ma chère bonne maman,
On est dans le brouhaha du jour de l'An. Oncle Amédée part pour Bordeaux. Tante Alix prépare les chambres, enfin tout est en l'air. Le jour serait grand si la médaille n'avait pas son revers. Le pauvre Brick est mort cette nuit, et la pauvre vieille Anna est bien près d'en faire autant. Elle s'est entêtée à aller à la messe de Minuit, et a pris mal. [Un] Engorgement des poumons en est résulté, et on l'a déjà administrée. Décidemment, la race des bons serviteurs s'éteint. Oncle Jules est bien bas, toutes ses filles sont autour de lui, on ne conserve guère d'espoir. Béatrix continue les accès, bien fatiguants pour un objet si petit. Le reste de la famille grouille, et vivote bruyamment et braillardement—Avez vous quelques lettres Espagnoles?! Il faut espérer qu'elles seront moins mouvementées que les autres. Papa traîne la patte, et sort après oncle Amédée attelé à une bécane. Il gèle ici, mais le soleil est si chaud et *brillant* que nous n'en souffrons pas. Tant il est vrai qu'on souffre du froid bien plus par les yeux que par le dos. Mais j'oublie le vrai but de ma lettre, qui est de venir d'un ton ému et maladroit, la grâce n'étant pas mon partage, vous offrir mes vœux de bonne année. Je les offre donc à vous et votre entourage, les plus sincères possible, mais les miens seuls (car les autres personnes Céleyranesques écriront pour

leur compte), et je vous prie d'accepter les mille et une embrassades de votre petit fils respectueux
H. de Toulouse Lautrec

P.S. Je prie Oncle Charles de m'écrire en me disant ce que le *Figaro* a dit sur *Cabanel*.

38 TO HIS MOTHER
[Paris, Spring 1882]

Ma chère Maman,
Je n'ai vu guère Papa ces jours-ci, et j'attends mes cousins de pied ferme. Papa m'a enfin dit que le Bosc était à ma tante, et que nous étions dehors. Vous savez mon opinion là-dessus. inutile de resasser ce sujet.
Vous me demandez pour mes journaux. Je continue à en faire, sans enthousiasme exagéré d'ailleurs, mais tous paraîtront ensemble, et on fera le texte exprès. Heureux littérateur, heureux public et heureux moi, si, comme je l'espère, ça me rapporte. Paris continue à être tiède et humide, avec quelques rares rayons de soleil.—J'ai enfin rencontré Lewis Brown qui a été fort aimable pour moi.—Que vont devenir mes cousins, dites moi votre opinion là-dessus. J'ai bien peur qu'elle ne soit pas brillante.
Dites à Louis que le billet ci-inclus le renseigne absolument. Quant à la galette, c'est du maximum c.a.d. 500^f que j'ai besoin *immédiatement*. Bien entendu, vous les aurez le 1er Juillet.
Et maintenant allons déjeuner.
Yours
Henri

39 TO HIS FATHER
Lundi 17 [April, 1882]

Mon cher Papa.
J'ai été reçu ce matin par les élèves de l'atelier Bonnat. Grâce aux recommendations de Rachou, l'ami de Ferréol, j'ai été bien reçu. Par chance un jeune américain de l'hôtel est entré avec moi. On nous a fait parler et payer un punch. Voilà tout. Ce n'est pas bien terrible. On fait assez de tapage mais on ne se boxe pas trop. Il y a beaucoup d'Anglais et d'Américains.
Me voilà donc absolument lancé. Dessiner, dessiner, c'est la question. M. Moore, le peintre américain sourd-muet a porté ici beaucoup de splendides bibelots du Japon. Ce jeune homme est son ami. Il a établi son atelier dans une des grandes chambres de Pérey.
J'ai vu hier Du Passage qui m'a demandé de vos nouvelles. Il a dessiné hier dans la Vie *Moderne* les diverses poses de sautage du cheval.
Princeteau est toujours à l'hôtel; il est charmant pour moi et m'encourage. Maintenant au travail!!
Adieu, mon cher Papa. Veuillez distribuer autour de vous nos meilleurs et affectueux souvenirs.
Votre fils
H de Toulouse Lautrec

40 TO HIS MOTHER

[Paris, Spring 1882]

Ma chère Maman,

C'est moi qui vais vous malmener un peu pour votre silence. J'ai été sur le point de vous télégraphier pour savoir ce que vous devenez. Je déjeune demain avec mon père et Rachou. Il a rencontré M. Verrier qui voudrait m'avoir à déjeuner (Il peut se fouiller). J'ai écrit à Bonne maman Louise pour lui souhaiter une bonne fête. C'est bien par hasard que je me suis rappelé. J'ai été un peu *contrarié par le temps, pour travailler dehors*. Dimanche mon repas chez les Nabab a été tellement copieux que je me suis mis à ronfler après dîner. C'est du propre!! sur ce je vous embrasse et Tata itou, en vous en voulant de me laisser sans nouvelles.

Peut-être votre lettre s'est elle perdue.

Henri

41 TO HIS MOTHER

[Spring 1882]

Ma chere Maman,

Vous êtes-vous cassé le bras, ou avez vous oublié l'existence de votre lardon? Un petit mot s.v.p. pour me mettre au courant.

Tout va bien ici, je travaille ferme.

Bien des choses, et poutounégeades.

Yours
H.

42 TO MME L. TAPIÉ DE CÉLEYRAN

Le Bosc, [August 1882]

Ma chère bonne maman,

Je n'ai pas voulu laisser passer la St Louis sans venir, mon rouleau de compliments sous le bras, vous la souhaiter bonne et heureuse (sigle classique). Je vous la souhaite donc de mon mieux!!! Voilà qui est fait, assez maladroitement peut-être, mais la grâce n'étant pas mon caractère distinctif, j'espère obtenir non des remerciements mais un pardon.

Peut être ne seriez vous pas fâchées de savoir comment nous vivotons ici dans les brumes ou plutôt la *bouillaque* de l'Aveyron, car il pleut dur. Je vous assure ça *déjute* pas (expression choisie qui dénote de ma part une profonde étude de la langue verte). Bonne maman . . . , que fait elle, Bonne maman? elle met des rideaux, et sent les nuages qui passent alternativement. Tante Emilie pique lesdits rideaux à la machine. Oncle Amédée massacre tout ce qu'il peut, et oncle Charles cherche des excuses (ô raffinement de diplomatie) à sa paresse qui montre plus qu'*un bout* d'oreille malgré ses protestations. Mamans fait, je crois, des découpures sur de la moleskine qui s'intitulent pompeusement nappe d'autel, et moi je divise mes loisirs entre la peinture et le mal aux dents, source inépuisable de jouissances variées. Kiki boude à tout ce qui n'a pas été baptisé blanquette, un baptême farineux. Mariette frise, et le Docteur Farguent est venu la cacheter. Un point c'est tout.

Nous vous embrassons tous, et *moi* je vous embrasse *vous*

votre filleul
Henri

43 TO HIS FATHER

Le Bosc, ce Jeudi [Sept. 1882]

Mon cher Papa,

Bonnat a congédié *tous* ses élèves. Avant de prendre une détermination j'ai voulu avoir les suffrages de mes amis, et, à l'unanimité, je viens d'accepter un chevalet chez *Cormon*, un jeune et déjà célèbre, auteur du fameux *Caïn fuyant avec sa famille* qui est au Luxembourg. Talent puissant austère et original. Rachou m'a télégraphié pour savoir si je consentais à y suivre q.q. uns de mes camarades, et j'ai accepté. Princeteau applaudit à ce choix. J'aurais bien essayé Carolus, mais *ce prince de la couleur ne fait que de médiocres dessinateurs*, ce qui serait la mort pour moi.

Et puis on ne s'épouse pas? et la gamme des maîtres n'est point épuisée.

Nous partons pour Respide, où nous comptons ne passer que q.q. instants pour aller reprendre le travail si nécessaire. Espérant réussir, je serai heureux de vous voir ratifier un choix qui n'est basé sur aucun préjugé, mais sur des arguments sérieux. Tout va bien ici, et nous avons tante Blanche. Nous vous embrassons tous.

votre fils respectueux
Henri.

44 TO HIS MOTHER

[Paris], 9 octobre [1882]

Ma chère Maman,

J'ai reçu votre bien peu gaie lettre, mais donnez moi, je vous prie, des details sur les incidents qui se sont produits. Etes vous rayée officiellement du gâteau familial, vous êtes vous renfermée dans le silence absolu? ou y a-t-il eu explication, et dans quels termes? Ecrivez-moi tous les détails, car je ne sais sur quel pied dancer, et ne voudrais pas faire de gaffe. Tout va ici aussi bien que possible. Je vais tâcher de me caser, mais ce n'est pas facile.

Je vous embrasse
yours
H.

Où est Jalabert. Donnez moi son adresse s.v.p.

45 TO HIS MOTHER

[Paris, November 1882]

Ma chère maman,

Ma vie est terne. Je turbine tristement, et n'ai pas encore causé avec Cormon. En tous cas je serai à vos pieds au 1er, avec mon ami Claudon qui est charmant, Ça nous refera un peu le tempérament.

Dora me fait l'effet d'être f . . tue. Vous trouvez Louis gros et gras. Tant mieux pour lui.

Je lui ai écrit pourquoi je ne l'avais pas vu avant son départ. Papa va partir??? Qu'il parte.
Je vous embrasse.

Henri

46 TO AMÉDÉE TAPIÉ DE CÉLEYRAN
[Paris], Vendredi 1er décembre [1882]

Mon cher oncle,
Nous voila de nouveau à nos moutons. Vous à vos machins et moi à mon fil à plomb. Mes affaires boulottent assez bien. Cormon m'a reçu avec bienveillance. Mes dessins surtout l'ont bien disposé, surtout (pardon) Odon avec les mains dans les poches, autrement dit: *raou plaou plaou*. Princeteau avait préféré la chauve souris, et Rachou *l'oncle Charles* appuyé sur la table.
Nous avons passé un temps de repos à Respide qui est vraiment un joli endroit, où l'on peut canoter avec ardeur. Louis bûche son bachot pour le 6. Pauvre petit: on m'a dit que Toto se décidait à forcer un peu. Ça n'a pas laissé dě m'étonner. Recommandez lui de ne pas trop forcer, ça a des inconvenients.
Mon nouveau patron est l'homme le plus maigre de tout Paris. Il vient nous voir souvent, et veut qu'on s'amuse à peindre en dehors de l'atelier le plus possible. Je n'ai pas encore vu Bonnat. Le verrai je!!!! Tous mes camarades m'étaient connus, alors pas de broche. Oncle Odon et tante O. sont ici. Les moutards sont partis pour Albi. Eux partent demain pour Florida. Ils font planter et bâtir. Ils ont déjà la gueule de bois. Que sera-ce au retour!
J'ai appris le mariage de l'oncle Bébert. Un homme à la mer . . . !!! de plus. Est il joyeux!! Puissent ces deux expériences et la mienne avec réussir!!!
Je présente mes hommages amitiés et *poutounégeades* à ces Dames douairières et demoiselles, et je vous serre majestueusement l'index.

votre nepveu
HMonfa

47 TO MME L. TAPIÉ DE CÉLEYRAN
[Paris, December 1882]

Ma chère bonne maman,
Je vous souhaite une bonne et heureuse année, et vous prie de distribuer mes souhaits autour de vous. Maman a dû vous raconter mes petites affaires, ainsi je ne me redirai pas car ce qu'elle vous dit, *nous* vous le disons ensemble. J'aurais espéré vous embrasser vraiment, mais j'avais compté sans les évènements. Si la barbe n'y est pas, le cœur y est, et bonne année.
Votre respectueux filleul et petit fils

Henri

48 TO HIS MOTHER
[Paris, 1882]

Ma chère Maman,
Je suis un peu en retard, mais je sais que d'abord le *fuss* du départ doit vous faire pirou-etter avec une agilité sans egale, 2° que Louis a dû vous communiquer mes intentions. J'ai tout à fait repris mon traitement. Gabriel est parti avec l'Abbé qui le menait à Lille(?) sans venir nous voir. Papa, toujours bouillant, a corrigé un artilleur qui criait après son cheval. Il fait un soleil superbe, et je vous embrasse avec l'espoir de la réalité prochaine.

your
Henri

P.S. Nous aurons à causer très sérieusement de la proposition de vente de Ricardelle. Papa m'ayant demandé mon avis, je me suis réservé prudem-ment. Ai je bien fait?

49 TO HIS MOTHER
[Paris, Spring 1883]

Ma chère Maman
J'ai été heureux des bonnes nouvelles que vous donnez à ma Tante Cécile qui prouvent que vous approuvez complètement mon transvasement. Tout en regrettant que votre retour soit retardé, je ne puis que vous approuver de profiter ample-ment de votre excursion. Je continue à dîner avec Princeteau. Un jour entre autres, chez Lucas la table d'hôte n'existant pas à cause de la pénurie de clients, j'ai été à Longchamps avec P. brouter l'herbe verte. Mon travail marche. Je finis le portrait de D'Ennery qui m'a posé avec une grande complaisance. Cormon est un peu abruti par les opérations du Jury terminées Samedi seulement.
Nous avons une température d'été, et le par-dessus commence à devenir un objet de luxe. Je m'arrête, devenant oiseux, et je vous embrasse, en vous priant de distribuer salamaleks et *poutounégeades* à qui de droit.

HTL

50 TO EUGÈNE BOCH
Château de Céleyran par Coursan (Aude)
[Sept. 1, 1883]

Cher vieux
Ne tremble pas devant la perspective noire de mon papier. Je vais tâcher d'être court . . .
Devant arriver à Paris le 1er Octobre, je désirerais savoir si Cormon n'a pas de projets voyageurs pour ce moment là, si l'atelier est terminé, prêt à abriter nos jeunes crânes frémis-sant du bouillonnement de l'inspiration, si les camarades sont rentrés, et lesquels.
Tu peux dire *ouf*. Voilà qui est fini. Je te dispense du récit de mes *vachages* aux soleil avec un pinceau à la main et des taches plus ou moins épinard, pistache, olive ou merde sur ma toile. Nous aurons le temps d'en parler.
Je te la serre cordialement, et j'espère recevoir quelques mots précis de toi pour m'esquisser la situation.

La jeune pourriture
H de Toulouse Lautrec

Château de Respide près Langon, (Gironde)
Samedi, 8 Septembre [1883]

Chère Maman,
Je viens de recevoir votre lettre pleine de sollicitude et d'affection, mais enfiévrée en diable. —Je trouve bizarre que, ayant rempli vos instructions de *point* en *point*, vous me reprochiez de n'avoir pas sacrifié mon après-midi à la poursuite d'un oncle affairé et insaisissable. Le voyage s'est effectué parfaitement malgré mon costume léger que j'avais renforcé d'un gilet à Paul et d'un châle de Madame Méjean. Nous avons pris un coupé, où j'ai été seul jusqu'à la fin, ayant quitté Paul et ma tante à Toulouse.
Ils sont aujourd'hui à Lourdes. La rougéole de Joseph est passée, et a été insignifiante. J'ai été hier à Malromé avec Louis et un vieil abbé qui a été d'un bucolique exquis. J'ai vu le timide Ballade qui m'a communiqué vos projets étranges que j'accepte pour vous être agréable. Je me ferais probablement de Malromé une idée tout autre, habitant un local agréable et gai. . . .
Le collier va au cheval que nous essaierons Louis, Philippe et moi.
Je vous prierai de me rappeler vos autres instructions oubliées.
Je vous embrasse tous et vous poutouniège
Henri de Toulouse Lautrec

P.S. J'ai vu Rachou qui sera Mardi à Paris. J'ai pris sur moi d'envoyer un tondeur à Malromé pour rafraîchir les crins de notre Bucéphale.
Adieu—et prière d'envoyer mes lettres . . .
HTL

[Paris *c.* Sept. 1883]

Ma chère Maman
J'ai vu mon doux père hier soir, il était fort gai. Princeteau est parti brusquement sans dire où il allait. C'est bizarre. Nous avons été à la gare à 10 h attendre les Odon qui ne sont arrivés qu'au train de 11h., ce qui fait que je les ai lâchés.
Vos nouvelles m'ont fait plaisir, en ce sens que vous me faites l'effet de vous sentir chez vous à Malromé. C'est énorme, et je pense Tata occupée à imprimer une odeur *sui generis* à la chambre de M. de Forcade.

Eau d'Addison	7/14
Petits pets	8 30
Aq. dist.	1 1/2
Tante Armandine	

Voila la dose.
Sur ce vous embrasse,
yours
Henri

Paris, 24 Décembre [1883]

Ma chère bonne maman
Je profite du Jour de l'An qui s'avance pour vous donner qq. nouvelles de notre petit train train. L'arrivée de mon oncle Odon et la famille nombreuse vient nous égayer un peu, car nous—ou plutôt Maman était assez seule. Elle, qui n'est pas prise dans l'engrenage de l'atelier, a de nombreux loisirs qu'elle emploie à devenir bas-bleu. Elle suit assidûment les cours métaphysiques de notre cher maître Caro (de l'Académie Française), et savoure la prose musquée de ce vieillard qui ne laisse pas d'être prétentieux.
Papa nous a lâchés pour aller voir son groom, qui, je crois, faisait danser l'anse du panier.
Et moi je travaille, et quitte mon petit atelier provisoire pour entrer dans un local plus grand que je vais meubler. C'est ici la place naturelle des remerciements que je vous dois pour les fonds que maman m'a remis de votre part, et qui vont m'être utiles. Ils passeront en tapis probablement. Vous avez, m'a-t-on dit goûté les charmantes attitudes et les souliers vernis de mon bel ami Louis. Vous devriez bien lui trouver une héritière, et la lui jeter dans les bras. Il n'est, je crois, pas bon à autre chose. Je vais racheter cette méchanceté en vous souhaitant une bonne année si sérieuse que je vous prie d'en distribuer des tranches à toute la famille, oncle, tante, cousins, cousines, et *abbés* . . .
Et je vous embrasse
votre petit fils et filleul respectueux
H. de Toulouse Lautrec
artiste en faux bois

[Paris, Jan. 1884]

Ma chère bonne maman
Je suis absolument coupable d'avoir différé jusqu'à ce jour mes vœux de bonne année, et pater pourra, sans craindre de paraître injuste, distiller les remonstrances les plus suraigues. Je courbe donc mon échine de rapin, car rapin je suis jusqu'aux oreilles. Je travaille comme un cheval, et n'ai même pas le courage de me promener le soir comme j'en avais contracté la douce habitude. Maman n'a pas l'air de s'ennuyer outre mesure. J'en suis heureux, car je craignais fort cet isolement relatif. Cela vaut encore mieux cependant que de la condamner à percher comme moi dans un quartier qui persiste dans son caractère coupe gorge. D'aimables farceurs s'attaquent aux femmes seules, et leur vident de l'encre dans le . . . cou. C'est d'un goût charmant. J'ai eu le chagrin d'apprendre la mort de mon pauvre ami le Docteur Rouilat mort en mer. Se sentant frit, il a voulu rentrer mourir à Paris et s'est arrêté en route. Louis Pascal va entrer au Comptoir d'Escompte. C'est une bonne fin pour ce têtard sympathique. Je vous engage à l'en féliciter.
Adieu, ma chère bonne maman. Je vous prie de présenter mes vœux à mon oncle et à ma tante et à Tata. Répondez avec équité des flots d'amitiés sur mes cousins, en favorisant Kiki.
Je vous embrasse.
Votre respectueux filleul et petit fils
Henri

P.S. Prière de dire à mon oncle que je ne l'oublie pas. Je ne suis pas encore fixé sur les chapeaux, sans ça j'aurais déjà fait ce qu'il m'a demandé.
HTL

[Paris, Spring 1884]

Ma chère Maman
 Comme je vous l'ai écrit dès que j'ai été fixé, le conseil m'a déclaré impropre au service, sans que j'ai eu à exhiber le moindre Certificat. M. Mullin a été aussi gentil que possible, et m'a fait passer avant mon tour avec des Auvergnats qui puaient des pieds.
 Le soir j'ai été à la fête donnée par Mayet dans son atelier, nous nous sommes couchés à 6 heures du matin, plutôt fatigués. Le beau Louis est invisible. J'ai pu, cependant, voir Bourges qui m'a rassuré sur son sort. Un nouvel oculiste lui a trouvé les yeux en très bon état, alors il a repris sa place au Comptoir d'Escompte.
 Quant à Paul il parait que les lézards ont envahi sa chambre et, de plus, l'insurrection ayant coupé les vivres, il a dû manger de la viande sans pain. Tout ça réuni l'a tellement séduit qu'il a bouclé ses malles et . . . son père a, je crois, l'intention de l'envoyer au Tonkin. Voila toutes les nouvelles. Je ne sais si vous avez lu l'accident du Comte et Comtesse de Nattes projetés avec leur voiture et leurs chevaux emportés contre le parapet de la Seine, en passant par les vitres de ladite voiture, tout comme Oncle Odon. Je n'ai pas encore vu ce dernier. Sur ce [je] vous embrasse et vous remercie, vous, ma tante et mon oncle, et Tata (places réservées) de vos attentions pour moi, qui en a si peu pour vous.

je vous embrasse
votre
Henri

P.S. Mes finances baissent, et je vais me trouver à sec bientôt. Je vous préviens pour que vous me fassiez parvenir de quoi vous attendre sans taper mes amis.
 Princeteau. Pas de nouvelles.

[Paris, Spring 1884]

Ma chère Maman
 J'ai reçu votre lettre peu rassurée. J'ai vu papa qui avait de bonnes nouvelles de Ricardelle, et Louis de mauvaises de Respide. Enfin, tout va bien pour nous.
 Il y a eu une revolution à l'atelier. Cormon à dégommé le massier pour en nommer un autre. Tout ça nous à passionnés plus que vous ne pourriez le croire. Rachou est notre patron, je crois vous l'avoir dit. Je dois radoter, car voila 5 journées que je n'ai pas quittée la Butte. Je peins une femme qui à la tête en or absolument. Mon dessin du *Figaro* n'est pas complètement terminé, mais il va assez. Ouf. Je viens de déjeuner très vite, et vais travailler.
 Je vous embrasse et Tata aussi.

Yours
Henri

P.S. Je ferai votre commission quand pourrai.

[Paris, June–July 1884]

Ma chère Maman
 J'ai reçu votre missive qui me donne espoir quant à Pérey. Vous viendrez au Métropolitain, et je vous y rejoindrai, ou je prolongerai un peu mon séjour chez Grenier qui est la perle des camarades et mieux est un ami. Nous avons reçu les envois multiples de Balade qui n'a envoyé malheureusement que fort peu de vin rouge, ce qui motivera de ma part la demande d'un second envoi, exclusivement rouge. Vous me parlez de mal de gorge. J'espère qu'à l'heure qu'il est c'est fini. Tante Armandine a eu tort de déménager. J'aurais été l'aider en Janvier, et lui voler le plus de choses possibles. L'atelier est en révolution, on veut nommer un massier. On m'offrirait ce poste ennuyeux, et je refuse avec entêtement.
 Je suis content de la satisfaction que vous donne ce que je fais.
 Je n'ai pas répondu à Louis, et ne lui répondrai pas.
 Cette obstination que met la majorité de la famille à me blaguer, me vexe beaucoup. Heureusement que vous avez droit à plusieurs voix à ce scrutin là.
 Je vous embrasse, et à part tante Armandine.

Votre fils H

Télégraphiez pour que j'aille vous chercher.

[Restaurant] Lucas, [Paris], Midi, 15 août [1884[

Ma chère Maman
 Si je ne vous ai pas écrit, c'est que j'ai été bousculé par le travail. j'ai travaillé tant que j'ai pu sur mon dessin du *Figaro*, mais, Rachou en ayant été mécontent, je ne l'ai pas envoyé au *Figaro*. Il m'a fait observer qu'il ne fallait soumettre au public que ce qu'on pouvait faire de mieux. Or, mon dessin aurait pu être mieux. Je pense que vous ne m'en voudrez pas d'avoir écouté ce sage raisonnement. Puisque jusqu'à la dernière minute, j'ai eté sur le chantier, j'allais travailler le soir au Bar. Enfin. Zut!!!
 Je n'ai point vu papa, et ignore s'il a fait vos commissions; je n'ai encore pu faire aucune des miennes.
 Je vous embrasse ainsi que Tata. Vais avaler une messe rapide, et regrimper là-haut où m'attend mon modèle.

Yours,
Henri

[Paris, late August 1884]

Ma chère bonne maman,
 Au milieu du brouhaha de ma pauvre existence, je me suis mis en retard, j'espère que vous me pardonnerez, pour vous souhaiter une bonne et heureuse fête. Je ne sais si vous êtes à Malromé en train de déguster notre pigeonnier. Dans ce cas, je vous prie de dire à maman que

Papa n'est point encore parti. Dans le cas où vous seriez au Bosc, je vous prie d'embrasser tout le monde, et particulièrement bonne maman Gabrielle pour moi, pauvre vieillard.

Je voudrais vous parler un peu de ce que je fais, mais c'est tellement spécial!!! J'aime mieux vous souhaiter simplement une bonne fête, et vous embrasser doublement comme petit fils et comme filleul.

votre petit fils respectueux
H. de Toulouse Lautrec

60 TO HIS MOTHER
[Paris], Mercredi [1884]

Ma chère Maman,
Je viens de recevoir votre lettre d'Albi. Vous trouverez, sans doute, à Respide Joseph qui part demain. Laura Pérey vous attend pour pendre la crémaillère à l'Hôtel, qui compte plusieurs nouveaux pensionnaires.

Je ne vous ai pas envoyé la photographie, et pense qu'à présent je puis attendre votre retour. Papa n'a point l'air de vous suivre à Malromé, je le regrette.

Je vous embrasse
H.

P.S. Prière envoyer l'argent pour payer *propriétaire*. Il vaut *mieux* ne pas le faire attendre. Adressez le chez Tante Emilie.

61 TO HIS MOTHER
[Paris], Dimanche [October 1884]

Ma chère Maman,
Je ne vous ai pas écrit plus tôt parce que j'avais plusieurs choses à définir. Papa m'a écrit *très aimablement* en me priant de retirer ses *colis* de chez Pérey où ils les avait laissés. Vous voyez donc que la rupture ayant fini en queue de morue ne sera peût-être pas aussi difficile à renouer que nous le craignions. Agissez calmement, et ne faites pas de *boulettes*. Je n'ai encore rien montré à Cormon, mais je l'ai vu, et il a été très gentil.

Je suis fort bien installé chez mon aimable camarade, si bien que je craindrais d'être indiscret si votre arrivée n'était à l'horizon.

Pas plus de choléra que sur ma main. Bourges m'a beaucoup bousculé quand je lui ai manifesté mes terreurs.

Mon pauvre Rabache est sur les dents, on lui a emporté la moitié de la mâchoire en taquinant une de ses molaires. Il boit du lait et broie du noir, et m'a reçu comme le messie. Rachou est à Toulouse.

Voila ma petite chronique succinte et precise.

Je vous embrasse férocement, et vais demain matin me mettre à la besogne.

Votre fils.

62 TO HIS MOTHER
[Paris, October 1884]

Ma chère Maman
Je sors de la messe d'une heure après avoir

déjeuné chez Lucas. Ça m'a un peu civilisé, car je ne bouge guère de mes hauteurs. J'ai vu Cormon ce matin. Il m'a plutôt félicité. tout en me faisant sentir mon ignorance. Ça m'a un peu remonté. Enfin nous n'avons pas perdu notre temps.

Rachou a été mordu à la main par un chien, ce qui l'a empêché de travailler. Il est à Toulouse, où il vient de commencer une serie d'études de chevaux.

Rabache est debout, et mon concierge va me lâcher pour se faire marchand d'huîtres, ce qui m'embête fort. Votre lettre m'a donné des regrets de ne pas vous avoir accompagnée, mais je compte décidément pousser une pointe à la fin de l'année. Dites le souvent.

Vous avez l'air fort satisfaite du contact du foyer, tant mieux. je n'ai aperçu personne sinon de loin les moustaches blondes de mon cousin Cupelet.—Voilà tout ce que le vide de mon cerveau me suggère de neuf. Embrassez fort mes deux bonnes mamans, et rappelez-moi au souvenir de tous. Quand Papa revient il? je suppose qu'il ne le sait pas lui même.

Je vous embrasse et voudrais vous voir (mais bien installée).

P.S. C'est le grand navet que Cormon a préféré. Ça m'a étonné.

H.

P.P.S. Notre cercle est mort. Je me couche à 9 h. Zut pour le Choléra!!

63 TO HIS MOTHER
[Paris, Nov. 1884]

Ma chère Maman
Il me semblait dans mes deux lettres avoir parlé de mes navets devant Cormon.—Il parait que je me suis trompé. Il a trouvé mes bœufs mauvais, les petits Laffitte pas mal, et celui sur l'herbe bien. En somme, tout ça est faible à coté des paysages qu'Anquetin a rapportés. Tout le monde est étonné. C'est dans une voie impressioniste qui lui fait grand honneur. On se sent bien petit garçon à côté de travailleurs de cette trempe. J'ai vu Papa Dimanche, et je ne saurais vous dire si mon oncle Odon est encore à Paris.

J'ai repris le train-train qui durera jusqu'au printemps, et alors je ferai, peut-être, des choses bizarres. C'est encore vague.

Je n'ai pas encore eu l'énergie d'aller chez le chemisier. J'ai la flemme à l'idée de déscendre. Il fait si bon le soir chez Grenier dans l'atelier chauffé. Vous feriez bien de me tricoter un bonnet grec et des pantoufles. Le café m'embête, déscendre me dérange, il n'y a que le sommeil et la peinture.

Je m'arrête, car je deviens prêchi prêcha, et embrasse les bonnes mamans, tantes et vous
Yours   HTL

J'ai vu oncle Ernest.

64 TO HIS MOTHER

[Paris, Autumn 1884]

Ma chère Maman

Votre lettre m'a fait plaisir; je vous vois jouer Junon Lucine avec conviction. Papa a piqué une pointe à Orléans, et je ne l'ai pas vu. Il s'est disputé avec les professeurs de Raymond qui ne veulent pas le lui donner.

Il fait ici un brouillard horrible, les tramways sont vaporeux et les nez rouges: C'est joliment triste.

Nous sommes dans le concours jusqu'au cou—on est gêné, il y a trop de monde. En somme c'est plus embêtant que les autres semaines simplement.

Vous seriez bien aimable de m'envoyer 4 boites de foies gras, ça doit être facile, et j'en enverrai 2 à Mme Dennery et deux à Grenier qui a fort apprécié l'autre. Ce serait une façon intelligente de reconnaitre leur gentillesse. Deux de plus ne gèneraient pas. *C'est très sérieux*—(je *soul*ighe) je voudrais aller partout pour voir des effets; le soir c'est terrible de se coucher à deux heures, pour se lever à 8 et à la chandelle, et Pourquoi??? . . .

Enfin nous causerons mieux les . . . joues . . . au feu—et bientôt j'espère.

Je vais pas mal, et j'ai envie de travailler. Zut pour le reste.

Je vous embrasse,
en vieillard désillusionné.
Yours
Henri.

65 TO HIS MOTHER

[Paris, 1884]

Ma chère Maman

Pas gr[an]d chose à vous annoncer. Je continue ma vie. Atelier le matin où Rachou corrige, et il n'est pas doux l'animal. Après midi plein air chez Rachou, et le soir le bar où je termine ma petite affaire. J'ai vu papa de loin en loin. Il a réussi à se brouiller avec Lucas!!! J'y vais t[out] de même. Quel drôle de bonhomme. J'ai raté les Odon. Ils sont capables de me deshériter. Je coupe court, car j'allais commencer une sortie,
et vous embrasse ainsi que Tata et Bonne Maman, mais vous surtout
votre rejeton chéri des grâces
Henri

66 TO HIS MOTHER

[Paris, January 1885]

Ma chère Maman,

Je vous aurais écrit une simple carte postale, mais M. Dufour ayant ce matin perçu (du verbe percevoir) le paiement de commencement d'année c.a.d. 3 mois d'avance, il en est résulté une baisse considérable dans mes finances. Je ne suis pas à sec, mais le serais si je payais ce que je dois. Je mène d'ailleurs une vie de coq en pâte, et le travail est en train. J'ai vu Bourges qui commence son examen de deux mois et qui s'embête ferme. Et voilà.

Je vous embrasse tous et vous prie d'excuser le caractère financier de ma missive. J'ai été sagement travailler chez un camarade, un pierrot femelle poudré à blanc. On m'a conseillé de commencer q.q. chose pour le salon: j'attends que Cormon lui-même m'en parle, mais je ne commencerai pas de peur d'une bourrade.

Tout ça est bien ambitieux et demande reflexion.

I kiss you.
Yours
HTL

P.S. Send money
Jeannette Hathaway.

67 TO HIS MOTHER

[Paris, January 1885]

Ma chère Maman

j'ai tout mis en ordre, ou à peu près, et puis vous donner des nouvelles. J'ai vu papa *une* fois. Il a été fort aimable, m'a donné de la galette et sa bénédiction. Nous avons été voir oncle Odon ensemble. J'ai vu ma tante, Raymond et Odette. Ça s'est tristement passé cette visite là, c'est bien navrant. Je n'ai pas encore vu Louis qui m'a écrit un mot sec. Je ne me suis pas pressé de lui répondre, alors un ton courroucé est survenu. J'y réponds par une invitation à dîner: on n'est pas plus aimable.

Bourges passe son examen, ses notes jusqu'ici sont brillantes. Cormon n'a pas encor vu mes navets. C'est pour demain matin. Il a différé le concours, car il y a encore du monde à la campagne.

Ah, Dayot s'est bien moqué de nous; nous avons posé au café de Bordeaux, nous y avons dîné à nos frais, et Deforges est arrivé fort tard nous dire que . . . enfin des raisons insuffisantes. Quant à Joseph, il eût très bien pu nous trouver, car nous sommes restés dans les mêmes dix mètres carrés toute la soirée. Tant pis pour nous.

Voilà, ma petite maman, ma chronique finie. Vous m'excuserez de n'avoir pas abusé de petits mots qui vous auraient poursuivie en vain.

Quand je reverrai Papa, je lui ferai vos commissions.

Je vous embrasse, et vous prie d'embrasser mes bonnes mamans.

Tachez de purifier un baiser aussi impur que le mien. Au passage gardez en un pour vous.
Yours
H
J'ai vu miss Braine, qui est toquée, je crois.

68 TO HIS MOTHER

[Paris, c. March 1885]

Ma Chère Maman

J'ai reçu de vos nouvelles par bonne maman. Il y a décidément une épidémie sur les chiens; deux des petits de Rachou sont morts. Le troisième est à l'hopital. C'est une espèce de choléra, ou diarrhée infantile.

Le temps s'est remis au beau, ce qui me permet de bûcher. Je me suis purgé ce matin. Aah . . . Tout le monde est dans le coup de collier pour le Salon. Bordes, Rachou, etc. Ce dernier vient d'avoir une commande de portrait d'un très joli prix. Je vous raconte tout ça, parce que j'espère vous intéresser. Je vous amènerai peut-être deux invités au lieu d'un. Vous devriez ramasser les jeunes filles du pays et leur apprendre à poser un peu pour que nous n'ayons qu'à nous y mettre. Voilà ma petite chronique terminée. Je vous embrasse, et les bonne mamans itou, si elles sont là.

your
H

Pas vu papa!!

69 TO HIS MOTHER

[Paris, April 1885]

Me chère Maman,

Je suis donc bien méchant pour que vous m'écriviez des cruautés pareilles. Je ne vous en veux pas. Je pense que la pluie joue un grand rôle dans votre mauvaise humeur. Ce que vous me dites au sujet de mes amis, me laisse croire que vous me trouvez bien bête, si tant il est vrai que vous me croyez capable d'introduire des loups dans votre pigeonnier. J'ai simplement voulu obliger un charmant bonhomme *très bien élevé*, et dont vous n'aurez certes pas à vous plaindre. Nous travaillerons de notre mieux, et ferons honneur à votre vin. Que voulez-vous de plus?

Passons à la seconde question.—Vous ne voyez donc pas que je n'ai pas voulu me laisser [charger] d'un vieux souvenir. J'ai un rendez vous certain aujourd'hui même avec mon expert, et n'aurai rien perdu pour attendre. Calmez Tata, je vous en prie. N'a-t-elle pas un peu déteint sur vous, et ne *trébadizez* vous pas un peu. Si cela est, je me claquemure dans la tour du nord avec mon ami et la vieille St Arnaude. Nous jouerons au bésigue avec deux morts, chose rare. Je voudrais bien emmener Grenier, mais il a l'air de se faire tirer l'oreille. Enfin, tout n'est pas perdu.

J'ai vu papa qui doit vous envoyer des pierres précieuses du Caucase.

Voilà, terrible Croquemitaine, tout ce que j'avais à dire.

J'attends la date de la foire de Langon avec ardeur, et vous embrasse, ou plutôt vous tends mon front d'enfant garni du bien peu de bourre que vous y avez laissé.

Votre indigne fils
Henri

Embrassez Tata pour moi S.V.P.

70 TO HIS MOTHER

[Paris, Spring 1885]

Ma chère Maman

Votre lettre est aimable, quoique ironique en ce qui concerne ma demande si légitime pourtant. Je n'insiste pas. J'ai vu toute la famille. Oncle Charles etc., etc., excepté oncle Amédée qui passe tout son temps à Puteaux, or je n'ai pas le temps de l'y poursuivre. Je passe tout mon temps à travailler, ce qui ne me permet guère d'avoir des choses nouvelles à vous raconter. Dites moi si vous allez au Bosc au commencement d'août. Je vous y joindrais, et, vers le 20 du même mois, nous rattraperions nos pénates, à moins que je ne fasse quelque chose d'après mes cousines. Refléchissez, et répondez.

Je vous baise les mains.

yours
Harry

71 TO HIS MOTHER

[Paris, Spring 1885]

Ma chère Maman

Votre lettre tardive m'a amusé fortement; elle est d'une gaité folle. Je suis tellement abruti par le chaud que je mène l'existence de ville d'eaux, la douche, le tub, plus le travail qui est fatiguant. Je résiste à Grenier et à Anquetin qui luttent à qui mieux mieux pour m'entraîner à la campagne, mais je sais trop que je n'y ferais rien.

Nous avons offert à Cormon une palme d'argent ridicule qu'il a reçu avec attendrissement.

Quels sont vos projets, et le Bosc garni de la couvée ne vous attirera-t-il pas bientôt? Si vous étiez là, quelles bonnes promenades nous ferions le soir . . . et nous jouirions bien plus de l'une de l'autre que l'hiver. Et dites donc que je n'ai qu'un cœur de pierre. Maintenant nous aurions à jouir de Papa qui s'obstine à ne pas m'assigner de rendez-vous, auxquels d'ailleurs il ne se trouverait pas.

Je vous embrasse en suant à grosses gouttes.

Yours
Harry.

72 TO HIS MOTHER

[Paris, June–July 1885]

Ma chère Maman

Votre question cheval est bien difficile à résoudre. Tant que vous confierez vos animaux à des *imbéciles*, il est inutile de chercher autre chose que des rosses, ce dont il est inutile que je me mêle.

Si vous êtes décidée à défendre qu'un autre que le *cocher* s'en serve, je veux bien m'en occuper. M. Anquetin ne demande pas mieux. Je suis donc à vos ordres cette restriction faite. Louis a dû venir vous voir, car il est à Respide. Vous avez donc pu vous expliquer avec lui. Pour ma part, je suis occupé à déménager, le travail en souffre, d'ailleurs la température est si lourde que les modèles dorment debout. J'ai vendu q.q. études—et suis en train de vendre d'autres. Papa ne bouge guère, mais j'ai bien peur que la chaleur nous expulse tous de Paris sous peu. Où irai-je? Je vais pour le moment canoter quelque fois à Asnières; ça sent bougrement

mauvais, et ne rappelle que de fort loin la mer
. . . plutôt que la *mer* . .

Ecrivez moi, et indiquez moi vos intentions,
pures ou autres, et je vous embrasse chaudement.
Yours
Henri

73 TO HIS MOTHER
[Paris], Vendredi [July 1885]

Ma chère Maman

Mon *entrevue* a eté relativement favorable, et
j'espère n'avoir pas besoin de faire appel à votre
largesse. Je suis toujours prêt à partir le 20 ou
22; vers le 30 nous passerons à Malromé et, après
un court arrêt, irons passer une 15ᵉ de jours à
Taussat ou *Caussat*. Je ne sais pas bien l'orthographe mais c'est très sauvage paraît-il. Chez
Robert Wurst. C'est décidé. Je verrai mes oncles
et tantes demain sans doute, le temps continue à
grincher, mais le départ prochain me rassérène,
comme si je faisais une bonne blague à St
Médard. Tant mieux que votre voyage ait
réussi, et à vous votre fils poutounégeade.
Harry.

74 TO HIS MOTHER
[Paris], Lundi soir [Autumn 1885]

Ma chère Maman

J'ai fait un excellent voyage, et ai eu la veine
de trouver Grenier chez lui; il repartait pour la
campagne où il voulait m'emmener. J'ai resisté
naturellement. Il m'a laissé à la tête de ses clefs
et de son lit, ce qui me permettra de me retourner.
Je pense aller chez Ottoz; comme le bonhomme
dont je vous avais parlé est encore là, ça me fait
un camarade, J'ai trouvé tout en place, mais il
paraît que j'ai un terme en retard(!), et j'avais mal
calculé c'est vrai—il n'y a qu'à gémir et à payer.
Je vous écrirai si ça presse, mais il faut attendre
que papa m'ait expédié des fonds.
Je vous embrasse tous, et vous surtout
Yours
Henri

75 TO HIS MOTHER
[Paris, Autumn 1885]

Ma chère Maman

Votre lettre est courte, et ne m'annonce rien
de bien neuf.—Moi j'ai été voir Grenier à
Villiers, il fait fort frais dans ce pays. Paris est
noir et boueux, ce qui ne m'empêche pas de
trottiner dans les rues après des musiciens de
l'Opéra que j'essaye de charmer pour me faufiler
dans le temple des arts, et de l'ennui. Ça n'est
guère commode. Je n'ai pas vu papa depuis
longtemps. Grenier doit aller en Sologne cet
hiver courrir le cerf, ou . . . se chauffer au coin
du feu.
Je fais le portrait de la belle sœur d'un de mes
amis, ce qui est fort amusant. J'y vais tout à

l'heure, et vous écris en sirotant mon café (alias
jus de chapeau).—
Je vous embrasse et vous attends,
Your boy
Harry

76 TO HIS MOTHER
[Normandy, late Autumn 1885]

Ma chère Maman,

Je viens vous dire que j'ai froid aux oreilles,
et que je bois beaucoup de cidre. Le pays est
assez poudré de frimas mais ne manque pas de
charmes. M. et Madame Anquetin sont charmants comme toujours. Nous chassons le cor-
beau avec ardeur mais sans succès. J'espère que
vous avez envoyé mon navet au grand journal. A
part ça rien de neuf, si ce n'est que je vous
embrasse, et vous prie d'en faire de même à ce
chiffon de papier qui me représente.
Your son
Henri

A demain (mercredi) soir,
minuit.

77 TO HIS MOTHER
[Paris, late Autumn 1885]

Ma chère Maman,

J'arrive de Normandie où j'ai été chasser les
corbeaux, journée charmante. Je vais revenir
avec Bourges au Crotoy chasser le Phoque. La
campagne est rudement jolie, et je comprends
bien que vous ayiez de la peine à la quitter. Je
vous raconterai à Rivaude les détails.
Papa est fort gai parce que Princeteau est là.
Il est devenu hypocondre, mais bien gentil tout
de même. Tachez d'obtenir Kiki si vous pouvez,
mettez toute votre diplomatie, et pensez ce qu'il
me serait agréable de trouver le grand air et le
travail réunis.
Je vous embrasse,
yours
Harry

78 TO MME R. C. DE TOULOUSE-LAUTREC
Château du Bosc, [December 1885]

Ma chère bonne maman,

Je vous écris du Château Bosc qui, pour le
moment, est loin de ressembler à celui de la belle
au Bois Dormant, étant donné le nombre des
jeunes mâles qui batifolent dans les longs
couloirs. Nous regrettons tous que vous ne
soyiez pas là pour présider à cette réunion de
famille, qui est la première à laquelle j'assiste
depuis bien longtemps. Nous nous distrayons
en photographiant les bêtes et les gens au grand
plaisir du cuisinier qui se trouve probablement
fort beau, car il fait des effets de cuisse devant
l'objectif.
Le temps (pour imiter la façon de Monsieur
Alary) est frisquet, quoique très clair. Nous

avons facilement la goutte au nez quand nous le sortons, et c'est la pipe, l'horrible pipe qui, séductrice, nous invite à faire la ronde autour de l'âtre que nous fumons en rang comme une exposition de Shouberski (le seul poêle à roulettes qui se trouve place de l'Opéra au prix unique de cent francs). Je relis ma lettre, et m'aperçois que j'ai oublié le but principal qui est, ma chère Bonne maman, de vous apporter mes souhaits bien sincères de bonne année. J'espère qu'il vous seront aussi agréables sortant de ma bouche barbue qu'ils l'ont été jusqu'à present. Veuillez, je vous prie, être mon interprète auprès de mon oncle et de ma tante si capitonnés dans leur nid, et merci de toutes les bonnes choses dont vous avez comblé maman à mon intention.

Je vous embrasse,
Votre respectueux petit fils,
Henri

79 TO HIS MOTHER

[Paris, Spring 1886]

Ma chère Maman

Mes tribulations amygdalesques ont fini, mais mon modèle menace de me lâcher. Ah quel sale métier que la peinture. Si elle ne répond pas à mon ultimatum, il ne me reste plus qu'à bâcler quelques illustrations, et à vous rejoindre au mois d'Août. J'irai me tremper à Arcachon. Papa m'a donné quelque argent, mais je ne sais si j'aurai assez pour payer mon terme et vivre. Dans ce vas vous m'aiderez, s'il plaît à votre seigneurie. Etant donné que nous passerions pas mal de temps à la campagne, ça équilibrera. Peut être viendrai-je passer le mois de septembre à Paris, et reviendrai en Octobre pour voir les mémères. Papa m'a reparlé d'un atelier coté Arc de Triomphe, et je lui ai bien expliqué que ce ne serait jamais qu'un salon. Peut être le prendra-t-il en me laissant le mien. Voila une combinaison toute nouvelle, et qui nous ouvre un horizon de five o'clock teas. Pensez à tout ca, et à votre garçon qui turbine tant qu'il peut, et vous embrasse dans sa barbe d'Auvergnat.

Yours
Henri.

Papa va tirer les canards à Rivaude.
Oncle Charles et son épouse vont bien.

80 TO HIS MOTHER

[Paris, Spring 1886]

Ma chère Maman,

Votre carte postale ne s'explique pas. Je vous avais écrit deux jours avant. Celui à qui j'ai confié ma lettre a dû l'oublier! J'ai vu papa qui prétend tirer le diable par la queue, et qui, par ricochet, me la fait tirer. Je vous dis cela franchement, quoique n'en souffrant pas assez pour vous appeler à mon aide. Nous reparlerons de tout ça—je passe. J'ai vu oncle Odon et tante Odette qui s'embêtent, et parlent (ne le dites pas) d'aller à Cannes.

Je vais faire des dessins, pour *le Courrier Français*.

Papa a toujours des velléités d'aller du côté de l'Arc de Triomphe. Nous avons même été voir des ateliers. Cela ne change en rien.

On me dit que vous venez avec Oncle Amédée. Est ce vrai? Rien de neuf à part ça. Cormon a été content de moi dimanche. Le concours sera jugé mercredi. Je vous embrasse ferme.

Yours
Henri

81 TO HIS MOTHER

[Paris, Spring 1886]

Ma chère Maman

J'ai enfin vu Louis—il a été fort aimable. J'ai vu Papa qui a un petit pardessus blanc qui est tout un poème. A part ça rien. J'ai diné dans la famille de Claudon avec sa mère et son frère; ils ont été très aimables. Tout le monde vous attend avec une certaine impatience et nous allons faire quelques petits diners joyeux, je l'espère. Il me semble que l'héritier fait des manières et se fait attendre. Anquetin va partir pour le Midi près de Nice. Voila qui m'embête, et si je me sentais assez fort je vous jure que je le suivrais; il fait noir ici.

Cormon est dans le marasme et n'a pas le sou.

M. Richard, mon éditeur, est en procès avec tout le monde. Tant mieux.

Quant à l'affaire Frayssinet la voici: M. Gervex, ayant fait le portrait de Mᵐᵉ de F. s'est vanté, disent certains, d'avoir partagé le bonheur du beau Jacques. Lequel lui aurait allongé une paire de claques, lesquelles ont été payées d'un coup d'epée. Il y a d'autres versions, que je vous dirai à vous.

Voila ma chronique
Je vous embrasse et les bonnes mamans.

H

82 TO HIS MOTHER

[Paris, July 1886]

Ma chère Maman,

J'ai reçu votre envoi en bon état, malheureusement je n'ai pu ajouter les 30 fʳ nécessaires au paiement du terme sans dessécher tout à fait mon escarcelle. Je paierai au premier jour quand je toucherai mon mois, Papa ayant été à Rivaude et disparaissant. Je me suis fort amusé ces jours ci au *Chat noir*. Nous avions organisé un orchestre, et nous faisions danser le peuple. C'était fort drôle, seulement on se couchait à 5 heures du matin, ce qui fait souffrir un peu le travail dudit matin. Je fais, en ce moment-ci, un dessin chez un sculpteur de l'avenue de Villiers, qui est fort joli garçon et d'une correction irréprochable. C'est très agréable, mais ça ne m'empêchera pas de me mettre au vert sans regret, et à Arcachon le *trempadou* est très indiqué.

Je suis un peu cuit, car il fait très chaud et même orageux (ah les nuages qui passent). Je n'ai pas encore trouvé la photographie demandée de Mgr Guibert. Je . . . , mais je sens que je vais vous répéter votre dernière lettre, ce qui est inutile. Je vous embrasse donc chaudement.

Yours
Henry

83 TO HIS MOTHER
[Paris, Autumn 1886]

Ma chère Maman
Je reçois votre lettre, et arrive de Villiers où j'ai passé une demi-journée. Robby est un vrai bijou, il semble un gros rat et commence à grogner. Grenier le gardera tout l'hiver. Je n'ai pas encore reçu de lettre de Papa et n'ai point vu Bourges. J'ai rendez-vous avec Roques, et ai presque mes entrées à l'Eden ça va donc pour le mieux, ce qui fait que je vous embrasse gaiment, quoique ayant un rhume qui me gonfle le nez. Embrassez les mamans

Yours
Henri.

84 TO HIS MOTHER
[Albi], Lundi [1886]

Ma chère Maman
Je vous envoie le bulletin albigeois qui comme vous le pensez est peu varié. Votre mère est guillerette et B[onne] Maman Gabrielle fort aimable—à mon endroit. Papa graillonne, et se frictionne de thérébentine. Invité aujourd'hui au Vigan, il a cané au dernier moment, et j'y vais seul avec bonne maman.
J'ai assisté hier à toutes les bénédictions archiépiscopales et papales C'etait fort beau. Raoul, gras, est arrivé avec sa femme qui a aussi de l'embonpoint, mais d'une autre espèce.
La machine à coudre a fait merveille. Il n'y a que Toto qui manque à l'appel, son congé étant remis à plus tard. Entre papa et moi il n'a rien été echangé de *significatif* encore.
Je vous embrasse.

Votre
H.T.L.

J'ai reçu *La Vie Parisienne*, merci.

85 TO HIS MOTHER
[Paris], Mardi [1886]

Ma chère maman
Pas grand'chose à vous annoncer. Je vois souvent Papa et Gabriel. J'ai recommencé à travailler!!! c'est pourtant bien dur de s'enfermer. Il fait un beau soleil, et, malgré l'air vif, je me promène le matin avec beaucoup de plaisir. Mon ami Lesclide a failli se perdre du Havre à Cherbourg. Les hommes terrifiés et malades et lui obligé de gouverner et manœuvrer seul par une mer épouvantable. C'est miracle qu'il en soit sorti.
J'ai dejeuné avec Gaston Bonnefoy et sa femme très aimable. Il commence pourtant à trouver que ce n'est pas une sinécure. Il se lève à 6 *heures*.

Raoul parti en découverte a deux propriétés en vue. Toujours sous le sceau du secret. Je vous embrasse, et vous remercie de vos raisins qui nous ont fait grand plaisir.

Yours
H

86 TO LILI GRENIER
[1886]

Duchesse,
Je viens vous rappeler que demain nous boulottons ensemble. Les garçons de l'Ermitage m'ont dit que l'autre jour vous·étiez avec un vieillard à nous attendre. Oubliez le s'il vous plaît dans une armoire.
Je baise vos petites mains

HTLautrec

87 TO HIS MOTHER
[Paris, Spring 1887]

Ma chère maman,
Je suis heureux de vous apprendre que Papa a pu chasser et tuer faisans et bécasses. Cela lui a donné beaucoup de courage, et il est docilement venu reprendre son traitement électrique que Bourges lui fait subir tous les jours. Il se fait masser par son cocher, et. exécute des mouvements de rotation du bras plusieurs heures par jour. Ces occupations, quoique peu récreatives, l'occupent et l'empêchent de se morfondre.
Je suis personnellement à pied du côté modèle de mon existence. Je me rattrape en mangeant beaucoup, mon appétit n'étant pas encore éreinté. Quant à l'appartement nous avons été le voir ensemble, mais il a l'air d'y trouver lui-même des inconvénients.
Donc tout va à peu près. C'est la grâce que je vous souhaite, et vous embrasse

yours
Henri

88 TO HIS MOTHER
[Paris, Spring 1887]

Ma chère Maman,
Cette fois-ci c'est vous qui avez laissé moisir votre encre de telle sorte que Papa ayant été passer je crois un ou deux jours à Orléans, me voilà tout à fait orphelin. Je travaille tant que je peux au soleil. Quant à aller chez Grenier, je pense que ça se fera dans une douzaine de jours, quitte à m'en aller si je ne travaille pas. A moins que je ne me décide à prendre un modèle avec Claudon et d'aller à Cernay. Tout ça est compliqué. Lui-même Claudon arrive de la campagne, où il avait commencé un modèle de Paris. Ils se sont disputés de suite.
Question sérieuse: si papa ne m'ajoute mon terme (ce qu'il n'a pas l'air de faire) je compte sur vous. Je vous télégraphierai *send money*, simplement en cas d'urgence, ce qui signifierait par télégraphe (27 rue Caulaincourt) les 335f, 33° nécessaires. Mes illustrations sont en plan grâce

au clicheur qui a fait ça noir comme le cul de Simon lui-même.

Tout va bien à part ça, et je vous embrasse en troupier fidèle.

Henri

89 TO HIS MOTHER
[Château du Bosc or Céleyran] 1er janvier [18]88

Ma chère Maman

Le premier de l'an est fort réussi, tout le monde va bien, et se congratule mutuellement. Il est vraiment regrettable que les circonstances aient hâté votre départ, car vous auriez fait bonne figure à la table de famille dont je suis le plus vieux mâle (l'abbé ne comptant pas pour tel). Ce cher homme a inventé une longue prière du soir avec préambule de son cru, qui donne des attaques de fou rire à Gabriel. Marraine me charge d'un tas de choses pour vous. Bonne maman Gabrielle est resplendissante. Il parait que le transfer à Albi va avoir lieu, l'appartement étant délivré des ouvriers. Ma filleule m'entoure de prévenances! Hosannah!!! Marie de Rivières entre au Sacré Cœur (n'ayant pas trouvé de mari). Cette réflexion est de moi, et je la crois juste. Voilà tout.

Nous allons grimper Miramont cette après midi, et c'est en le regardant que je vous embrasse. Rien de Papa.

Yours
Harry

90 TO HIS MOTHER
[Paris, January 1888]

Ma chère Maman,

Je suis, depuis deux jours, d'une humeur massacrante, et ne sais comment ça va tourner. Le ciel est inclément, et nous arrose avec une désinvolture qui prouve peu les faveurs des sentiments du père éternel à l'égard des peintres de plein air. A part ça les affaires vont. J'expose en février en Belgique, et deux peintres belges intransigeants étant venus me voir ont été charmants, et prodigues d'éloges hélas immérités. J'ai de plus de la vente en perspective, mais il ne faut pas *canta abaud d'avé fa l'iovu.*

Je vais à ravir, et vous embrasse. Gaudeamus.

Yours
Harry.

91 TO THÉO VAN RYSSELBERGHE
[Paris, January 1888]

Mon cher Théo,

Je viens vous remercier de l'invitation que je dois évidemment plus à votre recommandation qu'à ma valeur personnelle. J'ai fait des démarches auprès de Forain qui enverra très probablement, et je l'espère, car ses œuvres sont un vrai régal. Maintenant pourrai-je vous faire une demande sans abuser de votre complaisance? Un de mes bons camarades, Albert, qui a exposé aux In-

transigeants cette année à Paris, me prie de vous demander s'il y a encore des invitations à faire de songer à lui. Il serait très heureux de montrer sa peinture avec la vôtre et la nôtre. Je vous transmets sa demande, en vous priant de faire pour lui ce que vous avez si gentiment fait pour nous. Et en vous remerciant d'avance, je vous prie de me croire bien cordialement à vous.

H. de T. Lautrec

27 rue Caulaincourt.

92 TO HIS MOTHER
[Paris, January 1888]

Ma chère Maman

J'ai passé la journée avec papa qui est fort aimable, et me parait peu disposé à fuir le séjour enchanteur de la capitale quoique le temps soit orageux, c.a.d. passablement énervant. Le travail va assez bien, et je me remets assez pour exposer à droite et à gauche ce qui est le seul moyen de se faire voir. Je vais m'occuper de vous envoyer le portrait de Rachou. Quant à Miss J. Matheson, le mieux serait d'aller chez Mlle A. Dubos 56 rue du Rocher, je crois que c'est 10f. la leçon, mais c'est pas mal. (Entre nous, c'est une amie de Juliette.) Vous ai-je dit que j'exposais à Bruxelles au mois de février? invité par les Vingtistes. Sur ce, vous embrasse ainsi que bonne maman et Tata.

Yours
Harry

93 TO HIS MOTHER
[Paris, February–March 1888]

Ma chère Maman

Ma lettre a dû courir après vous, ce qui explique votre dépêche. Depuis ma lettre de dimanche je n'ai rien de neuf. Je livre des photos à Roques d'après mes panneaux du Mirliton. Qu'en adviendra-t-il, on ne sait que penser. Mon autre dessin a été déclaré mauvais à la réduction. C'est embêtant.

Je crois vous avoir écrit ce que Papa m'avait dit, et ce que j'en pensais. Miss Matheson ne m'a encore rien écrit. Que bonne maman ait *beaucoup* à faire, rien d'étonnant, mais qu'elle ne vous envoie pas ce que j'écris c'est moins drôle, car vos nerfs sont facilement en l'air et couve-poule et ce que fait votre canard vous intéresse, Nous avons eu un jour de neige vite fondue, ce qui m'a coupé bras et jambes. J'ai d'ailleurs eu une indigestion de pâté. Comme deux de mes camarades ont été également malades, nous supposons qu'un toxique quelconque en est la cause. Vert de gris ou viande douteuse? *that is the question.* Enfin c'est passé, et n'en parlons plus. J'ai *fusé* du haut et du bas avec profusion et parfums aussi variés que délicats.

Je continue mon train train, et vous embrasse ainsi que toute la société albigeoise.

Yours
Henri.

266

[Paris, Summer 1888]

Ma chère Maman,
Je suis sans nouvelles de vous de toutes parts, ayant vu souvent mon oncle et ma tante plus Papa. Quoi de neuf? sans doute plus que moi qui mène une vie plate. Si je n'avais les douches et le travail, je m'ennuierais à mort. Bourges souffrant va probablement aller au Mont-Dore? et je serai seul avec mon déshonneur. C'est gai. Tant pis?
Si vous étiez là, nous aurions la ressource de la voiture le soir aux Champs Elysées. Il y a là une idée à creuser, vous me verriez davantage, tout le monde ayant fichu le camp.
Your boy
Harry.

Villiers-sur-Morin, Vendredi 13
[July, 1888]

Ma chère Maman,
Le mauvais temps m'a tellement exaspéré que je suis venu chez Grenier à la campagne me consoler un peu. Tante Emilie a dû vous dire que mes dessins avaient paru. Je vous les enverrai Lundi. Nous partons toujours le 20 ou 22, que le diable emporte St Médard et son arrosoir. Quant à moi, je vais mieux depuis que je suis délivré de Paris et de mes modèles.
Il pleut d'ailleurs autant à la campagne qu'à Paris, mais je dors et digère sans tracas.
Your boy
Henri

Ecrivez moi à Paris, j'y reviens.

[Paris, Summer 1888]

Ma chère Maman,
Il fait un temps affreux qui me fait d'autant plus grogner que j'ai perdu deux jours en allant voir Grenier à la campagne. Vous devriez vraiment lui envoyer du vin, c'est vraiment promettre trop à ce garçon. J'espère que vous lui en enverrez du bon, plus une liste à moi pour savoir comment il pourrait s'en procurer et des échantillons si possible. Je fais faire la caisse pour le portrait de Rachou. Quant à mes projets il n'y en a guère, faites ce que vous voudrez, je m'arrangerai toujours. Je vous enverrai la note de Brédif (mystère) qui se monte à 114', si vous voulez m'envoyer directement la galette ou à lui.
Bourges est au Mont Dore pour ses bronches; il va revenir. Vous avez sans doute appris la mort de sa tante assassinée à Bordeaux.
Je vous embrasse, Tata et bonne maman et vous
yours
Henri

[Paris], Samedi [November 24, 1888]

C'est de mes 24 ans que je vous écris, ma chère maman, en vous remerciant d'abord de *tous* vos envois qui sont arrivés à bon port. La petite vérole est le point noir de la chose, car je me demande s'il faut risquer le paquet: n'ayant pas vu Bourges depuis deux *fois*. Il est installé à l'hôpital.
Gabriel vient souvent me voir, et a l'air de s'intéresser à ce qu'il fait. Tant mieux. Je suis d'ailleurs dans une bonne passe, menant trois études de front avec courage. Le ciel est d'ailleurs clair, chose rare dans cette saison et ici il me permet de donner libre cours à mes bonnes intentions.
Je verrai Papa demain, et ne l'ai point vu depuis qu[elques] jours, menant, une vie de reclus et le soir ne sortant que juste ce qu'il faut pour faire un peu d'exercice. Ça n'est guère varié, mais c'est fort satisfaisant. Donc pas de nouvelles, si ce n'est ma vieillesse qui vient de faire un tour, de plus, ce qui ne m'empêche pas de vous embrasser ferme.
Votre fils
Harry.

[Paris, Summer 1889]

Ma chère Maman,
je tremble en prenant la plume (afin de vous écrire ce mot de lettre comme disent les pioupious) de vous faire ressentir le contrecoup de la mauvaise humeur où je suis grâce à des abats d'eau qui n'arrêtent pas depuis 3 jours. Rien à faire qu'à regarder tomber la pluie. J'ai vu hier la famille. Oncle Charles achète poignards, arbalètes à rouet et autre menus joujoux destinés a encombrer son *hostel*.
Vos projets me semblent fondés sur des données vagues, vous ne devant pousser une pointe coursanaise, si vous croyez la chose urgente que vers la fin de septembre. Je doute fort que la smalah y soit encore ou du moins soit encore à Palavas. Je voudrais trouver une combinaison Arcachonnaise, mais il y a beaucoup de mais.
Je termine par un baiser mouillé jusqu'aux os.
votre boy
Henri.

Je relis ma lettre, elle n'est pas de trop mauvaise humeur. Tant mieux.

[Paris, September 1889]

Ma chère Maman,
Nous avons été absorbés par la grande joie du vernissage qui a été assez gai, malgré la pluie battante. Oncle Odon et ma tante y étaient et m'ont demandé quand et comment vous allez arriver. J'ai averti également Laura Pérey. Paul

et Joseph sont allés à Pauguiers, et nous les attendons demain. J'ai également rendez vous avec Charles du Passage pour aller voir la peinture. Princeteau n'a pas donné signe de vie. Bourges me fait des infidélités, il est obligé de rester à l'hôpital, tous les autres étant en villégiature. Son hôpital est d'ailleurs fort gai, plein de petits jardins. J'irai peut être y faire des études de bonnes femmes en bonnet blanc, qui leur donne un peu l'air de laitières.

En espérant vous voir bientôt, je vous embrasse.

Yours
Harry,

et Tata ne l'oubliez pas.

100 TO HIS MOTHER

[Paris, September 1889]

Ma chère Maman,

J'ai été fort peiné de savoir l'état malheureux de votre estomac, car je crains que le froid n'y soit pour beaucoup et que Paris et surtout Rivaude vous réservent des variations en courant majeur fort désagréables. Je suis heureusement hors d'affaire, ainsi que mon oncle Odon qui est reparti pour la Haichois nettoyé de fond en comble. J'ai déjeuné avec Papa aujourd'hui, nous avons été chez Du Passage qui a distillé sa salive bénissante sur mon jeune front. Je suis donc sauvé par l'imposition des mains de ce colosse gras. J'ai déposé mes hommages aux pieds de sa femme souffrante. Voilà tout ce que j'ai de neuf.

Mon travail n'est pas encore bien brillant, c'est si dur de s'y remettre. C'est a dégoûter du repos, parceque la réaction est vraiment pénible. Nous avons reçu le vin dont grand merci. Et maintenant, petite maman, écoutez votre vieux fils, soignez vous bien, et ne vous faites pas de bile surtout.

Yours
Harry.

101 TO MME R. C. DE TOULOUSE-LAUTREC
[Paris, January 1890]

Ma chère Bonne Maman,

Vous êtes, sans doute, au courant de nos petites affaires par Papa qui doit être auprès de vous en train de tisonner, (si je ne m'abuse), et c'est simplement pour vous embrasser en vous souhaitant un bon 1890 que je viens. J'espère, en ce faisant, ne pas vous communiquer l'influenza que j'ai eue *deux* fois, et que je traine encore. C'est à peine si je peux ouvrir les yeux, et, depuis quatre jours, je ne travaille guère, car dès que je suis en position et que je regarde mon modèle, je me mets à pleurer comme un veau, il n'y a pourtant pas de quoi. Maman n'y a pas échappé, mais s'en est tirée à bon compte. Voila bien des jérémiades, n'est ce pas?

Je vais à la fin de janvier porter la bonne parole, ou plutôt la bonne peinture(?), en Belgique—Pauvres belges!

Je consacre le papier qui me reste à bien vous embrasser, et vous prier de me rappeler à ceux de votre entourage qui s'intéressent un peu aux efforts de votre petit-fils respectueux.

HTLautrec

102 TO HIS MOTHER

[Paris, March–April 1890]

Ma chère Maman

Je suis encore sous le coup du second vernissage. Quelle journée!! mais quel succès. Le Salon a reçu là une gifle dont il se relèvera peut être, mais qui donnera à réfléchir à bien des gens.

Vous devez être tout a fait albigeoisifiée à present, et dans une douce torpeur faite de nourriture et d'ennui. Je regrette qu'il soit encore trop tôt pour aller braver les dangers du bassin d'Arcachon, car, ici pas grand chose à faire—Les modèles sont rares, et les modèles sérieux très rares. Tout ça manque d'intérêt.

J'ai vu hier le Dr Bonnefoy, très vanné par 8 jours de Paris qui m'a dit avoir une petite jument à vous vendre. Louis a l'air un peu sur la *corde noire*. Papa et Princeteau présidés par Nabarroy-Bey émaillent Lucas de l'éclat de leur présence. Mon domestique est décidément odieux, et moi je vous embrasse.

Yours
Henry.

103 TO HIS MOTHER

[Paris, June 1890]

Ma chère Maman,

Votre imprévu est un problème que je n'essaierai pas de résoudre. Pourquoi ce crochet à Rivaude? On se le demande. Je vais vous charger d'une mission! Pouvez vous me dire *certainement* si je pourrai travailler avec Juliette sans encombre, et si vous ne prévoyez pas d'interruption dans un travail suivi.

D'un autre côté, où la famille d'oncle Amedée passera ses vacances? Au besoin, vous pourriez emmener Kiki à Malromé pendant un temps, je pourrais peut-être faire quelque chose d'intéressant avec elle. Tout ça demande réponse parce que je me baserai là dessus pour partir de Paris au commencement ou à la fin de juillet, ce qui mettra mon retour définitif à Paris fin Octobre. Ce sont là de beaux projets. Quoi vous dire de moi-même? Je suis *tout seul*, aucun ami excepté mon voisin Gauzi, Bourges couchant à l'hôpital. Il a l'intention d'aller en Ecosse au mois d'Août. Princeteau s'est annoncé à l'hôtel Pérey.

Adieu ma chère Maman, et tâchez d'écouter votre imprévision pour être plus vite face-à-face avec cet être horriblement abject qui fait votre désespoir et qui signe.

yours
Harry.

Embrassez Tata qui restera probablement auprès de sa Tante.
Vous avez tort de la laisser partir.

[Paris, August 1890]

Mon cher Monsieur
J'ai oublié l'autre jour deux tableaux, l'un représentant une *femme assise en rose de face, un peu penchée en avant* l'autre une *femme rousse assise parterre, de dos, nue,* ces deux tableaux étaient à l'exposition des XX à Bruxelles cette année. Veuillez je vous prie m'en accuser la présence, j'en demande 300ᶠ. de chacun.
Cordialement votre
H. de Toulouse Lautrec

27 rue Caulaincourt

Taussat, mercredi 3 septembre
[1890]

Ma chère Maman
Je suis enfin rentré au bercail après une fugue bien amusante mais un peu fatiguante. Samedi Matin, départ de Taussat à 5 h. par chemin de fer, arrivé au Boucau, station avant Bayonne. A midi déjeuné avec un de mes amis qui fait un tableau de Toreadors. Départ pour Biarritz, pour retenir nos places à la Corrida. Diner, coucher après le Casino. Le lendemain matin, je suis parti pour St Sébastien avec des indigènes fort aimables (grâce à la présence de *Bordes* tout le pays était à moi). Déjeuner espagnol, et, à 4 heures, corrida avec 6 taureaux de 5 ans. Tapage, étripements, odeurs, rien n'a manqué, et retour le soir par un train de plaisir à Biarritz. Nous avons attendu *deux* heures en gare, empilés dans des wagons de troisième et par une chaleur!!!! Le lendemain j'ai été à Fontarabie (ayant couché à Biarritz) avec un journaliste parisien, et suis rentré le lendemain à Taussat. J'ai vu votre ville de loin, elle est très haut perchée. J'ai pris quelques bains de mer avec des lames qui roulent un peu vivement mais très agréables. Je reviendrai sans doute à Biarritz dans une 15ᵉ, enfin—nous aviserons. Je vous embrasse chaudement, car ici le soleil tape ferme aussi. Embrassez ma marraine.
Yours
H.

Taussat, Vendredi 11 [September 1890]

Ma chère Maman,
J'ai reçu votre lettre de Biarritz commençant à être inquiet sur votre sort. N'auriez-vous pas reçu ma lettre à Lourdes décrivant la course de taureaux et datée de Taussat où je suis à port fixe profitant des derniers beaux jours et bains de mer. Mon plan serait d'aller à Biarritz deux jours avant votre départ et d'aller visiter les usines du Boucau, puis vous accompagner même au Bosc pour huit jours. Voyez et combinez. Je partirais alors pour Paris. Je pense, si vos prévisions se réalisent que cela aura lieu à la fin du mois. Sinon j'irais quand même à Biarritz et de là à

Paris directement. J'ai été faire pêcher mes oiseaux dans les étangs où ils ont été fort brillants. Je termine en vous embrassant et vous demandant une réponse détaillée. Princeteau vient à Arcachon dimanche. J'irai l'y voir.
Embrassez ma marraine et dites-lui la part que je prends à son immobilité, sachant combien c'est peu agréable d'être cloué au lit sans bouger, et dites-lui tous les vœux que je fais pour sa guérison.
Your boy
Henri

Je n'ai de nouvelles de personne

[Paris, December 1890]

Ma chère Maman
J'ai fort bien reçu vos chaussettes, j'en ai assez pour le moment. Maintenant faites en faire encor 3 paires que vous apporterez à votre retour. J'ai donné de vos nouvelles à Papa qui a des ennuis avec ses tapisseries détenues comme gage par les propriétaires d'Altamoura dont papa avait sous-loué l'atelier. . . . Le voilà donc encore retenu. Je continue à travailler malgré le peu de lumière. Nous avons eu une glace fort épaisse, et, au moment où on inaugurait la fête des patineurs, le dégel est arrivé. Tant mieux mais quel gâchis.
Je vous souhaite un merry christmas, en attendant le new year, Embrassades genérales.
Your boy
Henri

[Paris, December 1890]

Ma chère Maman
J'ai reçu vos souhaits de bonne année, et ne puis que vous renvoyer la balle dans les mêmes conditions. Quant au miroir que vous m'offrez, je vous remercie d'abord, et vous prie de le garder sous votre aile jusqu'à nouvel ordre.
Nous avons, Bourges et moi, également fêté le piot envoyé par son frère de Bergerac. Les truffes, d'ailleurs, ne m'ont pas été clémentes, est-ce qualité ou quantité, mais j'ai dû restituer au seau ce que je devais au dindonneau. Sans souffrances d'ailleurs ni interruption de gaité. Vous voyez que je maintiens haut et ferme les traditions de famille.
J'ai eu avec papa une explication fort calme relative à mon peu d'empressement à aller voir mon oncle, et il m'a *approuvé pleinement*. Le tout très diplomatiquement d'ailleurs. Voilà donc une cause gagnée—qu'on se le dise.
Il continue ici à faire froid, si bien que Bourges patine tous les jours avec beaucoup d'enthousiasme. Il est fort inquiet des foies gras dont vous vous ruinez et les attend avec impatience. Y pensez vous?
Sur ce, je vais travailler, et vous embrasse encor en 90, sans préjudice de 91.

Je vais écrire aux mémères. Rappelez-moi l'adresse de Tante Armandine.

Poutounégeades, etc. etc.

Bonne année!!
Yours
Henri

109 TO JULES LÉVY
19 rue Fontaine.   [Paris, January 1891]

Cher Monsieur,

Mon ami Desmet m'a affirmé que vous écrire motivait une invitation au bal des Incohérents.

Je vous remercie donc d'avance, et vous prie de croire à ma haute considération.

H. de Toulouse Lautrec

110 TO HIS MOTHER
                                    [Paris, January 1891]

Ma chère Maman

Le papier manque, et je suis obligé de me servir de papier écolier. J'ai reçu les étrennes de bonne maman Louise et son pâté qui a passé un fichu quart d'heure. Dites-lui cela de ma part, en la remerciant bien.

Nous sommes ici avec un froid très sec, mais qui continue à nous peler. Bourges patine avec ardeur, et voudrait que ça dure éternellement. Il a failli cependant partir pour le Congo avec deux intrépides explorateurs pour *cinq mois*. L'affaire a raté, et il va se consoler en allant à Beyrouth faire un rapport sur le Choléra; chacun prend son plaisir où il le trouve. Papa va toujours parlant tantôt d'aller à Albi, tantôt de s'installer Cité du Retiro dans un atelier? Je pense toujours aller en Belgique et Hollande en février, mon exposition à Volney ouvrant le 26.

Donnez-moi une idée pour faire un cadeau à Kiki qui m'a demandé une *autruche* mécanique que je n'ai pas le temps de chercher. Je vous enverrai ce que vous penserez de mieux, et vous le lui ferez parvenir, ou remettrez en mains maternelles.

Je vous embrasse, et vous prie d'en faire autant à qui de droit.

Yours
Henri

Gaston Bonnefoy, retour de Saigon, a enregistré deux nouveaux accidents de voiture sans accident de personne. 1° Les Vathoin et les Massapin culbutés dans le même break. 2° la voiture des Lanure au cocher seul.

Je crois que votre idée de cocher est bonne.

111 TO HIS MOTHER
                                    [Paris, January 1891]

Ma chère Maman,

Je vois avec plaisir que la nourriture et les fioles vous aident à supporter vaillamment les intempéries, et que, loin de broyer du noir, vous cliquetez des mandibules.

J'ai failli cette nuit être rôti, le feu ayant pris à une poutre sous ma chambre. Heureusement les pompiers ont éteint le feu en un quart d'heure. La chose s'est d'ailleurs passée hier soir à 11 heures, et, quand je suis arrivé me coucher, je n'ai trouvé que beaucoup de fumée.

Est-ce Joseph Pascal qui se marie? Bourges a reçu une lettre signée Joseph sans nom de famille, et l'écriture ressemblant vaguement à la sienne? J'ai été stupéfait de savoir que j'avais oublié le texte de la carte adressée à Papa—Excusez moi. Répondez, je vous prie, à la question Béatrix. Ici tout le monde gèle—et gèlera encor. Qui sait quand je pourrai aller en Belgique! Embrassez grand-mamans et oncles et tantes et neveux, bien des choses à Papa.

Je vous embrasse
votre fils
Henri

Pouvez-vous nous envoyer un chapon albigeois, de bonne mine? Je l'espère et j'y compte ainsi que sur les foies?

Yours   H

112 TO HIS MOTHER
                                    [Paris, January 1891]

Ma chère Maman,

Je pense que le carnaval Albigeois n'a pas dû troubler outre mesure vos épanchements de famille. Ici peu de variété, sauf un encombrement des rues tel que j'ai traversé les grands boulevards, un officier de paix tirant mon cheval ou plutôt le cheval de mon sapin par le nez entre deux haies de sergents de ville, maintenant une foule hurlante et congestionnée qui donnait un peu la sensation de l'émeute, fort amusante d'ailleurs.

J'ai vu Gérard de Naurois au Moulin Rouge fort guilleret. Nous allons définitivement louer l'appartement du 21 de la rue Fontaine, qui est décidément l'idéal. Emile Pérey ne doit pas encore se marier donc pas de considération à prendre de ce côté-là. Louis ne m'a rien dit de Respide bien que me voyant tous les jours, puisque je fais son portrait. Pas d'autres nouvelles même à l'horizon. Je vous embrasse tous et vous surtout.

Your boy
Henri

Je vous envoie la coupure flatteuse oubliée la dernière fois.

113 TO HIS MOTHER
                                    [Paris, February 1891]

Ma chère Maman

La famille au grand complet, voilà donc la nouvelle du jour. Je crains bien que ma haute personnalité ne manque à cette petite fête. Nous jouissons ici d'un temps splendide, si bien que j'ai fait atteler le buggy et qu'avec Gaston nous avons été respirer l'air du bois de Boulogne deux ou trois fois. Je pense que Papa n'y verra pas d'inconvenient, au contraire, car cheval et voiture ont pris l'air—et moi aussi.

Je suis occupé de mon exposition, ayant en train 3 portraits. Gaston, Louis, et Bourges. Louis a deux situations sûres grâce à Msgr. Richard, soit des assurances, soit la Transatlantique. Tant mieux. Revenez vite, car je vais me trouver seul, Bourges allant en Afrique dans les premiers jours de mars, un mois à cheval jusqu'au sud avec promesse de chasse à la gazelle —quel dommage que je ne puisse pas l'accompagner. Papa pourrait, peut-être, y aller. Bourges le réclame, et me charge de ses meilleurs souvenirs pour lui.

Poutounégeades, et à vous your boy
Henri

114 TO HIS MOTHER
[Paris, Spring 1891]

Ma chère maman,

Pour une fois les journaux ont à peu près dit la verité. Le *typhus exanthematique* que nous avons est une maladie qui ne peut s'attaquer qu'aux gens mal nourris et enfermés dans des prisons ou collèges. Nous, plus heureux, sommes à l'abri de cette épidémie fort limitée. Je suis toujours flemmard, et attends l'inspiration. Je me promène au Bois tous les jours, et absorbe le plus d'oxygène possible. J'ai failli prendre le train, et aller passer une huitaine à Taussat, mais j'ai eu peur de ne plus pouvoir revenir. Je serai heureux de chercher une décoration pour le musée Rochegude, et ce serait drôle de figurer en peintre là où j'ai figuré jambes nues en jeune lévite.

Calmez vous donc, ne craignez rien et salamalekoz autour de vous

je vous embrasse
yours
Henri

115 TO CHARLES DE TOULOUSE-LAUTREC
[Paris], Pâques [1891]

Mon cher Oncle,

Tout va de mieux en mieux. L'appétit est plus que revenu, il est violent. Le docteur défend encore de se lever par excès de précaution. Mais probablement demain il le permettra. Maman est très gaie, et lit et cause avec plaisir. Embrassez tous.

Votre neveu
Henri.

116 TO HIS MOTHER
[Paris], Dimanche [May 31, 1891]

Ma chère Maman,

J'ai reçu votre mot—et ai déjeuné ce matin avec papa et ma tante de Gualy, fort cordialement d'ailleurs et avec grand appétit creusé par le froid qui sévit depuis hier sur Paris. J'ai été heureux de remettre mon paletot d'hiver, et ai rallumé le feu de mon atelier. Qu'en pensez vous?

Jeudi brillant vernissage avec trop de monde, mais quelques camarades. En somme bonne journée, à part ça rien de neuf. Notre ameublement avance à petits pas, à tout petits pas. Et je vous embrasse sur vos joues gonflées d'asperges, je le suppose du moins. Vous devriez nous en envoyer une belle botte.

Yours
Henri

117 TO HIS MOTHER
[Paris], Vendredi [June 1891]

Ma chère Maman,

Votre lettre nous a tous douloureusement impressionnés. Mais Bourges voudrait avoir des détails sur le genre de paralysie, si elle est localisée dans la bouche, l'œil, ou genérale de la face, ce dernier cas étant bien moins dangereux. Je connais plusieurs peintres qui ont été attaqués de la sorte, et qui vivent avec. D'ailleurs tous ceux qui travaillent en *plein air* y sont voués. L'avenir m'en réserve sans doute autant.

Tante Emilie, son époux et son frère sont arrivés, je ne les ai point ençore vus. J'ai revu Gabriel qui m'a dit avoir beaucoup travaillé, et profité de son expérience. Son père va venir. Ma jaunisse est *finie*, et vous pourrez compter me voir à la fin de juillet ou au début d'août.—Vous seriez bien aimable si vous pouviez, vers le 14 juillet, date memorable, m'envoyer quelques sesterces pour distribuer à des traficants de diverses espèces. Si vous le pouvez, vous me feriez g[ran]d plaisir, car M. Roques me fait attendre indéfiniment ses paiements, et que, n'ayant pas de conventions écrites, j'ai bien peur d'être dans le lac. Fiez vous à l'honnêteté des gens!!!

Je baise vos mains, si chères, et rappelez moi à Louis et ma tante.

Yours
Harry.

118 TO HIS MOTHER
[Paris], Lundi [June 1891]

Ma chère Maman,

Je suis heureux de savoir que le mieux s'accentue, et, après, que vous donnerez suite à votre projet de départ. Je ne peux pas vous dire mieux.

Je vous attends avec impatience, et vous embrasse

yours
H.

J'ai reçu le livre de Jalby, il est donc inutile de vous en occuper.

Est-il vrai que l'Abbé va devenir chanoine, ou est-ce un canard?

119 TO HIS MOTHER
[Paris, early July 1891]

Ma chère Maman

Je vous remercie d'avance de l'envoi des 500f destinés aux fournisseurs. Nous ne vous négligeons pas non plus, car demain matin je vais avec Gaston Bonnefoy conduire les 4 fils de Musotte à Maison Alfort pour leur faire couper les oreilles, ce sera vraiment une petite roquette. Votre futur toutou est grivelé, c'est-à-dire gris de fer avec des taches noires. Madame Bonnefoy nous avait invités pour nous présenter cette petite famille. Nous avons ici un soleil niçois, et Bourges a acheté un cheval. Ce sont les seuls événements marquants. Ma bonne s'améliore un peu, peut-être a-t-elle compris que j'allais l'exécuter. Madame de Montecuculli me fait l'effet d'être un peu dans la lune, j'écris à Papa dans ce sens.

Je vous embrasse, et vous prie de me donner des nouvelles du procès d'Emmanuel, dès qu'il y aura du neuf. Guibert sent que jamais il ne pourra se débarrasser de sa fidèle(?) compagne, et rit jaune. *Fallait pas qu'il y aille.*

Yours
H.

120 TO HIS MOTHER

[Paris, early July 1891]

Ma chère Maman,

Bourges parti hier soir pour Respide vous dira que je vais comme le pont Neuf.

D'ici une 15e et avant je serai en train de respirer l'air frais de Malromé. Je ne compte pas rester plus *d'un mois* en tout à la campagne. Nous irons dans le Narbonnais, au Bosc, etc. . . . rapido, presto, subito.

Tachez d'amadouer tante Cécile pour que nous amenions Louis avec nous dans ce Cook's tour. I kiss you.

Your Harry

121 TO HIS MOTHER

[Paris], Mercredi [July 1891]

Ma chère Maman,

Vous devez avoir reçu votre fille aux longues oreilles. J'ai été obligé de payer le port, cela fait donc 34f50 que vous me devez. Elle a l'air très *esperpil* et vivace. J'espère qu'elle fera bon ménage avec les autres perlons, et en tous cas elle est d'une race où l'on sait se défendre. Nous comptons tous aller à Nîmes, et même j'amènerai mon ami Guibert qui suivra comme le Docteur dans *l'Histoire de M. Cryptogame.*

Je profiterai de l'occasion pour voir Marseille, et passerai par Ricardelle. J'espère, d'ici peu, vous annoncer mon arrivée, car j'ai soif d'eau salée. J'ai été voir dimanche Grenier qui s'est cassé la jambe en tombant de voiture. Il va aussi bien que possible, et a été très aimable. Claudon est moins brillant, perclus de rhumatismes.

Donnez moi des nouvelles de la jeune fille, et je vous embrasse.

Yours
H.
P.S. J'aurai probablement besoin d'attaquer la forte somme pour régler des notes. Nous reparlerons de ça.

122 TO HIS MOTHER

Arcachon, 7 août [1891]

Ma chère Maman

Tout va bien. Je suis toujours en bateau, et ai reçu une longue lettre de Papa qui semble désirer que je m'occupe directement de Ricardelle au cas où Jalabert viendrait à mourir. Le sujet est gros et demande à être traité de vous à moi. Je vous ferai voir la lettre, et nous verrons ce qu'il y a à faire. Je viendrai Mardi ou Mercredi à Malromé.

Je vous embrasse.

Votre
H.

123 TO HIS MOTHER

[Arcachon, Sept. 1891]

Ma chère Maman,

Je crois qu'il est inutile que j'aille à Narbonne. Je vous attendrai donc à Respide, ou je viendrai vous chercher *lundi* si vous me le dites sérieusement. Tout ici est à la débandade. C'est sans doute le moment choisi par Papa pour venir quoique je n'y compte guère. Je suis donc à Arcachon jusqu'à Samedi.

Ecrivez moi

Your boy
Henri.

124 TO HIS MOTHER

[Paris, September 1891]

Ma chère Maman

J'ai fait une traversée magnifique mais, à mon arrivée à Paris, j'ai trouvé ma bonne couchée avec une fièvre muqueuse qui me privera de ses services, j'ai peur, pendant 1 mois à peu près. Je vais probablement la faire porter à l'hôpital dans une chambre, çà me coutera 4f par jour à peu près, et elle aura tout sous la main, de plus mon appartement ne sera pas ouvert aux voisins dévoués il est vrai—mais dont la présence me charme très-relativement.

Je ne m'attendais pas à cette tuile. La pauvre fille est triste à voir. Enfin, je vais tâcher de me débrouiller de mon mieux. J'espère que ma prochaine lettre sera moins fussy, en tous cas je vous embrasse

yours
H.

125 TO HIS MOTHER

[Paris, September 1891]

Ma chère Maman

Votre lettre m'est arrivée au moment où j'allais vous écrire. J'ai vu mon oncle A., Gabriel et Papa, qui est d'une humeur charmante. Il a ouvert sa caisse avec facilité. Quant à mon oncle et Gabriel ils sont rentrés à Rivaude jusqu'au 5, époque du commencement des cours. Gabriel habitera à l'hôtel, au Quartier Latin, l'adresse n'est pas encore décidée. Il a l'air heureux; quant à Papa, il est toujours sur son départ. Bourges a eu la jaunisse, et est d'une maigreur lamentable, tout à fait méconnaissable.

J'ai vu mes marchands. Il me revient 200ᶠ nets sur une étude, ce qui fait qu'elle a été vendue 300ᶠ, ce qui est une petite augmentation dans le tarif. Les affaires sont d'ailleurs dans le marasme. Grenier qui est venu hier à Paris est plus affolé que jamais, et Anquetin a failli être repris par ses rhumatismes. Mes hémorrhoïdes vont mieux grâce à l'onguent *populeum*. Mon atelier est livré au balai et aux ramoneurs, et moi ne suis encore pas bien décidé sur ce que je vais faire. Degas m'a encouragé en me disant que mon travail de cet été n'est pas trop mal. Je voudrais bien le croire.

Je termine en embrassant Tata et vous, et, me rappelant à Respide où vous pouvez dire à Paul que j'ai été présenté à M. Jouard,
vous embrasse
your Harry

126 TO HIS MOTHER
[Paris, October 1891]

Ma chère Maman
Je commence par vous rassurer sur l'état de papa qui a eu un peu d'influenza, et l'a traité par le Hammam. L'étuve l'a congestionné, et, après une courte syncope, il a été vite debout, grâce à quelques verres de Kümmel. Il se tâte encore un peu, mais a assez bonne mine.

Ce que vous me dites pour Louis ne m'étonne pas. Vous savez mon avis là-dessus depuis longtemps. Je crois que vous ne pouvez pas mieux faire que de l'aider. Je vous remercie des truffes en perspective. Si vous envoyez une volaille truffée écrivez sur l'adresse le poids:
Volaille tant
Truffes tant.
car les droits d'entrée sont exorbitants quand on ne prend pas cette précaution.

Autre chose. Faites moi adresser, vers la fin de la semaine prochaine et vers la fin de l'autre, une volaille, chapon ou poulet, le frère de Bourges, notre poulailler habituel, étant en voyage pour 15 jours.

La saison des foies est-elle ouverte? Si oui, pensez à m'en faire envoyer 12 boites. Je relis ma lettre, et lui trouve un caractère gastronomique. Mon affiche est collée aujourd'hui sur les murs de Paris, et je vais en faire une autre.

Souvenirs affectueux autour de vous à qui de droit.

Je vous embrasse
Yours
Henri

127 TO HIS MOTHER
[Paris, October 1891]

Ma chère Maman
Je vous demande encore un peu de temps pour me décider, *car* je viens d'avoir une attaque de névralgie *dentaire* très dure, ce qui m'oblige à suivre un traitement chez un célèbre dentiste *Cruet*, un ami de Bourges (J'aurai besoin de vous plumer un peu pour payer cet homme, qui est charmant mais cher.) Si tout va bien, comme je l'espère, je viendrai, sinon je vous préviendrai le 15 au plus tard, *et vous prendriez Louis*. Revers de la médaille, j'ai vendu la jeune fille qui avait figuré au Volney.

Je n'ai pas vu Papa, car je ne sors guère à cause de l'humidité. Adieu, et ne vous troublez pas. Tout ceci n'est qu'une affaire de patience. Je n'ai eu qu'un tort, c'est de ne pas m'y prendre plus tôt.

Votre boy
Henri

128 TO HIS MOTHER
[Paris, October 1891]

Ma chère Maman
Je vous avais accusé reception des 150ᶠ. Ma lettre s'est elle égarée? Je suis très content que votre sauvetage se soit exécuté sans encombre, et j'espère que vous n'allez pas tarder à venir ici, laissant Tata en bonne compagnie, pour venir un peu voir votre fils que vous lâchez avec pas mal de désinvolture—grâce aux nombreux impedimenta survenus il est vrai: mais il me semble que l'heure de la revanche est venue, et j'espère que vous n'allez attendre le jour de l'an pour vous transporter ici armes et bagages. Rien de neuf à part ça. Le temps est noir, et tout va son petit train. Papa parle de s'en aller sans conviction.

Les expositions commencent.

Et je termine en vous embrassant
Yours
H.
Arrivez vite.

129 TO HIS MOTHER
[Paris, October 1891]

Ma chère Maman
Je suis heureux de vous annoncer que ma réparation de mâchoire va beaucoup mieux quoique j'en aie encore pour un certain temps. Je pourrai *certainement* venir vous chercher et papa s'est *presque* offert à le faire ou du moins à m'accompagner. Ce que vous me dites de Respide est plus grave. Il est inutile de remâcher ce sujet si pénible, nous l'avons assez fait.

Mon traitement consiste à extirper ce qui est douteux et à arranger ce qui est potable. Grâce aux injections de *Cocaïne* [on arrive] à la suppression complète de la douleur. Quant à être reclus, heureusement il n'en est rien.

Bourges soigne une petite fille qui a le croup et vient de lui faire avec succès la *trachéotomie*.

Papa a des velléités de passer quelque temps chez M. Pothain. Il fait noir et il pleut. J'ai vendu mon affaire 200 f. en sus de la commission donnée au marchand. C'est à dire que je n'y perds pas mais je n'y gagne pas non plus.

Je vous embrasse
yours
Harry

130 TO HIS MOTHER
[Paris, October–November 1891]

Ma chère Maman

Je suis un peu en retard mais j'ai pour excuse les colères que mes nouveaux modèles m'ont fait faire. Décidément cette espèce est dangereuse pour la tranquillité des peintres qui malheureusement ne s'en peuvent passer. Papa a l'air d'avoir *vraiment* envie d'aller vous chercher. Il a des velléités cynégétiques avec M. Pothain. Réussirat-il à se déplacer, en tout cas il est aimable. Mon dentiste continue à m'instrumenter fort habilement. Gare la note.

Il commence à pleuvoir ferme. ce qui n'a rien de réjouissant.

Rien de plus à vous dire. si ce n'est que je vous embrasse.

Your boy
Henri

131 TO HIS MOTHER
[Paris, December 1891]

Ma chère Maman

Pourquoi ne venez vous pas ici? L'influenza existe, mais pas encore dangereuse. Venez donc au plus tôt, quitte à aller à Albi plus tard.

J'ai vu papa qui a été chasser!!! avec le prince de Bourbon. Tout va bien ici. Tous travaillent, et moi aussi. Je vous remercie de la confiture, fort bien arrivée. A part çà, rien de neuf. Je viens d'envoyer à Kiki un horrible enfant Jésus en cire acheté sur ses indications. J'espère qu'elle en sera satisfaite.

Je vous embrasse, et espère vous voir poindre un de ces jours.

Yours
Henri

132 TO HIS MOTHER
[Paris], 26 décembre [18]91

Ma chère Maman,

J'ai *eu* l'influenza. Grâce à ma médication énergique (Bourges m'a fait fuser par tous les bouts). j'ai retrouvé la vue, l'appétit, et la gaité après 24 heures seulement de maladie. C'est peu, et, avec un peu de prudence, j'en ai été quitte à bon compte, tandis que Gabriel l'a depuis pas mal de jours pas grave, il est vrai, mais lancinante. Nous venons d'ouvrir une boutique, sorte d'exposition perpétuelle, rue Le Peletier. Les journaux ont été fort aimables pour votre rejeton. Je vous envoie un extrait qui est écrit avec du miel broyé dans de l'encens. Mon affiche a réussi sur les murs, malgré quelques pataquès commis par l'imprimeur qui déparent un peu mon produit.

Il fait un beau soleil aujourd'hui. Bourges patine avec ardeur.—Merci de votre chapon arrivé à bon porté, je suis heureux de pouvoir le fêter dignement.—Quand pensez vous venir?! La vie ouatée d'Albi a bien ses charmes, mais voilà bientôt 3 mois que nous nous sommes lâchés, et je réclame un peu de viande maternelle.

Je vous souhaite Merry Christmas et New Year. Ce sera chose faite. J'écrirai aux bonnes mamans demain ou après.

Je vous embrasse

Yours
Henri

133 TO HIS MOTHER
[Paris], 25 janvier [1892]

Ma chère Maman

Je viens d'ouvrir l'exposition du Cercle où mes navets quoique placés le plus mal possible ont été notés favorablement par la presse.

On est d'ailleurs fort aimable pour moi dans les journaux depuis mon affiche. Le 'Paris' journal très républicain (n'en dites rien à la famille) a été jusqu'à me consacrer deux colonnes où l'on dévoile ma personne sans omettre un détail. Je pars pour Bruxelles le 3 février et serai de retour le 7 ou 8, *au plus tard*. Basez vous donc là-dessus pour faire vos malles. Vous avez encore le temps d'attraper quelques indigestions. Papa est rentré de Chambord avec un petit retour d'influenza, et très impressionné par la mort de son ami.

Adieu, ma chère maman, j'espère que cette lettre sera sinon la dernière au moins l'avant dernière et que tout se passera en chair et en os avant qu'il soit longtemps.

Distribuez mes mamours à qui de droit,
votre fils
Henri

134 TO THÉO VAN RYSSELBERGHE
[Paris, February 19, 1892]

Cher maître,

Pouvez vous m'envoyer les journaux (*Art moderne*) et (*Mouvement Littéraire*) où il est question des XX, j'en serais fort aise, et serais très heureux de voir ce que Picard et Verhaeren disent de nous. J'espère que cette corvée ne vous ennuiera pas trop.

Merci, et à vous en vous priant de ne pas m'oublier auprès de Mme Van Rysselberghe.

votre
H. T. Lautrec

135 TO ROGER MARX
[Paris, May 25, 1892]

Cher Monsieur,

Nous n'affichons que le 1er, dites-le je vous prie et tenez en compte pour faire passer la ligne que vous m'avez si gentiment promise.

Yours,
HT Lautrec

136 TO HIS MOTHER
[London], Charing Cross Hotel, 31 mai 1892

Ma chère Maman,

Me voici installé à Charing Cross après un voyage parfait, la mer comme un lac et un ciel de

Nice. Je suis déjà empoigné par le charme qui se dégage de la grande *activité regulière* Londonienne. Tout le monde est à son affaire, bêtes et gens, sans cris ni paroles inutiles. Les fiacres hansom sont d'une tenue à faire honte à bien des voitures de maîtres. J'ai mon ami Ricci, qui est, d'ailleurs, un compagnon de voyage parfait, reposé et de bonne humeur. Dites à Papa que sa lettre de recommandation ne pourra probablement pas me servir, les Sackville étant sur le Continent, et surtout notre séjour etant fort *limited*. Nous devons être de retour le 10 à Paris. Bourges avait reçu votre lettre avant mon départ, et a dû y répondre. Adieu ma chère maman, je vais jouer à '*breakfasting*', et entrer en campagne par le National Gallery. Je ne vous ferai pas de citation de tableaux pour éviter de ressembler à Adèle Bouscher.

Je vous embrasse

Yours
Henri

137 TO HIS MOTHER

[Paris], Samedi [June 1892]

Ma chère Maman

Je suis tellement abruti par le temps orageux depuis mon retour de Londres que j'ai, dormi *jour et nuit*, ce qui explique mon silence. Me suis reveillé depuis hier seulement, et en profite pour vous écrire. Au cas où cela ne durerait pas—je vous envoie mon portrait à bord sur le bateau de Douvres à Calais. C'est toujours un acompte. Je n'ai pas de nouvelles de Respide autre que des prix médiocres par lesquels il faudra en passer: 320 000ᶠ à peu près dont 280 dûs par ma tante. Je ne sais dans quelles conditions ces dames sont à St Médard.

Parlons d'autre chose. Jalabert me fait l'effet du hëron et du goujon—Je voudrais une réponse nette pour savoir ce que je vais avoir à toucher, étant au bout de mon argent, et ayant bien le droit de savoir à quoi m'en tenir, puisque j'ai vécu 2 ans avec 1 an. Dites moi ce que vous pensez de tout cela. Il faudra bien liquider à n'importe quel prix. Je suis ici indécis et ne sachant que faire—comptant aller à Taussat vers le 14 Juillet, à moins que ma presence ne soit nécessaire ici, ayant une affaire en train.

Je vous embrasse.

Yours
H.

138 TO HIS MOTHER

[Paris, June 1892]

Ma chère Maman,

J'ai fort bien reçu votre lettre. Mon inquiétude venait de ce que j'étais à *sec*, et attendais votre lettre avec impatience pour taper Jalabert, et vous n'avez guère eu l'air de comprendre mon impatience; *la plus belle charité commence par soi même.*

Ce que vous me dites de Respide était prévu, mais vous savez ma façon de voir là-dessus. Il n'y a *rien à faire*, laissez vos sentiments vous guider et écrivez-moi. Je suis, malheureusement, trop sceptique pour croire à la reconnaissance, mais il ne faut pas oublier que nous avons trouvé à Respide ce que nous avons vainement cherché ailleurs, un *home*.

Je lutte contre la pluie et les modèles sans aigreur, comme sans enthousiasme.

Nous allons déménager à côté, rue Mansart probablement, dans un appartement plus grand, Bourges ouvrant un cabinet à Paris. J'aurai une petite augmentation de loyer, mais çà n'est pas une affaire (200 ou 300ᶠ) qui sont bien compensés par le coulage que j'aurais étant seul. Tout ça nous vieillit.

Adieu, me chère Maman.

Ecrivez moi avec beaucoup de détails.

Yours
H.

139 TO HIS MOTHER

[Paris, June 1892]

Ma chère Maman,

Je voulais ne vous écrire qu'après avoir vu mon oncle Charles, mais il était si rompu que je n'ai pu lui souhaiter qu'un rapide bonsoir. J'ai vu Louis qui m'a fait voir votre lettre. Il est plongé dans une indifférence, malheureusement justifiable. A moins de passer pour un bourreau il ne peut agir (quitte à le regretter après?). Cette réflexion toute personele est bien fondée.

Revenons à *nos* moutons. Jalabert tient à ma disposition 11.000ᶠ avec un supplément aléatoire, ce qui, avec les sommes déja avancées me fait un lot de 20.000ᶠ. qui me permettra de vivre une bonne partie de l'année prochaine. Votre lot de 25.000ᶠ est donc supérieur au mien. Tout ceci est à noter. Nous nous entendrons toujours bien, je n'en doute pas. J'ai préféré laisser Jalabert dépositaire de l'argent, ne voulant pas d'abord avoir l'air trop goulu, et ensuite désirant m'entendre avec vous pour le placer ou le déposer en lieu sûr. Si vous croyiez, toutefois, que je doive réaliser (prudemment peut-être), écrivez-le moi en spécifiant ce que je dois faire.

Je vous embrasse fort.

Yours
Harry.

140 TO HIS MOTHER

[Paris, June 1892]

Ma chère Maman,

Ce que vous dites de Jalabert est ennuyeux sans doute, car je le crains un peu degoûté. Cet état d'ésprit est surtout terrible pour l'avenir, car, si on le rebute, il enverra tout promener. Tachez de provoquer une *heureuse* rencontre entre lui et vous, et essayez de lui faire voir les choses en moins noir. Je pense, dès que vous serez à Malromé, faire un aller et retour, et nous pourrons causer plus longuement, quoique notre rôle actuel consiste à attendre. Je suis dans les dessins jusqu'au cou et suis assez content. Juliette a, vous devez le savoir, donné le jour à un garçon

275

du nom de *Mare*. Cette marque de courtoisie coûtera sans doute quelques livres sterling à la famille.

Je vous embrasse.

Yours
Henri

141 TO HIS MOTHER [Paris, June 1892]

Ma chere maman,

Je reçois un mot radieux de Jalabert. Papa a fait une réponse *satisfaisante*, dit-il, et les travaux ont repris.

Hosannah (pour le moment).

Je vous embrasse.

Yours
H.

142 TO HIS MOTHER [Paris, June 1892]

Ma chère Maman,

Je comptais en effet sur des nouvelles indirectes qui n'ont pas manqué, d'ailleurs, et l'attente était bien plus de mon coté que du vôtre où était l'intêret. Bourges m'a mis au courant de tout. Inutile, n'est-ce-pas, de reparler du triste événement, et de broyer du noir. Je vous dirai seulement que j'ai été toute la semaine complètement ahuri, ayant un peu perdu le sens des choses et des heures. Dans quel état doit être Joseph.

Papa continue à parler de son départ imaginaire. Dites à Louis que je lui enverrai l'acte dès qu'on me l'aura donné. Demain probablement.

Dites-moi quand Paul et Jo doivent venir, et s'ils comptent user de notre hospitalité, plus écossaise que confortable. Et maintenant, répétez à tous ce que vous avez dû déjà dire, et ce qui, je l'espère, n'avait pas besoin d'être formulé, la grande part que j'ai prise à tout ce qui s'est passé, et . . . se passera

your boy
Harry.

P.S. Je vous demande pardon de vous poser une question financière, mais je vous serai reconnaissant de m'envoyer si vous le pouvez 500ᶠ, remboursables par moi le 1ᵉʳ Juillet.

your boy
H.

Je vous expliquerai pourquoi quand vous viendrez, et j'espère que ce sera bientôt.

143 TO HIS MOTHER [Paris, June–July 1892]

Ma chère Maman

Je suis le dernier des pignoufs de n'avoir pas répondu à votre lettre. Je pensais, un peu à tort, que Paul et Joseph ayant beaucoup écrit à Respide, vous auraient donné de mes nouvelles. Ils sont ici, et en butte à tous les embêtements des hommes de loi. Papa nous a fait déjeuner

dimanche et diner lundi, il a été fort aimable. J'ai vu oncle Odon, qui ne m'a rien dit de significatif. Quant à la façon dont papa m'a parlé du Bosc, c'était plutôt d'un ton fumiste. Je sais que tante Armandine est à Malromé. Savez-vous que Papa m'a annoncé qu'oncle Charles était décoré de l'ordre de Grégoire le Grand? Et Albi est en liesse. Mᵍʳ Fonteneau est un homme joliment habile. Tante Alix a aussi écrit à Papa, probablement pour adoucir l'amertume de la pilule. Que de diplomatie?—

J'attends avec impatience le beau temps. Il fait chaud, mais orageux. Tâchez de nous amener le soleil le plus tôt possible, et priez Tata d'intercéder auprès de St Michel, qui est, je crois, fort bien avec elle.

Embrassez la pour moi, et à vous mes baisers d'Auvergnat.

Yours
Henri

144 TO HIS MOTHER [Paris], 15 Juillet [1892]

Ma chère Maman,

Votre lettre assez peu gaie m'est arrivée ce matin. Il en ressort que le pouf imminent va nous gâter notre saison (triste!); j'ai vu Louis qui n'a pas l'air trop à plat. D'ailleurs Gaston a dû vous en donner des nouvelles. Papa gémit, ne trouvant pas où placer ses petites affaires.

Quant à mes projets, ils sont absolument vagues, se résumant à aller respirer l'air de la mer n'importe où! Quant à mon excursion dans le Tarn, ça tient toujours vers le 10 août à peu près. Ne pourriez vous pas garder les draps neufs, et m'en envoyer

(des vieux)   merci du vin.

(tout de suite)   je l'attends.

En somme le résultat de ces pluies est un grand énervement, que j'essaie de surmonter de mon mieux, mais difficilement.

Je vous embrasse.

Yours
Harry.

145 TO HIS MOTHER [Paris, late] Juillet [18]92

Ma chère Maman,

Les dernières nouvelles *très-vagues* nous apprenant que les Pascal sont à Soulac au bord de la mer. Dans quelles conditions? Je l'ignore absolument. Je voudrais bien m'en aller, mais ce n'est guère possible avant une 15ᵉ de jours.

Mes petits travaux ont parfaitement réussi, et j'ai attaché là le bout d'une filière qui peut me mener assez loin, je l'espère. Je comprends que malgré votre plaisir d'être au Bosc, vous ayiez le désir de rentrer dans votre nid. Je veux passer par Palavas pour voir un peu la mer bleue foncée avant d'aller vers l'Océan. Mais qui sait. Je vous serai bien reconnaissant de m'envoyer par retour du courrier la somme que vous avez à ma disposition. Louis est très philosophe, et ne pousse plus de cris inutiles. Je vais déjeuner avec Georges de Rivières et Suzanne Gonthier.

Je vous embrasse.

Yours
Henri

On va vous envoyer les photos.

146 TO HIS MOTHER
[Paris], 26 Juillet [1892]

Ma chère Maman

J'ai reçu votre envoi et vous en remercie. Votre lettre en ce qui concerne ma tante prouve que la fin est là, et je crains bien que les remèdes soient bien inefficaces. Louis seul, quoique peu gai, est capable de faire quelque chose. A quoi bon, d'ailleurs, parler, puisqu'il est même inutile d'agir sans avoir l'air de s'imposer. J'ai vu Georges hier condamnant mes victimes qui ont écopé de 1 mois à 15 jours de prison.

Voilà toutes les nouvelles. Je rencontre peu Papa qui déserte en été Lucas pour les bouillons en plein air qui ne me plaisent pas.

Je vous embrasse.

Yours
Henri

147 TO HIS MOTHER
[Paris], Samedi [July 31, 1892]

Ma chère Maman

Je vous écris en pleine fièvre de départ. Les Pascal n'ont plus *rien*. Ecrivez donc, quoiqu'il vous en coûte, pour offrir à ma Tante une pension *provisoire* chez Pérey, ce qui me semble le plus pratique. Les fils et belle fille s'installant chez Mr Niguet, Joseph s'arrangera avec Bourges comme c'est convenu. (Où trouveront-ils l'argent du voyage?) J'espère vous donner des éclaircissements à mon arrivée en Gironde, vers le milieu de la semaine prochaine, mais écrivez à ma Tante de votre coté, car, malheureusement, ce sont à des gens *à terre* que nous parlons à présent, ne l'oubliez pas, et mettez toute susceptibilité, *quelque fondée qu'elle soit*, de coté. Soyez charitable *tout à fait*.

Je vous embrasse.

Yours
Henri

A partir de Mardi, je suis à Taussat par Audenge (Gironde), chez M. Fabre.

148 TO HIS MOTHER
[Taussat, Summer 1892]

Ma chère Maman,

Votre lettre ne m'a rien appris de nouveau, mais je crois que vous exagérez en croyant ne pas devoir venir dans le pays. Je *crois* que vous devez venir à Malromé, quitte à nous réunir avec Bourges, et voir comment nous pourrons *aiguiller* la situation de ma tante au moment critique. Ecrire ne servirait à rien, tout a été dit, redit et ressassé. Tachez de franchir les ligues de

mineurs en délire, et *venez dans la Gironde*. Je profite du beau temps pour me tremper constamment dans le bassin. A part ça, rien de neuf.

Yours
Henri

Jalabert a un peu d'argent rentré, il a dû vous le dire.

149 TO HIS MOTHER
Taussat, 17 août [1892]

Ma chère Maman

J'ai passé 4 jours à Soulac avec mes cousins qui ont été charmants, et ma pauvre tante qui fait de son mieux pour ne pas avoir l'air accablé. Je lui ai dit que je tâcherais de vous faire venir, car les échanges de lettres, sévères mais justes, l'ont rendue très triste. Au cas où il ne vous siérait pas de voir Juliette, je pense que ma tante viendrait vous voir, soit à Malromé soit ailleurs, où vous pourriez (je pense) lui faire avaler la pilule de la séparation qui n'est pas encore entrée dans sa tête. Quant à ma pension, votre réponse catégorique ne me permet pas d'insister. Voyez pourtant ce qu'on pourrait faire et répondez-moi— ou arrivez à *Malromé; nous causerons*. Je suis d'ailleurs là pour vous appuyer, et je vous ai fait rendre justice en reconnaissant que vous êtes la seule qui ayez fait preuve de cœur. Quant au reste de la famille, *il n'est pas blanc.*—Je les ai laissés en présence de Suzanne Gonthier qui rehausse la plage de *l'éclat de sa présence*. Ils sont d'ailleurs installés à Soulac pour une somme plus que modique: 4 grandes personnes, une bonne et 3 enfants pour 35 F. par jour. Je ne crois pas qu'ils puissent vivre plus économiquement, et les racontars de luxe exagéré sont bien faux. Bourges trouve que pour le moment ce qu'ils ont de mieux à faire est d'y rester, attendant l'hiver pour *chercher* des emplois.

Venez donc à Malromé, c'est ce qu'il y aura de mieux.

Yours
Henri

150 TO HIS MOTHER
[Taussat], 20 [August 1892]

Ma chère Maman,

J'ai peu de nouvelles à vous apprendre depuis hier, et je viens simplement appuyer le lettre de Bourges qui vous met au courant de la triste situation de Louis avec chiffres à l'appui. Il faut que nous le sortions de là absolument, si vous ne voulez pas qu'il sombre definitivement, et que tout ce qui a été fait jusqu'à présent soit perdu. Il fait de son mieux pour vivre avec le peu d'argent qu'il a, mais il lui est matériellement impossible de liquider son arriéré si vous et mon oncle (à qui Gabriel écrit de son coté) ne le sortez pas de là. Envoyez donc, pour votre part, *deux cent* francs et nous ne vous demanderons plus rien pour lui avant le mois de décembre. Vous n'aurez donc qu'à vous occuper de ma tante quand Mme Niguet aura sauté, ce qui arrivera fatalement si le projet d'installation à Neuilly s'exécute.

Yours
Henri.

151 TO HIS MOTHER

[Paris], 13 Septembre [1892]

Ma chère Maman,

Vos doutes sur l'avenir ne me produisent pas une impression trop désastreuse, étant donné les misères que je vois. Les Pascal (*ceci entre nous*) ne s'en iront de Soulac qu'expulsés. Ils doivent leur hôtel et pension. Je tiens tout cela de Bourges qui a été à Soulac, ce qui m'a dispensé d'y revenir. Je pense qu'alors la famille n'aura pas le cynisme de les laisser poursuivre et condamner, et qu'on évitera à ma pauvre tante la honte de la *correctionnelle*. Voilà mon impression *sans fard*. Avouez que nous aurions mauvais grâce de gémir. Le comble est que Louis est tombé malade de crampes nerveuses, et qu'après un repos d'un mois à St Gratien chez le brave Gaston la compagnie sera obligée de lui acheter une machine *à écrire*. Tout ceci n'est pas une blague. Bourges a fait contrôler par des gens compétents, et j'ai bien peur que le pauvre bougre ne devienne tout à fait impotent; ça vous fera une dame de compagnie. Enfin, il vaut mieux ne pas trop noircir l'avenir, qui l'est assez naturellement et sans teinture additionnelle. Je vous raconterai tout cela vers le 27. Veuillez m'écrire et écrire à Balade, car j'ai intention d'aller pour 1 jour ou deux à Malromé vers le 25 avec Viaud et Fabre pour qu'on nous prépare des logements. Dites-moi comment faire, aussi, pour boire et manger. Fabre voudrait voir le pays, et est ami de l'acquéreur de Respide. Je ne peux pas lui refuser ça, il est trop gentil.—Adieu ma chère Maman et à bientôt.

Yours,
H.

Souvenirs aux gens qui se rappellent de moi.

152 TO HIS MOTHER

Paris Mardi matin [October 1892]

Ma chère maman

Il *faut* envoyer de *suite* la solde de ma tante à l'hôtelier *directement*, en demandant un reçu spécifiant que c'est le compte personnel de ma tante que vous payez.

Paul et Juliette *sont à Paris*, et Joseph et ma tante n'attendent que le règlement ci-dessus et l'argent du voyage de ma tante—100 francs, cent francs que vous lui enverrez directement avec l'adresse du couvent qu'il vous plaira, où elle est prête à entrer. Je l'y conduirai moi même. Tout va donc comme vous le désirez. Dépêchez vous d'en finir, et donnez moi des ordres.

Votre fils
Henri.

J'ai fait un très bon voyage.

153 TO HIS MOTHER

[Paris, October 1892]

Ma chère Maman,

Je comprends votre affolement, et malheureusement il n'y a que peu d'espoir. Si la pauvre Tata se tire de cette aventure, surmenée comme elle est, elle pourra remercier St Michel. Je suppose que vous n'avez pas encore reçu ma lettre où j'établissais le bilan des dépenses à faire pour ma tante Cécile, dont la situation passe au second plan, étant donné le regrettable dérivatif de la maladie de Tata.

Au cas où ma lettre serait égarée, je renouvelle mon addition: déboursé par moi *70^f* plus *100^f* qu'il me faut pour dégager les épaves de Respide, linge et effets d'hiver de ma tante, qui sont en souffrance à la gare.

Je regrette d'insister, mais c'est urgent, et, à moins de l'habiller à neuf, il faut en passer par là.

Je suis désolé que votre arrivée à Paris soit remise aux calendes grecques, et vous prie de vous soigner pour ne pas tomber malade à votre tour.

Embrassez Tata pour moi, et à vous.

Yours
H.

Répondez-moi par retour du courrier.

154 TO HIS MOTHER

[Paris], 19 octobre [1892]

Ma chère Maman,

Votre présence à Paris est urgente. Vos intentions sont pures, mais le résultat est négatif. Ma tante s'est vu refuser de l'eau chaude après 6 heures du matin, le bois n'étant pas compris dans la pension, et devant être payé à part. De plus la nourriture est malpropre, et les lieux sont semblables à ceux des casernes. Ou vous êtes mal expliquée avec l'administration, ou il y a mieux à faire, et, malgré toute la bonne volonté de ma tante, il est impossible de la laisser dans cet asile qui, malgré ses apparences, n'offre même pas le confort élémentaire. *Il faut* que vous veniez vous-même arranger tout cela, ce dont je suis tout à fait incapable. Il y a un tas de choses qu'un individu de mon espèce ne peut contrôler. Je compte donc sur vous pour la semaine prochaine, et vous embrasse

Yours   H.

155 TO HIS MOTHER

[Paris, October–November 1892]

Ma chère Maman,

Devant les motifs qui vous retiennent au Bosc, je n'ai qu'à m'incliner. Mais je vous prie de *relire mes lettres*, et de voir si votre présence à Paris, *n'était pas clairement indiquée*, car vous ne pouvez rester indéfiniment spectatrice d'un état grave il est vrai, tandis que votre présence ici est *urgente*. J'ai dû avancer à ma tante 100^f pour payer des raccommodages indispensables—de l'avis de Bourges et du mien. Je vous prie de me les renvoyer par le retour du courrier. De plus j'ai autorisé ma tante et ses fils à chercher dans les 300ᶠ par mois un couvent *ou family hotel* où on torturera un peu moins cette pauvre femme (on allait jusqu'à la faire cirer ses souliers). Et je crois n'avoir pas mal fait.

Je vous prie de venir arranger tout cela, car j'en ai *assez* et ne peux continuer à pallier une ligne de conduite que je trouve trop rigide. Le Couvent, c'est bien, mais par trop n'en faut. Venez vous en assurer de visu.

Je vous embrasse.

Yours
Henri

J'irais au besoin vous chercher si vous ne venez pas.

156 TO HIS MOTHER
[Paris], Vendredi [November 1892]

Ma chère Maman,

Je vais bien, et ai repris mes occupations, mais ma pauvre Tante Pascal est au lit avec une crise d'asthme, et ne peut dormir que grâce à la morphine. Mon ami Fabre de Taussat, étant venu faire un voyage d'agrément à Paris, est également cloué au Grand Hotel avec une crise de rhumatismes aigus. Bourges le soigne de son mieux, sans le soulager guère. Voilà un garçon qui n'a pas de veine.

Arrivez, on vous espère, et je vous embrasse.

Yours
Henri.

157 TO HIS MOTHER
[Paris, December 1892]

Ma chère Maman,

Guibert vous expédie en petite vitesse un bananier qu'on allait jeter au fumier. Il faudra observer ses instructions concernant cet arbre délicat. S'il crève tant pis.

Je travaille un peu; c'est très dur de s'y remettre. Il est si doux de ne rien faire. Je pense que Bourges gardera provisoirement l'appartement où nous sommes, en attendant une situation loin ou près de Paris, mais toujours hors Paris. Il est navré de me laisser seul, mais il fallait s'attendre à un changement, tôt ou tard. C'était trop beau. Je vais prendre un petit appartement dans le voisinage, et tacher de ne pas trop m'embêter; je garde provisoirement la bonne qui est parfaite. *Toujours le secret.*

Je vous embrasse.

Yours
H.

Ci joint un produit de Guibert.

158 TO HIS MOTHER
[Paris, December 1892]

Ma chère maman,

Commençons par un *merry* (relatif) *Christmas* et le *happy new year*, autrement dit les souhaits de saison. Gabriel a dû vous donner des nouvelles de moi, bonnes d'ailleurs. Il est regrettable que je ne puisse aller à Albi, car vous serez forcée de hâter votre déplacement parisien ou de ne pas me voir, ce qui serait fâcheux pour vous, et pour moi surtout, car, à part Gabriel, je ne vois pas grand monde, si ce n'est des indifférents.

Autre guitare. Je viens de faire mes comptes de fin d'année avec la maigre récolte de Ricardelle, j'arriverai à peine au mois d'avril, et sans faire de bêtises.

Il faudra donc que vous mettiez à ma disposition la fameuse réserve déja écornée. Ce qu'il y aura de mieux sera de les déposer au Crédit Lyonnais par exemple. Dites moi ce que vous pensez de tout cela, et embrassez les b[onnes] mamans à qui je vais écrire.

Your boy
Henri

159 TO HIS MOTHER
[Paris] Mardi 20 [December, 1892]

Ma chère Maman,

J'espère vous voir vendredi mais (et pardon du côté financier de cette lettre) Louis a un billet qui échoit le *23* et je vous prie au cas où vous retarderiez votre voyage de m'expédier au plus vite, en lettre chargée, 200 f. que nous considérerons comme le dernier arriéré de ce pauvre garçon qui est bien à plaindre car il est encore le seul qui gagne un fixe courageusement. Paul se débat avec beaucoup d'énergie contre les directeurs de journaux mais sans grands résultats. Je pense que vous ne trouverez aucun inconvénient à ce règlement dont d'ailleurs je vous avais parlé. Ma tante va mieux et dort un peu. Je suis guéri et vous attends, et en attendant vous embrasse.

Yours

160 TO AN UNIDENTIFIED MAN
[Paris], 2–6–[18]93

Cher Maître,

Voici quelques adresses d'amis de Bourges et de moi qui seraient heureux de rehausser de leur présence de votre représentation.

J'espère ne pas arriver trop tard et vous prie de recevoir avec mes remerciements ma plus cordiale poignée de main.

H de Toulouse Lautrec

161 TO FIRMIN JAVAL
[Paris], 25 juin 1893

Monsieur,

Je reçois une demande de M. Roques, directeur du *Courrier Français*, me demandant à reproduire mon affiche *Jane Avril*: comme vous êtes le premier auquel j'ai permis cette reproduction, je lui ai fait dire de s'entendre avec vous de façon à ce que vos numéros paraissent simultanément afin de ne pas déflorer la chose.

Cette lettre vous donne pleins pouvoirs, de telle sorte que si le *Courrier* vous faisait une saleté, nous puissions taper sur les doigts de son directeur, vous, moi et Kleinmann.

Veuillez, Monsieur, croire à mes meilleurs sentiments.

H. T. Lautrec

27 rue Caulaincourt

162 TO HIS MOTHER
[Paris], Lundi [July 17 or 24, 1893]

Ma chère Maman,

Vive la Russie!! Et chose curieuse il y a un tel élan patriotique ou international que ce 14 juillet de 8 jours n'a pas été fatiguant. J'ai bien eu des attentes de quelques demi heures par ci par là à supporter, mais il s'agissait de l'équilibre Européen, et j'ai fait bonne figure.—Les sergents de ville eux mêmes ont taché d'être aimables, et ce n'est pas peu dire. Enfin *ils* partent demain, probablement bien fatigués. Maintenant parlons sérieusement. J'ai loué pour un an au prix de 800ᶠ l'appartement du rez de chaussée de la maison contigue à mon atelier, même propriétaire. Ce qui me permet de voir venir: soit louer le rez de chaussée de mon atelier [aux] mêmes conditions, et m'installer complétement, ou trouver un autre atelier avec appartement. Je doute d'arriver aux mêmes espaces pour le même prix. L'avantage est que je connais les locataires, le concierge, le propriétaire, etc. . . . Bourges s'installera à Paris provisoirement avec sa femme dans notre appartement actuel attendant le poste probable de *Suez* (20.000ᶠ fixes), ce qui n'est pas à dédaigner. Il est très appuyé, et j'espère l'avoir.

Si vous pouviez me faire cadeau de 6 nappes de petite dimension, de quelques serviettes de table vous m'obligeriez beaucoup, car je vais être obligé de me monter. Je garde mon ancienne bonne, et trouve qu'avec une quarantaine de f. par mois de dépense j'ai tout avantage, raccomodé et déjeunant chez moi. Je compte prendre possession de mon logement à la fin de Janvier, car on va le remettre à neuf sous ma direction.

Je travaille le plus possible au milieu de ces combinaisons, et j'ai une affiche à faire pour le journal le *Matin*. Je suis heureux que Mˡˡᵉ du Chat soit aimable, et vous distraye un peu.

Je vous embrasse.

Votre
H.

Toujours le secret, bien entendu.
P.S. quelques couteaux de table très ordinaires feraient également bien mon affaire.
En somme je me marie sans femme. Le colis est très bien arrivé.

163 TO HIS MOTHER
[Taussat], Samedi [August–September 1893]

Ma chère Maman

Me voici de retour à Taussat, ayant fait un voyage magnifique et mouvementé. La dernière journée a été dure, les hommes ont dû passer l'embarcation sur de véritables rapides, sur des rochers. Nous avons fait tout le trajet de Cazaux à Mimizan avec nos propres ressources, campant et faisant la popote nous mêmes, les plus paresseux couchaient à l'hôtel(?), mais payaient ce confort relatif par des punaises et autres babaous. Moi, j'ai divisé mes plaisirs. Bourges était avec nous. Nous avons eu une chaleur remarquable, mais, avec deux ou trois bains par jour, nous avons pu la supporter. Je vais revenir là-bas dans 15 jours avec des cormorans.

Je viendrai à Malromé Mardi ou Mercredi, peut être Jeudi.

Je vous embrasse

Yours
H.

Le vin est bien arrivé.

164 TO GUSTAVE GEFFROY
[Paris], Lundi [October 23, 1893]

Mon cher Geffroy,

Pardon de mon retard à vous répondre, mais je voudrais vous parler demain Mardi à 6 heures. Je viendrai vous demander à *La Justice*, et j'espère n'avoir rien perdu pour avoir attendu.

Bien à vous
H. T. Lautrec

165 TO GUSTAVE GEFFROY
[Paris, October 1893]

Mon cher Geffroy,

Je viens de voir Joyant qui m'a dit qu'il viendrait avec vous, et qu'il était à notre disposition. Vous n'aurez qu'à le cueillir en passant. Je serai chez moi demain, mercredi, jeudi et vendredi *entre 4 et 5 heures*. J'espère que vous pourrez venir, car il y a urgence, et Valadon me trouverait bien en retard.

Cordialement à vous
HTLautrec

166 TO ROGER MARX
[Paris], Jeudi [October 19, 1893]

Mon cher Marx,

Maurin mon complice et moi aurons l'honneur de vous présenter demain vendredi matin à 9 heures une création inédite. Veuillez donner des ordres pour qu'on nous introduise. L'œuvre qui est de Maurin vous intéressera fort.

Bien à vous
HT Lautrec

167 TO GUSTAVE GEFFROY
[Paris], Mercredi [November 29, 1893]

Mon cher Geffroy

Mes dessins sont trop grands pour les transporter, mais je serai à mon atelier à *4 heures—aujourd'hui*, demain tout l'après midi. Venez les voir s.v.p.

Cordialement vôtre
H. T. Lautrec

Il faut être prêt le 2 décembre.

168 TO HIS MOTHER
[Paris, November 1893]

Ma chère Maman,

Je suis très heureux de votre dernière lettre qui prouve que nous avons bien fait de ne pas manifester. Je suis très occupé, et imprime à tour de bras.

Je viens d'*inventer* un procédé nouveau qui peut me rapporter pas mal d'argent. Seulement je suis obligé de tout faire moi même. . . . Mes expériences marchant à souhait. Nous venons de fonder un journal. Enfin vous voyez que tout va bien. Il n'y a que l'ennui de déménager et d'emménager qui est le point, pas noir mais gris, de mon horizon. Continuez à ne parler de tout ça à personne, et je vous embrasse.

Yours
H.

169 TO HIS MOTHER
[Paris], 21 Decembre 1893

Ma chère Maman,

J'attendrai, je pense, la fin du mois de janvier pour aller à la belle ville Albi. J'ai énormément à faire: deux affiches à livrer avant le 15 janvier, et qui ne sont pas encore commencées. J'irai aussi à Bruxelles en février vers le 4 ou 5—à peu près à mon retour d'Albi, ce qui vous permettra de rester encore un peu en famille. Louis va aussi bien que possible, quant au reste de la famille je ne vois que J. de temps en temps. Il est beaucoup amelioré, et est moins don Quichotte. Gabriel travaille ferme, nous dînons ensemble une ou deux fois par semaine. Je fais son portrait le dimanche. Nous n'avons pas encore eu de neige ici. Je vois à l'imprimerie Prouho, le veuf, qui s'est mis aussi à faire de la lithographie, et est bien brave homme. J'ai aussi eu la visite de M. de Mathan qui m'a présenté son fils, peintre. Je n'ai, d'ailleurs, assumé aucune responsabilité comme d'habitude.

Je vous embrasse, et vous prie de me dire ce qu'il faut pour Kiki. Faites le venir si vous avez une adresse, vous ferez ça mieux que moi.

Votre
H.

170 TO MME R. C. DE TOULOUSE-LAUTREC
[Paris], Vendredi 29 décembre [1893]

Ma chère bonne maman,

Je comptais aller passer le jour de l'an près de vous. Mais il m'est impossible de quitter Paris avant le 15. Alors je compte venir dans ma ville natale me reposer un peu les pieds au feu et le sourire sur les lèvres. Ce qui fait que c'est encore par correspondance que je suis obligé de vous souhaiter une bonne année. Vous verrez ou vous avez vu le célèbre Docteur Gabriel qui vous aura raconté nos nombreux travaux, lui sanguinaire et moi imprimeur. Il vous aura peut-être dit que mon camarade Bourges se mariant, je suis forcé de changer d'appartement ce qui n'est pas fort amusant, mais j'ai trouvé dans la maison même de mon atelier un local fort convenable. J'ai la joie ineffable de faire mes comptes et de savoir, le prix exact(?) du beurre, c'est charmant.

Je vous prie de me rappeler à tous autour de vous et vous embrasse et je vous prie de compter sur moi bientôt.

Bonne année.

Votre petit fils, respectuex
H. de Toulouse Lautrec

21 rue Fontaine
et à partir du 15 janvier 27 rue Caulaincourt

171 TO HIS MOTHER
[Paris], Vendredi [January 1894]

Ma chère Maman,

Il fait un froid qui pèle—12 degrés. Aussi, ce matin, suis resté au lit comme une marmotte, n'ayant pas le courage d'aller travailler. J'ai eu de vos nouvelles par Gabriel, mais j'ai peur que vous ne soyiez murée au Bosc comme dans le Pays des Fourrures. Je ne sais encore rien quant à mon voyage; ce serait fin janvier ou 1er février que je viendrais à Albi, et de là filerais passer une semaine en Belgique. Vous pouvez donc prendre vos aises, et n'arriver que vers le 15 février à Paris. J'ai rencontré à Paris par le plus grand des hasards le fils du Mme Bourgaux née Piedevache, qui a été si aimable à Barèges de funeste mémoire. Elle ne doit pas avoir changé beaucoup, elle est à Monte Carlo pour se consoler de la mort de sa fille, lui fait de la peinture.

Je vous embrasse fraîchement, et vais déjeuner.

Yours
H.

Bourges doit revenir le 15.

172 TO HIS MOTHER
[Paris, January 1894]

Ma chère Maman

C'est non votre fils, mais un glaçon qui vous écrit. Il neige, neige, neige, et, malgré tous les appareils modernes, le froid perce quand même. J'espère que dès que le dégel va arriver, vous en ferez autant, mais il serait vraiment scabreux de bouger avec un temps pareil. Le joyeux Fabre est ici, et combat les frimas par pas mal de petits verres. Je travaille heureusement en battant les semelles, mais se lever le matin est dur. J'ai des amis qui viennent poser, aussi j'attends lâchement qu'ils soient là pour me lever.

Rien de neuf à part ça. J'espère que votre

malade est en bonne voie, et escompte un peu le
fameux 'pas de nouvelles bonnes nouvelles'.
    A bientôt j'espère, et *poutounégeades* à la clef.
                                Votre fils
                                Henri

173 TO HIS MOTHER
                        [Paris, late January 1894]

Ma chère Maman,
    Il fait des pluies, et de trop, aussi je vais à
Bruxelles passer une journée pour prendre des
renseignements mobiliers complets. Mon installation avance à petits pas, aussi tâcherai-je
de finir bientôt pour vous venir embrasser. Je
viendrai, selon le temps disponible, en bateau
ou en chemin de fer. Tout va bien ici. Papa me
fait l'effet d'être comme Fabius Cunctator. J'ai vu
Louis et pas encore vu Juliette; on a fait venir
Rosalie pour pouponner le *cagonit*.
    Je fiche le camp, car l'heure presse, et vous
embrasse.

                                Yours
                                Henri.

174 TO HIS MOTHER
                        [Paris], Dimanche,
                        [January 28 or February 4, 1894]

Ma chère Maman,
    J'ai presque fini mon déménagement, reste la
question de l'emménagement. Je vais acheter
batterie de cuisine etc. etc., et, quand nous nous
verrons, vous me laisserez prélever sur l'argent
que vous avez à moi ces frais d'extra. J'espère
m'en tirer avec 5 ou 600f: meubles de bonne,
batterie de cuisine, vaisselle, armoire, etc. . . .
Quant à mon nouveau local il est assez vaste. Le
petit hôtel rêvé est toujours en espoir, mais le
propriétaire se fait tirer l'oreille pour des répara-
tions. *Autre guitare.* Dites à Balade de m'envoyer
du vin adressé 7 rue Tourlaque pour que je puisse
le faire mettre en bouteilles vers la fin du mois.
Qu'il s'arrange de façon à ce que je le reçoive du
10 au 15.
    Je vais à Bruxelles vers le 12, et serai de retour
15 au 20.—Je crois qu'il n'est pas opportun que
j'aille à Albi à présent, et je vous attendrai. Je
préférerais que vous vinssiez avant le 10 Février,
car mon absence sera très courte, et je serais bien
heureux de parler un peu avec vous—*et vous voir.*
Tachez d'arranger ça. J'irai voir les bonnes
mamans à Pâques avec Gabriel.
    J'ai ma pauvre tête pleine de chiffres, quoique
j'ai fait bien du progrès de ce côté-là.
    J'attends Bourges pour fin février.
                                À vous
                                'H.
Répondez moi vite.

175 TO ÉDOUARD KLEINMANN
                        [Paris, 9 February 1894]

Cher Monsieur
    Madame Jane Avril passera à 1 heure
aujourd'hui chez vous. Veuillez lui remettre
deux de ses affiches.
    Bien vôtre—
                                H. T. Lautrec

176 TO HIS MOTHER
            Amsterdam, Jeudi [February 15, 1894]

Ma chère Maman,
    Nous sommes, depuis 3 jours, au milieu de
Néerlandais qui ne vous comprennent guère.
Heureusement que le peu d'Anglais que je sais
et la *pantomime* nous tirent d'affaire. Nous sommes
à Amsterdam, qui est une ville extraordinaire, *la
Venise du Nord* parce qu'elle est batie sur pilotis.
Nous voyageons, Baedeker en main, an milieu
des merveilles des maîtres Hollandais, qui sont
bien peu de chose, à côté de la nature *invraisem-
blable.* Ce que nous buvons de bière est incalculable, et ce qui n'est pas moins incalculable est la
gentillesse d'Anquetin, que je cramponne de ma
petite et lente personne en l'empêchant de trotter,
et qui fait semblant de ne pas en souffrir.
    Et à bientôt les détails. Samedi ou Dimanche.
                                Yours
                                Harry

177 TO HIS MOTHER
            [Paris], Mercredi [February 21, 1894]

Ma chère Maman,
    J'ai trouvé vos lettres en arrivant à Paris hier
soir, et ai reçu la dernière ce matin. Pas de com-
mentaires n'est-ce pas, vous savez que je suis
avec vous de cœur, sinon en chair et en os, et, si
croyais ma présence utile, je serais avec vous.
Disposez, d'ailleurs, de moi comme il vous
plaira—ma désillusion a été grande de ne pas
vous trouver ici, comme bien vous le devez
penser.
    Mon *admirable* voyage a donc eu un fichu
retour. Il est inutile de vous énumérer les belles
choses que j'ai vues avec l'expérience peu-à-peu
acquise dans l'art, ce qui fait que j'ai eu une belle
leçon qui a duré huit jours avec professeurs
Rembrant, Hals, etc. Les Belges ont toujours été
gentils, comme d'habitude. Enfin, nous reparlerons de tout ça, un peu plus gais j'espère, et je
vous embrasse pour tous, et pour vous.
                                Yours
                                H.
7 rue Tourlaque.

178 TO EUGÈNE BOCH
                        [Paris], 21 Février [1894]

Mon cher ami,
    J'arrive de Bruxelles et Hollande pour
l'inauguration de la "Libre Esthétique" qui a
remplacé les XX. Maus, plus ronflant que jamais,
a présidé à la chose. Dis a MacKnight de venir
me voir à Paris, et nous pourrons peut-être
organiser quelque chose pour lui. Les Indépendants sont sans local, et cherchent vainement
à déposer leurs navets. Personnellement ça m'est
égal, car je suis tout à la lithographie. Les
peintres graveurs sont également chassés de
chez Durand Ruel, et les salons officiels sont
tellement peu avantageux. . . .

Enfin on tâchera de truquer, mais je n'ai pas grande confiance.

Adieu, mon ami, et à bientôt, j'espère. Mais profite du soleil tant qu'il y en a, ici il fait un froid de canard.

A toi
HTLautrec

27 rue Caulaincourt.

179 TO ÉDOUARD KLEINMANN
[Paris, 1894]

M. Kleinmann
est prié de donner au porteur les deux prog.[rammes] du Th[éâtre] Libre—avant la lettre

H. T. Lautrec

180 TO GUSTAVE GEFFROY
[Paris, June 21, 1894]

Mon cher Geffroy
Dès que vous aurez les épreuves d'Yvette, ayez la gentillesse de me faire signe. Je voudrais bien que nous terminions tout cela ensemble. Bien vôtre

H. T. Lautrec

181 TO HIS MOTHER
[Paris, Summer 1894]

Ma chère Maman,
Paul a été étonnant hier soir, ce qui confirme ce que je vous en ai dit. Ça lui fait beaucoup de bien. Louis est rentré, et est fort occupé. Il s'est mis à travailler affiches et bulletins avec une grande énergie.

Je ne viendrai que Lundi, Venez *déjeuner et me prendre.*

J'ai lu dans le Courrier de Narbonne: Ricardelle *10000 hect[ares] vendus, prix secret.* Je vous garde le numéro.

Et voilà. . . .

yours
Harry.

182 TO HIS MOTHER
[Paris], Samedi [Summer 1894]

Ma chère Maman
Je n'ai pas g^d chose à vous apprendre. Il fait chaud, chaud, chaud. Je n'ai pas reçu de nouvelles du manège Bertrand, et n'en demande pas. Mes tapissiers travaillent lentement.

Madame Bourges a perdu sa chienne qui a enflé, et est morte. Notre voyage a été superbe sur une mer comme un lac, ce qui n'a pas empêché Fabre, qui nous avait accompagné, de rendre tripes et boyaux, ce que c'est que l'imagination!! Pas d'incidents à l'horizon.

Je vous embrasse.

Yours
H.

183 TO HIS MOTHER
Grand Hôtel de la Paix, Puerta del Sol, 11 and 12,
Madrid, Mercredi [August 1894]

Ma chère Maman,
J'ai reçu, en arrivant, votre lettre. Après avoir vu une très belle course de taureaux Dimanche, nous sommes allés à Burgos où nous avons visité les merveilles de la Cathédrale et de deux monastères. Nous avons voyagé toute la nuit en sleeping-car, et nous voici débarqués à Madrid. J'ai des lettres de recommandation, et on va même chanter mes louanges dans les journaux du pays, ce que c'est que la gloire et le journalisme. Je pense que nous filerons Samedi soir ou Dimanche, après avoir été à Tolède. Envoyez moi tout *ici,* journaux etc. lettres.

Je vous embrasse.

yours
H.

184 TO HIS MOTHER
[Paris, October 1894]

Ma chère Maman,
Vous savez probablement la mort de ce pauvre Nini mort samedi à l'hôpital de l'Enfant Jésus, après d'atroces souffrances. J'ai été averti trop tard, et n'ai pu aller à l'enterrement. J'ai été hier avec Bourges voir Juliette et ma tante. Ces pauvres femmes sont bien abattues, et pas théâtrales du tout, la note comique est donnée par Joseph qui se figure avoir tout supporté, et n'est pas loin de s'imaginer que c'est lui qui est mort.

Bourges a vu sa femme très sérieusement pincée par une fluxion de poitrine. Elle a beaucoup maigri, mais est très guillerette, donc guérie. Quant à ma bonne, le mal était tout simplement une constipation opiniâtre, aussi l'ai-je vigoureusement recurée, et elle commence à bouger. J'ai un adjutorium très convenable, la bonne d'un de mes amis qui habite la maison, aussi suis-je débarrassé de ce côté-là. Je pense aller à Londres pour inaugurer l'exposition d'affiches à la fin du mois, mais pendant 2 jours seulement. Gabriel est ici, heureux et content, quoique Péan renouvelle son personnel en février selon l'habitude. Il a d'ailleurs, des travaux très intéressants en vue. Il paraît (ceci entre nous) que le mariage Odon s'indique avec beaucoup d'argent à la clef; tant mieux. Je vous embrasse.

yours
H.

Soyez donc assez bonne de m'envoyer un panier Chasselas et Malagas. Je voudrais en offrir à Robin qui m'a hébergé tous ces temps ci.

185 TO HIS MOTHER
[Paris, Early November 1894]

Ma chère Maman,
Je n'ai pas voulu vous écrire avant le retour de Gabriel ramenant E. J'espère que grâce à un

concours de circonstances très-possible tout va diminuer de proportion et tourner à une escapade où ni la patrie ni la famille n'ont à sombrer. Je suis toujours à mon train train habituel, coupé par des mots avec ma bonne, qui est au sévère régime d'entretenir mon atelier et mon appartement.

J'ai été passer la Toussaint avec Bourges et sa femme en Normandie chez M. Anquetin. Mon camarade Anquetin sculpte l'église de son village à l'instar des gens du moyen-âge.

Guibert va vous envoyer les splendides photos de Malromé, assez grandes pour que Philémon et Baucis soient appréciés par votre maman. Je ne vois rien de neuf de plus. Dites à mon oncle et à ma tante combien j'ai pensé à eux dans tout cela, et tâchez de leur inculquer un peu d'optimisme.

Je vous embrasse.

Bien votre fils
H.T.L.

186 TO HIS MOTHER

[Paris, Late 1894]

Ma chère Maman,
Je vous demande pardon d'avoir été si peu écrivassier, mais je suis débordé de besogne, et un peu abruti dans l'entretemps. Ce ne sont que marches, contremarches, rendez-vous, etc. etc. J'ai même débuté dans un nouveau métier, celui de décorateur. J'ai à faire le décor d'une pièce traduite de l'Hindoustani qui s'appelle *le Chariot de Terre Cuite*. C'est fort interessant mais pas facile. D'ailleurs, il ne faut pas chanter avant d'avoir pondu.

Je tâcherai de venir, après le départ des Odon, vous dire bonjour en Albi. Seriez-vous femme à rentrer avec nous??? Gabriel en serait. Le verglas a sévi hier dans Paris, il n'y avait que chevaux jonchant la plaine.

Je vous embrasse.

Yours
H.T.L.

187 TO HIS MOTHER

[Paris, Late December 1894]

Ma chère Maman,
Je suis très bousculé en ce moment par mon nouveau métier de décorateur; il faut courir à droite et à gauche pour ramasser des documents. Et c'est assez absorbant. Je pense que Papa doit gémir, sinon officiellement, au moins en dedans, car il est question de bâtir dans la Cité. Je crois que le gérant du Prince de Monaco lui a écrit dans ce sens. S'il ne vous en a pas parlé, n'abordez pas ce sujet scabreux qui doit le mettre hors de lui. Grandmaison a l'air fort guilleret, vu le gousset garni. Je ne sais si je pourrai m'échapper pour le jour de l'an, car la pièce de théâtre passe dans les premiers jours de janvier.

J'ai fait faire une nouvelle photo de moi, et vous l'enverrai bientôt. Elle est nature. Gabriel est un peu *influenzé*, et moi pas encore.

Je vous embrasse.

yours
H.
Je vous envoie Y. Guilbert dans le Rire.

188 TO EDWARD BELLA

[Paris, 1895]

Je prie M. Bella de bien vouloir faire connaître M. Hartrick à M. Bing, et le remercie de sa complaisance passée, présente et future.

H. de T. Lautrec

189 TO ÉDOUARD DUJARDIN

[Paris, June 6, 1895]

Mon cher Dujardin,
Alex Natanson s'excuse de ne pouvoir venir demain. Je le remplace avantageusement par J. P. Sescau. J'espère qu'il y aura des dames.

Votre HTLautrec

190 TO AN UNIDENITFIED CORRESPONDENT

[Paris, June 1895]

Cher Maître,
C'est pour Samedi—voyez Sescau pour que nous dinions ensemble, chez moi si vous voulez. Ayez un smoking blanc et teintez vous le visage —si possible.

Votre
HTLautrec

7 rue Tourlaque
27 rue Caulaincourt

191 TO HIS MOTHER

[Paris, July 1895]

Ma chère Maman
Je viens demander pardon de mon silence, mais ce silence était dû à un état d'exaspération qui commence, *heureusement*, à tomber. J'étais en plein déménagement. Tout est à peu près fini, mais je ne connais rien d'atroce comme ces transports dans la chaleur, poussière, et autres désagréables choses. Tout est laid et inconfortable, l'on a dit que *l'hôtel* devient un idéal dans ces moments là. Résumons: tout va être fini, et *Mardi* je quitterai le Havre avec le fidèle Guibert, ce qui nous met à Malromé jeudi ou vendredi. Nous passerons deux jours, et repartirons en bateau pour le Havre pour chercher Bourges qui fera le trajet avec sa femme, ce qui fera trois voyages en mer coup sur coup. Si je ne sens pas la morue, j'aurai de la chance. En tous cas à bientôt, et vous embrasse.

Yours
H.

Je vous tiendrai au courant par télégraphe.
Mon adresse est à présent 30 rue Fontaine.

192 TO LÉON DESCHAMPS

[Paris, July 12, 1895]

Cher Monsieur,
Ecrivez-moi 30 rue Fontaine, ma nouvelle adresse. Cordialement à vous.

H. T. Lautrec

193 TO ARSÈNE ALEXANDRE
Taussat, [September 8, 1895]

Mon cher Alexandre,
Henri Albert, directeur à Paris de la Revue *Pan*, qui publie une estampe de moi, viendra vous demander q.q. notes sur mon chétif individu. Comme vous avez été le premier à dire du bien de moi, je tiens à ce que ce soit vous qui clamiez mes hauts faits au delà du Rhin.
Cordialement à vous.
H. T. Lautrec

à Taussat par Audenge
Gironde

P.S. Quand paraît le conte Tristan Bernard au *Rire*? Soyez assez gentil pour me faire adresser ici les 4 derniers numéros de ce canard, les miens sont gardés par ma famille qui néglige de me les faire parvenir.

194 TO LÉON DESCHAMPS
[Paris, October 1895]

Mon cher Deschamps,
Je viendrai Mardi ou Mercredi à la Plume. Fixez-moi un rendez vous entre 4 ou 5 heures après midi. Ou portez-moi vous même la chose à 11 heures le matin chez Ancourt. Un mot s.v.p. *30* rue *Fontaine*, et non 27 rue Caulaincourt.
A vous cordialement
HTLautrec

195 TO LÉON DESCHAMPS
[Paris], Vendredi 11 [October 1895]

Pouvez-vous passer demain à 9 h. 1/2 chez Ancourt. J'y serai.
Commandez une pierre grainée.
Votre Lautrec

réponse 30 rue Fontaine

196 TO LÉON DESCHAMPS

Reçu de la Société anonyme 'La Plume' la somme de deux cent francs pour droits de reproduction d'une affiche demi colombier The Chap Book.

Paris le 14 novembre 1895
H. de Toulouse Lautrec

197 TO HIS MOTHER
Paris, 30 rue Fontaine Jeudi
[November–December 1895]

Ma chère Maman,
Après un voyage magnifique en tous points nous sommes arrivés à Paris ce matin. Tout est en ordre, et ma bonne non prévenue n'avait rien fait d'anormal. J'ai un petit de ma chatte qui est sevré. Si vous le voulez, on pourrait vous l'envoyer. Bourges est ici avec sa femme à peine guérie d'une chute de bicyclette, mais brûlant d'y remonter. Paris est noir et boueux, mais je vais travailler ferme. On m'attend dans divers endroits. Tante Alix m'a chargé de vous presser pour aller à Albi où vous l'aideriez à déménager. J'ai été à Creissels et à Roquebelle où tout le monde a été fort aimable, et s'est informé de vous.
Autre question: dites à Balade de préparer une barrique à envoyer pour que nous puissions le mettre en bouteilles, j'ai la place. Je consomme (d'après mes calculs) une barrique et demie par an.
Je vous embrasse.
Yours
H.

Papa a été réellement dans la Montagne noire d'où il a écrit; pas d'autres détails.

198 TO MAXIME DETHOMAS
[Paris], 30 rue Fontaine
[Autumn–Winter 1895]

Mon cher Dethomas,
Miss Belfort demande un époux pour sa chatte. Est ce que votre chat de Siam est mûr pour la chose? Un petit mot. s.v.p. et fixez-nous un rendez-vous. Nous irons chez Sescau à 2 heures ou ailleurs si vous voulez.
Votre
HTLautrec

199 TO ÉDOUARD KLEINMANN
[Paris, 1895]

Mon cher Kleinmann,
Veuillez donner à M. Rousselot un exemplaire de chacune de mes affiches à moi appartenant, et lui communiquer la liste de toutes celles que j'ai faites.
Votre
H. T. Lautrec

200 TO ÉDOUARD KLEINMANN
[Paris, 1895]

Mon cher Kleinmann
Je vous prie de confier (Polaire) à l'employé de M. Moline.
Voyez ce dernier pour les conditions de vente.
Votre
H. T. Lautrec

[Paris, January 1896]

Ma chère Bonne maman,

Je vous remercie des appétissants pâtés que maman m'a apportés de votre part. Nous allons les fêter de notre mieux en buvant à votre santé.

Je suis en plein travail toute la journée, et suis très heureux d'avoir un programme à remplir. Les étrangers sont décidemment fort gentils pour les peintres. Je viens de vendre deux tableaux au roi Milan de Serbie, je pourrai mettre sur mes cartes: peintre de la cour de Sofia, ce qui serait d'autant plus parodoxal que Milan est déchu. Il a l'air de prendre ça fort bien, et n'a plus peur du yatagan des anarchistes qui n'ont pas raté Stambouloff. Que vous dire de neuf, que mes cousins Pascal sont embarqués dans une histoire qui ne me semble pas très claire, et dont il me parait difficile de sortir les braies nettes. Peut-être ont-ils cru faire une brillante opération? . . .

Je vous prie d'embrasser Papa pour moi, et vous je vous embrasse.

Votre petit fils respectueux
Henri

[Paris, April 20, 1896]

Mon cher Deschamps,

La lettre d'invitation à venir rue Forest était bien pour vous. Nous comptons vous y voir.

Cordialement
H. T. Lautrec

[Paris, May 1896]

Ma chère Maman,

J'ai tardé à vous écrire, mais j'ai failli vous acheter un cheval, *admirable.*—Malheureusement je l'ai vu trop tard, et je crains qu'il ne dépasse les tarifs que vous auriez fixés. J'ai diné deux fois avec Mme Bourgaux qui est adorable. Elle descendra chez Pérey, et elle va faire de la peinture(?).

Je puis enfin sortir le matin, et je fais une cure d'air.

J'ai deux ou trois grosses affaires avec des compagnies velocipédiques, ça va, ça va.

Rappelez-moi le montant du fauteuil qu'on va me rembourser; votre tapis n'arrive que demain.

J'ai loué le bateau hollandais du 20 Juin au 5 Juillet. Je pense donc qu'on se rencontrera à Malromé le 14 Juillet.

La question cheval est toujours sur le pavé, je m'en occupe. *Poutounégeades* à tous.

Your boy
H.

Paris, Vendredi [Early June 1896]

Ma chère Maman,

Je croyais vous avoir dit que je rentrais de Londres dans deux jours. J'y suis resté du Jeudi au Lundi. Accompagné une équipe de velocemen qui sont allés défendre le drapeau de l'autre coté du détroit. J'ai passé 3 jours en plein air, et suis revenu ici pour faire une affiche annonçant *The Simpson's lever chain* qui est, peut-être, appelée à avoir un succès retentissant.

Paris, après deux jours de pluie, est redevenu assez rôtissoire. Je voudrais bien aller respirer un peu. Autre chose, Guibert et moi avons loué un chalet pour la saison arcachonnaise. Il faudrait, si vous pouviez, nous envoyer une demie barrique de vin à l'adresse de Mr. Brannen, agent de location à Arcachon, qui le ferait mettre en bouteilles. J'amène ma bonne. Guibert fera peut-être venir son boulet, mais je ne le crois pas.—Si vous envoyez le vin, faites le moi savoir pour que *j'agisse en conséquence*. Autre chose, vous me rappelez les biens que vous aviez mis à ma disposition—une galette. Si vous pouvez m'envoyer 500^f, ça m'arrangera pour liquider quelques dettes avant mon départ, le plus tôt possible sera le mieux. Autre chose: je ne sais pas quand je pourrai emménager, mais je crois que ce ne sera qu'en octobre. Autre chose: Inutile de parler de mon voyage à Londres, car vous pensez bien que je n'ai eu ni le temps ni l'intention de m'occuper de Raymond.

Je vous embrasse chaudement.

Yours,
Henri

[Paris], Mercredi [Summer 1896]

Ma chère Maman

Je viens de passer deux jours à bord du vapeur de Johnston, et j'ai assisté à la *grande pêche.* C'est extraordinaire, et je ne me lancerai pas dans des descriptions oiseuses. Dites-vous seulement qu'on rejette à la mer à coups de pelle pour 300^f de poisson de rebut par jour. On ne garde que la crème.

Les marins sont très gentils et nous ont fait manger des soupes au poisson redoutables. Gardez vous de parler de tout cela *à âme qui vive* car nous avons dû donner notre parole, Guibert et moi, de n'en pas parler même à Fabre et à Viaud. M. Johnston est criblé de demandes, et ne saurait à qui entendre si une fois il entrebaillait sa porte. Ce que vous me dites de la récolte n'est pas gai. Nous en parlerons de vive voix. Je vous embrasse.

Yours
H.

206 TO HIS MOTHER

[Arcachon, August 1896]

Ma chère Maman

J'ai reçu votre lettre ce matin. Pas de nouvelles ici. Bateau, manger, dormir. La pêche est tout à fait infructueuse malgré tous nos efforts réunis. Nous viendrons dans la huitaine lundi ou mardi, mais à notre aise, car Guibert et son frère gardent le chalet—et font venir leur cuisinière—je crois que l'idée de jouer un bon tour à la cousine n'est pas étrangère à cette combinaison. Elle est auprès de son père, et y restera le mois de septembre. Je renvoie Marie à ses chères études. Louis m'a remercié de l'envoi bien arrivé.

Quant à moi, ayez 2000 f. pour le 10 septembre à toucher. C'est tout ce qu'il faut à cette heure

Yours
Henri

207 TO HIS MOTHER

Taussat, 19 Septembre [1896]

Ma chère Maman,

Je suis rentré ici, et me prépare à aller avec Guibert vous voir vers la fin de la semaine. De là je partirai pour Paris en passant par Toulouse. Je vous avertirai par lettre ou dépêche de notre arrivée. Veuillez m'envoyer *tout de suite* par lettre chargée 500ᶠ en billets de 100 pour régler mes comptes.

Nous avons eu à Ste Eulalie un temps splendide; les oiseaux ont été très actifs, mais ont pris peu de poisson, quoique s'attaquant même aux brochets, ce qui est fort honorable.

Je vous embrasse.

Yours
Henri

208 TO AN UNIDENTIFIED
CORRESPONDENT

[Paris, 1896]

Mon cher Monsieur,

J'ai l'honneur de vous annoncer que j'ai à votre disposition des affiches de l'Aube (Ep. timbrées), chez M. Ancourt, au prix de 50ᶠ les 50. Je vous serai obligé de me faire parvenir l'exemplaire de la petite affiche américaine de moi. Nous pourrons faire un échange à ce sujet.

Je serai d'ailleurs chez Ancourt demain Mercredi à 11 heures.

J'ai bien l'honneur de vous saluer
H. de T. Lautrec

209 TO E. DEMAN

[Paris, December 2, 1896]

Mon cher Monsieur,

Merci des papiers, je ne les ai pas encore essayés. Je vous ai fait adresser une épreuve Lender; pour vous 30ᶠ, pour le public 50ᶠ. Ce vulgaire détail est simplement pour que vous ne le cédiez pas à moins.

Seriez-vous partisan d'exposer quelques dessins parus dans *le Rire*? ou me conseillez-vous d'envoyer ce lot à la Libre Esthétique? Un mot s.v.p., et à vous cordialement.

H. T. Lautrec

Adresse: 30 rue Fontaine

210 TO HIS MOTHER

[Paris, May 1897]

Ma chère Maman,

J'ai été encore dupé par la concierge du nouveau local, mais en fin de compte j'ai trouvé pour 1600ᶠ, *il ne faut pas le dire*, un appartement inouï. J'espère y finir mes jours en paix. Il y a une cuisine, comme à la campagne, des arbres, et 9 fenêtres sur des jardins. C'est tout le haut d'un petit hôtel à coté de Mˡˡᵉ Dihau; nous pourrons faire de la grande musique. C'est bien Mˡˡᵉ Suermond, non mariée que j'ai vu. C'est peut-être là le bonheur. *Chi lo sa.* En tous cas c'est resté une franche et bonne amie, et sans aucune prétention à la rareté comme cette pauvre Suzanne. Son mari est bien à plaindre d'avoir un pareil trésor.

Je vous embrasse

Yours
H.

Vous devez avoir reçu mon *Figaro*.

211 TO HIS MOTHER

[Paris, Summer 1897].

Ma chère Maman

Terrible chaleur qui nous a pris tout d'un coup. Je termine tout, et vais aborder le déménagement ou plutôt les déménagements. J'ai diné avant hier chez Bonnefoy avec Louis et Joseph qui se regardaient un peu en faience.

Mon ami Joyant a définitivement acheté la maison Goupil. Je termine un livre avec Clemenceau sur les Juifs—mon éditeur me doit 1200ᶠ. Il m'en donnera 300 demain. Dites moi si vous pouvez m'avancer 500ᶠ sur les 900 de reliquat. Remboursables dans les six mois. Si vous ne pouvez pas, je m'arrangerai autrement. J'espère placer ma bonne dans une bonne maison. Je sue comme un bœuf, et vous embrasse.

Your Boy
Henri.

Pardon de tous ces chiffres, mais les affaires sont les affaires.
P.S. Ja pense peindre un portrait d'ami à Malromé. J'ai naturellement invité le modèle, Mʳ Paul Leclercq. Un jeune homme du monde et du meilleur; comme çà, vous jouirez de moi. J'irai d'abord en Bourgogne.

Yours H

212 TO HIS MOTHER

[Summer 1897]

Ma chère Maman,

Nous sommes cuits. Il est impossible de rester dehors; on rôtit même en bateau, ce qui ne nous a pas empêchés de sortir en plein midi pour poursuivre les mules qui viennent s'épanouir sur le rivage. En deux coups de filet nous en avons pris 150, Fabre est en villégiature chez son frère près de Paris, ce qui fait que nous en sommes réduits à nous dire des choses pénibles entre nous, ce qui n'arrive d'ailleurs pas. J'ai reçu les chaussettes en bon état. Merci.

Soyez assez aimable pour m'envoyer *à moi* directement 200ᶠ, et à Louis, 32 rue des Mathurins, 100ᶠ. qu'il doit attendre. J'aime mieux envoyer la chose au tapissier moi-même, car j'ai à préciser certains détails. Cela fera donc en tout 300ᶠ. Si vous pouvez nous envoyer un peu de chasselas, cela nous aiderait à supporter la température. Adieu, ma chère maman, et à bientôt, j'espère. Je vous embrasse.

Yours
H.

213 TO HIS MOTHER

[Paris, end of 1897]

Ma chère Maman,

Je vous plains de vos névralgies; j'ai été moi aussi un peu aplati, mais par un trop bon diner. Je n'avais donc que ce que je méritais.

Je n'ai pas encore complétement emménagé, et couche toujours rue Fontaine. Le vin est arrivé à bon port. Je suis en train d'organiser une exposition à Londres pour le Printemps. N'en parlez pas, à cause des cousins plus ou moins épileptiques que je me soucie fort peu de sortir. Bourges a dû vous écrire au sujet des nippes du malheureux Joseph, j'ai de plus en plus envie de vous voir à Paris, car les soirées sont bien vides pour nous autres vieux garçons. Enfin, à bientôt j'espère; quant à aller à Albi, il n'y faut pas songer pour le moment.

Je vous embrasse.

Yours
H.

214 TO HIS MOTHER

[Paris, Early 1898]

Ma chère Maman,

Je ne vous ai pas écrit plus tôt, car je suis dans un état de lourdeur rare. Je savoure tellement ma tranquillité de l'avenue Frochot que le moindre effort m'est impossible. La peinture elle-même en souffre malgré les travaux que j'ai à exécuter, et préssés. Aussi, pas d'idées, et partent pas de lettres. Que vous dire de la mort de tante Isaure? Il vaut mieux pour elle d'en avoir fini avec l'existence végétative qu'elle traînait depuis déjà longtemps. Les volailles et co[mpagn]ie ont été appréciés et je vous en remercie, à nouveau. Transmettez le remerciement à qui de droit. Gabriel m'a dit que ma tante Alix m'envoyait un cadeau destiné à rehausser la beauté de mon intérieur. Remerciez-la par anticipation, je le ferai moi même directement dès que je serai un peu réveillé. Voilà, ma chère maman, un bilan bien tranquille. Devien-drais-je casanier? Tout

se voit et je n'ai guère qu'un voyage à Londres au mois d'avril qui me fera bouger.

Sur ce, je vous embrasse.

yours
Henri

215 TO ROBIN LANGLOIS

[Paris, Early 1898]

Mon cher ami,

Mercredi, je passe vous prendre à 11 heures. C'est une affaire entendue entre Jourdain et moi.

Votre cordialement,
H. T. Lautrec

15 av. Frochot.

216 TO ROGER MARX

[Paris, February 19, 1898]

Mon cher Marx,

Je vous ferai prendre le portrait de Sescau demain matin Dimanche. Donnez des ordres pour cela.

Bien à vous
HT Lautrec

217 TO FRANTZ JOURDAIN

[Paris] samedi 12 mars [1898]

Cher Monsieur,

Je vous remercie de votre aimable invitation, mais j'ai contracté un simili influenza qui m'empêche absolument de sortir le soir.

Croyez à mes regrets et présentez je vous prie mes valables excuses à Mme Jourdain.

A vous et à votre fils bien cordialement
H. T. Lautrec

218 TO EMILE STRAUS

[Paris], Tuesday [November 8, 1898]

Cher Monsieur

Je ne pourrai être chez moi demain à 4 heures pour vous montrer *les Forain*. J'y serai à 4 h. après demain jeudi et espère vous y voir 15 av. Frochot.

Mes hommages respectueux à Mme Straus et à vous.

H. de T. Lautrec

219 TO GUSTAVE PELLET

[Paris], 15 Novembre 1898

Cher Monsieur,

Le 30 courant, mon imprimeur Stern passera chez vous, et je vous prie de faire préparer pour les lui livrer *tous* les exemplaires en dépôt chez vous non vendus. Je vous prie également de vouloir bien lui régler ceux qui le sont. Il vous délivrera un reçu en règle signé de moi.

Veuillez, cher monsieur, agréer l'assurance de mes sentiments très distingués.
H. de Toulouse Lautrec

15 avenue Frochot.

220 TO ROGER MARX
[Paris, November 28, 1898]
Mon cher ami,
Voulez-vous m'indiquer le nom de l'aimable Conservateur du Musée Guimet qui nous a reçu admirablement. J'ai absolument oublié de le lire en lui faisant remettre votre laisser passer, dont je vous remercie encore.
à vous,
H de T- Lautrec
15 avenue Frochot.

221 TO GUSTAVE PELLET
[Paris], 30 Novembre 1898

Cher Monsieur,
Vous avez le 8 Juillet 1897, pris 25 épreuves en noir (*Intérieur de Brasserie*) à 10ᶠ prix net, et 12 épreuves *femmes dans la loge* à 20ᶠ net. Vous avez vendu 2 ép. *Brasserie* soit 20ᶠ, et une épreuve de *la loge* à 20ᶠ. soit total 40ᶠ.
Vous m'avez avancé sur le tout 200ᶠ; reste dû 160. Je vous laisse donc 8 épreuves de *la loge* en dépôt, et reprends possession du reste.
J'ai l'honneur de vous saluer
H. de Toulouse Lautrec

222 TO ROGER MARX
Pavillon d'Armenonville [Paris]
le 5 décembre 1898
Mon cher Marx,
Pourriez-vous nous recevoir jeudi matin à 10 heures Albert, mon ami Bouglé et moi. Nous viendrons voir vos bibelots et vous remercier de vos cartes d'introduction. Albert a l'intention de vous apporter des estampes de son cru pour vous remercier de votre gentillesse.
Mes hommages à Madame Marx
et à vous
HT Lautrec
Un petit mot s.v.p. 15 av. Frochot.

223 TO ROBIN LANGLOIS
[Paris, January 1899]

Mon cher Robin,
Venez me voir rue de Douai au plus tôt. Je vous y attends.
Votre dévoué,
HTL

224 TO HIS MOTHER
[Paris, Late January 1899]

Ma chère Maman,
Je vous ai télégraphié. Envoyez moi 100 f pour ne pas être obligé de demander l'aumône au concierge qui est grossier—par télégraphe si

possible. Tout va à peu près sauf le temps, il pleut.
[Je] vous embrasse.
Yours
Henri

225 TO EDMOND CALMÈSE
Monsieur Edmond
Calmèse
9 rue de Douai
[Paris, February 10, 1899]

Monsieur de Toulouse Lautrec prie M. Calmèse et sa mère à dîner pour ce soir le vendredi 10 Février—
Hommage et amitiés.
H. de Toulouse Lautrec

226 TO BERTHE SARRAZIN
16 avenue de Madrid, Neuilly,
[April 12 or 13, 1899]

Madame,
Je vous prie de venir, 16 avenue de Madrid, *le Matin*; et de m'apporter une livre de bon *café moulu*. Apportez-moi également une bouteille de rhum. Apportez moi le tout dans une valise fermée à clef, et demandez à me parler. J'ai bien l'honneur de vous saluer.
H. de Toulouse Lautrec

Apportez moi tout le courrier: Journaux, prospectus, etc.

227 TO HIS MOTHER
[Neuilly, April 16, 1899]

Madame A. de Toulouse rue du Manège Albi
Inquiet. Donnez moi nouvelles de grandmère et ordres pour Berthe

H. de Toulouse Lautrec. Neuilly
16 avenue de Madrid

228 TO HIS MOTHER
[Neuilly, April 20, 1899]

Ma chère Maman,
Je viens de voir Georges qui doit vous amener ici. Veuillez donner les clefs de mon atelier à mon ami Robin qui en sera le dépositaire, car lui seul connait les tréfonds de mon atelier. En attendant votre visite, je vous embrasse
Yours
Henri

229 TO HIS MOTHER
[Neuilly], Mardi
[Late April or early May 1899]

Ma chère Maman,
Jeudi je ne viendrai pas rue de Douai, car Georges m'emmène à Rueil déjeuner. Tâchez

donc de venir dans l'après-midi. Nous arrangerons nos petites affaires pour ne pas nous manquer.

Je vous embrasse.

> Yours truly
> Henri.

J'ai rendez-vous à l'imprimerie vendredi; pourriez vous m'avoir à déjeuner? même maigre.

230 TO HIS MOTHER
[Neuilly], Mardi,
[Late April or early May 1899]

Ma chère Maman,
Mon ouvrier Stern viendra rue de Douai pour prendre les clefs de l'atelier, et m'apporter divers objets. Faites-le accompagner par Berthe. Au point où nous en sommes, on ne saurait *hélas* trop contrôler. Je continue à prendre mon mal en patience. Pensez à toutes mes commissions, et venez souvent. Le prisonnier
> yours
> Henri

Bonnefoy est venu avec toute sa famille. Le Dr viendra bientôt.
P.S. N'oubliez pas mes couteaux de table
Faites demander à Robin où l'on achète l'*Eau Moscovite* fruitée. C'est inoffensif et très rafraichissant. J'en boirai *volontiers*.

231 TO RAOUL TAPIÉ DE CÉLEYRAN
Taussat, [Summer 1899]

Mon cher Raoul,
Je t'ai fait envoyer une petite bête en bronze. J'espère qu'elle te plaira.
Tu me demandes ce qui me ferait plaisir! Du vin. Nous le boirons ensemble d'ailleurs, j'espère. Voici ce que je ferai. Je vais voir q.qu. . . . échantillons de vin rouge. Je te dirai les tarifs, et tu m'enverras le nombre, de bouteilles que tu voudras. Peu mais bon.
> Cordialement à toi
> Henri
> chez M. Fabre

232 TO FRANTZ JOURDAIN
[Taussat, probably summer 1899]

Cher Monsieur,
Il m'est fort difficile de vous être agréable. J'ai déjà refusé de faire partie de la commission de placement. D'un autre côté s'il y a *jury*, je *refuse net*. Cette ligne de conduite je ne m'en départirai jamais. Envoyez-moi toujours les règlements Villa Bagatelle à Taussat, Gironde. Je voudrais bien vous être favorable mais après des livres sur la litho[graphie] dans le genre de celui de M. Bouchot du Cabinet des estampes je suis forcé de me tenir sur une réserve extrême, surtout là où le vieux clan a voix au chapitre.
Bien cordialement à vous et poignée de main à votre fils.

> H T Lautrec

233 TO HIS MOTHER
[Taussat], Dimanche [Summer 1899]

Ma chère Maman,
Nous avons fort bien reçu vos envois, et nous apprêtons à y faire honneur. Nous avons été à Arcachon, où Damrémont nous a reçus d'un air embarassé . .? . . . Encore une victime. Décidément le célibat a ses charmes. Ce pauvre garçon m'a fait de la peine. Il avait la mine du monsieur qui a foiré dans ses culottes, tout en se forçant pour dire des amabilités qui ne sortaient pas.
J'ai perdu un de mes cormorans qui a dû se mordre les palmes de m'avoir quitté, car les habitants d'Audenge l'ont reçu à coup de fusils, et son cadavre a jonché la plaine. Avez-vous envoyé le paillon!—si non, faites le.—Il arrivera un petit colis 'des clefs' à votre adresse. Gardez-le, ce seront les clefs de mon atelier. Je viendrai passer 24 ou 48 heures vendredi ou samedi, avec Viaud. Ma peau commence à reprendre, mais j'ai été cruellement décortiqué.

Je vous embrasse
> yours
> H

234 TO ANDRÉ ANTOINE
Bordeaux, [June 1900]

Monsieur Antoine,
tu es decoré!
c'est un honneur pour la maison, et çà fait toujours plaisir.
Je t'embrasse
> H. T. Lautrec

235 TO MICHEL MANZI
[October 1900]

Mon cher Manzi,
Félicitations sans commentaire et nous en prendrons un peu la part.
> à vous
> H T Lautrec

236 TO MME R. C. DE TOULOUSE-LAUTREC
66 rue de Caudéran, Bordeaux,
[December 1900]

Ma chère Bonne Maman,
Je suis à Bordeaux, et vous souhaite une bonne année. Je suis en train de partager votre opinion sur les brouillards de la Gironde, mais je suis tellement occupé que je n'ai guère le temps de faire des réflections. Je travaille toute la journée. Je figure à l'Exposition de Bordeaux avec 4 tableaux, et j'ai du succès.
J'espère que cela vous fera un peu de plaisir. Je vous souhaite une bonne année, et de la part d'un revenant comme moi cela compte double, comme qualité de souhaits.
Je vous embrasse
> votre petit fils respectueux
> Henri

APPENDIX I

237 FROM COUNT ALPHONSE DE
TOULOUSE-LAUTREC TO MICHEL
MANZI

Malromé, 15 septembre [19]01

Monsieur Manzi

Votre couronne mortuaire venue si exacte-
ment dire que votre cœur était avec nous lors du
douloureux trajet précédant la dernière séparation d'avec mon fils *unique* survivant de deux, ce
précieux autant qu'éphémère souvenir de vous
deux, car avec Joyant, vous êtes *Un* unis dans la
même pensée tutélaire de mon deshérité sinon
désespéré.

Ces fleurs de Paris méritaient un plus prompt
remerciement. Fleurs de Paris dis-je, *conquérant*,
dit-on, la gloire d'art quelconque dans toutes ses
variétés et ses révélations, voire déplaisantes à la
moyenne des oisifs qui peuvent croire avec

l'argent s'être fait une éducation de quelque
probité.

La sincérité, tout est là.

On peut critiquer la courte œuvre de celui qui
disparait, pas vieux par les ans, mais mûri par
tant d'épreuves natives et accidentelles.

Il croyait à ses croquis et vous avec lui.

Grâce à votre appui, il a percé, et il vous doit
d'avoir étouffé le courant malveillant.

Joyant disait à son camarade d'école: c'est un
tendre . . . qu'il soit permis au père d'ajouter, un
inoffensif.

Jamais il n'eut pour moi un de ces éclairs où le
fiel remplace le miel dans les relations de père à
fils.

Voilà la vie intime. Il est *votre* enfant pour l'art
encouragé.

LAUTREC

APPENDIX II

238 TO MADAME LA COMTESSE DE
TOULOUSE-LAUTREC

7 rue du Manège
Albi, Tarn   Paris, 4 janvier 1899

Madame la Comtesse

En rentrant hier au soir, je suis allée chez
Monsieur Henri. Il s'apprêtait pour venir dîner.
Je lui ai dit que Madame était partie. Il était très
en colère; il frappait sa canne par terre en jurant.
Il a pris une voiture, il est venu à la maison, il a
sonné à casser la sonnette. La concierge lui a dit
qu'il n'y avait personne. Il n'a même pas répondu.
Il est parti à la recherche de Monsieur Gabriel.
Stern m'a dit qu'il avait envoyé une dépêche
à sa tante. J'ai attendu Monsieur jusqu'à 11
heures dans son atelier; voyant qu'il ne rentrait
pas, je suis rentrée me coucher. Il est rentré à
minuit. Le concierge est allé le faire coucher ce
matin. J'y suis allée à 8 heures, il était bien plus
calme quoiqu'il dise toujours des choses qui ne
sont pas raisonnables. Il a encore brulé quelques
journaux dans la cuvette des cabinets, mais il est
bien mieux, tout de même.

Il m'a fait chercher les clefs de l'appartement.
Il croit les avoir perdues. La mémoire lui revient
un peu. Je crois que dans quelques jours il n'y
paraîtra plus. Il m'a dit qu'il ne comprenait pas
quel bateau on lui montait, pourquoi Madame ne
l'avait pas prévenu, que quand il y avait quelquechose dans la famille il était toujours averti le
premier. . . .

. . . Il n'est pas rentré encore. Je vais toujours
faire rôtir le dindon. Je pense que Monsieur
Gabriel viendra dîner. . . .

. . . Que Madame se repose et se tranquillise.
Je crois que tout ira très bien. Je ferai mon

possible pour justifier la confiance de Madame,
et soignerai Monsieur Henri de mon mieux. . . .
Berthe Sarrazin

239 TO MADEMOISELLE ADELINE CROMONT

Chez Madame la Comtesse de Toulouse
7 rue du Manège
Albi, Tarn   Mercredi, 9 hes ½,
[January 5, 1899]

Ma chère Adeline,

Je suis bien de votre avis au sujet de ce malheureux dindon. Il me reste sur les bras; personne n'est venu dîner, c'est un dindon de
malheur, aussi je n'ai pas envie d'en manger.
Monsieur est parti depuis ce matin, je ne sais
ce qui se passe, il n'est pas rentré; il m'avait bien
promis de venir dîner. Il m'avait fait mettre
quatre couverts, et personne. Je viens encore de
son atelier, et rien. Il y a une dépêche pour lui
là-bas et une ici. J'ai oublié de dire à Madame
que Madame Pascal était venue avec sa bru, elle
était toute surprise que Madame soit partie sans
prévenir. Cécile est venue aussi ce soir, ce qu'elle
m'a fait de questions; elle aurait bien voulu
savoir, mais je n'ai rien dit, elle a dit qu'elle
saurait bien demain par Madame de Bernard,
elle a fait toutes espèces de suppositions. Je vous
raconterai cela à votre retour.

Ma pauvre Adeline, Monsieur ne va pas mieux
allez, il a encore fait porter de la térébentine, un
litre; je l'ai reporté. Il ne fait que d'acheter un tas
de choses, des vieux moules à gâteaux, des
cuilliers de 20 fr. chez le marchand de couleurs,
mais je vais aller les reporter, et dire qu'il ne faut
rien livrer. . . .

le 5, midi

J'ai encore été bien ennuyée ce matin, Monsieur n'était pas rentré à 10h. J'ai pris une voiture, je suis allée chez Monsieur Gabriel, qui m'a dit qu'il savait où il était. Il lui a donné tout l'argent d'un coup, et je crois qu'il n'a plus rien ce matin. Il est rentré à 10h½, je lui ai demandé de l'argent pour le charbon, il m'a répondu que demain il en toucherait, ainsi il a dépensé mille francs dans sa nuit. Ne le dites pas à Madame. . . .

votre amie
Berthe Sarrazin

rue de Douai 9

240 TO MADAME LA COMTESSE DE TOULOUSE-LAUTREC

7 rue du Manège
Albi, Tarn   Paris, 6 janvier [1899]

Madame la Comtesse,

Il n'y a rien de nouveau. Monsieur est toujours à peu près plutôt mieux, quoiqu'il ne soit pas encore tout à fait dans son bon sens. Il fait toujours beaucoup d'achats de bibelots jusqu'à des poupées. Ce soir nous avons du monde à dîner, 6 couverts. Je pense que ça ne sera pas comme avant-hier. Je fais un poisson, un lapin, et la dinde froide, et une glace à l'ananas. Monsieur voulait (un) homard à l'américaine, bouillabaisse, foie gras en sauce, mais je lui ai fait comprendre que c'était trop compliqué, et que j'étais seule. Monsieur a reçu la lettre de Madame. Il est très content. Il me l'a lue. Tout va bien. Comme je n'avais plus d'argent, Monsieur m'a donné 100 f. Je marque tout. Madame comptera à son retour.

Je suis très occupée avec Monsieur. Hier, je suis allée huit fois; ce matin je suis restée jusqu'à midi. . . .

Berthe

241 TO MADAME LA COMTESSE DE TOULOUSE-LAUTREC

7 rue du Manège
Albi, Tarn   Paris, Samedi
               7 [January 1899]

Madame la Comtesse,

J'ai reçu la bonne lettre de Madame ce matin qui m'a un peu reconfortée, en même temps fait de la peine, car je vois que Madame est toujours aussi malheureuse. Elle le serait tout autant ici. Monsieur est toujours presque pareil, sauf qu'il ne touche plus au feu, mais, en revanche, il ne fait qu'acheter toutes sortes de bibelots. Ce matin, un homme en a apporté pour 172f, des petit bons-hommes qui m'ont paru en plâtre peint, plus il a donné au masseur 100 f. d'étrennes et la note qui m'a semblé être de 70 f. Bref, en une heure, près de 400 f. Il a beaucoup d'argent, il en a touché en mandat télégraphique. Ça me fait beaucoup de peine de voir gaspiller tant d'argent inutilement, sans compter que je ne suis pas toujours là, et ne peux tout voir.

Mon dîner a très bien marché. Ils sont venus 7.

Je n'avais pas fait beaucoup pour tant, aussi il n'est rien resté qu'un peu de dinde que j'ai donné à la concierge. J'en avais assez.

Ces messieurs sont restés jusqu'à minuit à fumer, à chanter; pendant ce temps Monsieur Henri dormait près du feu. Quand il s'est éveillé, il voulait coucher dans le lit de Madame. Je l'ai fait. Après, il voulait 4 chemises de flanelle, il fallait les trouver absolument, enfin tout le monde est parti, il ne restait que M. Albert qui a offert à Monsieur de l'accompagner à son atelier. Ils sont partis; ce matin je suis allée à 8 h. Monsieur n'a pas voulu me laisser entrer. Je suis retournée à 10 h. Il s'est donc passé ce que je viens de dire à Madame plus haut. Je retournerai à 5 h. Monsieur m'a demandé si j'avais des nouvelles de Madame. J'ai répondu non. Il m'a dit qu'il en avait reçu de très bonnes. Il ne se rappelait plus m'avoir lu la lettre. J'ai demandé à Monsieur s'il avait répondu, il m'a dit: 'non, jamais, il faut attendre'. Je crois qu'il est très ennuyé que Madame ne soit pas là.

Je voudrais faire quelquechose, mais je ne peux rien de plus. Quant à Calmèse, je suis allée lui dire, le jour du départ de Madame, de ne pas venir. Un heure après, il était chez Monsieur. Quant à Gabrielle, elle n'a pas reparu, Stern non plus. A demain, Madame, et bon courage.

Berthe

242 TO MADAME LA COMTESSE DE TOULOUSE-LAUTREC

7 rue du Manège
Albi, Tarn   Paris, 8 janvier [1899]

Madame la Comtesse,

Il n'y a rien de nouveau. Monsieur est toujours la même chose. Il continue à acheter des antiquités, à vernir ses tableaux à la glycerine, et il les frotte avec une chaussette. Ce matin il avait la figure rouge et enflée comme l'autre jour. Il déjeune chez Boivin avec Monsieur Bouchef. . . .

. . . Stern est venu ce matin. Il est resté avec Monsieur toute la matinée. Il ne parle pas de Madame du tout. . . .

. . . Il doit toujours continuer à boire; si on pouvait seulement le priver pendant 8 jours, je crois qu'il guérirait. Il est plus calme, et ne touche plus au poêle du tout. Il ne désinfecte plus non plus. Ce qu'il fait encore de déraisonnable (ce) sont ses achats de vieilleries. Il dépense beaucoup d'argent. les marchands en profitent pour lui vendre toute espèce de vieilles saletés. . . .

. . . Monsieur Gabriel m'a dit qu'il lui avait donné mille francs, et, comme le lendemain je demandais pour le charbon, Monsieur m'a répondu qu'il allait en toucher à la poste, qu'il n'en avait pas, et je sais que Monsieur a touché un mandat télégraphique. Je crois avoir dit à Madame que Monsieur m'avait donné 100 f pour la dépense. . . .

243 TO MADEMOISELLE ADELINE CROMONT

7 rue du Manège
Albi, Tarn   [Paris, January 9, 1899]

Ma chère Adeline,

J'ai reçu votre petite lettre ce matin. . . . Monsieur continue à être plus calme. Il déraisonne moins. Aussi il est venu déjeuner ce matin avec Monsieur Sescau. Monsieur Maurin devait venir aussi, mais il n'est pas venu. On a attendu jusqu'à 1 h. Hier Monsieur a passé la journée avec Monsieur Albert. . . .

On voit bien que Madame n'est pas là, il ne se gêne pas. Monsieur n'a rien acheté hier, je crois qu'il n'a plus d'argent. Il continue à frotter ses tableaux avec de la vaseline et de la glycerine. J'ai bien peur qu'il n'abîme tout. . . . Dites à Madame que ça va bien mieux, et qu'elle peut revenir. Je crois que Monsieur serait *très* content. . . .

244 TO MADAME LA COMTESSE DE TOULOUSE-LAUTREC

7 rue du Manège
Albi, Tarn   Paris, 10 janvier [1899]

Madame la Comtesse,

Je voudrais pouvoir donner à Madame de meilleures nouvelles, mais, malheureusement, c'est la même chose. Monsieur est, cependant, plus calme, par instant il raisonne très bien, mais il ne faut pas le contrarier. Ainsi, hier, au déjeuner il a voulu mettre du rhum dans la coupe aux confitures d'oranges, je voulais l'empêcher, il m'a bien remise à ma place. Il a dit qu'il était le maître. On est obligé de toujours l'approuver, dire oui tout le temps: autrement il n'est pas méchant. Il ne parle que de donner, faire des cadeaux à tout le monde. Monsieur continue à gâcher son linge. Il tire tout de l'armoire, jette tout par terre. Ce matin, je lui ai porté 8 mouchoirs de poche; à 10 heures, quand je suis retournée, il n'y en avait plus un seul. Il met de la vaseline sur ses tableaux, et essuie avec ses mouchoirs. . . .

. . . (Monsieur Mallet) me dit que Monsieur envoyait beaucoup de monde acheter sur son compte, et que, depuis 2 ans, Monsieur ne l'avait pas réglé, qu'il avait une très grosse note. Il n'osait pas la présenter, crainte de froisser Monsieur. . . .

. . . A 11 h ½ Calmèse a envoyé chercher Monsieur par son garçon d'écurie. Je crois qu'ils doivent déjeuner ensemble. Je vais retourner tout à l'heure. Je reste le plus que possible chez lui. Il parle, et il ne sort pas. Il oublie de boire, si on pouvait être toujours avec lui, l'occuper, il ne penserait peut-être plus à boire . . .

. . . Je ne porte que des œufs que Monsieur mange crus mélangés avec du rhum; çà ne peut pas lui faire de mal, et du café tous les matins. . . .

245 TO MADEMOISELLE ADELINE CROMONT

7 rue du Manège   Paris, 11 janvier 1899
Albi, Tarn   6 h soir

Ma chère Adeline,

Je ne vous ai pas écrit plus tôt, mais Madame a dû vous donner des nouvelles, elles ne sont pas très bonnes, c'est toujours la même chose. Que va-t-on faire pour Monsieur Henri? Il ne peut rester comme cela toujours, cependant personne ne s'en occupe. Je ne vois jamais Monsieur Gabriel ni personne, ce sont des étrangers qui le gardent, principalement Calmèse, ce n'est pas avec lui que Monsieur se guérira. Ils boivent autant l'un que l'autre. Le pauvre Monsieur est toujours le même chaque fois qu'il me voit, il me montre sa main, en disant ça va bien, c'est guéri, c'est fini. Il ne se rappelle de rien du tout; ce matin il me demandait si Madame savait qu'il s'était brûlée la main. Il ne touche plus au feu, il n'allume plus de journaux, il n'a rien acheté non plus hier et aujourd'hui. . . .

. . . Je viens de chez Monsieur. Calmèse dormait sur le divan avec son chien. Monsieur de Montcabrier était là aussi; vous savez, le petit jeune homme qui venait souvent. Monsieur me tourmentait pour avoir du rhum. Je lui ai porté le restant de la bouteille qui était dans l'armoire.

246 TO MADAME LA COMTESSE DE TOULOUSE-LAUTREC

7 rue du Manège
Albi, Tarn   Paris, 11 janvier 1899

Madame la Comtesse,

J'ai bien reçu ce matin la lettre de Madame et le billet de cent fr, mais je n'étais pas gêné puisque Monsieur m'en avait donné. Je n'ai pas encore tout dépensé. Je remercie bien Madame. Monsieur est beaucoup mieux, mais il n'a toujours pas de mémoire du tout; ainsi je lui ai demandé s'il y avait des nouvelles; il m'a dit qu'il avait reçu une dépêche, qu'il y avait amélioration. La dépêche que Madame a envoyée le lendemain de son départ, il croit qu'elle est d'aujourd'hui. Il a retrouvé aussi l'enveloppe de la dépêche qui lui annonçait un mandat télégraphique. Il m'a envoyé à la poste dire qu'on lui apporte l'argent à domicile. Je suis allée, je croyais que c'était un autre mandat, mais, pas du tout, Monsieur l'avait touché le 6 janvier. On m'a répondu à la poste que Monsieur n'avait pas beaucoup de mémoire s'il ne se rappelait pas avoir touché mille francs: alors il était furieux, et m'a envoyé chercher Monsieur Calmèse. J'ai fait semblant d'y aller. J'ai dit qu'il n'était pas là: il veut faire mettre en prison les demoiselles du télégraphe.

Monsieur est toujours fâché contre Madame. Il m'a dit que Madame l'avait laissé en plein travail, qu'il avait tout fait pour retenir Madame, mais qu'elle avait envie de voyager, que ce départ l'avait bouleversé et rendu malade, qu'il allait écrire une lettre de sa façon: il voulait même envoyer une dépêche, mais une minute après, il n'y pensait plus. Ce maudit Calmèse est toujours là, et ne quitte pas Monsieur. Ils déjeunent et dînent ensemble.

La marchande de vin en face de Monsieur (au Père François) m'a dit que Monsieur avait peur la nuit. Il est venu chercher leur garçon à 1 h. du matin pour lui faire regarder dans tous les coins de son atelier, voir s'il n'y avait personne de caché. Il leur a dit qu'il était mal avec sa famille, que sa famille voulait le faire enfermer, et qu'il avait peur qu'on ne l'emmène quand il dormait. A moi, il ne parle jamais de cela. . . .

247 TO MADAME LA COMTESSE DE TOULOUSE-LAUTREC

7 rue du Manège
Albi, Tarn   Paris, 12 janvier 1899

Madame la Comtesse,
    Monsieur n'a pas payé son terme d'octobre. La concierge m'a fait voir la quittance. Elle est de 409 fr. 85c. Elle n'a pas encore les quittances de janvier, mais elle croit que c'est à peu près la même chose. La concierge de notre maison n'a pas encore les quittances pour les frais de poste, elle me dit qu'elle avait envoyé 2 lettres recommandées, donc 80c.
    Monsieur est encore la même chose, il parle beaucoup, je suis encore restée toute la matinée à l'atelier. Monsieur m'a dit qu'il déjeunait avec ses cousins, des magistrats. Je pense que c'est avec Monsieur de Rivières. . . .
    Je rouvre ma lettre. J'ai vu Monsieur de Rivières dans la rue, je lui ai parlé, il m'a dit qu'il trouvait Monsieur beaucoup mieux, qu'ils avaient déjeuné ensemble, qu'il avait ecrit à Madame sous la dictée de Monsieur, que Madame se tranquillise donc. Je crois que tout ira mieux.
                                        Berthe

248 TO MADEMOISELLE ADELINE CROMONT

7 rue du Manège
Albi, Tarn   Paris, 13 janvier 1899

Chère Adeline,
    Je ne sais si vous aurez reçu votre verre à café. . . . Monsieur Henri, qui était mieux hier, est aujourd'hui dans un état. Il n'a fait que sortir et rentrer toute la nuit. Ce matin à 7 h il était déjà parti. Je suis allée à sa recherche. Il était avec Calmèse chez le marchand de vin de la rue Fontaine. Il est furieux contre Madame de ne pas recevoir de nouvelles. Il m'a dit qu'il ne remettrait jamais les pieds dans l'appartement, qu'il louerait un plus petit logement, et qu'il me garderait à son service. Il croit que Madame ne reviendra plus; il est très ennuyé.
    Je viens de quitter Monsieur que j'ai laissé avec Monsieur Bouchef dans son atelier. Je retournerai encore tout à l'heure. . . .

249 TO MADEMOISELLE ADELINE CROMONT

7 rue du Manège
Albi, Tarn   Paris, 13 janvier 1899

Ma chère Adeline,
    Rien de bon à vous annoncer encore. Je vous ai dit que M. Henri était dans un triste état hier toute la journée. Je suis retournée le soir, la grosse Gabrielle était là, cette sale grue lui a dit qu'il lui avais envoyé une dépêche de ne plus venir d'après les ordres de Madame, de sorte que Monsieur est encore plus furieux contre Madame. Vous voyez comme il faut se fier à ces sales femmes; elle doit tourmenter Monsieur pour avoir de l'argent. Il m'a demandé si j'en avais, j'ai repondu que Madame ne m'avait rien laissé, alors il m'a envoyé avec une lettre chez Monsieur Robin. Il n'y avait personne. Son concierge, le concierge de Monsieur, m'a dit que Monsieur n'avait fait que sortir et rentrer toute la nuit. Il n'est pas content, car çà l'empêche de dormir, Monsieur est resté toute la matinée chez Calmèse. Ils ont déjeuné ensemble au bureau de tabac en face de l'écurie. M. a reçu deux dépêches ce matin, que le concierge lui a portées chez Calmèse. Je suis allé porter une lettre chez M. Sescau. Je lui ai parlé, il m'a dit qu'il le trouvait plus mal, qu'il ne savait ce que ça deviendrait. Je suis venue apporter la réponse à l'atelier. Il y avait la Gabrielle, Calmèse, et, je crois, l'homme à Gabrielle. Comme vous voyez, une jolie compagnie, Monsieur va encore être beau ce soir, quel malheur, mon dieu.
    Je suis contente que Monsieur n'a plus d'argent; comme ces gens ne le suivent que pour cela, quand ils verront qu'il n'a plus rien, ils le lâcheront peut-être. Il faudrait que Madame ne lui en donne pas de quelque temps pour voir ce qu'ils feront, Monsieur a dit à M. Sescau qu'il allait se faire rendre des comptes, qu'il toucherait 3.000 f demain. . . .

                                    Berthe Sarrazin
Donnez des nouvelles à Madame ce que vous jugerez à propos.

250 TO MADAME LA COMTESSE DE TOULOUSE-LAUTREC

7 rue du Manège
Albi, Tarn   Paris, 15 janvier 1899

Madame la Comtesse,
    Monsieur n'a pas payé ses termes. Quand le concierge lui a présenté les quittances, il a répondu qu'il était mal avec sa famille, que d'ici huit jours çà s'arrangerait. Il ne fait qu'envoyer des dépêches. Il en a reçu de Coursan. Monsieur m'a dit qu'il allait partir en voyage. Il va aller à Coursan avec 2 agents de la Sûreté pour se faire rendre des comptes. Il dit que Madame n'y entend rien, que son père ne s'en occupe pas, et qu'on le vole. Monsieur continue à ne pas dormir la nuit, il est toute la nuit dehors. L'autre nuit, il est allé chez Monsieur Robin à 3 h du matin, ce matin à 4 h, il est sorti, il m'a envoyé chercher par une porteuse de journaux à 6 h. J'ai eu bien peur. J'ai cru qu'il était arrivé quelque chose. Pas du tout, Monsieur était en train de boire chez le marchand de tabac avec un cocher de fiacre. Stern est venu ce matin comme tous les dimanches. Je crois qu'ils sont allés déjeuner ensemble. J'irai demain chez Monsieur Bourges comme Madame me le dit.

J'écrirai plus longuement demain. J'ai peur de manquer le courrier. J'espère que Madame va bien, et lui souhaite du courage.

Berthe Sarrazin

251 TO MADAME LA COMTESSE DE TOULOUSE-LAUTREC

7 rue du Manège
Albi, Tarn   Paris, 16 janvier 1899

Madame la Comtesse,

Je viens de chez Monsieur Bourges à qui j'ai raconté ce qu'il en était. Il m'a dit qu'il ne pouvait rien du tout, qu'il fallait aller chez Monsieur Gabriel. Je suis donc allée chez Monsieur Gabriel, mais il était parti. Je retournerai demain matin. Monsieur est plutôt mieux, mais il est très ennuyé à cause de l'argent. Il m'a dit ce matin que Calmèse lui avait trouvé des prêteurs à trente pour cent. Il serait à craindre qu'on ne lui fasse faire de grosses folies. Je viens de chez lui. Il y avait 2 hommes que je ne connais pas; il m'a renvoyé. La Gabrielle attend chez le Père François jusqu'à 4 h, Monsieur doit la prendre, et moi je dois y retourner; aussi Monsieur m'a demandé si j'avais les clefs de la cour, il veut que je porte du vin blanc, du muscat. Il a fallu que je porte 2 petites bouteilles de muscat au bureau de tabac et une bouteille de cachet bleu. Je suis bien ennuyé. Il promet du vin à tout le monde, à la grosse Gabrielle, au garçon d'écurie. Il dit que c'est à lui. Je n'ai rien donné à personne encore, heureusement qu'il n'y pense plus.

Maintenant il ne veut plus voir Monsieur Gabriel. Il m'a dit que s'il venait de le mettre à la porte, que c'était un mouchard. Il m'a dit aussi qu'il venait de demander la main de Mademoiselle de Rivières, qu'il aurait un magistrat comme beau-père, qu'il lui ferait rendre des comptes. Mais il ne faut pas attacher d'importance à ce que dit Monsieur. Il n'y pense plus un instant après, que Madame ne se tourmente pas, je ferai au mieux de ses intérêts et ceux de Monsieur Henri, quoique, si je l'écoutais, je dépenserais bien 500 f par jour. Je vais donc tâcher de trouver M. Gabriel demain matin. Madame voudra bien faire mes amitiés à Adeline; à demain, Madame

Berthe

252 TO MADEMOISELLE ADELINE CROMONT

7 rue du Manège
Albi, Tarn   Paris, 17 janvier [1899]

Ma chère Adeline,

Je suis toujours bien embêtée avec toutes ces histoires. Quand cela finira-t-il? Monsieur était bien mieux hier soir, il m'a demandé lui-même à venir coucher dans l'atelier. Je suis donc allée, il est rentré à minuit, il s'est relevé 2 ou 3 fois; enfin à 5 heures il m'a dit qu'il allait faire un tour. Pensez comme j'ai dû bien dormir. J'ai attrapé mal aux dents et à un œil. . . .

. . . Ce matin Monsieur est encore dans un bel état; il m'a fallu porter six bouteilles de vin chez Calmèse. Je suis allée chez le marchand de vin; il était attablé avec deux sales grues. Ce cochon de Calmèse, on devrait le faire mettre en prison, il fera mourir ce pauvre Monsieur.

Je suis allée ce matin voir Monsieur Gabriel. Il a dit qu'il allait écrire à Madame. Monsieur Bourges m'a dit qu'il ne fallait pas dire à Madame tout ce qui se passait, qu'il fallait dire que ça allait mieux, car Madame s'affollerait. Je ne sais vraiment comment tout cela finira, ma pauvre Adeline.

Tous les amis de Monsieur blâment Madame d'être partie, d'avoir laissé son fils dans cet état à des mains étrangères. Entre nous, Adeline, je trouve qu'ils ont raison. La place de Madame serait plutôt ici. Le pauvre Monsieur n'est pas méchant, bien au contraire. Il n'a jamais été aussi gentil, il ne fait que me promettre. Ce matin, il m'a dit qu'il me ferait 3000 f de rente. Je n'ai pu m'empêcher de rire, j'ai vu le moment il allait se fâcher.

Ne faites surtout pas voir ma lettre à Madame. Dites que Monsieur va bien mieux, et que j'écrirai demain. . . .

Berthe Sarrazin

253 TO MADAME LA COMTESSE DE TOULOUSE-LAUTREC

7 rue du Manège
Albi, Tarn   [January 18, 1899]

Madame la Comtesse,

Rien de nouveau. Plutôt du mieux. Monsieur a l'air bien portant. Malheureusement il boit toujours un peu. Tant qu'il fréquentera Calmèse, ça sera toujours la même chose. S'il y avait un moyen de l'empêcher, si Madame écrivait, il est vrai que Monsieur n'a personne d'autre, on ne voit plus aucun de ses amis. Il n'y a plus que Calmèse et Gabrielle qui ne le quittent plus. Monsieur donne tout ce qui est dans son atelier, tous les bibelots à Calmèse et à Gabrielle. Il a même donné le coussin de son lit. Je ne sais où s'arrêtera cette nouvelle manie. Monsieur ne vient jamais rue de Douai. Il dit qu'il n'y mettera plus les pieds: quand je parle de Madame, que je dis qu'elle va revenir, il dit qu'il ne veut pas que Madame revienne; d'autres fois, il dit qu'il faut être indulgent, que Madame est malade. Il change d'idées 20 fois dans 2 minutes. Il ne fais pas attention à ces dires, mais, au fond, il est très fâché que Madame ne soit pas là. Il ne travaille plus du tout. Il ne frotte même plus à la glycérine. Il ne parle plus que de son affaire. Il va faire rendre des comptes à son oncle, que Madame a avantagé au régisseur. Le parquet est saisi, c'est Monsieur de Rivières qui s'occupe de cela. Il raconte tout cela chez les marchands de vin.

Monsieur me demande toujours si Madame m'écrit. Il demande à voir les lettres. Si Madame voulait m'écrire une lettre que je puisse faire voir à Monsieur pour voir ce qu'il dirait, que

Madame se tranquillise, il y a plutôt mieux que pire; si Madame pouvait revenir, çà irait peut-être mieux tout à fait.

Berthe

254 TO MADEMOISELLE ADELINE CROMONT

7 rue du Manège
Albi, Tarn   Paris, 19 janvier [1899]

Ma chère Adeline,
Je ne voulais pas écrire aujourd'hui parce qu'il n'y a rien de nouveau, mais j'ai réfléchi que Madame serait trop malheureuse si elle n'avait pas de nouvelles. J'ai vu Monsieur ce matin, 5 minutes. Il venait de rentrer avec la Gabrielle qui l'attendait déjà à 8 h du matin. Hier elle a attendu tout l'après-midi chez le Père François, mais Monsieur n'est pas rentré. Elle n'a pas pu lui prendre d'argent, c'est ce qui fait qu'elle était aussi matinale ce matin.
J'ai vu Monsieur Albert hier soir. Je le lui ai dit. Il m'a répondu qu'il la ferait arrêter. C'est malheureux, tout-de-même, de laisser Monsieur aux mains de cette coquine. Elle a tout déménagé les petits objets qui pouvaient s'emporter. Je suis retournée 2 fois cet après-midi chez Monsieur, mais il n'est pas là. Je vais encore y aller en mettant ma lettre. Je voulais vous demander, Adeline, où vous avez mis le satin de chine pour raccomoder le pardessus de Monsieur Henri, dites-le-moi. . . .

Berthe

255 TO MADEMOISELLE ADELINE CROMONT

7 rue du Manège
Albi, Tarn   Paris, 20 janvier 1899

Ma chère Adeline,
Comme je vous le disais hier soir, en revenant de porter ma lettre à la poste, je suis retournée. Il était chez le Père François avec Gabrielle et Stern, soûls comme je n'ose vous dire quoi. Ce matin, je suis allée à 8 h, il ne m'a pas laissé entrer. Le garçon m[archan]d de vin m'a dit qu'il avait porté du sablé (toujours son sablé), et qu'il était avec deux femmes dans son lit, la Gabrielle et une autre. Je suis retournée à 11 h, mais il avait mis le verrou. Je n'ai pas pu faire le ménage. Je viens d'aller chez Calmèse; il m'a dit qu'il ne voulait plus s'occuper de Monsieur qu'il le dégoûtait, qu'il avait fait ce qu'il avait pu, mais qu'il voyait qu'il n'y avait rien à faire, qu'il avait été méchant avec lui hier matin. Il m'a dit qu'il était en train de déjeuner avec ces deux femmes au bureau de tabac en face depuis 11 h, et il est 2 h. Il va encore être beau ce soir. Il n'avait pas d'argent hier soir. La Gabrielle a dit chez le marchand de vin qu'il lui restait 22 sous. Je ne sais si Monsieur Robin lui prête de l'argent, ou si M. Henri lui en a donné à garder; toujours est-il qu'il lui en a donné 50 f. . . .
. . . Tout le monde est étonné qu'il puisse résister à une vie pareille, vaut encore mieux que la pauvre Madame ne sache pas cela. Allez,

Adeline, c'est une charité que lui laisser ignorer. Que voulez-vous, il n'y a rien à faire, attendre qu'il tombe, ça ne peut être long. Vous me demandez s'il travaille, il ne fait plus rien du tout. . . .
. . . Il ne parle pas de Madame, ou s'il a fait allusion, c'est plutôt en mal qu'en bien. Ses amis se fatiguent de lui, je ne vois plus personne. Je crois que Monsieur Gabriel ne s'en occupe pas beaucoup. . . .

Berthe

256 TO MADAME LA COMTESSE DE TOULOUSE-LAUTREC

7 rue du Manège
Albi, Tarn   Paris, 21 janvier 1899

Madame la Comtesse,
Je n'ai pu faire le ménage de Monsieur hier. Il ne m'a pas laissé entrer de la journée. Je suis allée 6 fois. Il est allé coucher cette nuit chez Monsieur Robin. Je suis allée ce matin, j'ai vu Monsieur qui sortait. Il m'a dit d'apporter du vin, ce que j'ai fait. Monsieur aujourd'hui est inquiet, préoccupé. Il ne parle que de faire mettre quelqu'un en prison, je ne sais qui. Il est très réservé avec moi, je pense que la Gabrielle aura dû lui monter la tête.
Je dois prévenir Madame que Monsieur Robin lui est tout à fait hostile. Il dit que c'est la faute de la famille si Monsieur est comme cela, qu'il est abandonné, que personne ne s'en occupe, qu'il est bien à plaindre, et qu'il en a pitié. Je crois que Monsieur va aller rester chez eux, mais je crois que ça ne durera pas longtemps, Monsieur changera vite d'idée. J'ai dit hier à Adeline que Monsieur avait encore beaucoup bu. Aujourd'hui il avait l'air mieux. S'il pouvait rester chez Monsieur Robin, il boirait moins, mais, comme je viens de dire à Madame, ça ne sera pas pour longtemps. . . .

Berthe Sarrazin

257 TO MADAME LA COMTESSE DE TOULOUSE-LAUTREC

7 rue du Manège
Albi, Tarn   [January 22, 1899]

Madame la Comtesse,
Monsieur a encore couché chez Monsieur Robin. J'ai guetté sa sortie ce matin. Il est toujours fâché, et à l'air inquiet. Il m'a dit qu'il allait faire mettre beaucoup de monde en prison, que sa situation serait liquidée avant 3 semaines; c'est à sa famille et aux amis de sa famille qu'il en veut. Il ne va plus beaucoup à l'atelier. Je n'y suis pas rentrée depuis l'autre jour. Il m'a dit d'y aller cet après-midi, qu'il y serait. J'ai demandé à la concierge la note des termes que je mets dans la lettre. J'irai demain où Madame me dit pour l'argenterie, quoiqu'il n'y ait pas de danger ici, Monsieur n'y vient pas, et je ne l'aurais pas laissé faire, quand-même enfin ça sera plus prudent.

Je viens de l'écurie. Je crois que Monsieur est à dejeuner avec M. Calmèse chez sa mère.

Madame voit que c'est toujours la même chose. Il n'y a pas beaucoup de mieux, cependant Monsieur boit moins, et, comme il couche chez Monsieur Robin, il ne se relève pas pour boire. Il a encore sa figure rouge; tout de même, il faut prendre patience, pauvre Madame, espérons que Dieu aura pitié; je lui demande assez, il finira par nous exaucer, ne perdons pas courage. . . .

Berthe Sarrazin

258 TO MADAME LA COMTESSE DE TOULOUSE-LAUTREC

7 rue du Manège
Albi, Tarn   [January 23, 1899]

Madame la Comtesse,
J'ai fait la commission. J'ai porté l'argenterie ce matin chez Madame de Vismes; Madame trouvera la liste de ce que j'ai porté dans la lettre. Monsieur est toujours très en colère; ce matin il est venu chez le concierge rue de Douai; il a dit qu'il allait faire changer toutes les serrures de la maison. J'avais peur qu'il ne le fasse pendant que j'étais partie. Je me suis donc dépêche de revenir. Je suis allée à l'atelier, Monsieur y était, il a pris un tout petit chien chez le Père François, il a acheté un biberon, et il a mis le commissionnaire dans son atelier pour garder le chien toute la journée. J'ai renvoyé le commissionnaire, et je vais y aller. C'est ce qui fait que je me dépêche bien vite décrire un mot à Madame. Monsieur continue à coucher chez Monsieur Robin, il parle toujours de faire mettre tout le monde en prison. J'écrirai demain à Madame.

Berthe Sarrazin

259 TO MADAME LA COMTESSE DE TOULOUSE-LAUTREC

7 rue du Manège
Albi, Tarn   [January 24, 1899]

Madame la Comtesse,
J'étais pressée hier pour écrire à Madame. Je ne sais si j'ai dit que Monsieur avait fini par me laisser entrer chez lui dimanche soir. Il continue à coucher chez M. Robin, mais maintenant qu'il y a le petit chien il veut que je reste toute la journée dans l'atelier pour le garder, mais je l'apporte rue de Douai dans la cuisine.

J'ai vu Monsieur ce matin. J'ai attendu qu'il sorte de chez Monsieur Robin. J'ai demandé si Monsieur avait des nouvelles. Il m'a dit que Madame avait écrit. Il avait l'air fâché, il me dit qu'il ne voulait pas ce que Madame voulait, et qu'il voulait en finir, qu'il allait au Palais de Justice. Je lui ai trouvé mauvaise mine, le teint jaune, les lèvres pleines de croûtes jaunes aussi, et un peu maigri. Il m'a paru cependant moins surexcité que dimanche et hier. Il est vrai qu'il sortait seulement, qu'il n'avait pas encore bu. Monsieur est resté toute la journée d'hier avec Calmèse; il a déjeuné et diné. J'ai dit à Madame

que j'avais porté 6 bouteilles de vin blanc, Monsieur voulait encore que j'en porte 6 ce matin. Je ne les ai pas portées. Je vais voir si M. s'en rappellera. Je dirai que j'ai oublié. On ne voit plus la Gabrielle. Je crois que Monsieur Robin et Calmèse l'auront détourné d'elle, en lui disant qu'elle volait. C'est un bon débarras, mais il y a toujours ce Calmèse. En revanche Monsieur ne le quitte pas, et ils boivent toute la journée. Monsieur ne s'occupe plus du tout. Il ne travaille plus à rien. Il reste toujours chez Calmèse ou au bureau de tabac. Il ne se met pas en colère après moi, au contraire il est très gentil, mais il a disputé avec sa concierge de l'avenue Frochot, et il est venu aussi chez notre concierge rue de Douai faire des recommendations pour ses lettres. . . .

Berthe

260 TO MADEMOISELLE ADELINE CROMONT

7 rue du Manège
Albi, Tarn   [January 25, 1899]

Ma chère Adeline,
Je n'ai pas encore de bien bonnes choses à vous raconter. M. est toujours la même chose, plutôt plus mal ces jours-ci. Hier au soir il est venu rue de Douai voir le chien. Il a fait le tour de l'appartement, il a ouvert le buffet de la salle à manger, il a fallu que je lui fasse un paquet de deux boîtes de foie, une petite boite de truffes, le bout de saucisson, il voulait aussi un pot de confitures, mais ça faisait trop gros. Il m'a dit de porter tout ce qui restait chez M. Robin. J'ai dit que oui, mais je n'ai rien porté ce matin. J'ai tout caché. Je dirai qu'il n'y a plus rien. Je suis allée à l'atelier ce matin à 8 h. Je ne croyais pas trouver M. mais il y était quoique ayant couché chez M. Robin, mais dans quel état, grand dieu, il m'a fait très peur. Il était couché tout habillé sur son lit, il ne pouvait marcher. Je l'ai déchaussé, je voulais le faire mettre dans son lit, mais il s'est mis en colère, enfin peu à peu ça s'est remis, il m'a dit que je lui faisais perdre 30,000 f., que Madame Bourges lui avait commandé un tableau, et qu'elle ne voulait plus le prendre, que c'était de ma faute. J'ai été obligée de m'en aller un instant, quand je suis revenue il n'y pensait plus, il m'a parlé de M. Gabriel après qui il est très fâché et après son oncle. Il m'en a raconté à n'en plus finir: Calmèse a encore envoyé son garçon d'écurie voir ce que faisait M. (ils ne peuvent le laisser tranquille), cependant il m'avait dit qu'il ne voulait plus s'en occuper, et vous voyez! Monsieur a dit à Batiste, le garçon d'écurie, de prendre un commissionnaire, et de venir prendre tout le vin qu'il voudrait dans la cave, que c'était à lui, qu'il en faisait cadeau parce qu'il mariait sa fille, mais vous pensez bien que je ne veux pas laisser faire. Je serai peut-être obligée d'en donner un panier tout de même, je tâcherai de faire pour le mieux.

M. n'a plus un sou. Calmèse m'a dit lui avoir prêté 15 f. hier. Je n'ose lui demander pour le gaz, il y a 24f40 et la blanchisseuse 22. Dites-le à Madame. Ma chère Adeline, j'ai encore un peu d'argent à moi, si Madame veut, j'en avancerai.

J'ai tout depensé ce que Madame m'a envoyé, et ce que Monsieur m'a donné aussi. . . .

Berthe

261 TO MADEMOISELLE ADELINE CROMONT

7 rue du Manège
Albi, Tarn   Paris, 26 janvier 1899

Ma chère Adeline,

J'ai reçu votre lettre ce matin. Je vois que vous n'êtes pas tranquille, et que vous devez bien vous tourmenter; mais, que voulez-vous, ici vous seriez peut-être encore plus malheureuse, quoique je voudrais bien, de grand cœur, que vous soyiez revenue. Je vous assure que je trouve le temps long, mais il n'y a pas de mieux. Hier, toute la journée, Monsieur a été ivre à ne pouvoir tenir debout. Il a couché chez Monsieur Robin, et, ce matin, il avait l'air bien mieux. Il est toujours avec ce Calmèse, il y déjeune. J'irai voir tantôt. J'ai toujours le petit chien, j'en suis bien embarassée, il ne fait que crier quand je ne suis pas là, il fait partout; la concierge a peur que les locataires se plaignent. Je vais tâcher de le mettre chez Calmèse, si Monsieur veut. Cécile est venue hier soir, je n'étais pas là. J'étais bien contente qu'elle ne m'ait pas rencontré, elle a dit à la concierge qu'elle partait pour Albi pour quelques jours elle venait pour voir si Madame était rentrée pour avoir des nouvelles, vous allez la voir peut-être arriver un de ces jours. Dites à Madame, Adeline, que le Père François m'a réclamé 61 f. que Monsieur lui doit; il est aussi venu un marchand de couleurs avec une note de 19 f., mais ça ne presse pas, il peut attendre. Il fait très froid, il gèle depuis deux jours. . . .

Berthe Sarrazin

262 TO MADAME LA COMTESSE DE TOULOUSE-LAUTREC

7 rue du Manège
Albi, Tarn   Paris, 27 janvier, 1899

Madame la Comtesse,

Je crois que Monsieur va mieux. Je n'ai pu le voir ce matin, c'est Monsieur Robin que me l'a dit. Monsieur devait partir au Crotoy hier au soir avec Monsieur Joyant. J'avais fait la valise, mais il n'est pas rentré. Je crois qu'il a dû oublier. Je suis allée chez Monsieur Robin ce matin, Monsieur n'y était pas, pas plus qu'à son atelier.

Je ne sais où il aura dû coucher. J'étais bien inquiète, je suis retournée plusieurs fois, à la fin j'ai fini par savoir qu'il déjeunait avec Monsieur Calmèse. Je dois retourner ce soir chez Monsieur Robin. Il n'y a rien de nouveau autrement. J'ai pu me débarasser du chien, il est chez Calmèse. Adeline a dû dire à Madame pour le gaz de Monsieur, il y a 24f40c et la blanchisseuse 22f; si je peux voir Monsieur ce soir, je lui demanderai de l'argent, mais je ne crois pas qu'il en ait.

Monsieur m'a dit avoir reçu des nouvelles de Madame, mais il a dit qu'il me donnerait des nouvelles plus tard, que pour l'instant il ne

pouvait rien dire, que c'était très grave. Il déraisonne un peu moins. Je pense que ça va passer si Monsieur pouvait se remettre au travail, et qu'il soit ne pas toujours avec ce Calmèse: mais on n'y peut rien. . . .

Berthe Sarrazin

263 TO MADAME LA COMTESSE DE TOULOUSE-LAUTREC

7 rue du Manège
Albi, Tarn   Paris, 28 janvier [1899]

Madame la Comtesse,

J'ai vu Monsieur hier soir à 9 h. chez Monsieur Robin. Il avait un peu bu. Ce matin à 8 h. il était mieux, il avait passé une bonne nuit, mais à 11 h il était moins bien. Je viens de le quitter au bureau de tabac, il était avec un cocher de fiacre; ils viennent de partir dans Paris avec un monsieur à moustache rouge que je ne connais pas. Je voudrais pouvoir dire à Madame qu'il y a du mieux, mais je n'ose encore, c'est-à-dire que Monsieur a changé, il ne parle plus d'essence, il ne touche plus au feu, il n'achète plus rien, il raisonne même un peu mieux. Quoique cela, je ne le trouve pas bien, il a mauvaise mine, Monsieur Calmèse me dit dependant qu'il mange beaucoup Il a un clou sur la nuque, mais qui n'est pas grave, Monsieur Mallet l'a su, alors il ne parle plus que de son clou, il se met au cou en guise de foulard de la mousseline à cataplasme; il a perdu ou on lui a pris tous ses foulards.

Monsieur est toujours fâché après son oncle Monsieur Tapié, il dit que c'est un misérable, qu'il détourne Madame de lui, qu'il y a longtemps qu'il lui en veut, que Madame l'a avantagé, qu'il lui fera rendre gorge, enfin un tas de choses que je ne me rappelle plus, bien que je n'y fais pas attention. Il parle toujours de faire un voyage, je crois qu'il veut aller retrouver Madame. Madame me demande pourquoi Monsieur a fait une scène à son concierge, mais pour rien, il s'imagine qu'il y a des cambrioleurs, et qu'on est venu dans son atelier. Il n'y va plus depuis deux jours. Je crois qu'il a peur, c'est pourquoi il couche chez Monsieur Robin. J'envoie le mot que Monsieur m'a remis pour son concierge.

Quant au masseur, il n'est pas revenu depuis le jour où Monsieur l'a payé, et donné 100 f. d'étrennes. Je l'ai vu dans la rue, et je lui ai dit que Monsieur n'avait plus sa raison, qu'il ne devait pas prendre cet argent. Il m'a répondu qu'il était malheureux, qu'il avait six enfants, que ça lui ferait grand bien, enfin il n'a pas voulu le rendre. . . .

Berthe Sarrazin

264 TO MADAME LA COMTESSE DE TOULOUSE-LAUTREC

7 rue du Manège
Albi, Tarn   Paris, 29 janvier 1899

Madame la Comtesse,

J'ai bien reçu la lettre chargé ce matin avec 150

francs. J'irai payer l'assurance demain matin ainsi que le gaz de Monsieur. C'est toujours la même chose pour Monsieur. Il a encore couché chez Monsieur Robin, mais il veut venir coucher rue de Douai. Ce matin il voulait que je cherche un serrurier pour faire modifier toutes les serrures, je vais être forcé de donner les clefs pour l'en empêcher. Monsieur Robin le pousse à le faire. J'ai profité que c'était dimanche pour dire que je n'en trouvais pas, alors il est parti lui-même pour en chercher un. Il n'en aura pas trouvé, parce qu'il n'est pas venu. Il est 2 h, je vais aller voir où il se trouve, avant de finir ma lettre.

Je viens de voir Monsieur, il était encore à déjeuner rue Fontaine avec Stern. Il m'a parlé du serrurier, j'ai dit que j'allais chercher voir si je trouverais les clefs, qu'il patiente un peu. Il voulait une boîte de foie gras, j'ai dit qu'il n'en restait plus du tout. . . .

Berthe Sarrazin

265 TO MADAME LA COMTESSE DE TOULOUSE-LAUTREC

7 rue du Manège
Albi, Tarn   Paris, 30 janvier [1899]

Madame la Comtesse,

Je viens de recevoir la dépêche. J'irai demain matin chez Monsieur Gabriel chercher les clefs. J'ai été obligée de donner celle que j'avais à Monsieur hier soir, il voulait à toute force faire mettre d'autres serrures. Monsieur est venu coucher rue de Douai. Cette nuit, ce pauvre Monsieur est comme un enfant, il a fureté dans tous les coins, partout; il voulait tout emporter chez Monsieur Robin. Chaque chose qu'il trouvait, il la mettait sous son bras, il disait 'bon dans la pipe'; quand il avait trop de choses il me les rendait, je les remettais en place. Il ne pensait plus un instant après. J'ai rallumé le Cudé pour chauffer un peu, quoique Monsieur fasse un feu d'enfer dans la chambre de Madame. Il fait très froid, nous avons de la neige aujourd'hui pour la première fois. Monsieur Robin est venu chercher Monsieur pour déjeuner. Je suis allée payer le gaz et l'assurance. Je ferai les additions de chaque jour sur une feuille de papier que j'enverrai à Madame demain ou après, comme Madame me le demande. Monsieur est toujours très en colère après son oncle Monsieur Tapié, il dit qu'il y a captation d'héritage, qu'il le réduit à la misère la plus noire, qu'il est obligé de vivre d'emprunts et de mendicité par sa faute, mais il va aller faire un tour dans le Midi, et il y en a qui ne riront pas. Il en veut aussi à Monsieur Gabriel, il m'a dit que s'il venait, de le mettre à la porte à coups de balai, ou de l'enfermer dans une chambre, et d'aller le chercher, qu'il lui ferait son affaire. Madame voit que le pauvre Monsieur déraisonne toujours, par instants il y a des moments où il parle très bien cependant; heureusement qu'il ne m'en veut pas, au contraire il dit du bien de moi à tout le monde. Je ne le contrarie pas non plus, je fais ce que je peux pour lui être agréable. Je crois que si

Madame revenait, Monsieur serait bien content. Il dit à tout le monde qu'il n'a plus de mère, plus de famille, qu'il est dans la misère la plus profonde; les gens le plaignent, ils croient que c'est vrai. . . .

Berthe Sarrazin

266 TO MADEMOISELLE ADELINE CROMONT

7 rue du Manège
Albi, Tarn   Paris, 31 janvier [1899]

Ma chère Adeline,

J'étais encore bien inquiète ce matin. Monsieur n'est pas rentré coucher rue de Douai comme il me l'avait promis. Je l'ai attendu toute la nuit. Ce matin, à 8 h, je suis allée chez Monsieur Gabriel. J'aurais bien voulu le voir, mais on n'a pas voulu me laisser monter sous prétexte qu'il était trop tôt. Du reste Monsieur Gabriel avait descendu la clef pour qu'on me la remette. A 10 h. Monsieur m'a envoyé une lettre pour un serrurier me disant d'aller de suite à l'atelier. Monsieur avait fait défaire son verrou. J'ai donc prévenu le serrurier de faire semblant d'arranger (ce qu'il a fait). Rassurez Madame au sujet des cambrioleurs, Adeline, il n'y a rien eu du tout. Monsieur a, en ce moment, la manie de la persécution. On l'a volé tout de même, mais sur lui; il n'a plus sa montre ni son beau foulard, son épingle de cravate a disparu; aussi dites à Madame qu'il a tout de même de l'argent. Il m'a dit que des marchands de tableaux lui en avaient prêté. C'est Calmèse qui garde son portemonnaie. Il est entre bonnes mains, comme vous voyez.

Je suis allée chez Monsieur Mallet pour demander comment il trouvait Monsieur. Il m'a dit qu'il était bien mieux, qu'il le trouvait très bien depuis 8 jours, mais qu'il l'avait toujours vu comme cela. Monsieur sait que le frère de Madame est venu chercher Madame. J'ai été toute saisie ce matin, il m'a demandé qui était là quand Madame était partie. J'ai dit qu'il n'y avait personne; il m'a demandé si je n'avais pas vu un grand Monsieur avec des lunettes et la barbe grise. J'ai répondu que non. Je ne sais qui lui monte la tête contre ses parents. Il est toujours furieux contre Monsieur Gabriel. Il m'a dit qu'il avait dîné en face de lui hier soir, il ne riait pas: *Ah lui, s'il vient ici, allez chercher Monsieur Calmèse pour le mettre à la porte*, qu'il m'a encore répété. . . . M. m'a dit qu'il allait écrire à la Salubrité, qu'il ne voulait pas payer, qu'il ne fasse arranger sa maison, qu'il avait manqué être asphyxié par les cabinets. . . .

Berthe

267 TO MADEMOISELLE ADELINE CROMONT

7 rue du Manège
Albi, Tarn   Paris, 1er février 1899

Ma chère Adeline,

Je ne sais quoi vous dire. C'est toujours la même chose. Monsieur continue à boire, et devient méchant par moments. Monsieur Mallet dit qu'il le trouve mieux, mais moi je ne trouve pas. Voilà deux nuits que je ne sais où il couche. Il est venu ce matin Rue de Douai avec le chien. Il l'appelle Paméla. Ce pauvre Monsieur a encore fouillé partout dans les tiroirs, jusque dans vos affaires. Il voulait prendre votre couteau, ma pauvre Adeline. Je crois que ça ne lui passera pas, tant qu'il fréquentera ce démon de Calmèse. C'est qu'il ne le quitte plus du tout. Il ne va plus à son atelier. Il est toute la journée au bureau de tabac où il mange. Ce matin, il m'a fallu porter deux bouteilles de vin blanc, une muscat, le pot de confiture anglaise que vous aviez acheté, jusqu'au morceau de jambon qui restait dans l'armoire de la cuisine. Heureusement qu'il n'a pas vu celui qui est dans le torchon. Il lui aurait encore fallu. Comment tout cela finira-t-il, ma pauvre Adeline. . . .

Berthe Sarrazin

268 TO MADAME LA COMTESSE DE TOULOUSE-LAUTREC

7 rue du Manège
Albi, Tarn   Paris, 3 février [18]99

Madame la Comtesse,
    Comme je l'ai dit hier à Madame, Monsieur est resté dans la cuisine tout l'après-midi à cuire le jambon qui était dans le torchon. Je croyais qu'il ne l'avait pas vu, mais il savait bien qu'il était là. Il a mis une bouteille de vin blanc, une rouge, du vinaigre, du rhum, tellement de poivre, sel et le reste qu'il n'était pas mangeable; il m'a fallu le porter chez Calmèse 3 bouteilles de vin. J'ai dit à Madame que Monsieur était méchant. Il est rentré comme un furieux. Je ne l'avais jamais vu aussi violent, il voulait battre le petit concierge, il le tenait par le bras, et le secouait tant qu'il pouvait, en l'appelant toutes sortes de vilains noms. Il lui reprochait de mal garder la maison; à moi il m'a dit toutes sortes de sottises, qu'il me ferait mettre en prison avec sa famille. J'ai eu si peur que j'en suis toute malade aujourd'hui. Il dit qu'il va faire vendre le mobilier dans la rue, il y a des dettes, et on va saisir, il le fait exprès. Enfin, il en a tellement dit que je n'ai pu m'empêcher de pleurer. Quand il a vu que je pleurais, ça lui a fait de la peine. Il m'a demandé pardon, disant que c'était à sa famille qu'il en avait, mais comme personne de sa famille n'était là, que c'était moi qui avais supporté sa colère, mais qu'il ne m'en veut pas. Monsieur a couché ici cette nuit, il ne dort pas, il a fait du feu toute la nuit, il n'y aura pas de bois pour longtemps. Il est resté jusqu'à midi, il est venu nettoyer le fourneau à gaz en faisant couler de la bougie dessus, enfin il a fait toutes sortes d'excentricités qui seraient trop longues à raconter.
    L'autre nuit, on a manqué le mener au poste, c'est Guichard, le marchand de vin qui me dit cela. Il est venu prendre une chambre dans un hôtel de la rue Pigalle, il y avait un autre monsieur, et deux sales femmes. L'autre monsieur est parti un moment après, Monsieur est donc resté

pour payer, mais il n'avait pas d'argent, il avait beau dire: *Je suis le comte de Toulouse*, le logeur ne voulait rien entendre; alors Monsieur est venu réveiller Guichard qui a prêté les 3f50 qui étaient dûs. Monsieur n'a plus d'argent du tout. Je lui ai demandé pour le gaz, il m'a donné 20 f, ce qui fait donc 120 f que j'ai reçu de Monsieur. . .

Berthe

269 TO MADAME LA COMTESSE DE TOULOUSE-LAUTREC

5 Cité du Rétiro, Hotel Pérey
Paris
                            Paris, mardi 14, [February 1899]

Madame la Comtesse,
    J'ai eu des ennuis ce matin. Cet homme est bête comme une oie. Je ne crois pas qu'il puisse continuer à garder Monsieur. Il le laisse boire. Il ne sait pas du tout le diriger. Du reste, je n'ai pas osé dire à Madame de vive voix qu'il n'était pas convenable avec moi, c'est ce qui fait que je ne veux plus coucher ici. Ils sont allés à la Brasserie de la Souris, rue Bréda. Monsieur a dit à la patronne de cette sale maison d'envoyer chercher du vin, je ne sais combien de bouteilles. Ils sont venus à deux avec des paniers, un homme et une femme; je n'ai rien voulu donner, elle a renvoyé un petit garçon avec une lettre qu'il voulait remettre en mains propres. Je n'ai pas voulu le laisser entrer, mais je crains qu'elle ne fasse guetter Monsieur, et qu'il ne le sache, çà me ferait une jolie histoire. Je regrette bien Andrieux, il n'aurait pas laissé aller Monsieur dans cette maison. . . .
    . . . Monsieur a bien mangé à déjeuner, mais cet imbécile d'homme ne l'a ramené qu'à 1h½, je n'attendais plus; il est convenu qu'ils rentreront à 7h. pour dîner, ils sont partis en voiture. . . .

Berthe

270 TO MADAME LA COMTESSE DE TOULOUSE-LAUTREC

7 rue du Manège
Albi, Tarn   Paris, 13 avril [1899]

Madame la Comtesse,
    Je viens de voir Monsieur Henri. Il est toujours la même chose, plutôt mieux, surtout très calme. Il m'a bien reçu, et a été content de me voir. J'avais reçu une lettre de Monsieur par la poste ce matin, je la joins à ma lettre, pour que Madame [la] voie. J'ai porté du café, les pastilles de chocolat et les mouchoirs. Pierre se plaint qu'il n'y en a pas encore assez, que Monsieur en salit beaucoup. Je n'ai pas porté le rhum comme Madame doit bien penser, mais j'ai dit à Monsieur que j'en avais apporté, et que le concierge me l'avait pris en entrant. Alors il m'a dit de reprendre la bouteille en sortant, parce que le concierge le boirait à sa santé. Monsieur devait sortir hier se promener, mais je ne sais pourquoi on voulait le faire accompagner par le surveillant. Alors Monsieur a fait une colère, et n'a pas voulu sortir; il voulait que ce soit Pierre qui l'acompagne, Monsieur m'a dit que Madame allait

revenir bientôt, qu'il avait reçu des nouvelles, que sa grand'mère allait mieux. . . .

Berthe Sarrazin

271 TO MADAME LA COMTESSE DE TOULOUSE-LAUTREC

7 rue du Manège
Albi, Tarn   Paris, 17 avril [1899]

Madame la Comtesse,

Je suis allée ce matin voir Monsieur Henri, comme je ne recevais pas de lettre de Madame. Voilà trois lettres que Monsieur Henri me fait parvenir, une par M. Joyant, une autre par M. Dihau, et une par la poste. Il trouve le temps long. Je lui ai porté ce qu'il me demandait, soit de l'eau de lavande, du chocolat, du café, des petit beurres, de la cannelle en poudre, du sirop de limons, les six mouchoirs qui restaient et 4 paires de chaussettes. J'ai trouvé Monsieur très bien. Il ne m'avait pas encore semblé aussi raisonnable. Il m'a très bien parlé de Madame et de sa grand-mère. Il était très inquiet de savoir qu'elle était plus mal. Il a vite écrit la dépêche que j'ai envoyée hier. . . .

Je suis allée chez Mlle Dihau donner des nouvelles, comme Madame me le dit. . . .

Berthe

272 TO MADAME LA COMTESSE DE TOULOUSE-LAUTREC

7 rue du Manège
Albi, Tarn   [April 20, 1899]

Madame la Comtesse,

(. . .) Je suis contente que Madame Tapié continue à aller mieux, et que Madame revienne lundi. Je viens de voir M. Henri; je lui ai porté un petit pot de confiture d'orange de chez l'épicier, et différentes choses que je suis allée chercher dans son atelier. Monsieur continue à aller de mieux en mieux. Il doit sortir cet après-midi avec Monsieur de Rivières qui doit lui faire visiter une propriété que son beau-père lui a laissée. Pierre m'a dit que Monsieur ne parle plus en mal de Madame comme il faisait dans le commencement, ce qui prouve qu'il devient tout à fait raisonnable. . . . Il m'a dit aussi qu'il avait fait écrire à Madame par Madame de Vismes et par M. Joyant. Léon a mené Paméla à M. Henri, il l'a trouvée très belle, elle l'a bien reconnu, elle ne savait quelles caresses lui faire. . . .

Berthe Sarrazin

APPENDIX III

273 TO ARNOULD, COUNTERSIGNED BY LAUTREC
                                 Paris, 18 mars 1896

Monsieur Arnould,

Monsieur de Toulouse-Lautrec me charge de vous dire qu'il autorise à reproduire toutes les affiches que vous voudrez à condition de lui montrer les épreuves avant l'impression.

Je vous serre la main.

Edw. Ancourt

Vu et approuvé

T-Lautrec

Ex libris designed by Lautrec for Jules Renard.

Bibliography

ADHÉMAR, JEAN, *Toulouse-Lautrec, lithographies, pointes sèches, oeuvre complet.* Paris, 1965.

ASTRE, ACHILLE, *H. de Toulouse-Lautrec.* Paris, n.d. [1926].

ATTEMS, Countess [née Mary Tapié de Céleyran], *Notre Oncle Lautrec.* 3rd ed., Geneva, 1963.

BEAUTE, GEORGES, *Il y a cent ans, Henri de Toulouse-Lautrec*, Lausanne, 1964.

BÉNÉDITE, LÉONCE, *Catalogue sommaire des peintures et sculptures du Musée National du Luxembourg.* Paris, n.d.

CARCO, FRANCIS, *Nostalgie de Paris.* Paris, 1941.

COQUIOT, GUSTAVE, *Henri de Toulouse-Lautrec.* Paris, 1913. A second, expanded edition published as *Lautrec, ou Quinze ans de moeurs parisiennes (1885–1900)*, Paris, 1921.

DEGAS, EDGAR, *Lettres*, ed. Marcel Guérin. Paris, 1945.

DELTEIL, LOYS, *Le Peintre-graveur illustré.* Vols. IX and X: *Henri de Toulouse-Lautrec.* Paris, 1920.

DORTU, M.-G., MADELEINE GRILLAERT, and JEAN ADHÉMAR. *Toulouse-Lautrec en Belgique.* Paris, 1955.

GAUZI, FRANÇOIS, *Lautrec et son temps.* Paris, 1954.

GONCOURT, EDMOND and JULES DE, *Journal; Mémoires de la vie Littéraire*, ed. Robert Ricatte. Monaco, 1956.

HUISMAN, PHILIPPE, and M.-G. DORTU, *Lautrec by Lautrec.* English trans., New York, 1964.

JEDLICKA, GOTTHARD, *Henri de Toulouse-Lautrec.* Berlin, 1929.

JOYANT, MAURICE, *Henri de Toulouse-Lautrec.* Two volumes. Paris, 1926–1927.

LECLERCQ, PAUL, *Autour de Toulouse-Lautrec.* Paris, 1920.

MACK, GERSTLE, *Toulouse-Lautrec.* New York, 1938.

MARX, ROGER, Obituary Notice. *Revue Encyclopédique.* Paris, 1901, pp. 1174–5.

PERRUCHOT, HENRI, *La Vie de Toulouse-Lautrec.* Paris, 1958.

PISSARRO, CAMILLE, *Lettres à son fils Lucien*, ed. John Rewald. Paris, 1950.

REWALD, JOHN, *Post-Impressionism from van Gogh to Gauguin.* New York, 1956.

ROGER-MARX, CLAUDE, *French Original Drawings from Manet to the Present Time.* Paris, 1939.

Genealogical Chart

NOTE ON THE USE OF THE GENEALOGICAL CHARTS

Marriages between members of the three principal families connected with that of TOULOUSE-LAUTREC MONFA is indicated in bold numbers (1–6). The names of the partners are repeated in the charts of both families concerned. Descendants of these unions are to be found in the chart of the father's family. Generations are aligned in all four charts making the degree of parentage immediately apparent.

D'IMBERT DU BOSC

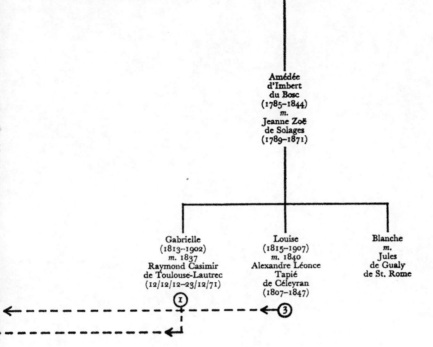

Amédée
d'Imbert
du Bosc
(1785–1844)
m.
Jeanne Zoë
de Solages
(1789–1871)

Gabrielle
(1813–1902)
m. 1837
Raymond Casimir
de Toulouse-Lautrec
(12/12/12–23/12/71)
①

Louise
(1815–1907)
m. 1840
Alexandre Léonce
Tapié
de Céleyran
(1807–1847)
③

Blanche
m.
Jules
de Gualy
de St. Rome

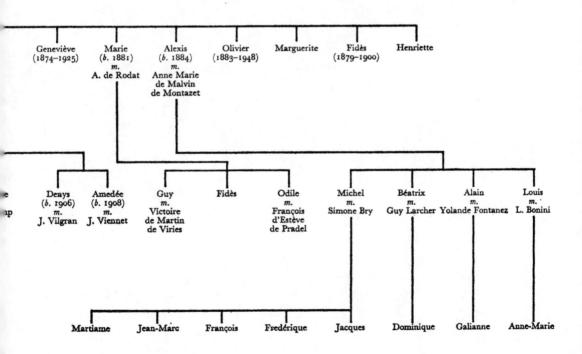

Geneviève
(1874–1925)

Marie
(*b.* 1881)
m.
A. de Rodat

Alexis
(*b.* 1884)
m.
Anne Marie
de Malvin
de Montazet

Olivier
(1883–1948)

Marguerite

Fidès
(1879–1900)

Henriette

Deays
(*b.* 1906)
m.
J. Vilgran

Amedée
(*b.* 1908)
m.
J. Viennet

Guy
m.
Victoire
de Martin
de Viries

Fidès

Odile
m.
François
d'Estève
de Pradel

Michel
m.
Simone Bry

Béatrix
m.
Guy Larcher

Alain
m.
Yolande Fontanez

Louis
m.
L. Bonini

Martiame

Jean-Marc

François

Fredérique

Jacques

Dominique

Galianne

Anne-Marie

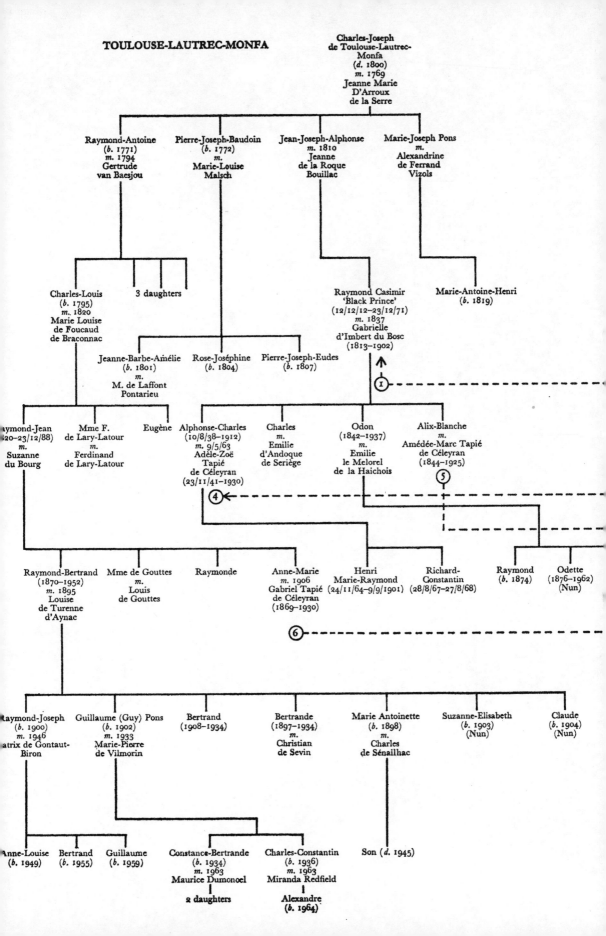

TOULOUSE-LAUTREC-MONFA

Charles-Joseph
de Toulouse-Lautrec-
Monfa
(*d.* 1800)
m. 1769
Jeanne Marie
D'Arroux
de la Serre

Raymond-Antoine
(*b.* 1771)
m. 1794
Gertrude
van Baesjou

Pierre-Joseph-Baudoin
(*b.* 1772)
m.
Marie-Louise
Malsch

Jean-Joseph-Alphonse
m. 1810
Jeanne
de la Roque
Bouillac

Marie-Joseph Pons
m.
Alexandrine
de Ferrand
Vizols

Charles-Louis
(*b.* 1795)
m. 1820
Marie Louise
de Foucaud
de Braconnac

3 daughters

Raymond Casimir
'Black Prince'
(*12/12/12–23/12/71*)
m. 1837
Gabrielle
d'Imbert du Bosc
(*1813–1902*)

Marie-Antoine-Henri
(*b.* 1819)

Jeanne-Barbe-Amélie
(*b.* 1801)
m.
M. de Laffont
Pontarieu

Rose-Joséphine
(*b.* 1804)

Pierre-Joseph-Eudes
(*b.* 1807)

①

Raymond-Jean
(*1820–23/12/88*)
m.
Suzanne
du Bourg

Mme F.
de Lary-Latour
m.
Ferdinand
de Lary-Latour

Eugène

Alphonse-Charles
(*10/8/38–1912*)
m. 9/5/63
Adèle-Zoë
Tapié
de Céleyran
(*23/11/41–1930*)

Charles
m.
Emilie
d'Andoque
de Seriège

Odon
(*1842–1937*)
m.
Emilie
le Melorel
de la Haichois

Alix-Blanche
m.
Amédée-Marc Tapié
de Céleyran
(*1844–1925*)

⑤

④

Raymond-Bertrand
(*1870–1952*)
m. 1895
Louise
de Turenne
d'Aynac

Mme de Gouttes
m.
Louis
de Gouttes

Raymonde

Anne-Marie
m. 1906
Gabriel Tapié
de Céleyran
(*1869–1930*)

Henri
Marie-Raymond
(*24/11/64–9/9/1901*)

Richard-
Constantin
(*28/8/67–27/8/68*)

Raymond
(*b.* 1874)

Odette
(*1876–1962*)
(Nun)

⑥

Raymond-Joseph
(*b.* 1900)
m. 1946
Béatrix de Gontaut-
Biron

Guillaume (Guy) Pons
(*b.* 1902)
m. 1933
Marie-Pierre
de Vilmorin

Bertrand
(*1908–1934*)

Bertrande
(*1897–1934*)
m.
Christian
de Sevin

Marie Antoinette
(*b.* 1898)
m.
Charles
de Sénailhac

Suzanne-Elisabeth
(*b.* 1903)
(Nun)

Claude
(*b.* 1904)
(Nun)

Anne-Louise
(*b.* 1949)

Bertrand
(*b.* 1955)

Guillaume
(*b.* 1959)

Constance-Bertrande
(*b.* 1934)
m. 1963
Maurice Dumonoel

2 daughters

Charles-Constantin
(*b.* 1936)
m. 1963
Miranda Redfield

Alexandre
(*b.* 1964*)

Son (*d.* 1945)

SÉRÉ DE RIVIÈRES

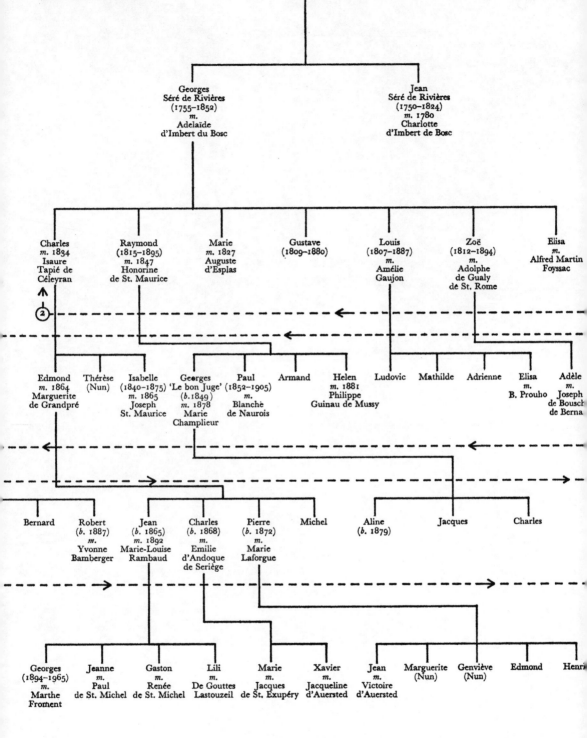

Georges
Séré de Rivières
(1755–1852)
m.
Adelaïde
d'Imbert du Bosc

Jean
Séré de Rivières
(1750–1824)
m. 1780
Charlotte
d'Imbert de Bosc

Charles
m. 1834
Isaure
Tapié de
Céleyran

Raymond
(1815–1895)
m. 1847
Honorine
de St. Maurice

Marie
m. 1827
Auguste
d'Esplas

Gustave
(1809–1880)

Louis
(1807–1887)
m.
Amélie
Gaujon

Zoë
(1812–1894)
m.
Adolphe
de Gualy
de St. Rome

Elisa
m.
Alfred Martin
Foyssac

Edmond
m. 1864
Marguerite
de Grandpré

Thérèse
(Nun)

Isabelle
(1840–1875)
m. 1865
Joseph
St. Maurice

Georges
'Le bon Juge'
(*b.* 1849)
m. 1878
Marie
Champlieur

Paul
(1852–1905)
m.
Blanchè
de Naurois

Armand

Helen
m. 1881
Philippe
Guinau de Mussy

Ludovic

Mathilde

Adrienne

Elisa
m.
B. Prouho

Adèle
m.
Joseph
de Bousch
de Berna

Bernard

Robert
(*b.* 1887)
m.
Yvonne
Bamberger

Jean
(*b.* 1865)
m. 1892
Marie-Louise
Rambaud

Charles
(*b.* 1868)
m.
Emilie
d'Andoque
de Seriège

Pierre
(*b.* 1872)
m.
Marie
Laforgue

Michel

Aline
(*b.* 1879)

Jacques

Charles

Georges
(1894–1965)
m.
Marthe
Froment

Jeanne
m.
Paul
de St. Michel

Gaston
m.
Renée
de St. Michel

Lili
m.
De Gouttes
Lastouzeil

Marie
m.
Jacques
de St. Exupéry

Xavier
m.
Jacqueline
d'Auersted

Jean
m.
Victoire
d'Auersted

Marguerite
(Nun)

Genviève
(Nun)

Edmond

Henri

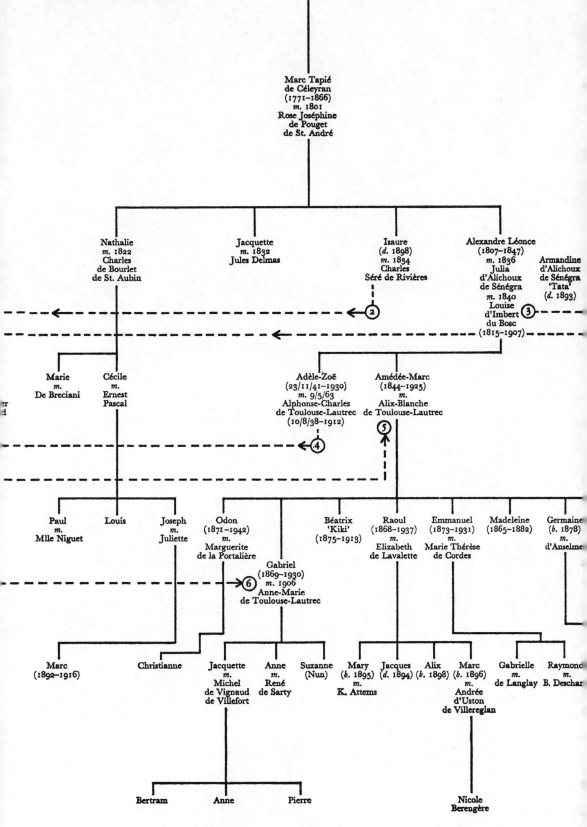

TAPIÉ DE CÉLEYRAN

Marc Tapié
de Céleyran
(1771–1866)
m. 1801
Rose Joséphine
de Pouget
de St. André

Nathalie
m. 1822
Charles
de Bourlet
de St. Aubin

Jacquette
m. 1832
Jules Delmas

Isaure
(*d.* 1898)
m. 1834
Charles
Séré de Rivières

Alexandre Léonce
(1807–1847)
m. 1836
Julia
d'Alichoux
de Sénégra
m. 1840
Louise
d'Imbert
du Bosc
(1815–1907)

Armandine
d'Alichoux
de Sénégra
'Tata'
(*d.* 1893)

②

③

Marie
m.
De Breciani

Cécile
m.
Ernest
Pascal

Adèle-Zoë
(23/11/41–1930)
m. 9/5/63
Alphonse-Charles
de Toulouse-Lautrec
(10/8/38–1912)

Amédée-Marc
(1844–1925)
m.
Alix-Blanche
de Toulouse-Lautrec

⑤

④

Paul
m.
Mlle Niguet

Louis

Joseph
m.
Juliette

Odon
(1871–1942)
m.
Marguerite
de la Portalière

Gabriel
(1869–1930)
m. 1906
Anne-Marie
de Toulouse-Lautrec

Béatrix
'Kiki'
(1875–1913)

Raoul
(1868–1937)
m.
Elizabeth
de Lavalette

Emmanuel
(1873–1931)
m.
Marie Thérèse
de Cordes

Madeleine
(1865–1882)

Germaine
(*b.* 1878)
m.
d'Anselme

⑥

Marc
(1892–1916)

Christianne

Jacquette
m.
Michel
de Vignaud
de Villefort

Anne
m.
René
de Sarty

Suzanne
(Nun)

Mary
(*b.* 1895)
m.
K. Attems

Jacques
(*d.* 1894)

Alix
(*b.* 1898)

Marc
(*b.* 1896)
m.
Andrée
d'Uston
de Villereglan

Gabrielle
m.
de Langlay

Raymond
m.
B. Deschar

Bertram

Anne

Pierre

Nicole
Berengère

Chronology

1864	24 Nov.	Albi	Born—Hôtel du Bosc, 14, rue de l'École-Mage.
1867	28 Aug.	Albi	Birth of brother, Richard de Toulouse-Lautrec.
1868	27 Aug.	Loury	Death of brother.
1871	28 Apr.	Céleyran	Earliest known letter.
	23 Dec.	Le Bosc	Death of Grandfather, 'Prince Noir'.
1872		Paris	Family takes up residence at the Hôtel Pérey, Cité du Retiro, rue Boissy d'Anglas.
	Oct.	Paris	Enters Lycée Fontanes (Condorcet), Classe de Mantoy.
	30 Dec.	Paris	Writes to grandparent.
1873	19 Jan.	Paris	Writes to grandparent.
		Amélie-les-Bains	Visits.
	23 Aug.	Céleyran	Writes to grandparent.
	Dec.	Paris	Returns to school.
1874	Jan.	Paris	In school—Premier Prix Thème latin, Version latine, Grammaire française and three Accessits. Cousin Louis Pascal and M. Joyant graduate in same class.
	29 Mar.	Paris	Letter to Cousin Madeleine.
	July	Paris	Leaves school. Studies under supervision of his Mother.
		Amélie-les-Bains	Visits.
		Nice	Visits. Pension de Famille Anglaise.
	30 Sept.		Letter to Aunt, with drawing of spider.
	23 Nov.	Paris	Returns to school.
	31 Dec.	Paris	Letter to grandparent.
1875	9 Jan.	Paris	Leaves school.
		Amélie-les-Bains	Visits.
	2 Nov.		Letter to grandparent.
1876	11 May		Passes exams.
	12 June		Première Communion.
1877	1 Mar.	Paris	Letter to grandparent. *Limping with my left foot.*
	July	Barèges	Visits.
	Dec.	Château du Bosc	Visits.
1878	9 Mar.		Letter of Dr. Gemeys about Henri's health —sulphur treatment.
	before 22 May	Albi	Hôtel du Bosc—fractures left leg. Letter dated 22 May to Raoul.

	June	Albi	
	Aug.	Barèges	Meets Devismes—stays at Maison Gradet.
		Amélie-les-Bains	
		Nice	
1879	Jan.–Feb.	Nice	
	24 Apr.	Albi	*Levée de l'appareil fixée au 24.*
	May	Le Bosc	Does water-colours.
	Aug.	Barèges	Fractures right femur.
	1 Sept.	Barèges	*Levée de l'appareil.*
	3 Sept.	Barèges	Mother writes *cette pauvre jambe.*
	Dec.	Céleyran	Letter to Cousin Raoul.
1880	13 Jan.	Nice	Letter to grandparent.
	16 Jan.	Nice	Letter to Mother.
	8, 11 Feb.	Nice	Letter to Devismes.
	Summer	Château du Bosc	Draws scenes of the Manoeuvres.
	Dec.	Céleyran	Letter to Aunt.
	30 Dec.	Céleyran	Letter to grandparent. Mentions *Ste Palette.*
1881	Jan.	Nice	Visits (sends 'Cahiers de Zig-Zags' sometime in 1881 from Nice to Cousin Madeleine Tapié de Céleyran).
	Apr.	Paris	Father and Princeteau *littéralement transportés à la vue des 'Chefs d'oeuvre'.*
	May	Paris	Mother reports he is copying a painting by Princeteau.
	July	Paris	Fails first attempt at baccalaureate.
	Aug.	Lamalou l'Ancien	Illustrates *Cocotte.* Stays at Hôtel des Bains.
	Oct.	Lamalou l'Ancien	Writes to Devismes.
	Oct.	Château du Bosc	Writes to Devismes.
	Nov.	Toulouse	Passes baccalaureate, second attempt. Abandons all formal study.
	22 Nov.	Albi	Letter to Mother, also to Devismes.
	Dec.	Paris	
	29 Dec.	Céleyran	Letter to grandparent.
1882	2, 17 Jan.	Céleyran	Writes to his Uncle Charles.
		Paris	Studies with Princeteau, 233, faubourg St-Honoré, Paris.
	end Mar.	Paris	First visit to Atelier Bonnat about a week after 22 March. Is admitted to follow instruction.
	Apr.		Mother writes to her sister *notre futur Michel-Ange.*
	17 Apr.	Paris	Letter to Father reporting on reception by fellow students of atelier.
	7 May		Letter to Uncle Charles saying that Bonnat judges his *dessin* to be *atroce.*
	Spring	Bosc	
	5 Sept.	Bosc	Visits, consecration of the new chapel of the Château.
	Sept.	Paris	Bonnat closes atelier. Cormon takes over

			atelier at 10, rue Constance (104, bd. de Clichy). Letter to Father announcing change.
	9 Oct.	Paris	Writes to Mother.
	28 Dec.		Letter to Grandmother (*has he lost in changing to Cormon?*) Makes acquaintance of Emile Bernard, Claudon, Raphael Collin, François Gauzi, Grenier, Adolphe Albert, Eugène Boch, Gustave Dennery, Descamps, Léon Mayet, Lucien Métivet, Louis Anquetin. Later, Van Gogh.
1883	10 Feb.	Paris	Letter to Uncle Charles about Cormon.
	20 May		Purchase by his Mother of Malromé.
	22 Aug.	Malromé	
	1 Sept.	Céleyran	Letter to Eugène Boch.
	8 Sept.	Langon	Visits Château de Respide. Letter to Mother.
	Oct.	Paris	
	24 Dec.	Paris	Announces his taking a studio.
1884	June		Chosen to work on illustrated edition of Victor Hugo.
	Summer	Paris	Moves in with René and Lily Grenier, 19 bis, rue Fontaine.
	July		Bourges passes the examination of the first part of the Concours d'Externat.
	7 Nov.	Paris	Outbreak of cholera, epidemic in Marseille and Toulon since June.
1885		Paris	Frequents Le Mirliton of Bruant who publishes *À St Lazare* signed Tréclau.
	Winter	Villiers-sur-Morin	Paints murals at the Auberge Ancelin. Visits Monet.
1886		Paris	Permanent display of some of his work at Le Mirliton, bd. Rochechouart.
		Paris	Takes an atelier of his own at 7, rue Tourlaque (corner 27, rue Caulaincourt) which he keeps until 1897. Gauzi and Zandomenghi also have studios there.
		Paris	Leaves the Cormon atelier.
	Aug.	Villiers-sur-Morin	Visits.
	Sept.	Malromé, Arcachon, Respide	Stays at Amédée's hunting lodge.
	17 Oct.– 19 Dec.	Paris	Exhibits at Salon des Arts Incohérents.
1887	Mar.	Paris	Rents apartment at 19, rue Fontaine with Bourges. Receives visit from Van Rysselberghe.
	Summer	Arcachon	*Partie de pêche à Arcachon: Cormorant tué par une anguille.*
1888	1 Jan.	Bosc, Céleyran	With Family.
	Feb.		Shows with fifth exhibition of Les XX in Brussels.

	Oct.–Dec.	Villiers-sur-Morin	Visits Greniers.
	24 Nov.	Paris	Writes to Mother.
1889	Jan.	Paris	Returns from Villiers-sur-Morin.
	June		Participates in show of the Cercle Artistique et Littéraire Volney.
	Summer	Arcachon	
	3 Sept.–4 Oct.		Exhibits in fifth Salon des Indépendants: *Moulin de la Galette*.
	Dec.		Influenza, letter.
1890	18 Jan.	Brussels	First trip to Brussels to attend exhibition of Les XX; defends Van Gogh against de Groux.
	20 Mar.–27 Apr.	Paris	Sixth Salon des Indépendants; exhibits *Mlle Dihau au Piano*.
	6 July	Paris	Lunch with Van Gogh at Théo's.
1890	30 Aug.–2 Sept.	Taussat	Trip to Biarritz, San Sebastian, Biarritz, Fuenterrabia and back to Taussat.
	Sept.–Oct.	Paris	Théo Van Gogh, manager of Goupil, 19, bd. Montmartre is paralyzed. Joyant named to replace him.
1891	Jan.		Moves to 21, rue Fontaine with Dr. Bourges.
	Feb.		Exhibits at Volney.
	20 Mar.–27 Apr.		Seventh Salon des Indépendants.
			Argues with Roques of *Courrier Français*.
	Autumn		Gabriel Tapié de Céleyran, his Cousin, arrives and becomes *externe* at St. Louis Hospital under Dr. Péan.
			Upon advice from Ancourt and Bonnard, begins working in lithography. Makes first original lithographic poster, *Le Moulin Rouge, La Goulue*, ordered by Zidler.
	Dec.		Exhibits at Le Barc de Boutteville with Bonnard, Anquetin, Bernard.
	26 Dec.		Writes to Mother.
1892	25 Jan.		Writes to Mother. Intends to visit Brussels, 3 Feb.–7 or 8.
	Jan.	Brussels	Exhibits with Les XX.
		Paris	Moulin Rouge reopens under Oller.
	19 Feb.		Writes to Théo Van Rysselberghe.
	19 Mar.–27 Apr.		Exhibits at eighth Salon des Indépendants.
			Poster: *Le Pendu*.
	Apr.		Exhibits at Cercle Volney and Le Barc de Boutteville.
	25 May	Paris	Writes to Roger Marx.
	31 May	London	Writes from Charing Cross Hotel. Returns to Paris in June.

Summer	Paris	Plans to go to Taussat in mid-July but is still in Paris July 15, 26, 31.
17 Aug.	Taussat	Writes to Mother, after four-day stay in Soulac with the Pascals.
13 Sept.	Taussat	Writes to Mother that he will visit Malromé with Fabre and Viaud about 25 Sept.
5 Oct.	Paris	Writes that he works at the printer's where proofs are being pulled.
23 Oct.	Paris	Writes that his Aunt Pascal needs further help.
19 Nov.	Paris	Writes that he is at the atelier 27, rue Caulaincourt.
19 Jan.		Writes to Roger Marx that the poster *Divan Japonais* is appearing the following day.

1893	Feb.	Brussels	Participates in show of Les XX and shows posters at Ixelles.
	Feb.	Paris	Exhibits at Boussod-Valadon (Joyant) together with Charles Maurin. Writes to Marty that a Cabinet Minister visits the show.
	25 Feb.		Writes to Geffroy about meeting Joyant.
	7 Mar		Asks Roger Marx for the name of Wiener.
	11 Mar.– 27 May		Four letters to R. Wiener in the first of which he gives his address as 21, rue Fontaine St-Georges. Suggests Rachou for drawing ornaments.
	Mar.		Writes to Marty asking him to announce Friday, 17 March opening of ninth Salon des Indépendants.
	18 Mar.– 27 Apr.	Paris	Exhibits at ninth Salon des Indépendants.
	Apr.	St-Jean-les-Deux-Jumeaux	Stays with Aristide Bruant.
	May	Paris	Exhibits at fifth Peintres-Graveurs show.
	4 May		Invites Marx to Zandomenghi show (May 3–20).
	2 June		Writes to Marty that *Jane Avril* poster will be issued on following day.
	25 June		Writes regarding *Jane Avril* poster.
	July		Bourges has recently been married.
	July		Begins work for *Figaro Illustré*, edited by Valadon of Goupil Gallery.
	July		Rents for one year the ground floor apartment next to his studio. Moves in January 1894.
	Aug.– Sept.		Trip with Bourges, Fabre, Guibert and Viaud from La Teste to Cazeaux and Mimizan.
		Taussat	Villa Bagatelle, writes to Wiener and to

			Marty. States he will return to Paris early in October.
	19 Oct.	Paris	Writes to Roger Marx.
	23 Oct.		Writes to Geffroy.
	1 Nov.		Travels with Dr. and Mme Bourges to see Anquetin in Normandy (Etrépagny).
	9 Nov.	Brussels	Les XX decide to ask their members whether the group should disband.
	26 Nov.		Octave Maus leads the group called 'Libre Esthétique' which replaces Les XX.
	29 Nov.	Paris	Writes to Geffroy.
	1 Dec.		Writes to Geffroy.
	9 Dec.	Paris	Café Concert (Montorgueil).
	10 Dec.		Writes to Marty about Yvette Guilbert and Geffroy.
	21 Dec.		Writes to Mother and states he has two posters to deliver.
	29 Dec.		Writes to Grandmother saying he cannot go South before 15 Jan.
1894	Jan	Paris	Moves to apartment at 27, rue Caulaincourt.
	9 Feb.		Writes to Kleinmann about Jane Avril.
	12–21 Feb.	Belgium	Second trip; also visits Holland.
	21 Feb.	Paris	States he returns after attending the first show of the Libre Esthétique.
	4 Apr.– 27 May		Tenth Salon des Indépendants.
	May		Writes to Mother about trip to Rouen and delays (of *Yvette Guilbert*).
	May	Paris	Exhibits at the *Dépêche de Toulouse*.
	5–12 May		Exhibits at Durand-Ruel.
	24 May		Writes to Geffroy.
	26 May		Writes to Wiener that *Yvette Guilbert paraîtra dans 10 ou 12 jours*.
	June	London	Visits. Stays at Marelles Hotel, Craven Street, Charing Cross, with Ricci.
	21 June	Paris	Writes to Geffroy of the expected proofs (*épreuves*) of *Yvette Guilbert*.
	early July		French series of *Yvette Guilbert* published by André Marty at the *Estampe Originale*.
			Arsène Alexandre asks him to give drawings for *Le Rire*.
	Summer	Malromé	Writes to Marty.
	Oct.	London	Exhibition of posters at Royal Aquarium, organized by Bella.
	20 Oct.	Paris	Writes to Marty.
	Dec.		Letter speaks of his new job as a decorator (*Chariot de Terre Cuite*).
	Dec.		Yvette Guilbert drawing in *Le Rire*.
1895	15 Jan		Draws *Nib* for *La Revue Blanche*.

22 Jan.		First performance of *Chariot de Terre Cuite*.
Mar.		Makes *Menu Sescau*, *La Bou illabaisse*, for 16 March, portraying Sescau and M. Guibert.
25 Mar.		Writes to Marty.
9 Apr.–26 May		Exhibits in eleventh Salon des Indépendants.
6–7 Apr.	Brussels	Third trip to Brussels; visits Libre Esthétique, exhibits five prints. *A visité avant le 7 avril.*
Apr.	Paris	Shows at the Salon de la Société Nationale des Beaux Arts.
Apr.		Shows at Centenaire de la Lithographie.
Apr.	London	Shows at the Royal Aquarium (Posters).
Apr.	Paris	Writes to Wiener about design for a binding.
2 May		Writes to Marty that he expects to introduce him to Degas at Zandomenghi show at Durand-Ruel.
May	London	Visits and meets Oscar Wilde, who refuses to pose. Portrait done from memory on return.
		Portrait of Whistler done in Chelsea.
	Dinard	With Dethomas at Dinard near Granville, Normandy.
6 June	Paris	Writes to Eduard Dujardin.
2 July	Paris	Writes to Tristan Bernard.
12 July		Writes to Deschamps, *30, rue Fontaine, Ma Nouvelle Adresse.*
	Valvins	Visits Natansons.
Aug.		Leaves Le Havre on 'Le Chili' for Arcachon. Goes to Lisbon and returns via Madrid with Maurice Guibert. Idea for *Passagère du 54.*
Aug.	Bordeaux	Visits.
8 Sept.	Taussat	Writes to Arsène Alexandre.
Oct.	Paris	Exhibits at fourteenth Salon des Cent, rue Bonaparte.
11 Oct.		Writes to Descamps from 30, rue Fontaine.
14 Nov.		Receipt for 200 francs paid by *La Plume* for *Chap Book* poster reproduction rights.
1896 Jan.	Paris	Exhibits at Manzi-Joyant, 9, rue Forest. Two locked rooms contain paintings not for general viewing (near 128, bd. de Clichy). Promises to be present with Joyant, 12 Jan.
20 Jan.		Writes to Edouard Dujardin.
Jan.–Feb.	Le Havre, Bordeaux	Visits.
	Arcachon	Visits.
Feb.	Brussels	Fourth visit, Joyant accompanying him.

			Exhibits at third Salon de la Libre Esthétique (*Passagère du 54*). Sees Van de Velde—Art Nouveau.
	18 Mar.	Paris	Authorizes Arnould to reproduce posters.
	22 Mar.		Writes to Deschamps.
	Mar.–Apr.		Makes drawings at trial of Arton and Lebaudy.
	Spring	Villeneuve-sur-Yonne	Visits Natansons.
	20 Apr.	Paris	Exhibition—rue Forest.
	22 Apr.		Fifteenth Salon des Cent, shows *Elles* series.
	June	London	Visits.
	late June–early July		Hires Dutch boat for Walcheren trip.
	July	Paris	Writes to Deschamps.
	Aug.	San Sebastian, Madrid, Toledo, Bordeaux	Travels with Fabre to San Sebastian, where they see a bullfight; goes to Burgos where they see the Cathedral and two monasteries; to Madrid where they stay at Grand Hôtel de la Paix. Returns after Toledo back to Bordeaux.
	Autumn	Arcachon	Visits.
	Nov.	Blois, Chambord	Visits with a group of friends.
	Winter	Paris	
	23 Dec.	Paris	The dinner for which he makes a lithographic stone evoking the Loire trip.
1897	Feb.	Brussels	Exhibits at Libre Esthétique.
	3 Apr.–31 May	Paris	Exhibits at thirteenth Salon des Indépendants.
	11 May		Leaves studio at rue Tourlaque and opens new one at 15, avenue Frochot.
	9 July	London	Visits. Letter to William Rothenstein from Charing Cross Hotel.
	Summer	Villeneuve-sur-Yonne	Visits Natansons.
	Winter	Paris	
1898	Early		Letter to Montcabrier complaining about *sale métier de Peintre*.
	25 Jan.		*Mon Premier Zinc*.
	Feb.		Eight Dry Point etchings.
	28 Mar.		Writes to Deschamps from 15, av. Frochot.
	Apr.		Show at atelier of the Cité Frochot.
	20 Apr.	Paris	Floury publishes *Au Pied du Sinaï*.
	May	London	Exhibits 78 works at Goupil Gallery, Regent Street. Falls asleep at opening. Stays at Charing Cross Hotel. Bliss and Sands publish *Série anglaise* of *Yvette Guilbert*.
	22 May		
	July	Arromanches	Visits.
	Sept.	Villeneuve-sur-Yonne	Visits Natansons; Vuillard paints him.

Autumn	Paris	
Nov.	Paris	Writes to Pellet.
28 Nov.		Writes to Roger Marx.
5 Dec.		Writes to Roger Marx announcing his visit with Albert and Bouglé.
Dec.		Writes to Grenier.
1899 Jan.		Comtesse de Toulouse-Lautrec leaves Paris with her brother Amédée around 3 Jan. for Albi. Floury publishes Jules Renard's *Histoires Naturelles*.
Jan.–Feb.		Berthe Sarrazin reports to artist's Mother, in Albi until at least 3 Feb. She writes again on 14 Feb. but now to Paris.
8 Feb.		Lithograph *Le Chien et le Perroquet*—dated on stone.
10 Feb.		Lautrec invites Calmèse and Calmèse's mother to dinner.
13, 15 Feb.		Lautrec's mother hires two male nurses.
between 27 Feb. and 13 Mar.		With at least his partial consent, is confined for an alcoholic cure in the clinic of Dr. Sémelaigne, 16, av. de Madrid, Neuilly, also known as 'La Folie St-James'. The internment lasts probably from February to 17 May.
Mar.	Neuilly	*Le Cirque* drawings started.
9 Mar.		Visit of Missia Natanson to the clinic.
17 Mar.		Writes to Joyant asking for lithographic stones and a box of watercolours.
Apr.		Bonnard and Vuillard try to visit him but are denied admission.
12 Apr.		Writes to Joseph Albert that he has seen his Mother and asks him to tell Joyant that the album is increasing.
13, 17, 20 Apr.		Receives visits from Berthe Sarrazin.
28 Apr.	Paris	Albert to take him to Dr. Cruet, the dentist.
17 May? certainly before 20 May	Paris	Released from institution. Letters to Antoine and Grenier. Travel to visit family with Louis Pascal.
20 May	Albi	Arrives. Letter by Aunt Emilie describes it.
June	Le Crotoy	Travels with Paul Viaud.
11 July	Le Havre	Writes that he expects to go on to Granville.
20 July		Cruise to Bordeaux, then stays at Villa Bagatelle, with Fabre, in Taussat.
Oct.	Paris	Member of jury for poster section, 1900 Fair.
1900 Jan.–Apr.	Paris	
Feb.		Makes a drawing and dates it Feb. 1900, in a volume by Nicholson published by Floury.

	15 May	Paris	Organizes his studio, arranges exhibition at 14, av. Frochot next to his atelier. Also participates in the Exposition Universelle Centenalle et Décennale de la Lithographie.
	late May	Le Crotoy	Visits.
		Le Havre, Honfleur	
	late June	Bordeaux, Arcachon	Visits.
	Sept.	Taussat	Visits, accompanied by Paul Viaud.
	Sept.	Malromé	With Mother.
	6 Dec.	Bordeaux	Writes to Joyant from 66, rue de Caudéran.
	Dec.		Writes to Mother.
	Dec.		Exhibits at the Exposition d'Art Moderne. Writes to Grandmother.
	23 Dec.		Writes to Joyant about *Messaline* programme.
1901	Jan.–Apr.	Malromé and Bordeaux	
	31 Mar.		Writes to Joyant about a sale of paintings.
	end of Apr. to July	Paris	Returns to sort his paintings and other possessions, accompanied by Viaud.
	15 July	Bordeaux	Leaves Paris for Bordeaux with Viaud to Arcachon and Taussat.
	20 Aug.	Malromé	Arrives.
	9 Sept.	Malromé	Dies and is buried at St-André-du-Bois, later transferred to Verdelais, Gironde.

List of Illustrations

The Editors and Publishers are grateful to the many official bodies, galleries and individuals mentioned below for their assistance in supplying illustration material.

1 Photograph of Lautrec, at the age of two years. In the Herbert D. Schimmel collection.

2 Lautrec: Early drawings, *c.* 1871. In the collection of Emile E. Wolf.

3 Château de Malromé. Photo in the collection of the Comtesse K. Attems.

4 Château de Céleyran. Photo in the collection of the Comtesse K. Attems.

5 Château du Bosc. Photo in the collection of the Comtesse K. Attems.

6 Autograph letter to his Godmother, 1871 (letter 1). In the Herbert D. Schimmel collection.

7 Autograph letter to his Great-Aunt Joséphine du Bosc, 1880 (letter 32). In the Herbert D. Schimmel collection.

8 Lautrec at the farm of Château du Bosc. In the collection of the Comtesse K. Attems.

9 Lautrec at the age of fifteen or sixteen, Nice, 1879–80. Photo in the collection of the Comtesse K. Attems.

10 Half-title page from Lautrec's Latin-French dictionary. In the Francis Kettaneh Collection.

11 Lautrec, his father holding falcon, and one of his uncles(?), 1887. Photo in the collection of the Comtesse K. Attems.

12 Comte Alphonse: Lautrec's father and two uncles on horseback. Pencil. In the collection of the Comtesse K. Attems.

13 Lautrec: Raoul Tapié de Céleyran on a donkey. 1881, Oil. Collection Maurice Lehman, Paris.

14 Photograph of the Comte Alphonse in armour standing on his horse. Photo courtesy M. J. Bourges.

15 Comte Alphonse(?): Lautrec riding. Pencil. In the collection of the Comtesse K. Attems. Photo Georges Beaute.

16 Lautrec: The Comte Alphonse as a coachman, Nice, 1880. Pencil. Photo courtesy of the Art Institute of Chicago.

17 Lautrec: Envelope with sketches. In the collection of Mr. and Mrs. P. Roland.

18 Photograph of Lautrec in a family group. Photo in the Herbert D. Schimmel collection.

19 Lautrec: Portrait of his mother, 1885. Charcoal. Photo courtesy Musée Toulouse-Lautrec, Albi.

20 Henri Rachou: Portrait of Lautrec, 1883. Oils. Photo courtesy Musée des Augustins, Toulouse.

21 Photograph of Henri Rachou, 1938. In the collection of M. Imart-Rachou.

22 Photograph of Cormon. Photo courtesy Lucien Goldschmidt.

23 Photograph of Bonnat. Photo courtesy Lucien Goldschmidt.

24 Lautrec in a group at Cormon's atelier. Photo courtesy Edita S.A., Lausanne.

25 Cormon: 'Cain'. Photo Giraudon.

26 A group from Cormon's atelier with Lautrec and Lily Grenier. Photo courtesy Edita S.A., Lausanne.

27 Autograph letter and envelope to

E. Boch, 1883 (letter 50). In the Herbert D. Schimmel collection.

28 Rue Fontaine, Paris, Photo Mme Simone Groger.

29 Rue Tourlaque, Paris. Photo Mme Simone Groger.

30 Lautrec asleep. Photo courtesy M. Imart-Rachou.

31 Lautrec: 'Mademoiselle Dihau at the piano', 1890. Photo courtesy Musée Toulouse-Lautrec, Albi.

32 Avenue Frochot, Paris. Photo Mme Simone Groger.

33 Lautrec: 'Portrait of Dr. Bourges', 1891. Photo Courtauld Institute of Art, Courtesy Pittsburgh Museum of Art, Carnegie Institute.

34 Page from Lautrec and Bourges' household accounts. Courtesy M. J. Bourges.

35 Lautrec in Japanese costume. Photo Phaidon archives.

36 Japanese statuette from Lautrec's own collection. In the Herbert D. Schimmel collection. Photo Nathan Rabin.

37 Madame Ymart-Rachou, 1890. Photo courtesy M. Imart-Rachou.

38 Lautrec: 'Portrait of Paul Sescau', 1891. Photo courtesy the Brooklyn Museum.

39 Lautrec and another looking at the Cheret Moulin Rouge poster. Photo courtesy Lucien Goldschmidt.

40 Lautrec: 'Portrait of Juliette Pascal', 1887. Photo Les Beaux Arts.

41 Lautrec: 'Madame Pascal at the Piano', 1895. Pencil. Photo courtesy Musée Toulouse-Lautrec, Albi.

42 Autograph letter to his mother about the Pascal affair, 1892 (letter 152). In the Herbert D. Schimmel collection.

43 Lautrec with Viaud and a sailor on a boat, c. 1899–1900. Photo courtesy Edita S.A., Lausanne.

44 Lautrec: 'La visite du Docteur', 1893, drawing. Photo des Musées Nationaux, Cabinet des dessins, Louvre.

45 Lautrec: Self-caricature. In the Lionel Prejger Collection.

46 Lautrec: 'Le salut'. lithograph. Photo Phaidon Archives.

47 Steinlen: 'Dans la rue', words by Bruant, inscribed to Lautrec. In the Herbert D. Schimmel collection. Photo Nathan Rabin.

48 Lautrec: 'Au pied du Sinaï'. Photo courtesy the Metropolitan Museum of Art, Bequest of Clifford A. Furst, 1959.

49 Lautrec: 'The Chap Book', Lithograph, 1896. Photo Ray Sacks, by courtesy of the Victoria and Albert Museum.

50 Lautrec: 'La Chaine Simpson', Lithograph poster 1896. Photo courtesy Musée Toulouse-Lautrec, Albi.

51 Autograph letter to Dethomas, 1895 (letter 198). In the Herbert D. Schimmel collection.

52 Lautrec: 'May Belfort,' Lithograph 1895. Photo courtesy Sotheby and Co.

53 Contract of employment of a male nurse, 1899. In the Herbert D. Schimmel collection.

54 Autograph letter to Berthe Sarrazin, 1899 (letter 226). In the Herbert D. Schimmel collection.

55 Autograph letter from Berthe Sarrazin to the Comtesse de Toulouse-Lautrec, 1899 (letter 270). In the Herbert D. Schimmel collection.

56 Autograph letter to his grandmother from Bordeaux, 1900 (letter 236). In the Herbert D. Schimmel collection.

In the Text: (p. 301) Ex libris of Jules Renard. In the Herbert D. Schimmel collection.

Index

Numbers in italics refer to illustrations and their captions.